CHINA

Yellow R.

Golmo

Sining

Birthplace of
the Dalai Lama

Kumbum

Lanzhou

A M D O

GANSU

(QINGHAI)

GOLOK

Dri Chu R.

Dege

S I C H U A N

Chamdo

Chengdu

K H A M

Litang

Mekong R.

Batang

Tatsienlu

Markam

Yangtze R.

Lhuntse
Dzong

(Tsangpo R.)

I N D I A

B U R M A

Drop sites
for Tibetan agents
and arms, 1957–1965

© A. Karl / J. Kemp, 1999

ORPHANS OF THE COLD WAR

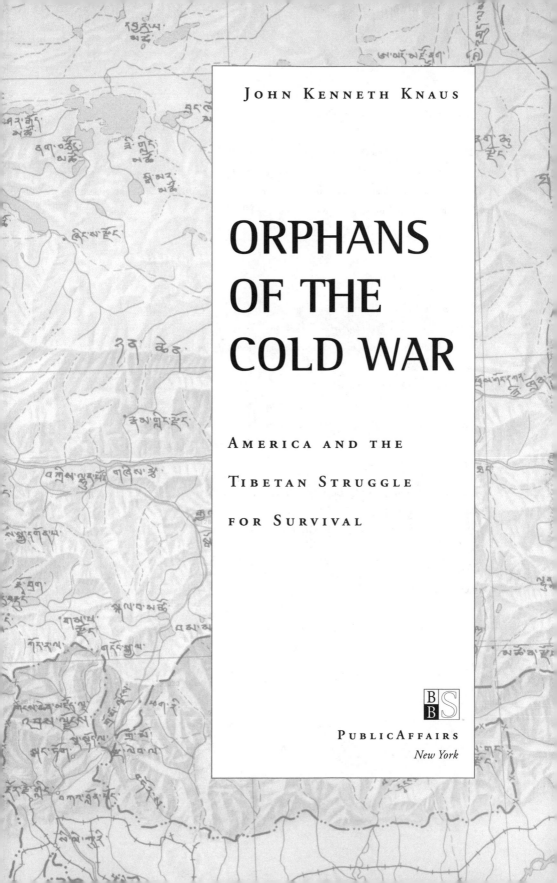

JOHN KENNETH KNAUS

ORPHANS OF THE COLD WAR

AMERICA AND THE

TIBETAN STRUGGLE

FOR SURVIVAL

PublicAffairs

New York

The detail from the map of Tibet that appears on the previous two pages was originally printed on parachute cloth and used by the resistance.

The drawings that appear throughout the book are from propaganda booklets written and drawn by members of the resistance. They took their booklets with them when they parachuted back into Tibet where they were distributed to their comrades and to potential recruits. The texts called for a united Tibet in the face of Chinese aggression and established the rules of conduct for the resistance fighters.

Copyright © 1999 by John Kenneth Knaus.

Endpaper map © 1999 by Anita Karl and Jim Kemp.

Published in the United States by PublicAffairs™, a member of the Perseus Books Group.

All rights reserved.

Printed in the United States of America

No part of this book may be reproduced in any manner whatsoever without written permission except in the case of brief quotations embodied in critical articles and reviews.

For information, address PublicAffairs, 250 West 57th Street, Suite 1825, New York, NY 10107.

Book design by Jenny Dossin.

LIBRARY OF CONGRESS CATALOGING-IN-PUBLICATION DATA

Knaus, John Kenneth, 1923–

Orphans of the Cold War : America and the Tibetan struggle for survival / John Kenneth Knaus.

p.   cm.

Includes index.

ISBN 1–891620–18–5

1. Tibet (China)—History—1951–   2. China—Politics and government—1949–

3. United States—Relations—China—Tibet. 4. Tibet (China)—Relations—United States.

I. Title. II. Title: America and the Tibetan struggle for survival.

DS786.K64   1999

951'.505—dc21   99–11836

CIP

First Edition

10 9 8 7 6 5 4 3 2 1

For my wife and the Tibetans who have enriched both our lives.

Contents

Preface

1 FIRST MET His Holiness the Dalai Lama in 1964. At that time he was in his fifth year of exile in Dharamsala, India, and I was a Central Intelligence Agency officer who had spent several years with the leaders of the Tibetan resistance in their fight to preserve their people's way of life, and, above all, their right to practice their religion and venerate the Dalai Lama as their spiritual and temporal leader. By then I had become identified with these people, whom my colleagues and I had trained and armed in their unequal contest against the Chinese while championing their cause abroad. I therefore had looked forward to that first audience with some awe and great expectations of meeting with this person whose gentleness, compassion, and friendly

humor were legendary. While I was not exactly expecting to be patted on the head for our good works, I had anticipated a welcome as a comrade in a common cause. That did not happen. While receiving me with his unfailing courtesy, the young ruler imposed a remarkably effective, though invisible, barrier between us. That quickly dispelled my illusion that this was to be a warm chat between friends about common objectives.

I left that meeting knowing that I had met a great person, but perplexed about the distance that he obviously wanted to preserve between himself and the representative of the agency that was sustaining his people's resistance against a common enemy. It took me some years to come to an appreciation of the profound moral dilemma our assistance had posed to him as a Buddhist leader committed to nonviolence, even though we had provided it in response to the fervent requests of his own people.

We did not meet again until 1995, again in Dharamsala, where the temporary military barracks of his refuge of the early 1960s had been replaced by the modest but substantial buildings of an established government-in-exile. In the intervening three decades the young man with an uncertain future had become an internationally respected religious and political leader and a Nobel laureate. During these years his once reluctant Indian hosts had been forced to accept him and his countrymen as allies in a confrontation with the Chinese. His original ally, the United States, had meanwhile gradually distanced itself from him and his people's battle for independence as its foreign policy objectives shifted elsewhere. Washington was ready to defer to his Indian hosts to assume the role of primary sponsor, and let its former protégé proceed on his own while it pursued more pressing concerns. The programs the United States had shared with the Tibetans, and the commitments made to him as their leader, were lost in the process.

For all these reasons I could have expected that the Dalai Lama might have even less interest in seeing me than when we had first met, and that we might have another perfunctory exchange of courtesies. This happily turned out not to be the case. I opened our conversation by recalling our earlier meeting and the irony that I personally dislike firearms but was then supplying them to his people. This must have seemed to be the embodiment of the moral quandary he had faced then and that continues to trouble him to this day. He smilingly agreed, and this time the discussion that I had hoped for some thirty years earlier took place. Together we examined the good and the bad that emerged from the relationship between this remarkable man and his people and the U.S. government.

Our conversation confirmed my belief that the long history of the U.S. government's relationship with Tibet deserves to be told in the full context of its origins and its evolution over half a century. It is also one man's retrospective evaluation of his own and his government's objectives in participating in these operations and their consequences.

ORPHANS OF THE COLD WAR

CHAPTER 1

Mission to Shangri-la

"W E ARRIVED SAFELY. Next time, please drop us fifty yards downstream because there was a house nearby with dogs who barked at us when we landed last night. We are well. We have cached our parachutes and are off to buy a horse to go to Lhasa tomorrow."

Cheers rang out in one of the buildings along the reflecting pool in Washington when this message was received on a crisp midautumn morning in 1957. It was one that the Central Intelligence Agency (CIA) had been anxiously awaiting. Two young Tibetans had tapped it out on a portable radio of the type issued to agents during World War II, its power cranked by hand. They were on a sand dune in the Brahmaputra River sixty miles south of the Tibetan capital. The senders were only a few miles from the spot where a U.S. Air Force B-24 Liberator had crashed fourteen years before, lost flying over "the Hump" of the Himalayas while transporting supplies to the Allied forces in China. Its American crew had been forced to parachute into Tibet by accident, but the American-trained Tibetans dropped from the second plane were on a guerrilla mission to support their countrymen's resistance against the Chinese. The Cold War had come to one of the world's most remote countries.

Since early in the nineteenth century the Tibetans had closed their doors to outsiders. Foreigners were considered threats to a way of life that had to be protected even to the point of slaughtering intruders. Natural obstacles reinforced this official hostility. This country of 500,000 square miles,[1] as vast as Western Europe, is bounded on the north by the towering Kunlun Mountains separating it from the Chinese province of Xinjiang, and in the west by the mighty Karakorum range on the border with Kashmir. The majestic Himalayas form a natural boundary with India in the south. Only to the east is there a gap to the outside world. Through it flow the headwaters of three of the world's great rivers, the Yangtze, the Mekong, and the Salween, cleaving great gorges on their way to China and southeast Asia. Within these formidable natural barriers Tibet is a sparsely populated wilderness of plains and mountain ranges of 16,000 feet or higher, a land later described by the Italian explorer Fosco Maraini as one of "dizzy extremes and excesses."[2]

Tibet is a land of Buddhism like no other. Over 1,300 years ago one of the great Tibetan kings, Songsten Gampo, introduced his subjects to Buddhism and determined the destiny of his country. At that time Buddhism had two forms, the Hinayana, called "the Lesser Vehicle," and the Mahayana, "the Greater Vehicle." It was the Mahayana, then spreading through northern India, Kashmir, central Asia, China, and Korea, with its abundant metaphysics, myriad celestial persons, and rich literature and art, that came to Tibet. It filled the solitude of that country's vast spaces and created a culture by compelling the Tibetan people to learn to read and develop a script of their own.

Mahayana differs from Hinayana Buddhism by its focus on the incarnation of an eternal cosmic Buddha and by its unique accompanying deities, saints, and emanations, rather than on the historical Buddha who died in the fifth century B.C.E. Its most unique characteristic is its emphasis on bodhisattvas, persons who have attained illumination but postpone the enjoyment of nirvana and remain active in the cycle of life until every sentient being has been delivered from suffering.

Tibetan Buddhism, like its Hinayana counterpart, which flourishes in South Asia, preaches a message of love and compassion. But this has not precluded violent battles, first with the defenders of Tibet's native Bon religion, then among the sects that grew up within the triumphant Buddhist community itself, and even among monasteries of the same denomination. These monasteries represented the principal route of advancement in Tibet, and almost every family sent at least one son to a monastery. Three of the four brothers of the present Dalai Lama were monks. The monasteries of Tibet were great centers of religious learning and prayer. They were also active participants in the commercial and political life of Tibet. The monks believed strongly in their religion and defended it with equal vigor against all challengers, foreign or domestic. If this meant using arms held in their arsenal, so be it.

Tibet's ruler, the Dalai Lama, belongs to the Yellow Hat sect,[3] which began as a fourteenth-century reform movement preaching discipline, celibacy, and temperance, and diminishing the role of lower gods and devils inherited from the native cults. The Yellow Hats established two of the features that have made Tibetan Buddhism unique—a supreme monk with equal spiritual and temporal authority, and the succession of this pontiff through reincarnation. The sect won power in Lhasa in the sixteenth century and then settled in to seal off Tibet from all challengers.

Tibet's self-imposed isolation was interrupted at the turn of the twentieth century when a Buryat Mongol monk named Dorjieff succeeded in winning the favor of the country's highest spiritual and temporal ruler, the Dalai Lama. Dorjieff had also been able to enlist the interest of his sovereign, Czar Nicholas II, whom he persuaded to invite the Tibetan ruler to Moscow.[4] When the Dalai Lama, despite the objections of his own xenophobic assembly, accepted the Tsar's overtures, Lord Curzon, the viceroy of British India and an arch-Russophobe, saw it as a revival of the nineteenth-century "Great Game"—the competition for control of central Asia—and a threat to his domain. Curzon subsequently dispatched Colonel Francis Younghusband with a military expedition to Tibet in 1904. It forced its way into Lhasa after several bloody and unequal battles against the Tibetans, which sickened even Younghusband himself. The thirteenth Dalai Lama fled to Mongolia, a Buddhist land that had been an early protector of Tibet, leaving the British victors an empty throne.

Within a decade the wheel of history had made a complete turn. The British signed an agreement with the Russians ending their competition in that final inning of the Great Game. The Chinese government collapsed after making one last fierce effort to impose its authority over this unruly country, which they claimed as part of their failing empire. The Dalai Lama returned to Lhasa from his second flight abroad, having fled this time to British India, where he had sought the protection of his former enemies. By 1913 the British were the preeminent foreign power in Lhasa, where the Tibetans were to manage their own affairs for the next thirty-seven years.

Until the Communist troops of Mao Zedong forced their way into Tibet in 1950, the U.S. government had taken little notice of Tibet. During World War II, Washington acquired a passing interest in this remote country prompted solely by its location. By May of 1942, the Burma Road, the only remaining overland route used by the military from South Asia into China, had been cut by a Japanese thrust. For Chiang K'ai-shek, the leader of the Chinese Nationalist forces, this meant the loss of his best hope of obtaining the large quantities of supplies he had been demanding from his allies since the attack on Pearl Harbor had brought the United States into the war seven months before. Seeking an overland route to supply his prickly ally, President Franklin D. Roosevelt commissioned the newly created secret intelligence organization, the Office of Strategic Services (OSS), to dispatch a reconnaissance mission into Tibet, large areas of which were literally terra incognita to the U.S. Army Map Service.

But the Tibetans had little interest in anything that might give their Chinese neighbors an excuse to increase their presence and thus reinforce China's historic claims to sovereignty over Tibet. The British were ambivalent. They saw the need for a road to get supplies to their new Chinese allies, but they were reluctant to do anything that might undercut their traditional policy of maintaining the isolated country as a buffer state between India and China.[5] The Foreign Office suggested that the way could be smoothed if Chiang could be persuaded to make a declaration recognizing home rule for Tibet, but this seemed unlikely. While Chiang had already gratuitously proposed that the British pledge independence to India and Burma after the war, London commented that "what is sauce for the Indian goose is not suitable for the Tibetan gander."[6]

The Lhasa government finally fixed on a compromise that would meet the allies' request while keeping their Chinese neighbors at bay. It would permit the transit of nonmilitary goods destined for China, with the term "nonmilitary" not to be interpreted too strictly. But its concessions were met by further Chinese demands to station "technicians" along the route to supervise the transport. The Chiang K'ai-shek government expected that the supplies coming over this backdoor route would not be sizable enough to be worth paying any political price in yielding its claims to Tibet.

THE TOLSTOY MISSION

Despite this unpromising background the OSS went ahead with its mission to obtain its own reading of the situation in Tibet. This intelligence project was an appropriate beginning to a unique relationship that for the next thirty years was carried out primarily through clandestine channels and based on covert operations. The initial project, code-named FE-2, was approved by President Roosevelt on May 12, 1942.[7] It was formally defined as a "reconnaissance mission via India to Tibet" whose purpose was "to move across Tibet and make its way to Chungking, China, observing attitudes of the people of Tibet; to seek allies and discover enemies; locate strategic targets and survey the territory as a possible field for future activity." All this in a country without paved highways and, of course, no railroads.

Although the Chinese and the British retained limited and residual representation in Tibet,[8] the Tibetan government still discouraged foreign visitors. In the years before World War II, only a handful of explorers and scientists had overcome formidable geographic and political obstacles to carry out limited expeditions to the border areas in the eastern and northern areas of Tibet. No American had made the difficult traverse over some of the world's most desolate deserts and highest mountains that would take the two OSS men 1,500 miles from the Indian-Sikkimese border to the Chinese border on the east. The man chosen to lead this mission was Captain Ilya Tolstoy, grandson of the great Russian novelist.

As a personable young Russian count who used his title even though he had become a U.S. citizen, Tolstoy's aristocratic lineage gave him entrée to the members of the British Raj in India who would be crucial to his success. He was also a man of ebullient charm and suffered from no want of self-confidence. These same credentials stood him in good stead with the generally pro-British Tibetan aristocrats and helped him deal with the arcane theocratic court in Lhasa. In contrast to the austere life in the Tibetan countryside, the clerical elite and noble families of the capital led a surprisingly pleasant and fun-loving existence.[9] Tolstoy easily made friends, including the only Tibetan member of the U.S. National Geographic Society, Tsarong Shape, who maintained what was probably Lhasa's most comfortable and modern household. The dashing former cavalry officer was thirty-nine years old at the time. Those who knew him, both during his OSS days and in his postwar career as a principal officer of Florida's Marineland and prominent member of the Explorer's Club, described him as full of life and ideas and fascinated by adventure.[10]

Tolstoy selected as the second member of the team a noted Far Eastern explorer, Lieutenant Brooke Dolan II, who was five years younger. Dolan was versed in the Tibetan and Chinese languages, as well as Buddhism. Independently wealthy, he had headed an expedition to northeast Tibet and western China ten years earlier for the Philadelphia Academy of Natural Science and returned with the first specimens of the giant panda. Two years later, he had journeyed to the high Tibetan plateau to collect fauna on a fifteen-month expedition that covered approximately 200,000 square miles. His trek with Tolstoy was nothing compared to what he had already accomplished.

The two left Washington in July of 1942 with instructions from the head of the OSS, General William J. Donovan to "keep in touch if you can."[11] Tolstoy later noted this was hardly possible since portable radio equipment light enough for them to carry was not then available. They spent the next three months in New Delhi while the British-controlled government of India negotiated with the Tibetan government to permit the two emissaries to bring gifts and a letter from President Roosevelt to the Dalai Lama and his government. The two men did not inform their British interlocutors that a previous request brokered by the Chinese government had been already been rejected by Lhasa.[12] Neither did they tell the Tibetans, or at least the British did not inform Lhasa, that their ultimate destination was Chungking and they had no intention of returning to New Delhi.

By the end of September 1942 the Tibetan government had granted Tolstoy and Dolan permission to proceed as far as Lhasa, and they set off in early October with the personal blessing of Vinegar Joe himself, Lieutenant General Joseph W. Stilwell, the legendary commander of the China-Burma-India theater.

Their first stop inside Tibet, as they made their way by foot and mule, was the trade center of Yatung. There they were entertained by Yangpel Pandatsang, a member of a prominent trading family from an area of eastern Tibet called Kham. Pandatsang had grown rich from the wool export monopoly he shared with another Kham family. The importance of the Tibetan government's foreign revenues from Pandatsang's wool trade had been sufficient to protect him when his brothers rose against the central government some years before. By the time he hosted Tolstoy and his party, Pandatsang had become the Customs Commissioner and de facto governor of the Chumbi Valley, which lies on the Tibetan side of the pass through which most trade was conducted with India. The Pandatsangs were later to play a role in the Tibetan resistance against the Chinese, and Tolstoy was charmed by them.

Following the route taken by a British military expedition thirty-eight years before, the American mission arrived in Lhasa in early December. On December 20, 1942, they were granted an audience by the fourteenth Dalai Lama. Tolstoy delivered the gifts and letters from President Roosevelt that were the ostensible reason for their visit. The Dalai Lama was then seven years old and had no way of knowing he would be one of the best known men in the modern world half a century later. He had reached Lhasa only three years before, newly proclaimed as the reincarnation of his predecessor, who had died in 1933. The boy was living in the Potala, the great fortress housing his apartments, a monastery, and the offices of the Tibetan government. In his autobiography, *Freedom in Exile,* the Dalai Lama describes the Potala, which had been begun in the tenth century and renovated in the seventeenth century, as "very beautiful, but not a nice place to live."[13] He was given the "pitifully cold and illlit" vermin-infested room on the top story of the Potala, which had been the bedroom of one of his distinguished predecessors, the "Great Fifth" Dalai Lama. His older brother, who had been his close companion, had been sent off to another monastery and the Dalai Lama was permitted only occasional visits from his mother and other siblings. It was a lonely life devoted to schooling in language, penmanship, and religion, preparing him for his ecclesiastical and temporal duties as ruler and spiritual leader of his country. Although regarded by his countrymen as a "god king," he enjoyed playing like any boy his age and he speaks fondly of the toys and gifts brought to him by foreign officials. He also had an intense curiosity about what lay outside his exotic but closed capital and must have looked forward to this break in his rigid regimen to meet with rare visitors from an unknown world.

At the State Department's insistence, the letter that Tolstoy brought from the president was addressed to the Dalai Lama in his capacity as religious leader of Tibet.[14] This was done to avoid "giving any possible offense to the Chinese Government which includes Tibet in the territory of the Republic of China." Roosevelt's letter introduced Tolstoy and Dolan as hopeful visitors to "your Pontificate," noting that "there are in the United States of America many persons, among them myself, who, long and greatly interested in your land and people, would highly value such an opportunity."[15] Like many Americans, Roosevelt was caught up in the mystery of Tibet. Earlier that year he guarded the secret of where American planes had taken off to bomb Tokyo for the first time by saying, "They came from a secret base in Shangri-la."[16] (Actually, they had come from an American aircraft carrier.) That was also the name chosen by Roosevelt for his retreat in Maryland's Catoctin Mountains now known as Camp David.

There was much less diplomatic anguish in the choice of the gifts Tolstoy and Dolan presented to the Dalai Lama and his regent. The president sent a photograph signed, "For His Holiness, the Dalai Lama from his good friend Franklin D. Roosevelt," and a gold chronographic watch. Tolstoy realized that since "President Roosevelt was Head of State he had to send something in gold to His Holiness," and he decided to obtain the best possible golden chronometer in existence at the time.[17] A jeweler in the Mayflower Hotel obtained one of only two such watches ever made, at a cost of $2,800. The British considered the Americans' offerings to the Dalai Lama unimpressive compared to earlier gifts to his predecessor.[18] But the Dalai Lama, who later became a collector of watches, described the gold chronometer in his autobiography as "magnificent" and valued it sufficiently to take it with him when he fled Tibet in 1959. According to his brother, Gyalo Thondup, he still uses it today.[19]

The gifts Tolstoy received in return signified a certain official pleasure on the part of the Tibetan cabinet ministers' new contact with the United States.[20] He reported they included four "very expensive and beautifully made religious tapestries (which took 300 women several months to make)"; a set of gold coins, a framed picture of the Dalai Lama, and a complete set of previously issued and current stamps, which the Tibetan Minister of Finance Tsarong Dzasa had run off at Tolstoy's request for the president's personal collection. The cabinet also expressed its "warmest appreciation of your good will." When Donovan forwarded this letter to Roosevelt, he responded with his version of the Gelett Burgess rhyme, "The Purple Cow":[21]

Dear Bill—
    Thank you for sending me the letter from the Kashag.

> I never saw a Kashag.
> I never want to see one.
> But this I know, and know full well,
> I would rather see than be one.

    P.S. I find that Kashag is a Cabinet. The above remarks still hold.

F.D.R.

The mysteries of the Tibetan government, about which the president jestingly expressed the desire to remain ignorant, were more politically sensitive than Roosevelt realized. While Tolstoy could not have been expected to detect the divisive undercurrents that were to lead to a bitter civil war between Tibet's top theocratic leaders the following year, this blissful ignorance about the dynamics of Tibetan politics still prevailed when the U.S. government launched its covert action programs in Tibet several years later.

The formalities completed, Tolstoy spent the next several weeks in Lhasa assessing local attitudes, sites, and assets for possible future operational activity. Tolstoy apparently decided that his mission did not include lobbying for the controversial supply route through Tibet. In his final report submitted to OSS headquarters the following summer, he said that he did not broach the subject of a motor road across Tibet with the government. He explained his restraint on the ground that "the present Tibetan government is most unfavorably minded toward any opening of Tibet," and regards "motor vehicles as modern and anti-Tibetan."[22] So much for the fundamental reason for the mission.

Tolstoy made a movie of Lhasa, one of the first of its kind, which served his intelligence task and pleased the Dalai Lama and his official household. The Tibetan government officially requested radio transmitters to communicate with its outposts, and Tolstoy endorsed this proposal to OSS headquarters, which passed it to the State Department, where in April of 1943 Alger Hiss, then an assistant to the State Department's adviser on political affairs, further endorsed it as "helpful to our war effort in the general area."[23] The Department nevertheless reasserted its old fears about offending the Chinese, so Donovan waited ten days and repeated his request. The State Department then apparently decided to wash its hands of the whole thing and leave it to General Stilwell as a military matter.[24]

TOLSTOY LEAVES LHASA

Tolstoy and Dolan celebrated the Tibetan New Year in February of 1943 in great style as the recipients of special invitations from the Kashag. After more than three months in Lhasa, the time had come to set off on the reconnaissance mission for which they had been sent to Tibet. They would have to head for China across northern and eastern Tibet.[25]

The OSS files are silent on how Tolstoy managed to obtain permission to head for China across an area previously closed to foreigners. An OSS field memorandum lists several cables concerning "certain [unspecified] action that the United States might take to cement its friendship with the Tibetan Government." Other cables indicate a certain amount of indecision about whether Tolstoy was to return to India or proceed to China.[26] This fuzziness may have prompted Tolstoy's venture into extracurricular diplomacy. According to the head of the British mission in Lhasa, Frank Ludlow, Tolstoy told the Tibetans he was recommending to his government that Tibet be permitted to send a delegation to the postwar peace conference. Tolstoy embellished his freewheeling statements, Ludlow reported, by telling the regent that "the American Government was in full sympathy with those weak and small nations who wished to retain their independence. He [Tolstoy] cited the case of the South American states whom the U.S. could overthrow and swallow in a very short time, but who were completely independent and free."[27]

However premature—the war would last another two and a half years—Ludlow also endorsed this prospect. When the Tibetans enthusiastically accepted it, warning only that it should be kept secret from the Chinese, Tolstoy quickly began to backpedal. He confided to Ludlow that he doubted his government would approve. If this ploy was ever reported beyond the British Foreign Office, which disapproved mightily, there is no record of any U.S. reaction.[28] It would not, however, have been out of step with the spirit of comradeship and unity of purpose for the Allied cause[29] that the U.S. government was at the time attempting to inculcate among the Tibetans. And in any case, it worked and earned the two travelers their passage across Tibet.[30] It was left to Ludlow's superior, Basil Gould, to disabuse the Tibetans a year later of any illusions that they were to be accepted into the international club.[31]

Tolstoy and Dolan set off from Lhasa at the end of February 1943, riding Tibetan ponies. They were accompanied by one monk, one lay official, and five soldiers provided by the Tibetan government against the "many dangers from robbers and thieves." While Tolstoy was en route, a U.S. naval attaché visited Xining, the capital of the ethnically Tibetan province of Qinghai. There he was informed by the local Chinese government that 10,000 Chinese troops had been moved toward the Tibetan border in obedience to Generalissimo Chiang K'ai-shek's order.[32] The U.S. embassy reported that Chiang had three objectives: to open a military supply route through Tibet on China's terms; to gain a foothold in the independent border provinces; and eventually to bring Tibet under effective Chinese control. China's pretext for all this, the embassy reported, was that Japanese agents were stirring up the Tibetans.

An aroused Winston Churchill warned Chinese foreign minister T. V. Soong at a meeting of the Pacific War Council in Washington on May 20, 1943, "that a disturbing rumor had reached him that China is massing troops on the borders of Tibet, and that he hoped it was in error, both because the borders of Tibet had been secure for so many years and, also, because it would mean diverting forces away from the true enemy—Japan . . . ."[33] Dr. Soong "stated emphatically that there was no truth whatsoever to the rumor, either that troops were being massed on the border or that China has any present intention of attacking Tibet. He stated however, that Tibet was not a separate nation; that it is a part of China and that eventually China may have to take necessary action to maintain her sovereignty, but that they have no intentions of taking such action at the present time."[34]

It must have been a lively exchange between the Harvard-educated Chinese banker and diplomat and the British bulldog as they both defended their threatened empires. Churchill did not, however, challenge Soong about the status of Tibet, even though only a month before the British government had informed Washington that "the Government of India [has] always held that Tibet is a separate country in full enjoyment of local autonomy, entitled to exchange diplomatic representatives with other powers." This aide-mémoire had gone on to assert that "the relationship between China and Tibet is not a matter which can be unilaterally decided by China, but one on which Tibet is entitled to negotiate, and on which she can, if necessary count on the diplomatic support of the British Government along the lines above."[35]

Churchill may have been inhibited by the State Department's chilly response, which held fast to its support for China's sovereignty over Tibet.[36] Preserving the frequently fragile alliance with Chiang was obviously of more immediate concern than the legal status of far-off Tibet. But the British Foreign Office, obviously losing patience, told Washington that if Chiang continued his saber rattling on the Tibetan border and contemplated withdrawing the autonomy enjoyed by the Tibetans, "His Majesty's Government and the Government of India must ask themselves whether, in the changed circumstances of today, it would be right for them to continue to recognize even a theoretical state of subservience for a people who desire to be free and have, in fact, maintained their freedom for more than thirty years."[37]

Unfortunately for the Tibetans, when this question became painfully relevant with the rise of the Communist regime at the end of the decade, the British either did not raise the question again or answered it more pragmatically.

✑

By the end of June 1943 Tolstoy had made his way to Lanzhou in the Chinese border province of Kansu. There the U.S. consul, John S. Service, an old China hand who had traveled into eastern Tibet as a young man with his diplomat father, gave him 200,000 Chinese dollars in cash to pay off his caravan. The money had come from the OSS representative in Chungking, who had given it to Service during his last visit on the authorization of a special logistical annex to FE-2. Service of course realized the dangers of carrying such a large amount of cash through an area infested with bandits. He bought several tins of tea and filled them with the bank notes, which he subsequently turned over to Tolstoy. When asked some thirty years later if there had been any significant return from the Tolstoy expedition, Service replied:

> None whatever that I know of. It was irrelevant, peripheral to the war. There were various rumors that had started that the Japanese had gotten into Tibet, into Lhasa, and that Japanese agents were active

there. There was apparently one Japanese Buddhist who had been in Lhasa for a good many years. But they didn't really prove that he was a secret agent or that he was very effective or that he subverted the Tibetans. So I don't think the operation accomplished anything. Maybe it accomplished a negative result in proving there wasn't anything to worry about, no Japanese subversion. The Japanese weren't about to take over Tibet.[38]

Service sent Tolstoy on his way to Chungking where he submitted his report to General Stilwell. Despite Service's dismissal of the mission's significance, Tolstoy's detailed and documented report was the first and probably the only comprehensive on-the-ground reconnaissance intelligence on Tibet that the U.S. government was ever to receive.

But despite the president's personal interest in a supply route to China through Tibet,[39] the matter remained unresolved for reasons of both international and internal U.S. government politics. In January of 1944 Tolstoy reopened the possibility of using the trans-Tibetan route, not to supply the Chinese but to provide supplies for OSS operations in China. He noted that the British authorities in India had estimated that "in a year's time of proper organization, transportation of 4,000 tons yearly could be handled over that route by pack animals."[40] He warned that the State Department would have to take preliminary steps to obtain the support of the Chinese and British, and said the Tibetans would have to be propitiated, too. Not only should the promised radio stations be delivered before the request was made, he said, but the U.S. government should buy Tibet's wool surplus, which amounted to no more than one shipload.

The OSS Far East Theater office grudgingly endorsed this proposal two months later with the following proviso: "OSS is having no difficulty in getting its small supplies into China. Recent relations with the 14th Air Force expedite matters considerably. Heavy equipment, such as transmitters, jeeps, trucks, machine guns, etc., are our bottleneck. If Major Tolstoy feels these can be moved through Tibet without much loss or breakage, I believe the plan should be pursued. If, however, the plan directs attention for the most part to OSS gadgets and special equipment, I do not feel that the extensive arrangements called for are justified by the facts."[41]

General Donovan, however, apparently felt that the project concerned more than just gadgets. He also may well have wanted to preserve the OSS stake in the China theater. He therefore forwarded Tolstoy's proposal to the State Department for action. Donovan conceded that the amounts that could be sent into China from India by pack animals would be of little material assistance to the U.S. armed forces but would be of "great use in OSS operations in China."[42] In what may have been a muted protest, he noted that the amount that could go overland would be double the OSS monthly supply allocation arriving over the Hump.[43] Donovan also pointed out that an overland route would also spin off an "intelligence byproduct" of value to the OSS.[44]

Donovan did, however, send along an accompanying memorandum from Tolstoy warning that recent Allied setbacks in Burma might make the Tibetans more wary of the road, while the Chinese might at the same time use the project as another lever in its campaign to reestablish control over Tibet. Tolstoy urged the United States to use its influence to relieve strains that could break out in open warfare along the border between Tibet and China.[45] The State Department had little interest in intervening in what could be a nasty local quarrel to obtain a route that was by then of marginal interest.

By this time, the whole question had been lost in the tactical debates over the best way to supply China by land or air, and the larger strategic question of how to drive the Japanese from China. The proposal seems to have been dropped in the summer of 1944, with only a minor victory for the OSS. In September of that year, the War Production Board granted a wool import quota to the Sadutsang brothers. They shared the Tibetan wool export monopoly with the Pandatsangs, to whom, Tolstoy noted in his memo, his mission was indebted "for their great assistance in many matters."

In November of 1944 the Tibetan government sent a letter of thanks to Tolstoy, reporting that the three transmitters and six receivers he had promised had arrived in Lhasa.[46] Getting them to work was something else. The Tibetans had insisted that the radio operators must be Tibetan, but there were few with even an elementary education who understood English well enough to grasp the technical details. Efforts by the British to open schools had been aborted several times under conservative local pressures. The Tibetan government reluctantly recognized this problem and permitted young Indians and Sikkimese to assemble and operate the radios.[47] Unfortunately, the generators sent by the OSS to power the sets did not produce enough electricity in the rarefied air. During all this the OSS was disbanded and transferred to the War Department, and it took another year for the appropriate generators, each weighing four hundred and fifty pounds and broken down into components, to reach Lhasa by pack train. When the radios, generators, and trained operators (from Sikkim and India) were finally assembled after the war, a network was in place.[48] But when China invaded eastern Tibet on October 5, 1950, the newly appointed governor general chose not to deploy the additional stations and operators available in his area, and thus one of the few tangible benefits of Tolstoy's mission was wasted.

⧟

What did the Tibetans gain from their first official encounter with the United States? They established a loose and ill-defined relationship and their own channels of communication with the country that was to be the most powerful in the postwar world. In the process they also were to acquire the interest, if not the commitment, of an eventual ally in their efforts to resist Chinese domination. Lhasa would no longer have to rely exclusively on the aloof and distant British to represent their interests to the outside world. Internally, they also acquired technical equipment ending their capital city's isolation from the rest of their own country. With this came the first official need to train a new generation in the rudiments of modern technology, which meant a potential challenge to an established system of beliefs that prized and defended isolation.

Watching the diplomatic tug of war over the negotiations to set up a supply route also should have given the Tibetans some insight into the constraints on the principal players, even in pursuing their common interest. The awkward retraction of Tolstoy's invitation to the postwar

peace conference must have increased the cynicism of the Tibetan foreign office, which well understood and had itself used such devices. This
must also have undercut the arguments of those in favor of emerging
into the modern world over the objections of Tibet's defenders of the
status quo. The clear lesson was that they had no choice but to make the
best deal they could in a world ruled by national interests.

As for the United States, it gained little of immediate value from the
Tolstoy mission, but its interest at that time was a limited one. The U.S.
government had neither need nor desire to challenge the traditional
interests of its British and Chinese allies there. Before the Tolstoy mission, America's knowledge of Tibet came largely from the National Geographic Society and its magazine, and the findings of the few American
anthropologists and naturalists who toured remote areas of the country.
Tolstoy and Dolan kept a daily log of their travels across Tibet, and it
became a report on the topography, altitude, climate, temperature,
weather, potential airfield sites, and Tibetan military installations. This
eighteen-part report was worthy of their nineteenth-century British and
Russian predecessors who charted the approaches to India and probed
the upper regions of the Oxus. The two men supplemented this data on
a hitherto unknown area with a remarkable collection of photographs.
While their contacts in Lhasa were confined to the lay and ecclesiastical
aristocracy, both men were keen observers and personable travelers who
also recorded the social and cultural outlook of ordinary Tibetans they
encountered on their way across Tibet's Great Northern Plain. Their
final report was the single greatest contribution to the basic country
studies that were then being assembled by America's nascent intelligence
services. When the Chinese Communists announced their intention to
"liberate" Tibet in 1949, H. E. Richardson, the British chief of the
Indian mission in Lhasa and an old Tibet hand, noted that "apart from
the Tolstoy report, there are no reliable maps and there never has been a
comparable geographical survey of Tibet."[49]

Through this mission the U.S. government, present and future, came
to know many people who were later involved in Tibet's efforts to
emerge with a new identity to challenge its aggressive Chinese neighbors. Though the American establishment had acquired only a surface

knowledge of these distant people and their society, it now knew them as real persons and not as inhabitants of Shangri-la. When it later served U.S. interests to encourage Tibetan resistance, the United States government had at least a small legacy of credibility and goodwill from Tolstoy's pioneering mission.

The first returns were modest but generally positive for both parties. But as the tangled history of operations will demonstrate, there were frustrations inherent in dealing with such a distant and landlocked country surrounded by neighbors of mixed sympathies and conflicting interests. The generally well meaning but inadequate perceptions of each other's limitations and objectives foreshadowed the complex and often disappointing relationship that was to develop during the next half-century of the Cold War.

CHAPTER 2

Emergence from Isolation

IT WAS TO BE FIVE years after Tolstoy's mission until the Tibetans made a serious effort to resume a relationship with the U.S. government. In the interim all the factors that were to make Tibet an orphan in the Cold War were emerging. Although the war had belatedly helped awaken the Tibetans to the outside world, their efforts to establish contact were hampered by regional enmities and crippling domestic political quarrels between and within clergy and laity. The Chinese civil war would replace an ineffective enemy with one capable of imposing a revolutionary and iron will by military force. Tibet's potential allies were preoccupied elsewhere with heavy and unexpected international responsibilities quite different from those they had imagined would be theirs in the peaceful world for which they had fought.

When World War II ended in 1945, Lhasa was embroiled in a struggle for power centered on the regency of the then ten-year-old Dalai Lama. Four years previous, Reting Rimpoche had resigned as regent in favor of Taktra, a respected monk in his sixties who was the Dalai Lama's tutor. Reting, an active but controversial individual, had been a principal figure in finding the Dalai Lama as a child. Ninety miles from Lhasa, at the sacred lake of Lhamolatso (in which the Tibetans believe prophetic images can be seen), he claimed to have had a vision in 1935 involving three letters of the Tibetan alphabet and certain geographical features forecasting the birthplace of the new Dalai Lama. When the fourteenth Dalai Lama was discovered two years later at a site matching Reting's vision, this further enhanced his political position. But in 1941, Reting, then only thirty-one, told government officials that he had had dreams foretelling his death unless he retired to a monastery for meditation.

The fourteenth Dalai Lama's older brother, Gyalo Thondup, believes that the regent's dreams may well have been generated by rumors and threats spread in Lhasa by Reting's theocratic enemies.[1] Reting was later to claim that Taktra had reneged on an agreement made between them, according to which the older man would resign once active opposition to Reting's rule subsided. But when Reting returned to reclaim his post in 1944, he found his successor quite unwilling to relinquish the regency and was forced to beat a humiliating retreat. Taktra, now his avowed enemy, at the same time moved against the ex-regent's political base in the powerful Sera Che College. Sera was one of the great monasteries of the Dalai Lama's sect, a small city housing several thousand monks and composed of colleges like a British university. The besieged Sera Che abbot fled to Chinese-controlled territory where he remained until the Communists took control of Tibet. This near-insurrection diverted attention, to say the least, from the great events outside Tibet that were shaping the postwar world and would in their own way affect the Dalai Lama.

Nevertheless there was a growing feeling in Lhasa that Tibet could no longer maintain its isolation. In October of 1945 the Kashag and clerical chiefs sent a mission to India and China to present gifts and letters of congratulations to the victorious wartime Allies. They had chosen to ignore the snub they received when the British made it clear that Tolstoy's unauthorized invitation to attend the postwar peace conference had been withdrawn. With the days of the Raj numbered, London, and therefore New Delhi, seemed to have little interest in receiving such felicitations from their former ward, but the Tibetans' real objective was to provide cover for discussions with China about their political future. Chiang had offered military supplies toward the end of World War II and issued a statement pledging that "if the Tibetans should at this time express the wish for self-government," China "would, in conformity with our sincere traditions, accord it a very high degree of autonomy." He even added that if, like Outer Mongolia, the people of Tibet fulfilled the economic requirements for independence, China would "help them attain that status."[2] The Tibetans were ready to put Chiang to the test.

The delegation was guided by strict guidelines drafted by the Tibetan national assembly in a letter to Chiang.[3] It stated Tibet's claim to independence, including the still-disputed territories on the eastern border with their ethnic Tibetan populations, reaffirmed that the Dalai Lama and lesser incarnate lamas were to be selected solely by the Tibetans, and asked that no more Chinese diplomats[4] be posted to Lhasa since discussions now could be carried on by wireless (a characteristically subtle dodge that was fully appreciated by their equally wily hosts). Foreshadowing later controversies, the letter also said that if Tibet needed to send envoys to China in the future, the Chinese government must recognize their Tibetan diplomatic passports and Tibet's own right to issue visas for traders and other visitors.

The delegation traveled first to New Delhi in March 1946, where it presented letters and gifts with the usual pomp and ceremony to the viceroy. Its members called on U.S. diplomatic representatives and presented letters of congratulations, photographs, and gifts from the Dalai Lama and the regent for President Truman. They were then delayed by a threatened quarantine because of an "infectious" skin disease, diagnosed as a heat rash. The Tibetans suspected that the British political officer in Sikkim was using the threat of quarantine as an excuse to obstruct their trip to China. This may well have been the case as the British officer with some prescience feared they would be forced to attend the National Constitutional Convention and be paraded as Chinese subjects.[5] Britain may have been withdrawing from Tibetan affairs, but it still wasn't ready to let the Tibetans provide the Chinese with tokens that they might use to reinforce their claim to sovereignty over Tibet.

The delegation proceeded to make its own travel arrangements and left the next month for China. It was accompanied by the Dalai Lama's elder brother, Gyalo Thondup, and his brother-in-law, Phuntso Tashi. Neither Gyalo nor Phuntso was a formal member of the delegation, and neither participated in the subsequent negotiations in Nanking. Gyalo, the only one of five brothers who was not a monk, was being sent to study Chinese and learn about the Nationalist government on the orders of his father, who wanted to prepare him to run the family properties in their native Amdo, part of the Chinese province of Qinghai. Reting, who at that time was hovering in the background hoping to return to power, had endorsed the father's decision to educate his son in China and opened his library in Lhasa to help Gyalo prepare for his studies in Nanking. Thondup's father was, in fact, a friend of Reting. The two shared a love of horses; the Amdo farmer was a former horse trader. Newly royal, he had rather greedily claimed and been generously awarded property and honors by the ex-regent. This association was later held against the family, especially Gyalo, when Reting attempted to reclaim this position.[6]

In Nanking, Gyalo split from the delegation to begin four years' study at the Central Political University. The delegation not surprisingly found the Chinese singularly uninterested in discussing the points raised in the Tibetan's letter to Chiang, and it soon became clear that independence was a long way off. The Chinese instead spent their time pressuring the Tibetans to support a declaration stating all present to be "subjects of the Chinese Kuomintang Government." The delegation left Nanking in March of 1947 without signing the document, but their hosts nevertheless gained a propaganda victory by the mere attendance of the Tibetan delegation in their colorful costumes, which the Chinese Nationalists photographed and distributed to the press. The Tibetans were learning about the traps along the paths of diplomacy, which they had avoided for so long in their closed world.

The Tibetans enjoyed one minor success in the autumn of 1946 at a semi-official conference of Asian countries sponsored by the Indian Council of Foreign Affairs. Jawaharlal Nehru—India's future prime minister, who was then in charge of foreign affairs of the interim Indian government—saw the New Delhi conference as a way for India to make its own way in the world. He invited Tibet to attend. The British representative in Lhasa who conveyed the invitation suggested that the conference would provide a forum to demonstrate Tibet's de facto independence.[7] Lhasa accordingly sent a delegation, ready to discuss Tibet's borders and political status, with the Indians, but Nehru rejected such talk. Phillips Talbot, then a correspondent for the *Chicago Daily News* and later involved in Tibetan affairs as U.S. assistant secretary for Near Eastern and South Asian Affairs during the sixties, recalled that the only notable incident involving Tibet was a Chinese protest at a huge conference map that showed Tibet as a separate country.[8] The Indians repainted the map overnight to blur the boundary, but the Tibetans returned to Lhasa satisfied at having been seated with their national flag and having had the opportunity to speak out like the other delegations.

WASHINGTON REDISCOVERS TIBET

The power struggle that had been festering for several years reached a climax on April 15, 1947, when Reting and two of his close supporters were arrested on charges by the national assembly of twice attempting to kill the regent Taktra and then seeking military support from Chiang K'ai-shek to overthrow the government. Reting's two collaborators confessed, while Reting would only admit that he had approved his fellow clerics' active opposition to the Taktra administration. He claimed ignorance of specifics such as the assassination attempts against the regent. The monks at Sera Che rose up in sympathy with their leader. Nevertheless, within days all three were found guilty by the assembly, but the case against Reting suddenly turned moot when he died in prison, probably poisoned. His two confederates were sentenced to have their eyeballs removed. This brutal punishment was later commuted to life imprisonment at Taktra's request, "for the benefit of the young Dalai Lama's long life."

Such plots and counterplots were more worthy of Florence under the Borgias than a Shangri-la of monastic contemplation. In Tibet, they hardly promoted the forward and outward vision that would be demanded by challenges from abroad. Washington, for its part, had remained largely ignorant of the complex and occasionally bloody politics of Tibet about which it would remain generally oblivious.

On January 13, 1947, George R. Merrell, the U.S. chargé d'affaires in New Delhi, belatedly forwarded to President Truman translations of the letters that the Tibetan victory mission had left with him the previous spring, prior to their departure to China. It had taken ten months for the letters to be forwarded to Washington, returned to New Delhi for translation, and then to be translated by British officials in Sikkim as a favor to their American colleagues. Merrell observed that the three letters from the Dalai Lama, the regent, and the Kashag all expressed a desire for friendly relations with the United States. The Dalai Lama also assured the president that "although I am young, I am doing my best to spread the Buddhist religion in Tibet."

Merrell reported that when the members of the delegation delivered these letters they had conveyed the impression that if the president were to send an official to Lhasa with a reply, he would be cordially received. Merrell then proceeded to make a strong case for extending such a reciprocal courtesy, noting that any opposition from the Chinese Nationalist government to such a show of U.S. official interest in Tibet would be irrelevant given the Nationalists' precarious position.

In language reminiscent of that used by British players in the Great Game a century earlier, the chargé cited Tibet's "inestimable strategic importance" because of its position "in a central continent threatened by Soviet expansionism." The Tibetans were people who "will probably resist Soviet influence and other disruptive forces longer than any other Asiatic people," he wrote, and the "conservative and religious nature of the Tibetan people and the relatively firm control exercised by their government combine to produce comparatively stable conditions." He then added a more dramatic inducement: Tibet, as a price of U.S. support for its independence, could provide "the only extensive territory where air and rocket-launching operations might be based" should the U.S. ever again find it necessary to send military forces to the mainland of Asia and be faced with opposition by potentially unfriendly or even anarchic new governments in India, Burma, Indochina, and China. In Cold War rhetoric already becoming familiar, Merrell added:

> Tibet may therefore be regarded as a bulwark against the spread of Communism throughout Asia, or at least as an island of conservatism in a sea of political turmoil, and a gesture of friendship from the United States might go a long way toward encouraging the Tibetans to resist possible Soviet or Communist infiltration into the Tibetan Plateau which, in an age of rocket warfare, might prove to be the most important territory of all Asia.[9]

Merrell's proposal reflected a rapidly changing international scene. Europe had been divided by the Cold War; the Communist forces in China were on the march, some of Merrell's foreign service colleagues were already being blamed for having supposedly "lost" China to Communism, and the British, exhausted by war, were dismantling their empire and yielding their geopolitical responsibilities to the United States in Europe and Asia. As far as Tibet was concerned, the British General Staff had already concluded in July of 1946 that "from a short term point of view there is no practicable means of aiding Tibet against a major enemy, and there is no real threat to India from that direction, and the Government of India [which was still under British control] do not propose further to consider at present the possibility of offering military assistance to Tibet. They will, however, continue to meet as far as possible reasonable requests for the supply of arms and ammunition."[10] This rationale for a minimal policy regarding Tibet was adopted by the new Indian government when it succeeded Britain in 1947.

It was three months before Merrell received a response. Washington was preoccupied with taking up the British responsibility of blocking the Communists from winning the civil war in Greece. Although the Truman Doctrine drawing the line against a Communist advance into

Greece and Turkey declared that "we must assist free peoples to work out their own destinies in their own way," the Tibetans were yet to qualify as threatened people, and Tibet was also far from central U.S. strategic concerns.

In its belated reply of April 14, the State Department told Merrell that the War Department had rejected his ideas for Tibet as a rocket base. A memorandum relaying the War Department's response ended: "On the facetious side, two possible uses for Tibet were envisaged: as a country offering great waste areas in which rockets could be tested, or as a final retreat (Shangri-la) to which peace-loving people could flee when atomic war breaks, for Tibet is too remote to be of significance in any war."[11]

Apparently the State Department shared their military colleagues' view of Tibet's peripheral strategic value but did not completely reject Merrell's plea for some diplomatic attention. Although it speedily backed away from anything even hinting of diplomatic recognition, it covered its bets by expressing the desire that the Tibetans regard the United States as "friendly and well-disposed." Merrell was advised that his superiors were preparing a reply to the Tibetans' request to establish relations with Washington. The response was to be forwarded "by readily available means of communication" to the Dalai Lama. Furthermore, the Department would be well disposed toward occasional "unobtrusive and unofficial" visits by foreign service officers to Tibet.[12]

The promised presidential reply was never sent, nor did embassy officers visit in order to find out what was happening in Tibet. Although Lhasa was close to civil war while this correspondence was underway, neither Washington nor New Delhi had much, if any, information on what was happening, apart from sketchy reports received and shared by the British mission. This lack of intelligence was to continue for the next two years while the combined resources of the Department's political officers and their colleagues at the newly organized Central Intelligence Agency began acquiring their own informants in Lhasa and news from travelers. Even then, the U.S. government was never to know or appreciate the full depth of the internal rivalries among the factions in Lhasa and between the capital and the regions of eastern Tibet bordering China.

THE HERMITS REJOIN THE WORLD

With the rebellion put down in Lhasa, the Tibetans took concrete moves toward establishing their own relations with the outside world. In June of 1947 the Tibetan foreign office wrote the U.S. embassy in New Delhi that Tsipon Shakabpa, the government's chief financial officer and long a member of Lhasa's political inner circle, planned to lead a trade mission to India, China, the United States, and Britain. Shakabpa brought with him one monk and two laymen, including Tolstoy's first host in Tibet, Pandatsang, the wool merchant and official from the controversial family of eastern Tibet. They asked the Americans to help organize "cordial talks there on arrival" with President Truman and other "high officials" to discuss trade between America and Tibet.[13] The embassy forwarded his request, reassuring Washington privately that it had done nothing to compromise China's claims to sovereignty over Tibet, meanwhile noncommittally inviting Shakabpa to visit the embassy when he was in New Delhi.

In a follow-up cable on August 21, the new ambassador to India, Henry F. Grady, reported the considerable misgivings of the British political officer in Sikkim, A. J. Hopkinson.[14] This patronizing remnant of the British Raj recalled how the Tibetans had been used by the Chinese during their visit to Nanking. He claimed that the trade mission also wanted to purchase gold to back Tibet's currency, which he suspected they wanted to obtain mainly "for the joy of the chase." Hopkinson feared the trade mission would only undermine Tibet's "simplicity and sincerity and its adherence to its own culture." Three months later Hopkinson embellished these reservations, suggesting that the mission was the brain child of Yangpel Pandatsang,[15] "the richest trader in Tibet," who seemed more interested in the personal gain of the members of the mission than the political objectives of the Tibetan government. "Despite their acumen as traders, members of the mission may prove to be 'babes in the woods' when they come face to face with foreign exchange and import/export restrictions," Hopkinson said.

The embassy duly forwarded his views but pointed out that the mission's negotiations—official or unofficial—were unlikely to make much of a dent in U.S. foreign trade either way. Nevertheless, the embassy asked the State Department to ensure a "courteous reception" and to "take such steps as may be feasible to prevent members of the mission from falling into the hands of unscrupulous persons." The new ambassador's motive was not particularly different from his predecessor's. He urged the government not to "throw away its unique opportunity to strengthen the friendly feelings which the Tibetans have exhibited" and revived the argument for recognizing the military importance of Tibet, rejecting the War Department's attitude as blinkered and conservative: "How many Army officers in 1935 would have taken seriously a prediction that ten years later a single aerial bomb could be utilized to demolish a city?" The ambassador also was ready to override Chinese objections, but the State Department was unmoved. It replied on November 21 that Washington could only receive the Tibetans informally through the Commerce Department and instructed the embassy to stamp only their visa applications and not their passports if the Tibetans carried Tibetan and not Chinese travel documents. State added a final caution about the restrictions on nonresidents purchasing gold and silver in the United States.[16]

Then began an extended and, on the Tibetans' part, cleverly executed diplomatic minuet demonstrating how misplaced the snobbish British diplomat's misgivings about the Tibetans' acumen were. The Tibetan government had protected its own identity for centuries by playing off foreign governments against each other, and these innocents from the mountains could have held their own at the Congress of Vienna. Shakabpa and his traveling companions well appreciated such symbols of sovereignty as visas, passports, the manner of receiving delegations, and, in finance, a gold reserve to back its currency and thus facilitate foreign trade.

Upon arriving in New Delhi, carrying the first official Tibetan passports ever issued for foreign travel,[17] the mission did the rounds of the Indian political circuit, calling on Prime Minister Nehru, the Raj's last viceroy, now a governor general, Lord Mountbatten, and Mahatma Gandhi. (Gandhi gave his guests a characteristic bit of homespun advice: He gently admonished them when he learned that the traditional ceremonial scarves that they had presented to him were made of imported silk. The Tibetans, Gandhi said, should be weaving their own cloth.[18]) The Chinese embassy predictably told its American colleagues that the Tibetans should travel only on Chinese passports. The American chargé in New Delhi was noncommittal and finessed the issue by advising the Tibetans to apply for U.S. visas at the U.S. embassy in Nanking or the consulate in Shanghai. They got no satisfaction from the Indians on their other concern, which was to unblock their own funds to buy U.S. gold. After fruitless negotiations with the new Indian government about its tariffs on Tibetan imports transiting Calcutta and the profits earned by Tibetan exports (the Indians put the dollars in the Reserve Bank of India and paid Lhasa in the equivalent amount of rupees), the Tibetans reached Nanking in February of 1948. They spent the next three months touring China, trying to arrange barter deals, and dodging Chiang's political land mines.

By the end of May, Shakabpa and his mission were ready to move on to their prime targets, Washington and London, but the problem of travel documents stood in their way. They had entered China by way of Hong Kong, using their Chinese passports at China's insistence. The Chinese had even offered to furnish them with all the foreign exchange they would need for their trip to the West if they continued using Chinese passports. The U.S. embassy, reluctant to challenge its Chinese hosts, advised the Tibetans they would receive U.S. entry visas only if they could present Chinese exit visas—which the Chinese government refused to place on their Tibetan passports.

The Tibetans then came up with a subterfuge, aided mightily by a bureaucratic snafu or possibly a maverick diplomat. They confided to the British ambassador that they would pretend to be returning to India without proceeding to London or Washington. The ambassador, either obliging or ill-informed, stamped visas to Britain and its colonies in their Tibetan passports.[19] London was furious, but it was partly the fault of Whitehall's own bureaucracy. The Foreign Office had neglected to send Nanking a copy of a telegram from the Commonwealth Office—which dealt with India—warning against issuing British visas in Tibetan passports. When the Tibetans then informed the American ambassador of their travel plans, he reported on May 29 that the mission was "traveling via Hong Kong in order to 'save face' by disposing of their Chinese passports there and proceeding on the Tibetan travel documents to which U.S. visas would have been affixed in Hong Kong."[20] In Hong Kong, the U.S. consul unaccountably placed their American visas on their Tibetan passports.[21] Perhaps the best explanation for his error can be found in John F. Kennedy's reaction when a U-2 went off course during the tense days of the Cuban missile crisis: "There's always some so-and-so who doesn't get the word."[22] Round One to the Tibetans.

The delegation finally arrived in San Francisco on July 9 where the British consul made the gratuitous but much appreciated gesture of meeting them. The mission proceeded by transcontinental train to Washington, where they were met at Union Station on July 19 by a Commerce Department official and two representatives of the Chinese embassy. Occasionally donning colorful official Tibetan robes, although generally appearing in business suits, these exotic emissaries from Shangri-la attracted interest wherever they went. George Yeh, the Chinese vice minister of Foreign Affairs, had already expressed his irritation to the U.S. ambassador in Nanking at having been outmaneuvered by the Tibetans, and the Chinese embassy also complained to the State Department in Washington. The Department quickly reassured China's ambassador in Washington, Wellington Koo, that the United States still recognized Chinese sovereignty over Tibet and informed him, incorrectly as it turned out, that the mission's U.S. visas had not been issued on Tibetan travel documents but on "U.S. Government standard forms."[23] Mollified, the Chinese diplomats nevertheless insisted on assisting in "arrangements" with the trade mission. The embassy apparently wanted to stop these supposed "babes in the woods" from pulling any more diplomatic fast ones on their turf. The State Department tried to dodge that move by pointing out that the Tibetans were mere businessmen and were being treated as such by the Department of Commerce.

But three days later the issue of diplomatic recognition was joined when the Department sounded out the Chinese embassy counselor on a potential problem: the trade mission's request for an appointment with the president. The Department's China Affairs officer explained that the mission had brought along a photograph of the Dalai Lama inscribed to

President Truman and wanted to present it to him in person. He assured the Chinese diplomat that the Department did not want to make an appointment "without the prior knowledge and acquiescence of the Chinese Embassy." On the other hand, State "did not wish to refuse the request without thorough consideration, as the Tibetans had been extremely courteous and helpful to American Army officers traveling in Tibet during the war . . ." The counselor deftly said that he could perceive no objection, indeed he would like to assist by setting up the appointment with the president through the Chinese embassy, with Ambassador Koo accompanying the Tibetans to the White House.[24]

With exquisite courtesy, the counselor called back the next day to express Koo's appreciation to the Department for bringing the meeting to his attention, but the ambassador felt it necessary to refer the matter to his own superiors in Nanking. Within three days the U.S. ambassador in Nanking reported that the Chinese foreign minister had asked that the president refuse to receive the Tibetans. The foreign minister, undoubtedly still smarting at having been outwitted by Shakabpa, cited the Tibetans' unacceptable travel documents and accused the mission of trying to "act as independently as possible and by any means available to acquire recognition of its separation from China."[25]

By now exasperated, the State Department delivered a diplomatically concealed punch to the Chinese, assuring their embassy's minister that the United States would do nothing to "call into question China's *de jure* sovereignty over Tibet."[26] Use of this phrase for the first time drew a pointed distinction between the legal status the Chinese claimed over Tibet and the actual authority they exercised there. Later in this conversation, the U.S. official took off his gloves and noted that the Chinese government "should recognize that the fact that it exerts no de facto authority over Tibet is the root cause" of the dilemma. He reminded the Chinese that Washington had not invited the Tibetans, but now they were here, they "must be received with the courtesy due high-ranking representatives of far distant countries" and "could rightly be affronted if they were not received by the President."

He warned the embassy, which was acutely aware of the Nationalists' public image, that the U.S. press was showing considerable interest in the Tibetans' visit, and if it should come out that the Chinese government had frustrated their intention to call on the president, it could expect very bad press. He concluded with two substantive clinchers. "Such a story might be raised in light of self-determination which is a popular concept among the American people." To this lightly veiled threat that the U.S. might move to a new public position on Tibet's legal status he added that President Truman himself had expressed a personal interest in greeting the Tibetans.

The undoubtedly shaken Chinese diplomat was then asked to resolve the dilemma with "Chinese ingenuity" and was warned that without it, the U.S. government might act unilaterally. The Department's plain-speaking officers then bucked the problem back to Ambassador Leighton Stuart in Nanking. He was instructed to bring the Department's arguments to the attention of the Chinese foreign office, not with the "wish to add a mite to Chinese current preoccupations" (the military tide was beginning to turn against the Nationalist government), but to emphasize that the Department was "confronted with a practical problem which discourtesy will not solve." The Chinese in effect stonewalled, proposing that Ambassador Koo request an appointment with the President to present the members of the Tibetan mission and also insisting that any written replies to the letters the Tibetans planned to present to him be transmitted through the Chinese government.

The stonewalling worked. The administration was apparently unwilling to engage in a public quarrel with the beleaguered Nationalists that could turn into a domestic political issue in the U.S. presidential elections only three months hence. On August 2 the State Department sent Fulton Freeman, the assistant chief of the Division of Chinese Affairs, to try to persuade the Tibetans to accept Koo's formula.[27] Shakabpa objected, resolutely insisting that his mission was purely commercial and nonpolitical, and that the purpose of the call was simply to greet the president in the name of Tibet and present the letters and photographs they had brought from the Dalai Lama and the regent. He pointedly reminded Freeman that the Chinese had not been consulted five years earlier when Tolstoy and Dolan had been received by the Dalai Lama and presented similar letters from President Roosevelt. Freeman nevertheless warned that it would be "very difficult if not impossible" to arrange an appointment with the president without Koo. A heated discussion ensued among the Tibetans themselves, and at that point Freeman threw in the possibility of a private meeting with Secretary of State George Marshall. Such a private appointment with the secretary might, however, be possible only if the mission yielded and permitted the adhesive Chinese ambassador to accompany them in any call they might make on the president.

But within the State Department, the pendulum, for unexplained reasons, then swung back in favor of the Tibetans. On August 4 a stern message went to Nanking instructing Ambassador Stuart to inform the Chinese that Koo's formula appeared "somewhat disingenuous" since he already knew from his discussions with the Tibetans that they would not agree to visit the president under his sponsorship.[28] Thereupon followed two days of diplomatic scurrying in an unsuccessful effort to find a compromise. On August 6 the Tibetans and Secretary Marshall met at Blair House, the president's temporary residence while the White House was being renovated. The Chinese were not present, and the discussions were confined to matters of trade and an exchange of photographs, letters, and small gifts.[29]

Thus the meeting that had previously been held out as bait to induce the Tibetans to bow to Chinese demands had been granted without the Tibetans yielding or the Chinese being consulted. Marshall undoubtedly recalled Chiang K'ai-shek's bitter intransigence three years earlier when the American had unsuccessfully tried to shape a compromise that would stop the civil war now raging in China. He may well have decided to ignore the Nationalists' stubborn complaints and proceed on his own to receive these unusual guests.

Shakabpa told Marshall that the mission's primary purpose was to improve trade relations, and that Tibet wished to purchase gold and silver bullion, machinery, and other merchandise. Marshall asked whether they could pay in U.S. dollars. Shakabpa fudged, and the next day he sent a letter complaining that the new Indian government compelled the Tibetans to surrender dollar-export earnings for rupees. If the United States wanted to sell goods to Tibet, the shrewd Tibetan finance official said, it could press the Indian government to free Tibet's dollar earnings. He also asked the secretary to issue a permit to the Tibetans to buy 50,000 ounces of gold for shipment to Tibet. (Three weeks later the Department notified Shakabpa that the Tibetans could buy the gold they desired, but it declined to intervene with the Indians about releasing dollars to them to buy it.[30])

The Tibetans then left for New York, having given up hopes of seeing the president. There they spent their time informing a condescending press that Tibet was an independent country. Questions from reporters generally concerned the use of yaks' tails for Santa Claus whiskers and the inevitable question about whether they had seen the movie *Lost Horizon*.[31] Undaunted, Shakabpa raised the possibility of American businessmen, tourists, journalists, and officials visiting Tibet. He also visited Tolstoy, who introduced him to the Eastern Establishment, whose interest in remote countries was mostly channeled through the American Museum of Natural History in New York. Many of the museum's members served as senior officers of the State Department and the Central Intelligence Agency, and they also had extensive contacts with the U.S. academic community. Tolstoy arranged visits with Prince Peter of Greece and Denmark, who was planning an anthropological expedition to Tibet for the University of Copenhagen, and with the writer and broadcaster Lowell Thomas, who wanted to visit Tibet with his son. The most important of their calls was on Dwight D. Eisenhower, who was then president of Columbia University. The victorious supreme commander in Europe during World War II thanked them for the courtesy shown by their government in aiding the U.S. pilots who had been forced to abandon their plane over Tibet five years earlier. No one there could foresee that they were meeting with the man who would be president ten years later when Tibet's revolt against the Chinese made U.S. support even more critical.

Tolstoy turned the visitors over to Henry S. Evans, the public relations manager of *Business Week,* who arranged for a screening of the film Tolstoy had made in Tibet during his mission. At the delegation's request he also set up a showing of *Lost Horizon,* which turned out to be a disappointment because it had little authentic footage on Tibet, and the English dialogue was incomprehensible to the Tibetan visitors. They delayed their departure to witness the presidential election on November 5, 1948, but were refused an audience and photograph with the Republican candidate Thomas E. Dewey at his campaign headquarters because his press spokesman, James Hagerty, responded that "since Mr. Dewey is practically president, they will have to be cleared by the F.B.I."[32] The Democrats felt no such compunction, and the mission was able to witness from his party's national headquarters the excitement of the surprise reelection of the man they had been unable to meet personally.

Shakabpa had sent a message on election day to Secretary Marshall thanking him for "the help and cooperation so kindly extended by the Department"[33] that had enabled the mission to contact wool importers and the suppliers of American goods. Punctiliously, he also sent a telegram congratulating President Truman on his reelection. To this gesture he received no reply, the Department's chief of protocol having included his telegram on a list of messages on which no action had been taken "because of insufficient information as to the name of the sender or the address."[34] (The president eventually managed to send Shakabpa a photograph of himself in a silver frame inscribed "To His Holiness the Dalai Lama from Harry S Truman.")

The mission then set sail, provided with Mother Sills pills by Tolstoy's friend Evans, who discovered the night before they sailed that, having never traveled by ship before, they were completely ignorant of seasickness. The Tibetans left with some sense of satisfaction. These amateur diplomats had more than held their own against the professionals of the Nationalist embassy. While they did not gain an audience with the president, they had met with his most trusted foreign policy adviser. The amateur diplomats had come away with U.S. stamps in their Tibetan passports and had gained the privilege of buying gold to back their currency, thereby laying claim to the rudimentary trappings of sovereignty. Countering this semblance of success, the actual results were less apparent. While they had been granted permission to buy the gold, the U.S. government was not going to lend them the money to make the purchase. The president had wanted to meet them, but he had yielded to the Chinese demands that made the meeting impossible. They had obtained U.S. visas in their passports, but the State Department denied this fact to the Chinese to whom this paper recognition of Tibet's special legal status was a vital issue.

↪

On December 10, 1948, the mission left England after three weeks of protocol visits and another contretemps over its now-expired visas, which were extended after the irate Shakabpa threatened to cancel his visit and proceed home via France. On their way back through India they were able to persuade the Indian government to release $250,000 to buy a portion of the gold the U.S. Treasury had made available, supposedly for the purchase of machinery. The Tibetans came up with another $175,800 from their own sources to purchase a total of $425,800 worth of gold, which was eventually carried to Tibet by pack animals. Neither the Indian government nor the U.S. State Department knew where the Tibetans obtained the $175,800, but the historian Melvyn Goldstein says that it is "certain" that at least part of the gold was purchased with the private funds of the mission members for their own use. The diplomat/traders apparently saw no conflict of interest in pursuing both their official and private roles.[35]

When they finally returned to Lhasa to report on their efforts to establish Tibet as a member of the world community, they had been gone for a year, and the results, while mixed, made it seem a year well spent. They had visited the four countries that were to play the critical roles in Tibet's efforts to gain international acknowledgment of its independence. In each they had encountered the complex domestic and foreign policy issues that were to influence and at times plague their efforts at recognition. They had again witnessed the dogged, unyielding resistance of the Chinese Nationalists even as great stretches of China and the industrial heart of Manchuria were falling to the relentless Communist forces. Their losses undoubtedly made the Nationalists even more determined to refuse to acknowledge that these frontier mountain people were no longer part of the "Chinese family." Their territorial claims were one issue on which both the Nationalist government and its Communist successors agreed, even to this day. The visit had other tangible benefits. For the first time the U.S. State Department took note of the principle of self-determination in the context of Tibet. This was to be of crucial importance. The correctly cool reception they had received from the British, who would not even record the Tibetans' reception by the Lord Chamberlain in the *Official Gazette,* should have provided a useful—if painful—education in political reality. They could, they realized, expect little from England, to whom they had looked for support for the past three decades. Moreover, the newly independent Indian government had no intention of picking up the "white man's burden" that the British had dropped in Tibet. They would therefore have to look to the United States, while the Americans began to look closely, for the first time, at them.

CHAPTER 3

Caught in a Bigger Game

D URING 1947 and 1948 Europe was being turned into two armed camps by the Soviet conquest of the eastern half of the continent and the formation of the North Atlantic Treaty Organization (NATO). But the battle lines in Asia were drawn in a different way and on a different schedule. The Communist victory in China was not complete until the autumn of 1949, and it was not until North Korea's attack on the South in June of 1950 that the Cold War truly came to Asia.

When Shakabpa arrived in New Delhi on his way back to Lhasa to report on his attempts to gain international recognition for Tibet he called on Loy Henderson. The new U.S. ambassador was to become one of

Tibet's most ardent champions in its resistance to the Chinese Communists. Henderson's staunch anti-communism dated from his early assignments in Latvia and Russia in the twenties and thirties, and to his assignment in Moscow during Stalin's show trials of his political enemies in 1936. He frequently crossed swords even with the relatively moderate Soviet foreign minister Maxim Litvinov, and had never hidden his distrust of the Soviet system. This resulted in his removal as chief of the East European desk in 1943 under pressure from Litvinov, then the Soviet ambassador to Washington, and from those in the White House who were anxious to get rid of hard-liners like Henderson in the interest of greater cooperation with Moscow as America's wartime ally.[1]

After the war, the controversial but highly respected Henderson became director of the Department's Office of Near Eastern Affairs, where he was one of the architects of the 1947 Truman Doctrine asserting the U.S. interest in defending Greece and Turkey from communism. Henderson believed strongly in that doctrine's corollary of supporting free peoples resisting subjugation. Paradoxically, he was also an outspoken opponent of the creation of the state of Israel. This led to his bureaucratic exile as ambassador to newly independent India in the summer of 1948, removing him from Washington lest he become an issue in the presidential campaign that fall.[2]

When Henderson met Tsipon Shakabpa and his colleagues in January 1949, as a professional diplomat he was still toeing the line on China and hence Tibet. With Chiang still clinging to power, he refused to support Tibet's independence. He informed the Tibetans that the United States recognized China's sovereignty over Tibet, and that their relations with Washington "would have to be strengthened by indirect means."[3] No more than four months later, with the Chinese Nationalists fighting to hold their capital at Nanking, he bit the bullet. An April 12 memorandum of the State Department's Office of Chinese Affairs described the ambassador as arguing that if the "Communists succeed in controlling all of China, or some equivalent far-reaching development takes place, we should be prepared to treat Tibet as independent to all intents and purposes."[4]

The April memorandum on Tibet was in the form of a balance sheet updating the recommendations of Henderson and his predecessors, which now were put into high relief by the impending Nationalist collapse. The arguments in favor of recognizing the independence of Tibet included its new ideological and strategic importance relative to China; the Tibetans' conservative and anti-Communist outlook and their "stamina to withstand Communist infiltration"; the Dalai Lama's authority over Buddhists in neighboring countries; the unlikelihood that the Nationalist government would again be able to assert authority in Tibet; and the new interest the Tibetans were showing in establishing relations with the outside world. The counterarguments were that recognition could lead to China's gradual dismemberment; that it might undercut U.S. objections to Soviet efforts to detach territory from China's northern regions, and might backfire by intensifying Soviet efforts to take Tibet itself into the communist camp. The memo also argued that Tibet could not be held for the West without "far-reaching practical measures"; that Tibet's dubious military potential and sparse mineral resources would hardly make such efforts worthwhile; and that India's cooperation to make Tibet "a bastion of the West" would be as necessary as it was unlikely.

These last three, essentially pragmatic, arguments proved to be correct. The State Department also faced a domestic dilemma. It knew that the Nationalist government's authority over mainland China was fading past, but feared to be seen hastening its demise when the Truman administration and especially former Secretary of State Marshall and his successor were already under attack by their political opponents for "losing China." In New Delhi, closer to the scene, the embassy was more concerned about the threat in neighboring Tibet than about the problems of the retreating Nationalists. It sent a telegram to the Department warning that "if we make no effort to demonstrate a friendly interest in Tibet until a Communist-dominated regime consolidates its hold on China, the impression will be created among the Tibetans that we were moved only by a desire to contain Communism and not to develop cordial relations with the Tibetan people."[5] Henderson was right. Almost fifty years later both the Dalai Lama and his elder brother told me that they felt the United States had used Tibet as a pawn in the Cold War and they still resented it.[6]

Finding no good solution, the Department temporized. It concluded that for the present the United States should keep its policy flexible by avoiding references to Tibet's legal status while maintaining a friendly attitude toward Tibet in ways short of giving China cause for offense. This meant informing but not asking the Nationalists about any U.S. moves concerning Tibet, supporting the Tibetans in obtaining foreign exchange from India, and sending American officials to Lhasa to "secure first-hand information as an indication of our friendly interest." It added that if the Communists ruled all of China proper—as they would in only seven months—and the Nationalists disappeared, it would then be "clearly to our advantage" to deal with Tibet as an independent state. If the Nationalists continued to exist, the question would have to remain open—and it did when they fled to Taiwan.

U.S. Missions to Tibet

Three months later, Henderson noted that the Nationalist Chinese government was "nonfunctioning." He suggested that this presented a unique window of opportunity to send a prominent American to Lhasa and leave behind a small foreign service mission.[7] It took the Department almost a month to respond. It was preoccupied not only by a forthcoming white paper blaming Chiang K'ai-shek for losing authority in China, but also by rising Republican party criticism of the Truman administration's China policy. Publicly recognizing Tibet's independence would only underline the disintegration of the Chinese state, so the Department suggested a compromise—send a covert American mission to Tibet in the venerable tradition of the Great Game.

Washington made two suggestions. One would be to send either the embassy's second secretary, Jefferson Jones, perhaps accompanied by a British representative of similar middle rank, for two weeks to survey the political situation and prepare recommendations for opening a consulate. The other was to send an experienced explorer-scholar of China such as Schuyler Cammann of the University of Pennsylvania. Jones, ostensibly on leave, would return to write a preliminary report while Cammann remained in Tibet for the "major portion of a year under sci-

entific cover but observing political trends."[8] The U.S. embassy preferred the all U.S. scholar/diplomat combination to a joint British-
American team. It expressed doubts that "Tibet would be pleased" by
the latter and reported that India had already discouraged the British
from sending a similar mission earlier that year.[9] In any case it was too
late in the year to put together a visit before the trails into Tibet became
impassable, and the project was stillborn.

America's rediscovery of Tibet was left to the author and newscaster
Lowell Thomas, who had made his reputation by dramatizing romantic
figures in history, most notably Lawrence of Arabia. While the diplomats dithered, Thomas and his son were already on their way to Lhasa.
They had established a personal connection with Tibet via Shakabpa
during his mission to the United States the year before. In the book he
wrote about his trip to Lhasa, Lowell Thomas Jr. acknowledged that "at
the psychological moment, when the top Tibetan officials were debating
what would be the best way to inform America of the Red threat to
Tibet, our request to travel to Tibet arrived." The Tibetans, he wrote,
"decided to take a gamble—and we were invited to Lhasa."[10]

The Thomases received their invitation in mid-July and by early
August were making their way to Lhasa along the same route used by
their friend Colonel Tolstoy six years earlier. They were welcomed in
Lhasa by their sponsor Shakabpa, who expressed his disappointment
over the meager economic results of his trade mission to the United
States the year before. The father and son then met with the senior ministers of the Kashag, who asked whether they thought Communism had
come to stay in China and whether it would keep spreading across
Asia.[11] They turned the Thomases over to Tibet's two foreign ministers—one lay, one monastic, in the tandem Tibetan system—who got
down to the business that had caused Lhasa to welcome the Thomases'
visit. The ministers stated Tibet's case for independence and then asked
directly what was on everyone's mind at the time: What help Tibet
might expect if the Chinese Communists invaded?

At first, reported H. E. Richardson, the officer in charge of the Indian
mission in Lhasa, the senior Thomas made "excessively optimistic statements to the Foreign Bureau and the Kashag about Tibet's position,

alleging that they were safe for ten years."[12] Richardson was an old Tibet hand who had been asked to stay on in 1947 after the British ceded their responsibilities in Tibet to India. He said that after he told Thomas that an invasion was a far more imminent threat, the renowned commentator became more aware of the urgency of the position and promised to do all he could to enlist U.S. aid "if it could be done in time." The Thomases by their own account became more cautious in their replies, either because of Richardson's sobering advice or their own recognition of complexities they had not seen before arriving.[13] They backed away from making any promises, pleading that they were only unofficial visitors and that the U.S. policy process was complex. The Tibetans must have begun to conclude that they could not rely on decisive U.S. assistance if faced with a Chinese invasion.

The Thomases' visit concluded with an audience with the Dalai Lama, at which they presented him a Siamese tiger skull set with gold and silver, an American raincoat, and the inevitable timepiece—a folding clock.[14] The Dalai Lama in return gave them a scroll for delivery to President Truman. His message expressed the hope that the Thomases' visit would make the American people more aware of Tibet as "a holy, independent and religious country." He concluded that "we are eager to have it known that here in Tibet, a land that is especially dedicated to religion, all of our peoples, both laymen and monks, are earnestly praying that God will grant happiness and everlasting peace to all humanity."[15]

Although Thomas wrote later that he and his father realized the overwhelming logistical and political problems of bringing American aid to Tibet, this did not prevent the elder Thomas from publicly suggesting three months after his return to New York that the United States could give the Tibetans more modern weapons and advise them on guerrilla warfare, "which would make it more difficult for the Chinese Communists to approach on the North."[16] He gave the same advice to Secretary of State Dean Acheson privately the following February. According to Acheson's version, Thomas told him that the Tibetan "terrain was admirably suited for guerrilla operations, and Tibetan forces could put up strong resistance through such operations to any military force that could be sent into Tibet." He proposed sending a mission headed by a military man to encourage the Tibetans to resist. He suggested "a younger version of General Wedemeyer"—Albert Wedemeyer, one of the more vocal critics of the administration's alleged loss of China. Thomas also offered his own assistance to the point of sending his son back to Tibet.[17]

Acheson said such a mission might have merit, but remained wary. He asked Thomas about the capabilities of the Tibetan army and noted that India seemed reluctant to help. And he pointed out that "a major difficulty was that of avoiding publicity which would draw Chinese Communist attention and probably serve to hasten their move against Tibet." He may also have been aware of charges in the Soviet press that the Thomas visit was part of a "dirty adventure" to detach Tibet from China and establish it as a "colony and military base" directed against the new Chinese Communist government, which had been proclaimed on October 1, 1949.[18]

The Tibetans had little choice but to seek help from every possible source. Within six weeks after Mao's Zedong's historic victory declaration that "the Chinese people have stood up," Lhasa began receiving reports that the Chinese Communists were moving troops into areas of Tibet on the eastern frontier with China. Surkhang Shape, an alumnus of the 1948 trade mission and one of Lowell Thomas's hosts in Lhasa, delivered a message on November 19, 1949, from the Tibetan foreign bureau to the U.S. State Department asking for extensive civilian and military aid.[19] Lhasa also wrote Mao asking him to respect Tibet's territorial integrity and warning that it would be defended by all possible means.

The Tibetans had discussed this letter with Richardson. In his regular report the "old pro" British mission head noted that the Tibetan government had belatedly addressed the Chinese threat "after about five weeks, which were devoted to the annual entertainments." Richardson and Harishwar Dayal, the Indian political officer, both advised the Tibetans against provoking the Chinese by raising the issue of independence. The Englishman urged the Lhasa officials to turn their attention to their own defenses because "if matters were left until an invasion had occurred it would be too late for anything to be done." By Richardson's account, the Tibetan foreign office pondered his advice but sent a confrontational letter to Mao anyway in the belief that "a declaration of independence would improve their position in the eyes of the world." They apparently did accept Richardson's advice on defending themselves, reporting they were raising the strength of the Tibetan army from 13,000 to 100,000 men and asking the Indian government for arms, ammunition, and training.[20]

But when the British talked to their American diplomatic counterparts in New Delhi, they discounted the immediacy of the threat reported by their former colleague. While there was a nostalgic reluctance to opt out completely, the British wanted to do nothing that might encourage their former wards in Tibet to provoke the Chinese. They fell back on recommending rhetoric "to bolster the courage of the Tibetans," meanwhile trying to dissuade the Indian government from writing off Tibet.[21] Meanwhile, the highly emotional debate then in progress in Washington over whether to recognize the new regime in Beijing did not augur well for any favorable response to requests from the Tibetans for open support. Washington and London accordingly coordinated their equivocal replies to the Tibetans' appeals for material and political assistance.[22] At the same time, the State Department warned the Tibetans that they could expect both Russia and China (in the seat held by the Nationalists) to veto their request for membership in the UN. In a bit of advice that proved to be sadly lacking in prescience, it suggested that the Tibetans might better lie low lest they jeopardize their de facto freedom by "any obvious move at this time to complete separation from China in form as well as substance."[23]

Throughout this exercise of responding to the Tibetans' request for help, both the United States and Britain deferred to the Indians as the only nation that was in a geographical position to give any meaningful military support. Both assumed that any significant supply of arms that could be delivered to the Tibetans without attracting attention would have to be sent overland through India with that government's consent. Having almost totally abandoned their obligations to Tibet, and facing severe financial straits, the British sought to fashion a new policy that would enable them to regain some of their former influence in China.

Providing arms to the Tibetans would not serve this objective. And the United States, even had the political will existed, did not then have the capability to deliver significant loads of arms over long distances in covert fashion (something that was to be developed later by the Pentagon and the CIA as a consequence of the Korean war). Even that normally aggressive diplomat Loy Henderson backed away from his original proposal to send an official mission to Lhasa. He argued that it might appear to the Russians and the Indians as the first move toward an American foothold in Tibet and "cause the Communists to expedite execution of their program for the conquest of Tibet."[24] As for American aid to Tibet, Henderson argued, "It would be unfair for the U.S. to take any action which might encourage them to resist because of a mistaken idea of help from the US." He was unwilling to raise false hopes among the beleaguered Tibetans and tried to instill these same scruples among his officers. In 1951, when the embassy was urging the Dalai Lama to flee, Nicholas G. Thacher was sent as a junior officer to negotiate with the Tibetans. Years later, after retiring as an ambassador, Thacher recalled that during his 1951 mission one of his principal concerns was to discourage the Tibetans from harboring unrealistic hopes that American arms could save them.[25]

Henderson did, however, want the Indians to know that Washington was seriously concerned about the fate threatening their northern neighbor. He accordingly informed the Indian foreign secretary that the U.S. had put aside a plan to send an official party to Lhasa to avoid "any move concerning Tibet which might render more difficult the success of the present Indian Government policy of encouraging the Tibetans to preserve their autonomy without stimulating Chinese Communist moves against Tibet." The agile Nehru, Henderson's equal at diplomatic sparring, responded by thanking the ambassador for this courtesy. But he ignored the American attempt to make him define Indian policy on the legal status of Tibet.[26]

Most surprising, and obviously unexpected by Henderson, was the Indians' decision to continue delivering the small arms they had been providing the Tibetans. In June of 1949 they had delivered 144 Bren submachine guns with 360,000 rounds of ammunition, 168 Sten guns with

204,238 rounds of ammunition, 1,260 .303 rifles with 252,000 rounds of ammunition, 42 Verey pistols with 630 rounds of ammunition, and an additional 3.5 million rounds of ammunition. They had also permitted twelve Tibetan soldiers to receive training in the use of the Bren and Sten guns by the Indian troop detachment stationed at the Indian Trade Agency in Gyantse in southern Tibet.[27]

In January of 1950 the Indian foreign minister told Henderson that "in light of recent events" India would continue to expedite this small arms supply (for which the Tibetans paid India in cash).[28] Nehru was practicing his own kind of neutralism. Aware of India's relatively weak military situation, he made a virtue out of a necessity. Acceptance of the new Communist government in Beijing would be the best way to influence events in Asia. But while admiring a fellow victor over the old order, he was wary of this new neighbor. The delivery of the weapons and the training that accompanied them foreshadowed India's policy of taking quiet steps that might preserve some equity in Tibet without arousing the full force of the Chinese Communists. Nevertheless, as the Tibetans debated the impending threat from Beijing at the end of 1949, they could also see the limits to the help they might expect from their southern neighbor.

SHADOW BOXING WITH MAO

On January 7, 1950, General Liu Bocheng announced that the Chinese Communist army, having crushed resistance in southwest China, would now "liberate our compatriots in Tibet." Liu was responding to instructions Mao had cabled him from Moscow, where he was negotiating with Stalin over China's new role as a leader in the Communist world. And in its New Year's message, the Chinese Communist Party's Central Committee had proclaimed the "glorious fighting task . . . in 1950 is to liberate Taiwan, Hainan and Tibet," a goal that was given implicit Soviet endorsement by its publication in the Soviet military journal, *Red Fleet.*[29] To the Tibetans, this confirmed that their days were numbered as they waited in vain for substantial help. To give added urgency to their requests, they had informed the State Department that they were sending a special mission to Washington to present their case in person. They also dispatched a delegation to open negotiations with the Chinese Communists, and on January 30 they began broadcasting from Lhasa for a half-hour daily in Tibetan, Chinese, and English denying China's claims to Tibet, which they declared was an independent, theocratic, and peace-loving state.

The Tibetans were reacting to conflicting messages from both their potential allies and the Chinese. One of the principal channels for transmitting these messages was Gyalo Thondup, the Dalai Lama's elder brother who had returned to India in June 1949 after four years of study in China. There he had become a protégé of Chiang K'ai-shek, who told him that he wanted Thondup to pursue his education in the United States and then return to Tibet as an adviser to the Dalai Lama. Chiang told Thondup[30] that, with the British gone from Tibet and with him as a well-educated protégé, he would feel "China's back door" would be safe enough for him to grant independence to Tibet—a promise that was easier for him to make than to deliver.

Thondup asserted that the Tibetan government had started pressuring him to return to Tibet almost as soon as he arrived in Nanking in 1946. This pressure began when his father died from one of those mysterious ailments that often befell Tibetans whom the ruling elite found troublesome. Instead of complying, Thondup had sent back his brother-in-law, Phuntso Tashi, who had been dispatched to China with him as companion and keeper. In 1947, after the Tibetan assembly had passed a bill of particulars falsely charging Gyalo with lobbying in China on behalf of the recently deceased ex-regent, Thondup found a decoded cable from the Kashag lying on a desk in the Tibet Bureau in Nanking. It warned that Thondup's extended presence in China might harm Tibet's interests and instructed the bureau to persuade him to return to Lhasa "whatever the cost" by playing on his sense of obligation to the Dalai Lama and Thondup's family, now alone in Lhasa. The bureau was authorized to promise him his father's title of Yabshi Kung, a duke of the Dalai Lama's household. Thondup took the cable into the next room, where the bureau's officers were absorbed in their usual game of mah-jongg. He told them to advise the Kashag to stop quarreling and to allow him, then only a young man of eighteen, to continue his studies in China so he could return to help his brother in Lhasa as a political adviser.

When Tsipon Shakabpa came to Nanking as head of the trade mission in 1948, he too tried to persuade Thondup to return to Lhasa. Thondup resisted on the advice of his mother, Gyayum Chenmo, the "Great Mother" who stood aside from court intrigue but was amazingly perceptive about Tibetan politics. She believed that Thondup's return might aid those around the regent who were plotting to depose the Dalai Lama and replace him with Ketsang Rimpoche, the high lama who had led the search party that discovered the boy. They feared that when the young man assumed his full powers he might punish those responsible for the previous regent's death. Thondup's presence abroad made them uneasy because he might be able to rally international support for the Dalai Lama, particularly from the Chinese Nationalists. His mother therefore warned him that both his and the Dalai Lama's lives might be in danger if he returned to Lhasa. Although he never told me so, Thondup may also have been in no hurry to have his new wife, the daughter of the Chinese general Chu Shih-kuei, face an uncertain reception by his family and Tibet's old guard.

Thondup finally fled Nanking in April of 1949 after the fall of the Chiang government. He had admired Chiang as a person but had seen his government collapse from the inside and was prepared to help his brother deal with the impending Chinese invasion. This was the beginning of his life's work as both a political adviser, urging the Tibetan government to reform in order to deal with the modern world, and his government's principal emissary in negotiating with foreign governments. While he waited in India for nine months during 1949 and 1950, he was contacted by Prime Minister Nehru, Ambassador Henderson, and the Chinese Communist military leader, Zhu De. All tried to use him as a conduit, with results ranging from the useful to the bizarre, due in part to Lhasa's long history of isolation and lack of understanding of a world which had suddenly found its own uses for Tibet.

During the long hot summer and early autumn of 1949, before Mao finally assumed power in Beijing, Henderson twice asked Thondup to relay his request to the Dalai Lama to send two officials to New Delhi to discuss what the U.S. government could do to help the Tibetans. But the Tibetans apparently did not recognize what an effective advocate they had in Henderson and turned directly to Washington. The Tibetan foreign bureau sent letters directly to the State Department seeking aid, followed by letters to Truman and Acheson on December 22, 1949. The letters to the president and his secretary of state announced that, inasmuch as Chinese Communist forces had occupied the Tibetan areas of the border provinces of Qinghai and Sichuan, they were sending two senior Tibetan officials to Washington to seek aid.[31]

In an enterprising follow-up two weeks later, the Tibetans also sent a message to the U.S. ambassador-at-large, Philip Jessup, inviting him to visit Lhasa on his trip to southeast Asia. They expressed their pleasure over a recent speech, which they chose to interpret as extending the Truman Doctrine to Asia. They cited a broadcast that apparently carried a speech Jessup made to the World Affairs Council and the American Association for the United Nations in San Francisco on December 19, 1949. The Tibetans noted that they had heard Jessup say that Asian nations "need U.S. assistance to stop the spread of Communism"[32] and must have decided to lose no time asking him to include them.

Their letter to Jessup said: "Tibet has decided to oppose Communist aggression. For this reason, special missions of the Tibetan Government will shortly leave for the U.S. and other countries to ask for help. Nevertheless, we do hope you can include a visit to Tibet in your program after leaving India." The letter optimistically concluded: "After a favorable decision, kindly inform us beforehand by what means you will be traveling to our capital Lhasa."[33] Richardson reported that the naive Tibetans had even asked Heinrich Harrer, the Austrian mountaineer who had found refuge in Tibet, to supervise the building of a temporary landing field for Jessup's plane.[34] (Years later, the Dalai Lama said that he had watched from his rooms in the Potala while a rough airstrip was built in the winter of 1949–1950. Smiling, he asked if I had been one of those out there building it. When I replied no, but that my colleagues had arranged for the construction of an airfield for contingent uses, he wryly noted that when it came time for him to flee nine years later, he had been forced to rely on the traditional Tibetan pony.[35])

The seven-year-old Fourteenth Dalai Lama Tenzin Gyatso, when he met his first Americans in Lhasa in 1942.

The Potala with a carved stone pillar in the foreground bearing the words from a treaty signed by Tibet and China in 822 A.D. The treaty stated in part: "Tibet and China shall abide by the frontiers of which they are now in occupation . . . on neither side shall there be waging of war nor seizing of territory. Between the two countries no smoke nor dust shall be seen . . . and the very word enemy shall not be spoken. This solemn agreement has established a great epoch when Tibetans shall be happy in the land of Tibet, and Chinese in the land of China." An identical pillar was erected in China.

ABOVE: Reception party meeting Major Tolstoy outside of Lhasa, 1942. The British and Chinese (Nationalist) Mission chiefs are the first two men from the left in the front row and the British Operator of the Mission Radio, Reginald Fox, is behind them.

MIDDLE RIGHT: Major Ilya Tolstoy (right) and Captain Brooke Dolan (left) flanking one of their noble hosts, Tsarong Dsasa, while the British Mission Chief Frank Ludlow looks on, Lhasa, 1942. The two American OSS officers were sent to show the flag in this previously closed country.

BOTTOM RIGHT: F.D.R.'s presents to the young Dalai Lama. While the British scorned the offerings as too paltry, the gold chronograph pleased him and he still has it today.

Reting, the former Regent of Tibet at his monastery palace, 1943. He died in prison four years later after a bitter civil war with his successor.

Taktra, the Regent of Tibet at the time of Major Tolstoy's visit.

Major Tolstoy and Captain Dolan at Amo Chu in southern Tibet as they begin their reconnaissance mission across previously uncharted territory.

The Tolstoy mission near the sources of the Yangtze and Mekong rivers.

Yangpel Pandatsang (right), was from one of the powerful trading families of eastern Tibet and a member of the Lhasa establishment. He, his wife, and Betty Tsaraong of the Lhasa nobility are shown at the lunch they gave for Tolstoy and Dolan.

George Patterson, the young Scottish missionary sent by the Pandatsangs from their stronghold in eastern Tibet to seek Western aid in resisting the Chinese.

RIGHT: Robert Ford, the British radio operator, with Rapgya Pandatsang in Chamdo just before the Chinese crossed over the river to invade Kham in 1950.

Chamdo, the site of the final battle with the Chinese when their troops crossed the headwaters of the Mekong into Tibet in October 1950.

Monastery at Yatung in southern Tibet where the Dalai Lama took refuge in December 1950 while he decided whether to return to Lhasa or accept U.S. offers of support if he sought asylum abroad.

The Tibetan delegation, led by Ngabo Ngawang Jigme, signing the Seventeen Point Agreement, which ended Tibet's political independence, Beijing, May 1951.

Gyayum Chenmo, "the Great Mother," in Chinese Communist-controlled Lhasa, 1952.

The entire episode no doubt perplexed the U.S. embassy in New Delhi. It did not forward the letter to Jessup via Washington for three weeks, and there is no record of any response from him. By then Acheson had attempted to play on China's Russophobia. In a speech January 12, 1950, he expressed concern that Stalin might be outmaneuvering Mao by detaching Chinese territory during the prolonged talks between the two leaders of the communist world then underway in Moscow.[36] It would not have been a propitious time to welcome a delegation seeking support in Washington for Tibetan claims to territorial and political independence from China. That same day the Department instructed Henderson to discourage the Tibetans from sending their proposed special envoys requesting aid to meet the threatened Chinese occupation of the Tibetan regions along the upper Yangtze. It cited the publicity it would engender which "might hasten Chinese action against Tibet." Washington warned that it was "unlikely the U.S. would be prepared to extend aid to Tibet, particularly in view of the attitude of the Indian Government respecting Tibet and the key position India plays with regard to Tibet."[37]

As an alternative, the Department suggested that discussions with the Tibetans might better be conducted in New Delhi. That met with a cool reception from the Indian government, which also was not keen about any public display of diplomatic hospitality toward the Tibetans despite New Delhi's covert offers of help. In another instance of India's schizophrenic policy, Nehru had sent the Indian ambassador to China, K. M. Panikkar, to meet Thondup in Kalimpong during the summer of 1949. This unlikely emissary brought messages from the Indian prime minister urging the Tibetan government to remove all its historic and cultural treasures to India for safekeeping and to mobilize the Tibetan populace against the threatened Chinese invasion. Panikkar promised that if the situation worsened, the Tibetans could use India as a base and a supply of arms. Nehru also urged Thondup to tell Lhasa not to panic, and promised a plane to fly the Dalai Lama out of Lhasa if necessary. While the primitive airstrip constructed in Lhasa the following winter was never used, Nehru did send a plane to take Thondup from Kalimpong to New Delhi. There the prime minister personally reaffirmed Panikkar's commitments.[38]

Nevertheless, Thondup did not receive instructions from Lhasa to follow up with the Indians on these surprisingly bold pledges. In any case the Indians soon withdrew to their more characteristically skittish position. When Henderson called on K. P. S. Menon, career head of the Indian foreign office early in 1950, the Indian diplomat vetoed the American plan to short-circuit the mission the Tibetans wanted to send to Washington by meeting them in New Delhi instead. He used Washington's own argument that the inevitable publicity might only arouse the Chinese.[39] He displayed annoyance at the British for also "passing the buck to India" in discouraging the Tibetan mission from traveling to London. Whitehall had used the excuse that British policy on Tibet was determined in consultation with the Indians.[40] Menon said he had told the U.K. high commissioner that India felt the British still had responsibilities in Tibet. In London, the British Foreign Office took note, sending Menon's comment to the Commonwealth Relations Office (CRO) with the advice that "we shall have to be careful in our dealings with the Government of India over Tibet not to give the impression that we are washing our hands of all responsibility in that quarter; I think that they appreciate that it would be best for us to keep in the background, however, and will be satisfied if we are, for example, forthcoming in meeting their requests for replacement of arms."[41]

Menon's unwillingness to shut the door completely on the Tibetans while not wanting to accept responsibilities for their situation reflected India's moral and political dilemma. On the one hand it was supplying Tibet with arms, but it was anxious that the Tibetans use them only to resist and not to challenge the Chinese. The Indian political officer in Lhasa, while doubting that the Tibetans would be able to organize an effective resistance, vowed he would resign if India formally attempted to dissuade the Tibetans from resisting, lest he personally be "placed in the invidious position of telling the Tibetans that the Indians, who for the past two decades have proclaimed themselves to be the best friends of Tibet, are unable to come to their assistance in time of need."[42]

Nehru was at the same time receiving contrary advice from influential foreign friends. Lester Pearson, Canada's External Affairs minister, reported that Nehru "let his hair down" in a talk on January 13, 1950, wondering whether India should act against the Chinese threat to Tibet. Pearson, a future Nobel Peace Prize–winner but also a practitioner of realpolitik, told Nehru that in his personal view India should do nothing because the country "was so remote that it was of little practical importance whether or not the Communists moved into it." Nehru apparently found this counsel congenial, because Pearson confided to the U.S. ambassador in Colombo that the prime minister was inclined to agree. When the Canadian told Sir Roger Makins of the British Foreign Office of his advice to Nehru, the pragmatic Makins said the Canadian at least should have encouraged Nehru to send agents to Tibet to find out what was going on there.[43]

India nevertheless decided the following month to continue helping Tibet with supplies and training. The British encouraged the Indians, although they opted out of any active involvement. In reporting the Tibetans' welcome for even this limited help, the Indian mission in Lhasa noted that "a small but advanced section of Tibetan officials is trying to urge upon the Tibetan Government the necessity of opening up the country immediately for modern communications with India, with the ulterior object of bringing military supplies for defending Tibetan independence." The Indian mission warned that "any such hurried and drastic measures, however, are not likely to appeal to the Tibetan mind."[44]

The British spent much diplomatic and bureaucratic energy debating and evolving a morally ambiguous position arising out of the remnants of desire to play a role in a part of the world where they were once the imperial power. The British admitted to their State Department colleagues in Washington that the Tibetans deserved "moral encouragement even though it was not possible [for Britain] to extend material aid,"[45] insisting that the Indians "should take the lead on this problem."[46] The soul-searching going on in Whitehall was apparent in various Foreign Office minutes.[47] One option was to "advise India to encourage Tibetan resistance by any means short of military operations." The drafter suggested this might be achieved by increasing supplies of small arms and inviting Tibetan soldiers to train in India. He noted that "in the mountainous terrain of Tibet such a policy might effectively defeat any but a highly organised Chinese attack." He noted, however, if Britain was prepared to do no more than take diplomatic action in and outside the UN and was "prepared to abandon the

Tibetans to their fate," then it should also not mislead them to expect support from London lest the Chinese call everyone's bluff. The next day another officer noted that it would be better for the Indians to take the lead in any public action involving Tibet's defense since the Indians had better credentials in Beijing. While this debate continued the Foreign Office sent the message to the Tibetans asking them not to send their proposed mission to London "since there was no possibility of Tibet being admitted to the UN and the U.K. was not in a position to extend direct assistance to Tibet."[48]

The Foreign Office had assumed that Britain at least would be willing to provide replacement matériel if the Indians did not have adequate supplies. But the British military balked at providing replacement rifles, mortars, and ammunition for what the Indians would supply to the Tibetans, arguing that the arms would not really add much to Tibet's capacity to resist and would eventually fall into Chinese hands.[49] The diplomats had argued that India's policy of "bolstering up the lamas" had been taken "against the advice of a considerable body of opinion in New Delhi, only after we had advised them to do so."[50] To back out now would cast doubts on London's sincerity in encouraging the Indians to assist the Tibetans against the Communist threat.[51] The Chiefs of Staff finally agreed that they would "be able to make a certain amount of equipment available, if it is considered that there are strong political arguments in favor of supplying Tibet with arms."[52]

The question eventually became moot because the Indians never asked for the arms. The mortars, Bren guns, and ammunition suggested by the British to supply one brigade group for six months would have required 7,000 mules to deliver across the Himalayas, and the beasts were unavailable in such huge numbers. But the Tibetan commander in chief went secretly to Gyantse, the Indian trading post in southern Tibet, to learn to operate Sten guns and other modern small arms. In fact, this assistance may have been precisely what Nehru had in mind in his pledge to Thondup.

THE MISSION TO BEIJING

By early 1950 the problem of Tibet had been put on hold. The period was reminiscent of the eight months of the "phony war" in 1939–1940 while France and her allies waited for the inevitable German blitzkrieg with a combination of resignation and wishful thinking. The Tibetans had been turned aside by potential supporters preoccupied with their own problems. Acheson was under attack for his support for the former State Department official Alger Hiss, who was suspected of being a Communist spy. Senator Joseph McCarthy, a Republican demagogue from Wisconsin, had begun his attacks on that "group of untouchables" in the State Department "who have delivered China to communism."[53] On January 6, 1950, the British offered formal recognition of the Communist government and were then confounded by a singular lack of response from the Mao government.

The Tibetans' attempts to deal directly with the new masters of China had gone nowhere. It had taken them four months to reply to Zhu De's pledges to Gyalo Thondup that the Communists would maintain the same relationship with Lhasa as their Nationalist predecessors and would disclaim any intention to invade Tibet.[54] Zhu De's messages had arrived during the two months prior to the Communists' assumption of power. Although Thondup was skeptical, he believed his government should have responded immediately, at the very least in order to determine whether there was room for negotiation before the Communists began their moves toward Tibet.

The official chosen by a divine lottery to head the mission that Lhasa finally decided to send to Beijing was Tsipon Shakabpa, the man who had hoodwinked Mao's predecessors with Tibetan passports when he led the 1948 trade delegation. This time his instructions from the regent were to meet with the Chinese somewhere near the border and discuss the defiant letter that the foreign bureau had sent to Mao Zedong the previous November and the "atrocious radio announcements" threatening Tibet. He was also to secure from the Chinese their pledge to respect Tibet's territorial integrity and the Dalai Lama's independent rule.[55]

Shakabpa arrived in Kalimpong on his way to Beijing in March of 1950 but made little progress. In a repeat of their 1948 performance the British and Indian governments used a number of specious excuses, ranging from visa problems to fear of heat rash, in frustrating the Tibetan attempts to meet the Chinese in Hong Kong.

Gyalo Thondup became discouraged by the delays and he left India in April of 1950 to go to Beijing to conduct his own negotiations in the hope of forestalling an invasion. The British also denied him a transit visa for Hong Kong, so he flew to Manila and tried unsuccessfully to enter China through Macao. He finally gave up and went to Taiwan, where he told the United Press International (UPI) that he planned to visit Japan, the United States, and possibly Europe to rally support and arms to repel the Chinese Communists. "The Tibetan terrain is ideally suited for defensive warfare," he said.[56]

In London, the Foreign Office professed perplexity about the contradiction between Shakabpa seeking to negotiate with the Chinese Communists to forestall an invasion while Thondup was talking in Taiwan about the need to defend Tibet. The British diplomat Guy Burgess, notorious for his defection to Moscow a year later, was then serving in Whitehall and commented: "it will all come out in the debacle."[57]

But Thondup was sandbagged by his friend the generalissimo's efficient intelligence service, which had learned of Zhu De's communications to him. Unbeknownst to him, one of Thondup's in-laws had photographed the letters when they had been fellow houseguests of Thondup's Chinese father-in-law. When Thondup arrived in Taiwan the generalissimo and Madame Chiang expressed their fears to him that an untrained political amateur such as he would be exploited by the Chinese Communists if he went to Beijing. More likely, they were really worried that their skillful young protégé might make a deal on Tibet's status that would compromise their own claims. In any event, they made it impossible for Thondup to leave Taiwan. Their enforced hospitality kept him on the island for the next sixteen months. In order for him to leave, and only for the United States, Secretary Acheson had to intervene on Thondup's behalf.[58]

Meanwhile, a frustrated Shakabpa had apparently decided to make one more effort to enlist American support by playing the Russian card. He sent word to the U.S. government through his own private channels (probably Tolstoy or the Thomases) that he might soon either negotiate with the Chinese or go to Moscow, having "more or less given up hope of getting effective support from the West."[59] While the Department thought this was merely a maneuver, it could not ignore the possibility that this might represent a genuine intention to negotiate with the communists. Washington accordingly asked Henderson to reassure Shakabpa of Washington's sympathy. It held out the hope that in the absence of any overt Western action, that the "cost of a full-scale Commie military expedition against Tibet in the face of the geographic and logistic difficulties might lead to an indefinite delay in Commie military action, particularly, if the Tibetan military capacity to resist is quietly strengthened." Henderson, himself skeptical that Shakabpa would risk traveling either to Moscow or Beijing lest he be held hostage in either place, was told by Washington to tell the Tibetans they could count on the continuing interest of the United States but to look for military help from India.[60]

THE PATTERSON MISSION

In the middle of this uneasy period, early in March of 1950, a young Scotsman presented himself at the Office of the Deputy High Commissioner for the United Kingdom in Calcutta. He told an extravagant story involving Chinese Communist aggression, political intrigue, revolt, and tribal rivalries in the Kham area of eastern Tibet.[61] George Patterson, a Plymouth Brethren missionary, had spent the past three years living in Tatsienlu, the principal city of what the Chinese regarded as the province of Sikang and Lhasa considered the Tibetan area of Kham. There Patterson had become a protégé of Topgay Pandatsang, the head of one of the big four trading houses and families in Kham. These Khampa trading families, the Pandatsangs, the Gyadutsangs, the Sadutsangs, and the Andutsangs had emerged during the reign of the thirteenth Dalai Lama as merchant princes of Tibet. They had used their new wealth to purchase titles, grudging respectability, and limited political leverage in Lhasa. As traders they had been among the few Tibetans who had lived outside Tibet. They had already witnessed the twentieth century democratic challenges to the established order in China and India.

Many of these new merchant princes had returned to Tibet eager to convert the isolated traditional theocracy into a modern national state. Their aim was not to promote democracy for itself, but to see the establishment of a more effective government administered by men selected on the basis of competence instead of family or monastic connections. Their support for administrative reform and the reduction of the power of the established aristocracy put them at odds with the central government in Lhasa. Thus the bourgeois political revolution of eighteenth- and nineteenth-century Europe was arriving in Tibet.

The Pandatsangs were the most notorious among the challengers to the established order. They also had maintained the closest ties to whomever was in power in China. Topgay Pandatsang's father had accompanied the thirteenth Dalai Lama into exile in 1910 and been accordingly rewarded when he returned to Tibet, where he built up a large trading concession with India. Topgay's brother Yangpel, who had built the family business into one of the greatest trading houses in Tibet, would be a member of Shakabpa's 1948 trade mission. While Yangpel had become a member of the Tibetan establishment, his two brothers, Topgay and Rapga, had been leaders of an armed revolt against the Lhasa government in 1934 that was part of the jockeying for power after the death of the thirteenth Dalai Lama. Topgay had been defeated by an unlikely combination of Tibetan troops sent by Lhasa to assert its remote authority, Chinese Nationalists defending Chiang's uncertain claims, and Chinese Communists who were just then passing through the territory on their Long March to Yenan. By World War II, however, Topgay had reestablished both his political and economic position in Kham and was made a colonel by Chiang K'ai-shek, responsible for the Khampas of the region.

In 1947, Patterson arrived in Tatsienlu to begin work as a medical missionary. Young and handsome, he won the respect of Topgay and his Khampa supporters by his medical attentions, his horsemanship, and his abilities as a crack shot. Topgay confided his plans for a new revolt being organized by himself, his brother Rapga, and two Tibetans from the Amdo area. One was Geshe Sherab Gyatso, a relative of the Pandat-sangs and a well-known dissident monk allied to the Chinese National-ists. When the Chinese Communists invaded Tibet, he had no problem becoming a propagandist for them.

The plan was for Topgay to take over the Kham area, while the two Amdowas took over their province (known by the Chinese as Qinghai). The rebels would then propose to the Lhasa authorities that they officially recognize the two provinces as part of Greater Tibet and join in a united fight against the Chinese for Tibet's independence. If Lhasa refused, Topgay and his coconspirators would then march on the capital, calling on their fellow Khampas and Amdowas in the army and monasteries to fight alongside them in taking over the Tibetan government.[62]

The encroaching Chinese Communists soon learned of the plans for the revolt and demanded that Topgay agree not to oppose their own advance into eastern Tibet. In return they promised arms, ammunition, and money to support Topgay's insurrection under the label of the "East Tibetan People's Revolution against the corrupt, reactionary govern-ment in Lhasa." Patterson said the Chinese Communists' deal was in effect an ultimatum that made it clear the "liberation" of Kham was merely a first step in a plan. Tibet would fall to Communism in one year, followed by Nepal, Sikkim, and Bhutan within three years, and finally India by the end of five years.

According to Patterson, Topgay soon concluded that he could tem-porize with the Chinese for no more than six months. He thus decided to withdraw to a remote area north of the Kham capital while he sent word of the Chinese plans to both the British and representatives of the Tibetan government in Lhasa. Patterson was sent as a messenger because he was more likely to be believed than a member of the suspect Pandat-sang family. Patterson was then to arrange to ship food and medical sup-plies to Topgay's stronghold in Kham so he could resist the impending Chinese invasion.

This was the account Patterson laid out to the British official in Cal-cutta, David Anderson.[63] Patterson had expected to be brushed off as a wild-eyed romantic, and he was therefore surprised when Anderson not only seemed to take his story seriously but also introduced him to a CIA officer at the U.S. consulate and a local Indian security official.[64] Both Anderson and the CIA officer eventually told Patterson that their respective governments could provide Pandatsang with little material support. By the time the story reached London, the Foreign Office dismissed as optimistic at best "any idea that the Pandatsangs or any other of the big Tibetan commercial families are likely to form a bastion against Communism, or indeed to act from any other motive than immediate self-interest . . . "[65]

Patterson proceeded to Kalimpong, the principal border trading post in India. The thirteenth Dalai Lama had spent four years there in exile, and the place continued as a site of Tibetan intrigue even four decades later. Shakabpa, waiting there for visas, received Patterson courteously and promised to relay his warning of an imminent Chinese invasion. Despite Shakabpa's close ties with Yangpel Pandatsang, Patterson probably believed, rightly, that Shakabpa harbored suspicions of Yangpel's brothers' plots in Kham, and that his report to Lhasa reflected this distrust. Whatever his doubts, Shakabpa did not hesitate to occupy the house of one of the suspect brothers in Kalimpong. The Tibetan mind has many compartments.

Having delivered the warnings to the British, the Americans, and the Indians, all of whom proved to be either unwilling to believe his story or unable to provide support, Patterson assembled the supplies for Kham. He planned to join his patron in battle against the Chinese, but a devastating cyclone forced him to cancel these arrangements, and Patterson was thus stranded in India when the Chinese Communists marched into the Pandatsang homeland early in October of 1950.

Patterson remained for some years in India where he subsequently was involved in several covert operations either planned or conducted by the U.S. government. CIA officers who worked with Patterson at that time described him as a "bit of a romantic," but "a direct, honest and decent person."[66] They had, however, no knowledge or appreciation of the complex motivation and personalities of his sponsors, who over the next ten years would collaborate with both the Chinese Communists and the Tibetan resistance. The Pandatsangs combined political opportunism and clan loyalty, which made them flawed proponents for the modernization and reforms of the Tibetan governing structure that they espoused. This was only one spectacular instance of Tibet's culture that was little understood by the Americans, who had only recently happened on what seemed to them to be a simple scene of a frontier drama with the good guys trying to get rid of bad guys. These fluctuating loyalties and mixed objectives on the border, plus the chasm between the hinterland and Lhasa, would frustrate Tibet's efforts to mobilize support, at home and abroad, to resist the Chinese. This left the Tibetans with a divided government confronting an announced invasion that both they and their allies wishfully professed to think might not happen at all.

The Americans should have been warned off their simplistic image of Shangri-la by the shocking death on April 29, 1950, of Douglas S. MacKiernan, the former U.S. vice consul in Urumchi, the capital of the neighboring Chinese province of Xinjiang. The international press had been following MacKiernan and his small party on their seven month odyssey fleeing the Communists in China across some of the world's most formidable terrain. When they arrived at the border, MacKiernan was shot and killed by a party of nomads and six mounted Tibetan border guards, who confiscated their supplies and belongings.[67] The painful irony is that he was killed by the very same people whose leaders were seeking help from Washington against the Communists. In New Delhi, Ambassador Henderson's immediate reaction was to form an escort party headed by Patterson, the sort of man of action Henderson liked. The Tibetan government, mortified and apologetic, hurriedly sent assurances that it would care for the survivors of the MacKiernan party and send them on to India guided by experienced Tibetan mountaineers. (The Tibetans accompanied this offer with a note of concern that the Chinese were making "baseless allegations" of foreign, "especially American, designs on Tibet.") Henderson accepted the Tibetan offer. "Since there is little we can do for Tibet, we should not insist upon the Tibetans agreeing to steps being taken which might prejudice Tibet's position with the Chinese Communists," he wrote.[68]

No one questioned why notification of the long-expected arrival of MacKiernan's party was not received by the Tibetan guards until two days *after* they killed him, nor voiced the ugly suspicion that they had done so simply because they wanted the goods he and his party were carrying.[69] Washington was still willing to give a potential ally the benefit of the doubt. In a gracious gesture to indicate that the U.S. government harbored no ill will, embassy officials who met the escort party at the Indian border gave it 400 cc of procaine penicillin. The embassy believed the antibiotic "would be welcomed in Tibet where VD [venereal disease] is understood to be prevalent."[70]

THE COLD WAR COMES TO ASIA

On June 16, 1950, only a fortnight before the outbreak of the Korean War was to change the nature of diplomacy in Asia for forty years, the State Department called in representatives of the British embassy to discuss U.S. proposals to "encourage and support Tibetan resistance to Communist control." The State Department paper acknowledged that the Chinese Communists had the military strength to capture Tibet but noted that the terrain presented formidable logistical problems to an invader and favored guerrilla resistance. It concluded that "comparatively little assistance in the form of specialized military instruction and supplies might stiffen Tibetan resistance and make a Chinese Communist military expedition so costly that it would not be undertaken, particularly in the absence of a manifestation by the Western states of extraordinary interest in Tibet or an attempt to alter its international status."[71]

State's plan was to have the Indians supply Tibetan guerrillas in secret, and have the British persuade their former wards to do so. Left unsaid was the Department's doubt that its own embassy in New Delhi would have much influence with Nehru's government. (It was still smarting from a speech Henderson delivered in April to the Indian Council on World Affairs denouncing India's nonalignment policies. The outspoken ambassador had criticized those "who shrink from close cooperation with the United States lest such cooperation create hostility toward them on the part of the powerful forces of the world which feed on human poverty and suffering, which rely on force and terror to achieve their ends, and which look with disfavor upon any association of free nations that might be effective in overcoming poverty, liquidating strife, or discouraging aggression."[72] The atmosphere was hardly conducive to initiate a joint U.S.-Indian covert operation.)

No CIA representatives are listed among the participants at the June 16 meeting with the British, but guidance was certainly available from the Office of Policy Coordination (OPC), the CIA's center for covert action. Moreover, the operational approach recommended was basically identical to that which the CIA was using in Eastern Europe. The British embassy official at the meeting "at once" wanted to know who would provide the money and supplies if his government agreed to support the guerrillas. He doubted London would go along because Britain's special interest in South Asia had ended two years before with Indian independence. This position was immediately confirmed by the British Foreign Office, which deemed intervention "impracticable and unwise."[73] Whatever the U.S. might want to do about Tibet, it would have to go it alone; its wartime ally no longer had the heart for endeavors affecting areas that were now only remembrances of an empire past.

While this unproductive exchange between Washington and London was going on, Joseph Stalin, Mao Zedong, and Kim Il Sung had already agreed on North Korea's attack on the south.[74] When North Korean forces invaded South Korea on June 25, 1950, Asia gained equal status with Europe as a theater of the Cold War. The CIA was instructed to initiate psychological warfare and paramilitary operations against Communist China, and this would affect Tibet in due course.[75]

Two weeks after the North Korean invasion, Washington informed Henderson that State and "other interested agencies" were considering an approach to Shakabpa and his mission "with a promise of secret U.S. aid in the hope that this would help the Tibetan authorities to resist Chinese Communist encroachment on Tibet."[76] The Tibetans were still cooling their heels in New Delhi. Henderson doubted that the Korean invasion would change the Indians' mind, but he agreed with Washington that the Indians might find it difficult to refuse a request from the Tibetans to procure arms from abroad on their own.[77] The State Department confirmed one week later that it was "now in a position to give assurances to the

Tibetans re U.S. aid" and that Henderson should inform them that the U.S. was "ready to assist in the procurement and financing" of such assistance.[78] The Tibetans would, however, have to try to obtain the Indian government's cooperation. The Department noted that Acheson's rejection of Nehru's proposal to give China's UN seat to Beijing as an inducement to end the war in Korea would not leave India any better disposed toward U.S. efforts to help Tibet. The Tibetans would therefore have to ask on their own to buy Indian military equipment without letting the Indians know that Washington would pay the bills.

Shakabpa got the word from U.S. embassy representatives on August 4.[79] They tried to disabuse him of any hope that their aid would mean the dispatch of foreign troops and planes to Tibet to fight against an invasion, or even the delivery of equipment to airfields in Tibet that Shakabpa offered to have constructed. Equally, they discouraged Shakabpa's proposal for planes to take off from Pakistan or Burma to help Tibet if the Indians refused to cooperate. Shakabpa finally accepted that the Tibetans would have to follow the Department's formula of first asking the Indians for additional aid, and if refused, then attempting to seek the Indian government's cooperation in permitting free passage of aid to Lhasa from abroad. Shakabpa agreed to relay the U.S. offer to Lhasa but warned the American emissaries that he did not expect a reply for at least fifteen days.

However badly Lhasa wanted help, the delay was understandable. The Tibetan capital was suffering from an acute case of war jitters, which makes its victims irresolute. The Nepalese government was reporting that Lhasa was "paralyzed with fear, and the bickering and indecision among the Tibetan authorities themselves may well be more instrumental in bringing about an early downfall of the regime than an invasion from the outside."[80] The *New York Times* was similarly reporting that disaffection among the ruling elite was dividing efforts to confront the "liberation" Beijing Radio was threatening.[81] Among the troublesome situations cited by the *Times* was a campaign against the resistance by the Sera monks, still angry over the imprisonment and death of their leader, the former Regent Reting; the continuing intrigues of the Pandatsang brothers in Kham; and the agitation sponsored by the

Chinese in favor of their claimant to the throne of the Panchen Lama, traditionally the Dalai Lama's political subordinate but co–religious leader. The government was also said to be worried about the Amdowas, the other principal tribal group along the border, whom Lhasa hesitated to arm lest they go over to the Communist side.

On September 9, more than a month after the original approach, Shakabpa officially confirmed to Henderson that the Tibetan government "has taken a firm decision to meet any Chinese Communist incursion with force," and expressed its deep appreciation of the U.S. offer of military assistance. As suggested, the Tibetans would first solicit Indian cooperation, and Lhasa was dispatching two officials with "full instructions" under the cover of a trade mission to New Delhi.[82] The Department reaffirmed the scenario on September 15, asking for a detailed and realistic list of Tibet's requirements, to be compiled with the help of the embassy's military attaché.[83] Washington was even prepared to provide the Tibetans with a transmitter to expedite communications and a special internal indicator, "Totib," for embassy cable traffic. But it declined to exchange communications in code with the Tibetans, who seem to have caught on surprisingly quickly to international diplomatic practice and privileges.

The Indians were not surprised when the Tibetans made their first pitch for arms, since Henderson had filled in his British counterpart back in August on the terms of the U.S. offer. London, which really wanted nothing to do with this whole operation, had immediately expressed concern lest the Indians be caught unaware by the U.S. offer when it came because they were busy trying to persuade the Chinese not to invade Tibet.[84] On August 14, Henderson had accordingly informed Nehru's senior Foreign Office adviser, G. S. Bajpai, that in response to inquiries made by Shakabpa earlier that summer, he had told the Tibetans that in the event of an unprovoked invasion by the Chinese, the U.S. was ready to send military supplies if the Tibetans could transport them through India.[85] Bajpai thanked Henderson for the advance notice but said he would wait for a request by the Tibetans. He added that he had received no reply to the strong representations that Ambassador Panikkar in Beijing had been instructed to deliver to the Chinese earlier that week urging them not to invade Tibet.

The players were therefore all in position as Shakabpa received reports from Lhasa of Chinese troop concentrations along the eastern border, ready to move without further acclimatization, and favored by summer and autumn weather. The Chinese had been signaling their aggressive intentions throughout that summer. In late July, General Liu Bocheng had announced that troops under his command would soon march on Tibet to "bring that mountainous land of the lamas back into the Chinese family."[86] Liu knew the terrain of eastern Tibet from the days of the Long March, and he knew how to appeal to the local Tibetan populace with promises of regional self-government and protection of the monasteries. He assured the Tibetans that the Chinese occupation troops would follow the vaunted Mao formula by paying their own expenses and that "pro-imperialist and pro-Kuomintang" local officials would be allowed to continue in their posts "if they submitted peacefully."

Meanwhile Shakabpa, while brokering the preliminary arms negotiations, had been going through the motions of trying to pin down the Chinese ambassador in New Delhi on the status of Tibet. When pushed, the Tibetan envoy admitted to Henderson that his government wanted independence but was afraid to demand it lest it provoke the Chinese into an invasion and alienate the Indians. The embassy believed that Shakabpa was trying to hint to the Chinese that the Tibetans were ready to fight for their independence in the hope of ultimately negotiating a compromise to preserve the status quo.[87] The Chinese ambassador to India was equally skilled in the art of temporizing. After protracted meetings in September, he told the Tibetan delegation that he was unable to conclude an agreement and they must go to Beijing for final negotiations.

Then the Tibetans suddenly turned tail. On October 16 two officials who had arrived from Lhasa made an unannounced call on Henderson, who told them to return two days later when the officer handling military aid would be there to meet them. At the appointed hour, the embassy received a letter canceling the appointment because of "urgent works" and expressing the hope that the two would see Henderson on their next visit.[88] A week later a mystified Henderson told Washington that a resumption of discussions on military aid had been completely upset by the mission's departure from New Delhi the day before, "with nothing more than telephone advice from them." Menon, the Indian foreign secretary, later stated categorically that the Tibetan delegation had never raised the question of additional military aid with the Indian government, a formality demanded by the United States. While suspicious of Menon's denials, Henderson concluded that the attitude of the Indian government had made the Tibetans lose heart, and the "question of military aid for Tibet is therefore dead."[89]

Shakabpa later said that he had received several cables from Lhasa, starting on the day of the canceled appointment.[90] They first informed him that the Chinese had invaded eastern Tibet and instructed him to try to stop it, then followed up with conflicting instructions, obviously from a government in great disarray, instructing him to negotiate the three concessions demanded by the Chinese ambassador to preclude an invasion. Under the Chinese terms, Tibet first would have to yield its claim to independence by acknowledging that it was part of China; permit the Chinese army to be deployed on all its international borders; and grant China the right to handle its foreign trade and political affairs. At first the Kashag informed Shakabpa he was empowered to accept the critical point acknowledging that Tibet was part of China. But the Dalai Lama overruled the Kashag and appealed to the state oracle, which confirmed his strong view that acceptance of Chinese sovereignty over Tibet was unacceptable.

Shakabpa was then instructed to reject all three Chinese demands but proceed with his delegation to Beijing by October 26. The two Tibetans charged with negotiating military aid checked in with the U.S. consulate in Calcutta; they confirmed Henderson's suspicions about India. They reported that earlier in the month they had met with Nehru to make the pro forma request to India for arms in accordance with the American formula. Nehru, however, had been so negative that they retreated without ever bringing up the U.S. offer to provide military assistance if he would allow it to transit India. When they finally raised the issue of military aid with the External Affairs ministry, they were told that Nehru called the shots but the ministry would try again. But the Tibetans expected the Indians to refuse and had not even asked if India would object to an approach for arms from foreign governments. They then apparently huddled with Shakabpa and decided that, in view of the urgent instructions he was receiving from Lhasa to negotiate with the Chinese, they would have to stand aside until Shakabpa's political negotiations either succeeded or failed.

Shakabpa was therefore on his way to negotiate with the Chinese when it was announced that their troops were "advancing toward Tibet."[91] The period of wishful thinking was over.

CHAPTER 4

The Invasion of Tibet

THE FALL OF CHAMDO

The first target of the Chinese attack was Chamdo, the Tibetan administrative center at Kham on the eastern border. The frontier they crossed had been established by their Manchu predecessors in 1727 and roughly paralleled the headwaters of the Yangtze River.[1] This boundary still separates the Tibetans. Forty-six percent of them, according to the 1990 Chinese census, live in political Tibet, the traditional area ruled by Lhasa and now known as the Chinese Tibet Autonomous Region. The remaining 54 percent of Tibetans live on the other side of the river in four Chinese provinces, where they have generally stood aloof from the affairs of their brothers on the Western side of the Yangtze.

The inhabitants of the southern part of this vast border region of remote alpine valleys lying on both sides of the Yangtze, known as Khampas, are a distinct breed of Tibetans. Robert Ford, an Englishman then living in Kham and operating one of the old OSS radio sets for the Tibetan government, described them as "tall and broad-shouldered, strong and hardy, sometimes almost Aryan in appearance."[2] They have their own dialect, dress and culture, and most carried arms to hunt, intimidate others, and protect themselves. Ford, like most Westerners who came in contact with the Khampas, admired them for their "independence and lack of servility."

The Khampas were divided into competitive clans ruled by chieftains dedicated to preserving their individualistic, frontier style of life. This meant frequent quarrels among the neighboring clans and an occasional battle on a larger scale to throw back a venturesome Chinese general or challenge a Chinese governor. They were fervently devoted to the Dalai Lama, but paid only nominal allegiance to the distant Tibetan political establishment and its lay and clerical aristocrats, whom they generally held in contempt. They were Khampas first and then Tibetans.

In the two centuries since the Manchu emperor Yung Ch'eng had fixed this border, the area had been a generally autonomous region of locally governed fiefdoms. In 1910 a Manchu general occupied Chamdo on his way to Lhasa with his troops. They were expelled the next year when the Chinese nationalist revolution broke out. In 1928 the Nationalist government attempted to quell the persistent fighting between Tibetan clans and the Chinese troops in the provinces east of the Yangtze and incorporate the area into a Chinese province called Sikang. This province existed on official maps but the Chinese troops rarely ventured from the capital of Tatsienlu. Throughout the following years the Nationalist government, confronted by warlord domination of the provinces, invasion from Japan, World War II, and civil war with the Communists, was far too preoccupied with its own existence to make any effective efforts to control the area.

Mao and his Red Army further alienated the Tibetans in 1936 as they moved through the region foraging for food on the long march to Yenan. Mao later told Edgar Snow that this was the Chinese Communists' "only foreign debt," which some day they must repay.³ The repayment came in 1950 when Mao's troops returned to "liberate" these Tibetan areas east of the Yangtze. Throughout that summer they moved through the region making preparations to accord this same privilege to the Tibetans on the western bank of the river.

Before the Chinese arrived, Rapga of the ubiquitous Pandatsang family had spent a few days in Chamdo in consultations with the governor. He slipped back across the river to the mountain stronghold where he and his brother Topgay waited. Ford, who continued to operate the radio and thus maintain Chamdo's only link to Lhasa, said it was generally believed that Rapga had gone to parley with the Chinese on behalf of the governor to delay the attack.⁴ If that was his mission, he was unsuccessful, but he and Topgay continued their ambiguous roles as resident middlemen in that area for the next several years. The Khampa clans on the other side of the river were yet to make common cause with their kinsmen, and they generally waited out the battle for Chamdo except for a few whom the Chinese had persuaded to join what would clearly be the winning side.

The battle for Chamdo and the defense of Tibet was pitifully unequal but mercifully short. The Chinese crossed the river with well-trained and -equipped armies of soldiers. On the western side five hundred Tibetan soldiers were stationed at Chamdo, lacking heavy weapons and leadership.⁵ They were augmented by another garrison of surprisingly well-disciplined soldiers, which came to the defense of the provincial capital, but it was far from enough. The recently arrived governor, Ngabo Ngawang Jigme, put up an inept defense and was captured while fleeing to Lhasa. Some local Khampas, who had been recruited to augment the defense, turned to marauding when abandoned by the retreating governor. It was all over in less than two weeks.

When on October 24, 1950, the Chinese formally announced the invasion that they had actually begun some weeks earlier, the Indian government reacted with a sense of outrage. Beijing had repeatedly assured New Delhi it was still negotiating with the Tibetans. Defiant and unremorseful, the Chinese told the Indians it was none of their business, adding the gratuitous insult that "outside influences" had caused the Indians to delay the Tibetan negotiators. Several rounds of mutual and public recriminations followed, ending in a show of defiance by a frustrated Nehru, who told Beijing that Indian military and civilian personnel had been "instructed to stay at their posts" at Lhasa and in southern Tibet.[6]

Henderson, who had described Nehru to Washington as "a vain, sensitive, emotional and complicated person," might be forgiven if he had gone to Nehru with the attitude of we told you so. But he warned the State Department against such smugness and acknowledged that Nehru "in spite of his vanity and of his petty snobberies, is a man of warm heart, of genuine idealism, of shrewd discernment, and of considerable intellectual capacity."[7] Moreover, Henderson had not forgotten that, after his impassioned pleas three months earlier, the Indians had endorsed the U.S. resolution at the UN that provided the international legitimacy for American troops to resist the North Korean attack on the south.

Nevertheless, on Tibet, Henderson reported that despite Nehru's irritation with the Chinese, he found no evidence that India's leader would "take such drastic steps as to terminate India's chosen role of best friend of Peking among the non-Communist powers."[8] When they met on November 2, Henderson merely agreed that the Chinese action "was not in the interest of peace"[9] and asked how Washington might help with a burden that "geographic and historic factors" had thrust mainly onto India's shoulders. Nehru said the United States could be most helpful by doing nothing and saying little for the moment lest it lend credence to Beijing's charges that the great powers had been scheming in Tibet.

In public, however, Nehru partly excused China's invasion on the same ground, suggesting that Mao may have acted on misinformation from Moscow about "Anglo-American intrigues" to create an anti-Communist Tibet.[10] For Nehru to have confessed that Beijing had betrayed him while he was arguing for the Communists to take the Chinese seat at the UN would have meant admitting to flawed judgment. But he was also a realist and a politician under attack at home for not confronting the Chinese about their attack on Tibet. Aware that India did not have the military capability to take on the Chinese, he believed that his only viable geopolitical choice was his policy of nonalignment. This did not preclude quiet efforts to help Tibet, including continued arms and training. He also immediately took steps to develop Indian intelligence and security capabilities along India's 2,000-mile northern border.[11] It was an untidy policy that did not appeal to the forthright Henderson, but he quietly acquiesced in the prime minister's advice that the U.S. hold its public fire on Tibet for the time being.

The Tibetans literally found themselves in diplomatic limbo: Their delegation to Beijing was trapped in India after the invasion. In Lhasa, meanwhile, the frightened government expected the Chinese soon to occupy their capital. Plans were made to advance the grant of full powers to the still teenaged Dalai Lama. On November 13, the Tibetan cabinet and national assembly appealed to the United Nations to restrain Chinese aggression. They assured Secretary General Trygve Lie that "Tibet will not go down without a fight, though there is little hope of a nation dedicated to peace resisting the brutal effort of men trained to war." The United States thought it tactically wise to avoid taking the lead at the UN so that Tibet would not be dismissed as just another item on the Cold War agenda. And whereas Washington was ready to support any diplomatic initiative taken by the Indians at the UN, New Delhi had no interest in taking the lead.

The British, at odds among themselves, continued to be indecisive. The War Office decided that Chinese control of Tibet "would not appreciably increase the military threat to neighboring countries."[12] The Foreign Office, however, was not so easily able to slough off the complex political issues that would soon be brought before the United Nations. Whitehall conceded that Tibet's autonomy qualified the country as a state within the definition of the UN Charter,[13] but Britain's UN representative in New York, Sir Gladwyn Jebb, challenged his home office: "Politically, I have no doubt at all that what we want to do is to create a situation which does not oblige us in practice to do anything about the Communist invasion of Tibet."[14] That was too much for even the lawyers to swallow. The Foreign Office's legal advisor, Sir Eric Beckett, supported by Attorney General Sir Hartley Shawcross, argued against wriggling out of Britain's diplomatic responsibilities to Tibet by mere legalisms.[15] But like Washington, London would defer to New Delhi.[16]

The Tibetans therefore found no ready champions at the UN. But while the United States, Britain, and India were deferring to each other, El Salvador surprised everyone on November 15 by demanding an immediate debate in the General Assembly. Ernest Gross, who as deputy U.S. representative had shepherded the UN resolution on Korea five months earlier, explained that as a loyal Catholic country, El Salvador had responded to the personal interest of Pope Pius XII and to the Vatican's consequent action behind the scenes to have Tibet's case heard by the international community.[17]

Gross was instructed to support the resolution by a less idealistic State Department. His instructions suggested that the debate might yield a propaganda advantage by "marshalling world opinion against Chinese Communist aggressive actions in the Far East."[18] This might help the U.S., now in dire military straits in Korea as human waves of Chinese soldiers forced back American troops who had advanced close to the Chinese border. Nevertheless, Gross was to defer to the Indians to take the initiative, and they—particularly their opportunistic UN ambassador—remained ever reluctant to lead. On November 24 the UN General Committee, which sets the Assembly's agenda, unanimously voted to postpone consideration of the Tibetan appeal based on the assertion of India's ambassador that Beijing's latest note pointed toward a peaceful settlement. The United States supported the postponement, a welcome respite for everyone but the Tibetans.

Although Tibet would eventually be seen as an opportunity to challenge the Chinese on terrain disadvantageous to them, for the time being it carried a distinctly lesser priority than the main event in Korea. There were also intelligence reports of increased Chinese support to the Vietminh in Indo-China, which prompted the U.S. to undertake a major military aid program for the French fighting there. President Truman saw it all "timed to coincide with the attack in Korea as a challenge to the Western world . . . aimed at intensifying the smoldering anti-foreign feeling among most Asian peoples." Secretary Acheson believed that the U.S. was closer than it had yet been to a wider war,[19] and intelligence estimates concluded that the Chinese intended not only to make the Western position untenable in Korea but with Russian support were prepared to face a war against the United States. Washington's problems were compounded by pressure from the British[20] to negotiate a cease-fire in Korea, to come to terms with Beijing on a seat in the UN, and above all, to revert to a policy emphasizing Europe (which would leave little room for peripheral countries like Tibet).

Within the State Department the Office of Chinese Affairs conducted a three-month debate with its colleagues in the Office of United Nations Affairs, arguing that even if the United States could not prevent the Chinese occupation it should "lay the groundwork for keeping Tibet stirred up" in order eventually to challenge Communist control. The UN Office countered that the world organization was unable to mount substantial help for the Tibetans, and consideration of their UN appeal might jeopardize efforts for a cease-fire in Korea. (Ironically, among those in the China Office who championed strong action against the Chinese Communists on Tibet was Oliver E. Clubb, later to become one victim of Senator McCarthy's charges against State Department officers who had supposedly "lost" China to communism.[21]) Unfortunately, the distracted Tibetans again dropped the ball, failing to apply for the visas that they had been notified were waiting for the delegation named to present their case in New York. Nor could the State Department find much support for the Tibetans. In a poll conducted by seventeen U.S. embassies in Asia and the Middle East, the Department found a general indifference and a uniform lack of enthusiasm for any UN action.

But American resolve to confront the Communists on all fronts was stiffening. In a review of the world situation dated January 15, 1951, the Joint Chiefs of Staff concluded that the nation faced "one of the greatest dangers in its history. The Korean war could be the first phase of a global war between the United States and the USSR."[22] The nation's military leaders assumed that the Chinese intervention in Korea had been undertaken with an "appreciation of the risk of general war between the U.S. and Communist China and perhaps in expectation" of it, most likely with the assurance of effective Soviet support. They recommended a military buildup to support the policy of containing communism, plus propaganda, psychological warfare, and special operations "against Kremlin-dominated communism everywhere." This was to call forth what Franklin Lindsay, chief of operations for the CIA's Office of Policy Coordination,[23] called a worldwide "explosion" of anti-Communist operations, which were to include Tibet.[24]

WASHINGTON ENGAGES THE DALAI LAMA

With the world's attention focused on the humiliating retreat of American forces in the bitter winter cold of Korea, the Dalai Lama withdrew to Yatung in southern Tibet with fifty principal officers of his government and gold and silver bullion from the Potala treasury. Yatung, twelve miles from the Indian border, is where his predecessor, the thirteenth Dalai Lama, had spent his last night before crossing into exile in India while fleeing the Chinese occupiers of Lhasa forty years earlier.

The decision to move was made shortly after Thubten Jigme Norbu, the Dalai Lama's brother, arrived in Lhasa in November 1950 from the Chinese-occupied areas of eastern Tibet bringing frightening news.[25] As a child Norbu had been declared to be a reincarnation of a famous monk, Takster, whose seat was at Kumbum Monastery in the Amdo region near to the family's birthplace; Takster Rimpoche was his title. As the district's ranking prelate and, more to the point, the Dalai Lama's eldest brother, he had become a prime target of the Chinese Communists for political conversion when they occupied this region the previous year. The Chinese occupiers made sustained efforts to convince Norbu to travel to Lhasa and persuade the Tibetan government to welcome the Chinese troops as liberators. They offered to make him governor general of Tibet so he could assist in a socialist reconstruction that would rid the country of its "antiquated religious beliefs." If his brother the Dalai Lama resisted, the Chinese suggested that "in the interest of the cause," fratricide would be justified. A horrified Norbu pretended to accept their mission so that he could get to Lhasa to warn his brother of the full and sinister extent of China's intentions for subjugating Tibet.

When Norbu arrived in Lhasa he immediately went to his brother and shared his experience of the past year under Chinese occupation, including the proposal for murder if necessary. Norbu wrote a report of the Chinese proposal, which he planned to circulate only to his brother and the cabinet. Unfortunately someone leaked it, probably in an attempt to drive Norbu from Lhasa. He therefore made it available to the Tibetan assembly, but then it was time to get out of Tibet. In mid-December Norbu decided to retreat to Yatung accompanied by his mother, two sisters, and his youngest brother. They were followed two days later by the Dalai Lama and most of the senior officials.

On the advice of his senior ministers, the Dalai Lama had assumed full governing powers in November, two years in advance of the traditional age of eighteen. One of his first acts was to pardon those officials imprisoned during the bitter warfare between the regents in 1947. His assumption of full powers, the amnesty, and the now generally recognized sense of peril, produced a greater unity within his government. But unity did not mean unanimity. Members of the clerical old guard had not been enthusiastic about his departure and appealed to the Dalai Lama to accept the Chinese terms presented in October to the captive Tibetan governor of Chamdo, Ngabo Ngawang Jigme. These terms for "peaceful liberation" promised to respect existing government and religious institutions and Tibetan customs and property. The old guard was willing to accept Chinese overlordship if it meant they could preserve the status quo. This pressure for accommodation was to add to the Dalai Lama's problems in the coming months as the UN pigeonholed his appeal for moral support and he faced the agonizing choice between a return to Lhasa or exile.

Disappointed by the UN's snub, the Dalai Lama sent two emissaries in January of 1951 to sound out the Chinese ambassador in New Delhi about opening negotiations to forestall a resumption of the Chinese invasion, which had halted after the capture of Chamdo. They were impressed by the ambassador's assurances that the invasion would not proceed if the Tibetans negotiated with Beijing. The desperate Tibetans agreed, dispatching Ngabo from Chamdo accompanied by two officials from Lhasa who carried vague and unrealistic negotiating points. Two similarly uninstructed officials went from the Dalai Lama's provisional headquarters at Yatung, and the Dalai Lama's brother-in-law Phuntso Tashi accompanied the group as an interpreter. No one in the delegation was authorized to conclude an agreement; the Tibetans were still hoping to buy time.[26] Washington meanwhile searched for means to keep the young leader from becoming a tool of the Chinese.

ᔥ

As part of its new resolve Washington decided it was time to take more active measures on Tibet, unilaterally if necessary, lest it "go by default, particularly in view of the UN action re Korea and also the need for checking Chi Commie advances where feasible."[27] The State Department accordingly solicited Henderson's views. What would be the effect on Tibetan resistance if the Dalai Lama were to flee to India? Could the young Tibetan ruler become a rallying point for internal resistance if the Chinese took Lhasa? How should the dormant UN appeal proceed? What could be accomplished if the Indian government changed its position against active involvement in Tibet? The Department was convinced that the Chinese conquest, which seemed to be on hold for the moment, would soon extend throughout Tibet. "Every feasible effort should be made to hinder the Commie occupation" and ensure that Tibet's case received a hearing at the UN, the cable declared. It pledged that the U.S. government "still stands ready to extend some material assistance if appropriate means can be found for the expression of Tibetan resistance to aggression."

This doughty statement of policy had been supported in a legal sense during the previous week by an extraordinarily generous American reading of Tibet's status made at the request of the British.[28] Washington forthrightly told London that the "United States, which was one of the early supporters of the principle of self-determination of peoples, believes that the Tibetan people has the same inherent right as any other to have the determining voice in its political destiny."[29] It went on to make the surprisingly sweeping judgment that "should developments warrant, consideration could be given to recognition of Tibet as an independent state." In the meantime, the U.S. government recognized Tibet's autonomy in fact if not yet in law, and that provided the basis for any UN consideration of what China was doing to Tibet.

Such sweeping statements provided ample policy approval for a program of active support for the Tibetans. Operationally it was difficult to launch one. Henderson, as much of a realist as he was an activist, gave the Department a bleak assessment of the possibility of organizing a resistance effort around the Dalai Lama if he sought asylum in India. He concluded that "unless there is an immediate future indication that Tibet might receive moral as well as substantial military aid from abroad, the Dalai Lama might depart from the country [Tibet], and with his departure all effective resistance would probably collapse."[30] And even if he were to seek asylum, the ambassador believed that the Indian government would not permit him to direct a resistance movement from India. While Washington was not prepared in the winter of 1951 to offer "substantial" military aid, it was moving toward more active political support. The aim was to preserve the Dalai Lama as a potential rallying point for his own people and a symbol of resistance to Chinese Communist aggression for all his fellow Buddhists in Asia. It was to take some months for these operational proposals to take shape.

On March 29, 1951, two visitors called at the embassy to seek Henderson's advice on how the Dalai Lama should deal with a situation in which he felt increasingly trapped. James Burke, New Delhi bureau chief for *Time* and *Life* magazines,[31] brought the young man's former tutor, Heinrich Harrer, who had fled Lhasa with the Dalai Lama. Harrer described his prized pupil as more intelligent and better informed on world affairs than any of his advisers, and one who trusted the United States more than any other country. According to Harrer, the Dalai Lama had reluctantly sent the delegation to Beijing and had withheld full negotiating powers from its members because he feared that they might be forced to yield to Chinese pressure. He had doubts about returning to Lhasa, but some of his monastic advisers were insisting that he must come to terms with the Chinese and go back to rule under the country's new overlords. "The Dalai Lama does not know which way to turn for advice," said Harrer.[32]

Henderson was convinced that Harrer was telling him the truth. So was Burke, who had interviewed the Austrian at length. The ambassador quickly realized the nature of the Dalai Lama's dilemma. His treasury had been sent across the border to the Indian protectorate of Sikkim for safekeeping, but if he returned with it to Lhasa, both he and his funds would fall into the hands of the Chinese Communists. If he returned without the money, the Indian government might freeze the funds, but he had no guarantee of asylum in India.

"Unless someone in whom this young man might have confidence should give him advice, he will fall into the Chinese Communist trap, or he will be in an extremely unenviable position in India," Henderson cabled Washington. He then proceeded to fill this avuncular role himself. The ambassador reported that he had sent two couriers with an unsigned letter on nonidentifiable Indian stationery. The couriers were instructed to tell the Dalai Lama that the message was from him. The letter itself preserved deniability by stating that it came from "a high foreign official who had recently visited Asia and who had sympathy for Tibet and deep concern for the welfare of His Holiness and His people" and was therefore sending his earnest suggestions.

Probably recalling his own experience with Soviet absorption of the Baltic states, Henderson began with a warning that no concessions by Tibet could alter the Chinese Communist determination to gain complete control over the country. The Chinese, he wrote, prefer to accomplish this by "trickery rather than through force," and any agreement that would establish Beijing's representative in Lhasa would only speed the takeover. Henderson therefore warned the Dalai Lama under no circumstances to return himself or his treasury to Lhasa "until changes in the world situation would make it difficult" for the Chinese Communists to take over Tibet. In the meantime, the Dalai Lama should start arranging for asylum in Ceylon, and if that proved impossible, he was "certain of finding a place of refuge in one of the friendly countries, including the United States, in the Western Hemisphere." Henderson also suggested that the Dalai Lama send a delegation immediately to the UN to make a direct appeal, reminding him that U.S. visas awaited his emissaries.

In his covering letter to the Department, this professional diplomat, who in his later years was known as "Mr. Foreign Service," acknowledged that his bold and unauthorized action involved a considerable amount of risk. But it was "better for this risk to be taken than to see the Chinese Communists succeed by trickery in taking over Tibet and in gaining control of the Dalai Lama and his treasures." He explained that he had not wanted to chance a leak, and in any case his tactics left the Department free to disclaim responsibility if the message became public. He added a bit of retroactive diplomatic cover by assuring the Department that he recognized the dangers of officers in the field acting on their own initiative, but this was "one of the rare occasions" when he felt he "should move forward fast and take the entire responsibility for the consequences."

In the event, Henderson suspended the delivery of his letter until the Tibetan negotiating mission left for Beijing, which gave the Department time to countermand it. On the contrary, it enthusiastically approved,[33] except for the appeal to the UN because a recent poll of potential supporters for UN action on Tibet did not turn up enough votes. The letter itself did not reach Tibetan hands for transmission to the Dalai Lama until May, when Henderson sent First Secretary Fraser Wilkins to Kalimpong to meet with Tibetan foreign secretary Thupten Tharpa Liushar. Liushar had described the government's deep disappointment over the lack of response to its appeal to the UN and the consequent sense of fatalism about the inevitability of China's control of Tibet's defense, foreign affairs, and communications; only internal affairs would be reserved for the Dalai Lama. Despite this bleak and unfortunately accurate forecast of Tibet's prospects, Liushar assured Wilkins that "Tibet would in the long run emerge unscathed . . ." Meanwhile the foreign secretary hoped that the U.S. government "would not be disheartened by little actions which they [the Tibetans] might be forced to take."[34]

Henderson's activist embassy responded by proposing help both overt and covert. It would facilitate Tibetan wool marketing in the United States, conduct marketing surveys for other Tibetan products, buy up unspecified "strategic Tibetan products which otherwise might go to China," offer Tibet economic aid, conduct more frequent informal liaison with Tibetan representatives in Kalimpong, provide information and assistance to the Tibetan language newspaper there, offer military assistance to the extent permitted by Indian law, lend further support to Tibet's UN appeal, and publish "in proper form at a proper time a statement by the United States Government with respect to its recognition of the autonomy of Tibet." It was far from what the Tibetans had hoped for, but it was a start.

CHAPTER 5

The Dalai Lama's Dilemma

THE OCCUPATION AGREEMENT

Although the Dalai Lama thought he could prevent his delegation from committing itself in Beijing, the Chinese announced on May 26, 1951, that his representatives had signed an agreement that effectively ratified the Chinese occupation of Tibet. Henderson's letter with its offer of support had not yet been delivered to Yatung and the Tibetan delegation had been bullied and essentially overpowered by the Chinese negotiators. The signing had actually taken place three days before it was announced.

Phuntso Tashi, the Dalai Lama's brother-in-law and a member of the delegation, said that from the very beginning the Chinese made it clear that their terms were the only basis for negotiation.[1] They accused the Chinese Nationalists, the British, and the United States of forcing them to defend their borders, now of course expanded to include Tibet. Whenever the Tibetans attempted to contest a point, the Chinese would angrily beat the table with their fists and ask whether the Tibetans wanted the "liberation" of their country to be peaceful or violent. They had been told to sign or "there would be war," Phuntso later told his family. He added that throughout their stay the members of the delegation were continuously watched and followed, and felt they were "as in an iron box." At one point the beleaguered Tibetans threatened to break off negotiations and leave. But they caucused that evening and decided it would be more dangerous to Tibet if they did not reach an agreement, thus giving the Chinese a free hand. They therefore acceded to the Chinese demands without asking Lhasa.

Ngabo Ngawang Jigme, the chief of the delegation, objected to signing the agreement without the official seal, which he did not let the Chinese know that he had brought with him. The Chinese brushed this objection aside and made personal seals, which they forced on the delegates. Accused later of being a Tibetan quisling,[2] Ngabo explained to the Dalai Lama that he had concealed the state seals so the Chinese would be forced to fabricate invalid substitutes. That, he said, would allow the Dalai Lama to repudiate the agreement later (as he immediately did when he went into exile in India in 1959).

The seventeen points of the agreement ended the de facto independence of Tibet. As Tibet's foreign secretary Liushar had predicted a few weeks earlier, the Tibetans ceded control of their defense and foreign relations, and their army was to be incorporated into the Chinese People's Liberation Army. There would be a Chinese committee of civilians like the committees that administered the major regions of China, although the Chinese did promise that the existing political system in Tibet and the powers of the Dalai Lama would not be changed. The Chinese had achieved their objective of establishing control over Tibet without the further use of military force.

The agreement included a series of protocols, known only to the negotiators and their principals, which have never been published. While some questions remain about their specific contents, there is a consensus among knowledgeable Tibetans and scholars that one protocol stipulated that the main agreement would remain in force if the Dalai Lama should prefer to remain outside Tibet and, further, that he might assume his full status and authority if he decided to return later. Two members of the delegation cited another protocol dealing with a Tibetan police force and another phasing out Tibetan currency gradually.[3] The son of the delegation leader said two more protocols limited the Chinese forces in Tibet to one army corps and reserved the formal definition of the frontier between China and Tibet for later negotiation.[4]

The Dalai Lama was stunned when he heard the Chinese broadcast the agreement. He contested the broadcast's phrase, "return of the Tibetan people to the big family of the Motherland—the People's Republic of China," and he was shocked that the delegation had exceeded what he thought was its limited powers. Forty years later he took a more resigned view and characterized Ngabo as a Tibetan patriot who had been forced to sign under duress. But at the time, the Dalai Lama could only wait for the return to Yatung of the delegation to find out what had happened in Beijing and how to deal with it. His own position was crucial. If he returned, he would legitimize Chinese control, but he might be able to run interference for his people. If he crossed the border into exile, he would preserve the institution of his office and perhaps become a rallying point for an effective challenge to the Chinese, but his people would feel abandoned and he risked becoming an irrelevant international relic. He was caught in a painful political and moral tug of war, pulled in several directions by his own conscience, the demands of his new Chinese overlords, the uncertain promises of his newly found American friends, the concerns of his family, and the divided counsel of his advisers.

Even before the Beijing announcement, Shakabpa had requested conversations with Fraser Wilkins, the U.S. embassy's political officer whom Henderson had sent to Calcutta and Kalimpong to sound out Tibetan officials on the Dalai Lama's plans. Shakabpa, who had gained some knowledge of the ways of the outside world from leading the 1948 trade mission, asked Wilkins what Tibet should do when the anticipated breakdown in the Beijing talks occurred. He said Liushar had shown Henderson's letter to the Dalai Lama, and the foreign secretary was on his way to discuss it with the young ruler. Shakabpa said that the Dalai Lama was willing to concede Chinese control of defense and external affairs over the Tibetan area east of the Yangtze, but that the young ruler would leave Tibet if the Chinese insisted on the same authority over the "heart of the country" in which Lhasa had traditionally exercised control.[5]

But just how far did Washington's commitments go? How would the U.S. government help if the Dalai Lama sought asylum abroad? Should Tibet renew its appeal to the UN, and would the U.S. support it? Would the U.S. approach the Ceylonese government for asylum? And if the Ceylonese refused, could the Dalai Lama expect asylum in the U.S.? How would he be received there and would the U.S. government pay his expenses? Would Washington provide military assistance and money "when the time is ripe" for Tibetan resistance groups to rise up against the Chinese Communists?

For the present, Shakabpa asked the U.S. to establish some form of representation in Kalimpong to facilitate negotiations. The Dalai Lama was worried about the safety of his eldest brother Thubten Jigme Norbu (Takster Rimpoche). He believed Norbu's refusal to play ball with the Chinese had made it unsafe for him to remain in Lhasa. Would the U.S. receive him if he could not find safe haven in India?

The embassy forwarded all these questions with recommendations for positive but qualified responses: The U.S. would support a UN appeal; receive the Dalai Lama as an "eminent religious dignitary and head of the autonomous state of Tibet" if asylum in Ceylon didn't work out; help him live in a "modest and dignified fashion"; provide military assistance if the situation warranted and the aid did not violate Indian law; help the resistance by taking "action which might be effective in encouraging the Tibetan regime and maintain [ing its] autonomy;" send U.S. officials to Darjeeling and Kalimpong but not as representatives accredited to a government-in-exile. Finally, the embassy proposed telling Shakabpa that Takster Rimpoche would be welcome to visit the United States if he believed he would not be safe in India.

The State Department's reply was sent after China's imposed agreement with Tibet became known. It opened with a sturdy declaration that "the Tibetan people should enjoy certain rights of self-determination commensurate with the autonomy Tibet has maintained since the Chinese Revolution [of 1911]."[6] The Department reserved its final judgment until it could determine whether the Tibetans signed under threats of personal violence, but assuming that was the case, Washington generally endorsed the embassy's recommendations while disclaiming American "responsibility [for the] guidance of the Tibetan government." But it was less generous in offering financial support for the Dalai Lama in exile, suggesting he use his own funds. Only "limited assistance in terms of light arms" would be given to a Tibetan resistance movement, but it would have to organize itself without outside help. The U.S. contribution would be determined by what "the attitude or the government of India makes possible." Eventually the Department backed down from its puritanical demand that the Tibetans pay their own way in exile, but the other commitments and conditions remained during the crucial next two months of trying to woo the Dalai Lama to the West.

Henderson was ready to move when he got the word. He sent his young political officer, Nicholas Thacher, with his wife and young baby, on an extended "vacation" to Kalimpong to maintain contact with Shakabpa and Liushar. A CIA officer was already on the scene, having been introduced to the Dalai Lama's mother by a well known Kalmuk monk, Geshe Wangyal. She had sent "Geshe-la" to the Calcutta consulate seeking assistance in her efforts to persuade her son to leave Tibet for India because she believed his life was in danger. Assisted by other American diplomats, Thacher kept in touch with Tibetans in a position either to influence the decision of the Dalai Lama or to arrange for the logistics of his flight, if he chose to make one. Heinrich Harrer and George Patterson also served as go-betweens. It all made for a busy summer with U.S. officers shuttling among New Delhi, Calcutta, the picturesque hill station of Darjeeling, and Kalimpong, the trading center from which caravans had for centuries set off across the pass to Tibet.

Thacher said one of his primary considerations was to keep these activities secret from the Indians.[7] It is highly doubtful that he succeeded in the goldfish bowl on the border, where the Indians were becoming increasingly anxious about events on the other side. Henderson's energetic action reflected the increasingly hard line being taken against China by the Truman administration in Washington under intense Republican pressure. Truman's firing of General Douglas MacArthur in the spring unleashed a Republican torrent, and the U.S. military recovery in Korea under the command of General Matthew B. Ridgway set the stage for negotiating a cease-fire from a position of strength. Anything to demonstrate the administration's resolve in thwarting the Chinese Communists would now receive a welcome reception, even backing the Dalai Lama in the distant land of Tibet.

The negotiations over Korea, which had begun that summer, did little to dampen Washington's enthusiasm for support of the Tibetan case. Vigorous efforts were made to persuade the Dalai Lama to repudiate the agreement with Beijing and leave Tibet so that he might be used as a symbol to rally Asia's Buddhists against Chinese Communist expansion. As assistant secretary of state for Far Eastern Affairs, Dean Rusk was calling the shots on U.S. policy in Tibet at that time. Four decades later, the soft-spoken, determined Georgian reaffirmed to me his belief that American support of Tibetan independence in Asia fit within the prevailing Truman doctrine in Europe.[8] He confirmed that both Secretary Acheson, who was a realist but staunchly anti-Communist, and the president had been kept fully informed of and approved the efforts being undertaken to extend the doctrine to the Tibetans.[9] According to Rusk, Washington believed that if the Dalai Lama could be removed from Tibet and established in a nearby Buddhist country he "might make a go of it" in his claim for an independent Tibet. In any event this action would serve the U.S. purpose of doing anything possible "to get in the way of the Chinese Communists," even over the anticipated objections of the Chinese Nationalist government, which had withdrawn to Taiwan and was still recognized by the United States as the government of China.

Into High Gear

Early in June Henderson exercised his relatively free hand to utilize his well-positioned team in a series of negotiations with the Tibetans.

First he tried to convince Bajpai, the Indian foreign secretary, that Asia would gain if the Dalai Lama refused to accept the treaty.[10] A resigned Bajpai agreed that Henderson might be right, but he said that, in the interest of correct relations with Beijing, the Indian government was refraining from attempting to influence the Dalai Lama. Henderson felt under no such constraint.

On June 10, Wilkins returned from Darjeeling and Kalimpong, where he had met Shakabpa to give him the official answers to his questions.[11] Shakabpa gave him the news that the Dalai Lama had telegraphed from Yatung that he and his government did not recognize the agreement with the Chinese and that the Tibetan delegation in Beijing had been instructed to tell the Chinese it was unacceptable. He also reported the ominous news that the Tibetan government had been informed that a ten-man Chinese delegation was on its way to Yatung to "congratulate" the Dalai Lama on the agreement and that some members of the Tibetan negotiating team would probably return with them. Shakabpa said that Tibetan negotiators would therefore probably not renounce the agreement until they were safely outside China.

On the final day of their negotiations, Shakabpa told Wilkins that he had just received an urgent message from the Dalai Lama, which he interpreted to mean that if there were any prospect of strong political support from the U.S., the Dalai Lama was prepared to leave Tibet. But if no assistance was forthcoming, there seemed little hope that Tibet could successfully resist the Chinese terms. Declaring himself "extremely pleased and happy" even with the carefully hedged replies from Washington that Wilkins had just delivered, it was apparent that the experienced trader had just begun to bargain. He said it was crucial that the Dalai Lama leave Yatung for India. U.S. assistance would be essential to the formation of resistance groups inside Tibet, because the Tibetans, not expecting to have to swallow the Chinese pact, had not recently approached the Indians for help. He pressed for a more definite statement about the amount of the financial aid and loans the Tibetans might expect in order to organize and sustain a resistance movement. Wilkins hedged again but reassured Shakabpa that the U.S. "was prepared to give consideration to action which might be effective in encouraging Tibet to regain and maintain autonomy." On this point Shakabpa would seem to be out ahead of the Dalai Lama, who consistently showed little heart for a military response to the Chinese. This is not surprising as these negotiations were conducted through irregular communications between negotiators with uncertain briefs and a principal who was surrounded by advisers with varying agendas.

That same day Takster Rimpoche arrived from Yatung with a letter from the Dalai Lama declaring that he sought close relations with Washington and its assistance. Washington and the embassy swung into high gear. The embassy proposed that Washington issue a statement of sympathy and support immediately after the Dalai Lama's anticipated public disavowal of the agreement with China. New Delhi was authorized to inform the Tibetans that upon disavowal, "official reference to this action, indicating sympathy for the Tibetan position, could be expected." [12] The Department left itself some latitude by adding that the "tenor and timing of any comment would depend on the character of the Tibetan announcement." The Department arranged for the CIA-supported Committee for a Free Asia to sponsor a visit to the United States by Takster Rimpoche, who was by then very much out of favor with the Chinese. It also notified the Thai government that the United States would underwrite the expenses of the Dalai Lama and his entourage if he was unable to settle in India and decided to seek asylum in Thailand. Shakabpa, however, exercised a pocket veto over the Thai option by simply not forwarding it to Yatung.

The embassy meanwhile was growing impatient that Shakabpa had received no response from Yatung to the offers made two weeks earlier. It became concerned that Henderson's pledges of support had not reached the Dalai Lama, and arranged on June 24 to forward the assurances through "other sources,"[13] later identified as Heinrich Harrer. The Dalai Lama later confirmed indirectly that he had received the messages,[14] so his ominous indecision about whether to go into exile was not just a matter of bad communications.

Now it would be Takster's turn to bargain on behalf of his brother, this time with the U.S. consul general in Calcutta, Evan M. Wilson, and members of his staff.[15] Takster said that his brother had asked his advice about how to respond to American appeals to disavow the agreement and flee Tibet, inasmuch as the Tibetan government was powerless and there were no signs that the U.S. would help in any concrete way. Wilson pointed to the promise of American support for the Dalai Lama's disavowal of the agreement once he actually did so, but he expressed his understanding of the Dalai Lama's reluctance to do anything that might jeopardize his delegation until it was safely out of China. But now that the delegation was in Hong Kong, it was time for him to make his move. He also pointed out that it was highly important for the world to know exactly where Tibet stood, especially if it was contemplating another approach to the United Nations (which the U.S. would support). Takster said that with this assurance of American readiness to speak out on behalf of the Tibetans, he thought the Dalai Lama would probably disavow the agreement.

The consul then discussed places of possible asylum for the Dalai Lama. The U.S. preference, based on proximity to Tibet in a country sympathetic to Buddhism, was for India, followed by Thailand, and finally Ceylon. If none of those three was acceptable, the U.S. would be glad to receive him and a small group of followers both as an eminent religious dignitary and "Head of the Tibetan State." Wilson finessed the proposal for a secret agreement contained in the Dalai Lama's letter by deferring to Washington where the proposal got lost.

While the consulate was trying to pin down Takster on his brother's intentions, Thacher was engaged in equally intense but equivocal negotiations with Shakabpa in Kalimpong.[16] Both Washington and the embassy in New Delhi were becoming increasingly anxious. The Dalai Lama would have to make his declaration and flee to India before he was forced to confront the Chinese in Yatung, who would not be shy about pressuring the young holy man. Thacher warned that the chances of U.S. assistance "were rather slight" if the Dalai Lama accepted the Chinese agreement. The foreign service officer temporarily abandoned his usually scrupulous caution and urged the Tibetans to consider active resistance to the Chinese occupation. While temporizing about whether the U.S. government recognized Chinese suzerainty over Tibet, he reaffirmed that the Dalai Lama would be received in the U.S. should he go there as a "great religious leader and as leader of an autonomous state." Thacher could not be accused of having fallen under the spell of his clients, at least those advising the Dalai Lama. He ended his report with the observation that "there is much opportunism among the Tibetans" who "may forget broader duties to save their own skins—very hesitant and strongly tempted to come with their gold and jewels to Kalimpong for safe haven, rather than take the risks and hard work of opposing China."

Thacher's hedge on suzerainty showed foresight. The Department answered his follow-up request for a definitive statement by saying it did not "wish to commit itself on what it may or may not say re Tibet's legal status."[17] Washington needed to keep its options open pending the reactions of the Chinese Communists and the Nationalists if the Dalai Lama fled abroad. Both claimed Tibet as Chinese territory with equal vigor.

ℝ

On July 1 the Chinese delegation, accompanied by members of the Tibetan delegation, arrived in Calcutta en route to Yatung. Takster, who had earlier expressed what the consulate considered were justified fears for his personal safety in India, sent word the next day that he had just received a telegram from the Dalai Lama asking him not to leave India.[18] The request from his brother came in response to Takster's telegram summarizing his conversations with the consulate and urging the Tibetan government to issue a statement disavowing the agreement. Takster told the consul that the Dalai Lama's decision to receive the Chinese delegation at Yatung, however, made it all the more necessary for him to seek asylum in the United States. If the Dalai Lama lost his freedom of action, Takster wanted to be out from under the thumb of the Chinese and available in Washington to maintain direct contact with the U.S. government. Takster's concerns about the Dalai Lama's personal liberty had probably been heightened by his conversation the night before with his brother-in-law, who had told him of the restraint imposed on the negotiating team when they were in Beijing.

The following days were full of what the consul general later called "cloak and dagger."[19] His officers worked with George Patterson to keep Takster out of sight while they obtained the necessary exit papers and reservations for him on the Pan American flight leaving Calcutta, by appropriate coincidence, on July 4. (Patterson had been brought into these operations a few weeks before by the Dalai Lama's mother when she, Takster, and two of his younger siblings had arrived in Kalimpong, ostensibly on a pilgrimage.) There were two final anxious days in Calcutta after the first plane reservation was canceled because the Indians refused to accept the travel documents issued by the U.S. In the meantime Phuntso Tashi learned of Takster's plans to flee and had to be sworn to secrecy. He had failed to persuade his brother-in-law to return to Tibet to avoid incurring the wrath of the Chinese.

Takster, by then shaken, had one more frightening encounter when Zhang Jingwu, the head of the Chinese delegation en route to Yatung, peremptorily summoned him to meet with the Chinese ambassador.[20] Zhang urged Takster to return to Lhasa, where much work awaited, and, declaring expansively that Nepal, Bhutan, and Sikkim remained to be "liberated," promised him a good job in one of these future Chinese provinces. Takster attributed this surprisingly crude offer—curiously like the previous one of the post of governor-general of Tibet if he would assassinate his brother—to typical Chinese arrogance. The ambassador joined in, adding that Takster could also go to Beijing or Moscow if he preferred. Finally, he challenged Takster's excuse of being in India for medical treatment, suggesting that Beijing had far more advanced medical facilities. Takster was able to put off the skeptical ambassador, and, evading the men he and Patterson had seen tailing them, made his way undetected that same evening to DumDum Airport and the midnight Pan Am flight to London.

When Takster finally arrived in Washington he was greeted in his native Amdo dialect by Colonel Robert Ekvall, who had learned the language as the son of missionaries to Tibet. Ekvall had been selected by the Free Asia Committee to shelter and reassure him while he recovered from the traumatic events in Calcutta and negotiated with the State Department and the CIA. Their officers met with him on July 12 and provided him with the most comprehensive and authoritative statement of American commitments so far produced for the Tibetans—but not in writing.

According to the account of the session at the State Department that was relayed to the field, these assurances began with the declaration that "the U.S. Government believes Tibet should not be compelled by duress to accept violation of its autonomy and that the Tibetan people should enjoy the rights of self-determination commensurate with the autonomy Tibet has had [for] many years. This has consistently been the position of the U.S." Furthermore, the "U.S. will therefore indicate publicly its understanding of the position of the Dalai Lama as head of an autonomous Tibet, and will similarly endeavor to persuade other nations to take no action adverse to the Dalai Lama's position as head of [an] autonomous Tibet."[21]

The Department then spelled out its specific offer to pay all the costs of transporting the Dalai Lama and his entourage from India to Ceylon and to solicit the cooperation of the Indian government in arranging the move. It offered the further inducement of promising that "friends of Tibet in the U.S." would provide appropriate support in Ceylon for the Dalai Lama, his family, and an entourage of one hundred people or slightly more who would hopefully be chosen for their "political influence and effect." The U.S. also committed itself to support a resistance effort against the Chinese, but considered this a "long range problem limited by physical [and] political conditions in Tibet and in adjoining areas, over which the U.S. of course has no control."

Washington's commitments depended on the Dalai Lama leaving Tibet, publicly refusing to accept "the Tibet-Chi Commie agreement, his continued opposition to Commie aggression, and his continued willingness to cooperate generally." It added that "implicit in this understanding, however, is U.S. support for the Dalai Lama's return to Tibet at the earliest practical moment as head [of an] autonomous non-Commie country." Finally, Takster was assured that the commitment was "basic and longstanding" and unrelated to the war in Korea.

This commitment was surprising since it was made when truce talks had just begun in Korea to end what was becoming an unpopular war at home and with America's allies. Washington's willingness to lend public support to the Dalai Lama, thereby risking the much-desired cease-fire, points to its strong desire to preserve him as a means of opposing further aggression by the Chinese. Had the Dalai Lama left Tibet at that point and become a visible rallying point against the Chinese Communists, he also would have played an inadvertent role in domestic politics as a symbol that the Truman administration was not "soft on Communism." This tangential benefit would not have been immediately apparent as much of the U.S. role in inducing the Dalai Lama to seek asylum abroad was covert. But the generation that shaped national security policy in both the White House and Congress contained a heavy ingredient of Wilsonian idealism with its emphasis on self-determination. A kindred soul, Supreme Court Justice William O. Douglas, who was traveling to India, was asked by his Washington friends to urge the Dalai Lama not to return to Lhasa lest he become a vassal of the Communists.[22] The Dalai Lama left Yatung, however, before the justice could reach there to press his case. It was probably a combination of this idealism and the anticipated future political benefits of having this appealing victim safely out of the grasp of the Chinese Communists that outweighed the risks of imperiling the still uncertain outcome of the cease-fire talks.

THE DALAI LAMA DECIDES TO RETURN

The Chinese delegation left Calcutta en route to Yatung via Kalimpong on the same day Takster departed for the U.S. By plane, jeep, and then pony, it took them a week to reach the young ruler, who was torn by conflicting advice on whether to seek asylum or return to Lhasa. One of those closest to him was the head of his personal staff, Phala Dronyerchemmo, who had encouraged his young charge to leave Lhasa to save his life and now was urging him to accept the U.S. assurances and proceed to India. Phala came from an aristocratic family that had served the Dalai Lama's predecessors. Takster described him as an outstanding exception to the self-seeking officials surrounding the Dalai Lama in Yatung.[23] Although steeped in Tibetan literature and culture, he was unfamiliar with the ways of the outside world. This did not prevent him from deciding that the man to whom he was personally and theologically devoted was better off out of Chinese hands. Phala gave Takster a secret code to communicate his negotiations with the Americans. His counsel, encouraged by both Takster and Shakabpa on the basis of the commitments they had received from Washington, was supported by the Dalai Lama's mother. Her argument for exile was a mother's simple and strong concern for her son's safety, reinforced by her keen sense of politics in both Lhasa and Beijing.

But an equally strong phalanx of government officials and representatives of the leading monasteries, fearful that they might lose the only way of life they knew, along with its attendant privileges, were urging their ruler to return. They argued that he could do more for his country by returning to bargain for the best possible deal with the Chinese. Gyalo said his sister and her husband Phuntso Tashi seconded this advice, warning the Dalai Lama he could expect little support in exile from either India or any other country. They, too, were prepared to take their chances on returning to Lhasa and resuming their comfortable lives there.

The New Delhi embassy had made one more effort to persuade the Dalai Lama to leave by sending another emissary off to Yatung with another unsigned document reiterating the promises of U.S. support.[24] It went further than previous communications in specifying that, if the Dalai Lama left Tibet and organized resistance to the Chinese, the U.S. was prepared to send light arms through India, although, again, the Tibetans would first have to ask the Indians for arms or permit the U.S. to do so. If the Dalai Lama was able to organize resistance within Tibet, the U.S. would also "give consideration to supplying you with loans of money to keep up the resistance, spirit and morale of the Tibetan people," something that "is important if Tibet's autonomy is to be maintained or regained in the event you should feel impelled to seek asylum outside of Tibet." The embassy also told the Dalai Lama it was ready to discuss military assistance with the Tibetans "when you tell us who your representatives are." It was the most explicit statement of the U.S. government's willingness to lend active support to a resistance movement that the Dalai Lama was to receive. Those making these offers of arms did not seem to consider the moral dilemma they presented to the young Buddhist ruler whose whole being represents an abhorrence of violence.

The statement reached the Dalai Lama on July 6. On July 12 Consular Officer Robert Linn in Kalimpong sent a message warning the young ruler that "if Tibet is to be saved from the enemy of all religions, Communism, it will be necessary for you to show the highest courage and act at once." Linn noted that "we have been told that you are courageous." He also added one new enticement by assuring the Dalai Lama that the Indian government had promised the embassy it would assist him in leaving if he sought help through the Indian representative just across the border in Sikkim.[25] The following morning Shakabpa asked Linn for details of the Indian promise of help, indicating that the Dalai Lama was interested in going to India but remained under "the strongest pressure" to stay in Tibet. A frustrated Linn repeated that Shakabpa must contact the local Indian political officer, Harishwar Dayal, the only authoritative source available on what the Indians could offer. A skeptical Shakabpa, who was resignedly packing to join the Dalai Lama in his return to Lhasa, reluctantly agreed to call on Dayal at his Sikkim headquarters en route to Yatung, although he was sure it would do little good.[26]

This apparently hopeless situation did not deter American officials. When Washington received word from Shakabpa via the consulate in Calcutta that the Dalai Lama had decided to meet the Chinese delegation and then return to Lhasa on July 20,[27] it assumed he was acting under duress. In retrospect, Takster believes that his brother, discouraged by the absence of any support from either the Indians or the UN, had by then decided on his own that it was his duty to return to Lhasa to do what he could for his people.[28]

Washington, fearful that the Dalai Lama "was no longer a free agent," launched a frantic campaign to persuade him to change his mind.[29] The State Department illogically proposed that he ask Indian permission to cross the country to asylum in Ceylon, and asked the embassy to seek British assistance in a joint appeal to the Indians, ignoring the lack of British interest in his case all summer. The Department optimistically suggested that if the Indians offered an airplane to the Dalai Lama for his flight into exile, he should accept. If they did not, U.S. "citizens' funds," presumably from the CIA, would be made available.

On July 15 the two Calcutta consular officers operating in Kalimpong gave Shakabpa a written copy of the oral assurances provided to Takster in Washington. Shakabpa was to take this document to Yatung, where presumably he would convince the Dalai Lama to wriggle out of the supposed clutches of the Chinese and flee to India. The document contained the Department's forthright declarations of American support for Tibetan "self-determination commensurate with the autonomy Tibet has had for many years" and its willingness to declare this support openly and encourage other nations to take similar action. But again, it was an unsigned blind memorandum whose official genesis could always be denied.

In preparing the message, the consulate noted that references to autonomy had been included "although it may be difficult to convey to the Tibetans exactly what the Department has in mind, in view of the fact that the Tibetan language does not differentiate between the concepts of autonomy and complete independence."[30] George Patterson, who was used by the consulate in Calcutta to draft various messages, had persuaded the consul in previous discussions with the Tibetans to drop the reference to the Dalai Lama as head of an autonomous state to avoid any misunderstanding originating from the imprecise Tibetan word used to convey the concept of autonomy. This term was nevertheless included in later commitments made by the Department of State, which seemed either oblivious to these semantic distinctions or less concerned about limiting the Dalai Lama's expectations. Patterson, when referring to autonomy, was forced to use the Tibetan word *rang-mang* meaning "free to choose or decide," a word that he knew the Dalai Lama and his brother would recognize and agree with.[31] As this word could also have been used at that time for autonomous, sovereign, suzerain, or independent, the imprecision of the Department's position may actually have been conveyed more accurately than it intended.

The Dalai Lama's brother-in-law, Phuntso Tashi, hand-carried this communication to Yatung along with a real surprise package—an American-backed escape plan[32] offering three options: a quiet departure at night by the Dalai Lama and a "small group of faithful followers presumably for India"; a surreptitious departure for India under escort; or, if these more modest schemes were not feasible, a more elaborate one. Patterson and Heinrich Harrer, in disguise, would meet the Dalai Lama at a prearranged location near Yatung and escort him out of Tibet across the border into the semi-independent country of Bhutan a few hours away.[33] Patterson had secured the agreement of the Bhutanese prime minister Jigme Dorje and his still powerful dowager mother to provide temporary refuge to the Dalai Lama and his party until they could be flown out by small planes from an airstrip on a Bhutanese tea plantation to permanent asylum.[34]

The plan was conceived in Kalimpong, and Patterson said the principal Tibetan involved was Yangpel Pandatsang. As the more respectable member of this maverick family, he was the Tibetan trade agent in southern Tibet and Kalimpong, and thus had quasi-governmental status in the Yatung region as well as command of a small troop of Khampa guards. Pandatsang later said he had agreed to participate in these negotiations despite his grave reservations that it could have been a mistake for the Dalai Lama to deprive Tibet of his leadership during this time of crisis.[35] Harrer claimed the right to participate in exchange for the use of maps he had made while living in the area. The only Tibetans who knew of the plan were Pandatsang, the Dalai Lama's mother, and Phuntso Tashi, whose willingness to participate in this escapade was probably designed to redeem his credentials. At Yatung, the Dalai Lama's junior clerical tutor, Trichung Rimpoche, was the channel for getting these daring proposals to his ward.

In the end, the Dalai Lama rejected the scheme, ending what must have been one of the more audacious proposed ventures ever sponsored by the State Department and its colleagues in the CIA. Today it would be inconceivable to obtain official American support for a proposal to have two foreigners hijack a prominent foreign leader even with his agreement and conduct him across the frontiers of two independent countries. India would surely have disapproved lest it offend its Chinese neighbor, whose sensitivities were particularly acute so soon after Takster's escape from under their noses in Calcutta. Approval had come from people of a generation whose memories of the can-do spirit of

World War II were still fresh as they faced what they considered an equal peril worthy of the risks involved.

But the conscientious young leader had already decided to return to Lhasa. He felt he could protect his country at home better than from abroad, and in any case he was under strong pressure from the privileged officialdom of Lhasa. Moreover, the chief abbots of the three largest monasteries had arrived in Yatung and demanded that the Dalai Lama consult the state oracle. The oracle had emerged from his first trance with a command to return to Lhasa. The Dalai Lama insisted on a second session, and the state oracle emerged from his second trance with the same answer: Return to Lhasa.

Four decades later Dean Rusk ruefully recalled that this intervention from the gods overruled assurances by the most powerful country on Earth. His version of the decision was that the Dalai Lama had swung two balls of mud in a basket until the one marked "Return to Lhasa" dropped out—"so he went."[36] His Holiness was greatly amused when I related this account to him.[37]

In his autobiography, the Dalai Lama cites more worldly reasons for his decision.[38] His reasoning was that the most likely outcome of a deal with Washington would be war and great bloodshed. Moreover, while the United States was a very powerful country, it was thousands of miles away while China was Tibet's neighbor, overwhelmingly superior in military force. This would mean a prolonged war, which he doubted the Americans would be prepared to sustain with its high casualties. The Chinese would inevitably prevail, leaving the Tibetans on their own again, and even weaker after the loss of countless lives. This pragmatic idealist also stressed years later that he never saw a written statement of the U.S. promises that were being made at that time, and he was skeptical about verbal assurances unsupported by an officially signed document.[39] He was also apparently even more suspicious of what he could expect from the Indians if he sought asylum from them, and probably rightly so. Nehru had written off Tibet with great regret, but an explicit offer of asylum at that time would not have helped his courtship of Beijing as joint leader of the nonaligned world.

Several further attempts to persuade the Dalai Lama to leave Tibet were made even after he was on the trail back to Lhasa. Convinced that influential members of the Tibetan cabinet were not aware of the commitments made by the U.S. government, Evan Wilson, the persistent consul general in Calcutta, enlisted a Tibetan courier to ride after the Dalai Lama's party with another unsigned letter spelling them out. The pony rider caught up with the travelers after a "rigorous 35-hour ride" and showed the letter to the Dalai Lama's defense minister Ragashar Shape, whom Wilson believed favored asylum for the Dalai Lama. Ragashar's reaction was one of "incredulity" that, if the U.S. government was willing to make such commitments, it would not do so in a signed document.[40] Without one, Ragashar said he would not stand a chance of convincing the skeptics in the cabinet. The defense minister assured the courier that there was no danger of the letter falling into Chinese hands, since the only Chinese then in central Tibet were the five members of the Chinese delegation traveling separately to Lhasa. Both the chargé acting during Henderson's absence in New Delhi and the Department in Washington were unconvinced. They vetoed Wilson's appeal for a signed letter.[41]

When the more audacious and determined Henderson returned to New Delhi to turn over his embassy to Chester Bowles he accepted a compromise. Heinrich Harrer proposed that Yuthok Shape, a relative of the Sikkimese royal family and former Tibetan official living in Kalimpong, return to Lhasa to try to persuade his old lay colleagues to overcome monastic opposition to the Dalai Lama's departure from Tibet before the Chinese arrived in force in Lhasa. He proposed that Yuthok be shown a letter signed by Henderson on official embassy stationery outlining the commitments previously made orally.[42] He could then swear to its existence and thereby ensure his credibility "since Tibetans attach great importance to such oaths." This time the Department approved, and Wilson and Harrer met with Yuthok in the Calcutta consulate after closing hours on the evening of September 30 to show him the document.

The letter spelled out all previous commitments and added three key assurances.[43] It promised that an "essential part of our cooperation would be a public announcement by the United States that it supports the position of Your Holiness as head of an autonomous Tibet. The United States would also support your return to Tibet at the earliest prac-

ticable moment as head of an autonomous and non-Communist country." It reaffirmed that this position was "fundamental and will not be
affected by developments in Korea or by the Chinese intervention in that
area." At the Department's request it did hedge on providing aid to resistance groups which "would be furnished as was feasible under existing
political and physical conditions." Yuthok took notes on the letter,
which was then locked in the consulate safe, where it would stay. He said
that he planned to leave for Lhasa, where he would meet with Ngabo, the
man who had negotiated and signed the occupation agreement,
Ragashar, the two prime ministers, and the Dalai Lama's older brother
Lobsang Samten. Two weeks later the Department decided that Yuthok
might not be a reliable channel so the Henderson message was shown to
the Dalai Lama's mother in Kalimpong.[44] Leaving no channel uncovered,
the Department told Gyalo Thondup, who was then in Washington, that
the U.S. government recognized both the Nationalists' claim to suzerainty
over Tibet and Tibet's claim to de facto autonomy, adding the hint that
Washington might upgrade its recognition of Tibet's legal status should
relations with the Nationalist government change.[45]

Throughout this whole summer the British had maintained a sniffy
reserve about its American cousins' muscular diplomacy. They considered it a cynical effort to use the Dalai Lama's departure from Tibet as a
propaganda stunt. The Indians were also demonstrably irked at being
informed belatedly by the U.S. about moves that they obviously already
knew about. They were not about to make an unsolicited offer of asylum to the Dalai Lama.[46] After strong representations from the embassy,
the Indian foreign ministry intimated that its willingness to grant him
asylum had been communicated to the Dalai Lama by the Indian trade
agent at Yatung, though the agent admittedly did not have direct access
to him. Whether it was due to botched communications or a genuine
reluctance to take a potentially embarrassing diplomatic initiative, the
Tibetans today, including the Dalai Lama, still resent what they feel was
a failure by the Indian government to provide any formal assurance of
asylum at that time.

The Dalai Lama therefore returned to his capital disappointed. He
could take some comfort from the repeated U.S. assurances that it rec-

ognized Tibet's special status, but the commitments were not in writing. The strongest written statement had entertained the further possibility that "should developments warrant, consideration could be given to recognition of Tibet as an independent state,"[47] but that statement had never been given to him. It was contained in the memorandum that the State Department had given privately to the British and the Canadians earlier that year when the situation in China was more uncertain. The "developments" that might have triggered recognition of Tibet's independence were probably the disappearance of the exiled Chinese Nationalist government and continued civil unrest on the mainland. These events never took place, so the U.S. government never had the opportunity to consider this ultimate card.

CHAPTER 6

Occupied Tibet

THE DALAI LAMA
RETURNS TO LHASA

On August 17, 1951, the Dalai Lama and
his cabinet returned to Lhasa in a caravan of
nine hundred mules. His leisurely return
journey to the capital from his retreat in
Yatung took about a month, slowed by the
acclaim expressed to him by his relieved subjects. With their spiritual and temporal ruler
back in his capital, they could hope that life
would go on as before—as long as they could
ignore the ugly fact of the Chinese presence.
One of the Dalai Lama's final acts before
reentering the capital he had left eight
months before was to escort his old tutor,
Taktra, to his monastery outside of Lhasa.

Taktra had come to Yatung to offer advice to his former pupil, and the Dalai Lama's public act of courtesy toward the man who as regent had been the center of controversy four years earlier should have helped to consolidate the government in a time of trouble. But it was to take more than this gracious gesture to unify a ruling elite that remained dedicated to a governing system ill-equipped to meet the divisive tactics of an overwhelming foreign rule.

The chief of the Chinese occupation administration, General Zhang Jingwu, had made his presence known by establishing his military and civil occupation headquarters in Lhasa on the eve of the Dalai Lama's return in mid-August. One month later the first contingent of People's Liberation Army troops arrived in the capital. Late in October the Dalai Lama formally accepted the agreement signed by his hapless representatives in Beijing six months before. The Tibetan leadership began a period of uneasy accommodation with their new overlords.

By December of 1951 the Indian mission in Lhasa reported that the growing size of the Chinese forces had alarmed even "the usually quiescent Tibetan Kutras,"[1] the official families of Tibet, who feared that the Tibetans would become a minority in their own country. When these old aristocrats expressed their concerns, they were not reassured with the bland reply of their occupiers that, although Beijing had originally planned to introduce "only" 50,000 Chinese troops into Tibet, the shortage of supplies was forcing them to make substantial alterations. Citing security, the Chinese refused to disclose the present strength of their forces, but they warned that a number of border posts still had to be manned.

But while the Chinese forces had already imposed a punishing load on Tibet's limited resources (affecting most harshly poorer Tibetans) the Kutra aristocrats were prospering. The occupiers arrived with an ample supply of silver dollars—Phuntso Tashi years later described it as a "rain" of coins[2]—which the obviously British-trained Indian political officer said they "squandered with the liberality of princes and the sleek abandon of rakes." Among the limited real estate belonging either to the government or to absentee leading families, at least thirteen houses had been leased or obtained as gifts by the Chinese. The old families were the principal beneficiaries: the Sadutsang house fetched 170,000 rupees and the Trimon house 100,000 rupees. The Chinese also obtained an outbuilding of the Tsarong compound, Dzasa Sampho's house, and Dzasa Yuthok's, formerly the Chinese Nationalist mission. At a time when the average annual income of an Indian civil servant was about 1,200 rupees,[3] these would have seemed very handsome prices indeed to the Indian diplomat reporting the sales.

Similarly, on four successive days in mid-November, the Chinese military commandant, Zhang Gwohua, entertained the principal officers of the government, the abbots of the two leading monasteries, the tutors of the Dalai Lama, "incarnate lamas of fame and ill-fame and Tibetan ladies." Not surprisingly, the Indian reporting officer found Zhang boorish but noted that "this mode of making friends of erstwhile enemies, of introducing strangers over a cup of wine, has much indeed to commend itself, but what is more it testifies to the consummate political skill of the Chinese Communists whom the ill-informed prefer to under-estimate." The Dalai Lama also contributed to the festivities himself. On November 19 he threw a party for all the Chinese officials in Lhasa. A few days later the indefatigable Zhang held another party, a reunion of all the Tibetan officials who were at Chamdo when the Chinese captured the town the previous year. While this anniversary celebration might have appeared to be in questionable taste, it was apparently accepted by the attending guests as either the price of defeat or another token of their occupiers' benevolence.

The attitude shown by Lhasa's prime aristocrat, Dasang Dadul Tsarong, gave further evidence of the success of the Chinese velvet glove approach, the willingness of the old guard to delude themselves that they could continue living in their old ways, the remarkable ability of the gentry to accommodate to overpowering Chinese authority, or all three. Tsarong had been commander-in-chief of the Tibetan army under the thirteenth Dalai Lama, who had replaced him at the demand of the Lhasa establishment, which feared his reformist efforts in the army and the government. Tsarong had retired to a prosperous life of trade, managing his estates and enjoying his reputation as Lhasa's most cosmopolitan figure. Because of his considerable influence in Lhasa, he was a member of the national assembly. It had been called into session to debate whether the Dalai Lama should accept the Chinese offer to become chairman of the Administrative and Military Committee through which the Chinese were governing Tibet. The Indian officer in charge of the mission S. Sinha, who had replaced his British predecessor Hugh Richardson, reported that Tsarong, "the wily old fox, known for years as the most pro-British of Tibetan officials, took the lead in advocating that the Dalai Lama should accept the post and bow to the wishes of Beijing."4 He noted that this demonstration of loyalty to China earned Tsarong overnight the reputation of being the most pro-Chinese official in Lhasa, but "Tsarong is a shrewd judge of the political climate and he knows his views, however unpopular, will not bring him retribution but acclaim from the Chinese." He had already taken the precaution of entertaining them at dinner and dance parties.

The Chinese also made some efforts to ingratiate themselves with ordinary people by opening a dispensary offering free medical treatment, a bank, and a hospital. They provided free cinema shows, first for the Tibetan troops and the Lhasa police and then for the public. These entertainments were also taken to the nearby villages, where they were welcomed by the villagers but not by the local monks, who disapproved of such vulgar amusements. It soon became apparent that there was another side to the Chinese occupation beyond bread and circuses. Sinha noted that despite their generosity, "the Chinese leave the impression that they have entered Tibet like swarms of colonists to make this their permanent home . . . [like] land-hungry peasants in the thin disguise of liberation uniforms. . . ."5 Such observations were prompted by the greed of the occupation troops, who had appropriated all of the fallow and grazing land in and near Lhasa and turned it over to the army for cultivation. The Indian official trenchantly commented that if Tibet's own landed aristocrats had allowed their peasants to cultivate the fallow land, they would have gladly done so. Why, he asked, had the land gone to "alien soldiers from afar and not [been] let to the Tibetan peasants?"

The heavy burdens of feeding a large number of Chinese occupation troops brought rising prices and a shortage of essential goods that squeezed ordinary Tibetans, primarily in Lhasa and the surrounding villages. Their always marginal economic situation rapidly become insupportable, and misery was exacerbated by influenza and smallpox epidemics, which resulted in large numbers of deaths among an already weakened populace. The seeds of popular dissatisfaction were thus being sown.

Disgruntled victims of the occupation organized a series of local protest rallies called *mimang tshongdu* (people's assemblies),[6] which produced a petition asking the Kashag, the Tibetan cabinet, to help them. According to Lhamo Tsering, who was later to become one of the principal figures in the Tibetan resistance movement, the petitioners belonged to an organization called the Chudruk Lhasa Mimang Tshopa (Water Dragon Lhasa People's Association), which had been founded by a monk from Sera monastery named Dhamchoe Sonam. The petition was delivered to the Kashag on March 5, 1952, and its demands were as much political as economic. First and foremost, they asked the Chinese not to assume the powers of the Dalai Lama and not to confiscate Tibet's monasteries. And while they accepted that the Chinese might need some civil officers and military forces in Tibet, they asked that those in excess of their needs be returned to China.

The activities of Dhamchoe's group were supplemented by four Tibetans who drafted anonymous letters of grievance. The best known of the drafters was a ne'er-do-well businessman named Alo Chondze,[7] who, along with another lay person named Besur and two monks, assumed leadership in the Mimang (People's) movement. Posters and slogans saying The Chinese Are Very Bad, Chinese Go Home, Long Live the Dalai Lama, and The Dalai Lama Is Tibet's Legitimate Leader, popped up and were shouted in public places.[8]

The Chinese denounced these challenges to their authority as the work of reactionaries encouraged by foreign countries and demanded that the Tibetan government arrest the leaders and disband the organization. In a visible show of force, the Chinese began entrenching their troops and placing machine guns behind sandbags around the buildings they occupied. The shops closed in the Barkhor, the market street in front of Lhasa's principal temple, and the situation became tense. Despite denials by the Tibetan government of official or foreign instigation, the Chinese remained adamant, and the Mimang Tshopa leader

Dhamchoe and his colleague Lobsang Dawa were arrested and ordered to disband their organization. These actions to stifle popular dissent were part of the Chinese agenda for imposing political control that soon smothered the Tibetan government.

Chinese policy in Tibet paralleled Communist policy to consolidate power in China.⁹ It was one of balance, and at times contradictions, reassuring key local groups while establishing firm organizational control. The Chinese were particularly adept at trapping Tibetan officials into carrying out the policies of their occupiers. Under the 1951 Beijing agreement with Tibet, the Chinese administrative committee responsible for the occupation was to be a purely Chinese affair. By early 1952 it had been transformed into a joint Chinese-Tibetan advisory body with power to recommend reforms and legislation. Neither the unwilling Tibetan appointees nor the government were in a position to reject the committee's advice but were forced to participate in formulating policies aimed at transforming their country into a Chinese province.

The Chinese further demanded that the Tibetan government empower two senior officials with full authority to deal with them on all matters affecting the administration of the country. The government made the obvious choices of Ngabo and Defense Minister Ragashar, who had the reputation of being independent-minded and unsympathetic to collaboration. Both men tried to wriggle out but were eventually forced to accept. The following month the Chinese governor, Zhang Jingwu, officially opened the headquarters of the military region and announced the appointment of General Zhang Gwohua as commander-in-chief. Ragashar and Ngabo were named vice-commanders. This headquarters was one of the two agencies established to ensure the implementation of the Seventeen Point Agreement. Two prominent Tibetans had been co-opted against their will to lend authority to the occupation, now reinforced by additional Chinese troops in Lhasa. The Indian mission reported that there was a growing realization among the intelligent people in Lhasa, including even Ngabo Ngawang Jigme who had negotiated the occupation agreement, "that it will not be long before the Chinese sound the death knell of the old order through revolutionary reforms."¹⁰

Thus, by early spring the Chinese had nearly completed the process of eliminating and demoralizing the few independent Tibetan government officials upon whom the Dalai Lama could depend. On April 1, 1952, a scuffle took place near Ngabo's compound. The Chinese claimed that Tibetan rebels, part of a secret organization led and inspired by "imperialist agents," had raided Ngabo's house as part of a plot against them and certain Tibetan officials. These "rebels," said the Chinese, had been overpowered by Chinese guards. The Tibetan version, not surprisingly, was quite different. A Chinese soldier from Ngabo's house had for some time been sneaking into the adjoining compound, which was occupied by three Tibetan soldiers, to steal radishes. When the vegetable thief made his regular nightly incursion, the Tibetans were waiting and rushed into the garden, partly dressed, firing at random in the darkness. This brought the Chinese guards from Ngabo's house to the aid of their comrade, who had vanished in the dark. In the melee the supposed rebels, who were actually members of the regular Tibetan army, were captured and brought before Ngabo, who turned them over to the Chinese.[11]

The full significance of this petty dispute became apparent only afterwards. The Dalai Lama's two plucky prime ministers protested to the Chinese occupation commanders, Generals Zhang Jingwu and Zhang Gwohua, about the growing violations of the Seventeen Point Agreement. This was a particularly sensitive subject as the twin proconsuls had themselves been involved in negotiating the agreement, and the two Tibetan politicians were called in for a two-hour harangue.[12] The two Zhangs warned the courageous, but powerless and hapless, ministers that if they failed to bring the rebels to account and halt growing dissidence, the peaceful methods being used to "liberate" Tibet would be replaced by force. The Chinese list of those suspected in the supposed outrage included the two prime ministers themselves, Nepalese traders, members of the Dalai Lama's family, the Indian mission, Surkhang Shape (an adviser who had urged the Dalai Lama not to return to Lhasa), hostile monks, and the stock "imperialist agents."

The first 3,000 additional troops the Chinese governor had called in to tighten up security began arriving in Lhasa ten days after the incident in the radish garden. The next installment disclosed the real objective of the Chinese political drama. The two troublesome prime ministers were hauled by General Zhang Gwohua before the Kashag and accused of numerous crimes. These included such treasonable views as believing in the independence of Tibet, opposing the Chinese, and aiding village rebels with whom they maintained secret relations. If all this had happened in China, Zhang added menacingly, the penalty would have been death. While these charges made the two men popular heroes, the Tibetan political establishment was duly intimidated and scurried to negotiate on behalf of the accused prime ministers. They came back with the alarming news that the Chinese were prepared to back their demands by summoning an additional 5,000 troops to Lhasa. This ultimatum was accompanied by a warning to the Dalai Lama that he was being held personally responsible for the conduct of his prime ministers, and that any delay in their dismissal would open him to similar charges.[13] After a stormy session with one of Zhang's subordinates, General Fan Ming, plus pressure from the intimidated Kashag, the Dalai Lama yielded and tearfully dismissed his bold defenders.

The Indian mission officer reported that "with one adroit stroke the Chinese have eliminated all official opposition to them in Tibet." The crude use of political muscle, he wrote, had left the Tibetan government thoroughly cowed, resembling "an army which has lost all its generals after a series of tactical defeats on the field, they are leaderless, without morale and rapidly disintegrating." Several of the more responsible key officials had either been forced to resign or had asked for leaves of absence. Most of those left were understandably reluctant to assume responsibility for attempting to govern under the Chinese fist. The Kashag was powerless, and the foreign bureau practically out of business. While some of the old guard accepted the price of accommodation, it was in these months that the Tibetans lost irrevocably any hope or claim to self-government. In his monthly report for June 1952, the Indian mission officer wrote that the "situation here sadly reminds one of the last days of the Kuomintang."[14]

Gyalo Thondup's Return to Lhasa

It was in the midst of this period of popular dissension and governmental upheaval that Gyalo Thondup returned to the capital he had left seven years earlier as a venturesome teenager. He came back as a man with a mission and a plan.

His sense of mission had crystallized during the six months that he had spent in the U.S. after his involuntary stay on Taiwan. He was determined not to repeat the history of his Chinese Nationalist hosts, who had failed to rally the support of their citizens and consequently lost their country. He had traveled throughout the U.S. and become impressed with the benefits of a modern free society then bursting with determination and optimism. These travels had made him even more angry at the rule that the Chinese were imposing on Tibet and increased his sense of urgency about getting back to Lhasa before the Chinese occupation was firmly established.[15] He was convinced that Tibet's traditional rejection of foreign ideas and rulers and its universal devotion to a religion that crossed all social lines would unite all Tibetans, in opposition to the Chinese. He was also counting on the harsh terrain and climate of Tibet to prevent or at least delay the Chinese in bringing their full force to bear. Thondup hoped to provide the political leadership to unite young Tibetans motivated by devotion to their country and their religion, while prodding their leaders into carrying out the reforms that would block the Chinese from consolidating their occupation and exterminating Tibet as a nation and a culture.

Like Sun Yat-sen, the spiritual father of the political philosophy he had absorbed in his studies during the last days of the Chinese Nationalist government in Nanking, Gyalo had a three-objective program.[16] The goal was to develop a unified country capable of meeting the challenges of the modern world. His program called for reform of Tibet's political, economic, and educational systems. This would mean an end to the clerical and lay autocracy, restructuring the unequal system of land tenure, and broadening the curricula of the monastic school system as well as the almost nonexistent secular schools.[17]

This reform package was sure to antagonize both the entrenched interests in Lhasa and Tibet's new Chinese overlords. The occupiers had their own program and wanted no hometown populist to compete with them. Gyalo's determined personality and leadership style did not make his job easier. Like Sun Yat-sen, democracy to him was a means and not an end in itself. Furthermore, he had acquired his political education under the autocratic Chiang K'ai-shek. Holding town meetings or even consultations with important politicians, whether monastic officials or established laymen, was not Gyalo's style. He had neither the time nor the temperament to build a constituency. He also had no patience with those who could not or would not see how their own interests would be served by his reforms. He would fight alone for what he believed his brother's government must do if Tibet was to survive.

With this sense of urgent duty Gyalo set off for Lhasa in early February 1952 accompanied by this mother, elder sister, younger brother, and the faithful Lhamo Tsering, who was to be his lifetime companion and adjutant in the struggle. They left from Kalimpong and plowed through the bitter winter cold. Soon after his arrival Gyalo had a long reunion with his younger brother, now holding full powers as ruler of Tibet. He gave the Dalai Lama details of a reform program designed to preempt the Chinese from imposing their own revolutionary system on Tibet.

- After an inventory of the lands held by the three main monasteries and officials of the Tibetan government, land titles would be confirmed but holdings would be limited.

- Salaries for government officials would be realigned according to their rank and responsibility.

- Debts to monasteries and government officials would be validated, but excessive and long-standing obligations that had forced poorer Tibetans into debt bondage would be forgiven.

- A new tax system would abolish outdated and excessive rates.

- The Dalai Lama's family would voluntarily surrender its properties outside of Lhasa, retaining only one property inside Lhasa and turning over the huge family residence to the government for a school.

The Dalai Lama and most of his family approved Gyalo's proposals. His mother and brother Lobsang Samten accepted them as both a necessary and wise price to preempt the Chinese from imposing their harsh regimen on the rest of Tibet. But as Gyalo went about visiting the family's property near Lhasa and putting his ideas into effect, the old guard—with the exception of the two prime ministers, who were soon to lose their jobs—was appalled at the radical proposals that this young iconoclast was promoting and actually carrying out. Gyalo later recalled that the government-appointed trustees of the family's holdings, Thongbo Shape and his lay counterpart Sharsur Kalon, regarded him as a lunatic for depriving his own children of their inheritance, which had been built up by Gyalo's materialistic and status-seeking father. The old guard with some reason felt threatened by the loss of its traditional prerequisites. Here was a man in his twenties who had returned from abroad with foreign ideas, asking them to give up the only way of life they and their forebears had known for generations. The nobles spread the word that Gyalo Thondup was "more Red than the Chinese." He gained few followers.

The Chinese proconsuls Zhang Jingwu and Zhang Gwohua regarded the return of this radical Tibetan nobleman with ambivalence. Gyalo decided to take the measure of the Chinese proconsuls and called on Zhang Gwohua. The military commander welcomed him home and noted that since he had studied in China, he should work to use his knowledge to establish a new Tibet under his brother's rule. But then he proceeded to deliver an ominous tirade warning Gyalo that the People's Liberation Army, having stabilized the southwest frontier of China, now was ready to get rid of Tibet's retrograde system. The bombastic general seemed to be the one designated to browbeat the Tibetan establishment. He said the Chinese army could remove the last elements of foreign imperialism from Tibet, and as a former military man who had fought the Kuomintang he knew just where they were. He then pointedly remarked on the absence of Gyalo's wife, dismissing his excuse that she had remained in India because she was pregnant, offering to provide doctors to meet her at the border and escort her to Lhasa.[18]

Nevertheless, when the two Chinese generals heard that Gyalo had turned over the family residence in Lhasa for public use, burned old debt contracts, and distributed land on the family estates south of Lhasa, they began to entertain hopes of using this well-connected radical in their own cause. They offered him and the Dalai Lama support against the nobility and the traditional government. While he regarded the nobility as an outdated institution, Gyalo was not prepared to sell out his countrymen or allow himself to be used by the Chinese. Still, he feared that if he continued to refuse collaboration he would jeopardize the position of the Dalai Lama. Gyalo discussed this dilemma with his mother, whose astute political sense he valued.[19] Mother and son agreed he should flee to enlist foreign support that might temper Chinese expansionism or at least inform the world of its consequences in Tibet.

Meanwhile the Chinese governors, eager to use Gyalo to further their political objectives, were nervous about being able to control him. Zhang Jingwu, the senior Chinese officer responsible for enforcing the occupation, was particularly angry about his support for the more openly obstreperous Prime Minister Lukhangwa and denounced Gyalo as "mentally disturbed." Zhang recognized that whatever made Gyalo a valuable tool—his modern education, political skill, and his close family and personal ties to the Dalai Lama—made him an equally dangerous threat in Lhasa. Zhang Jingwu therefore seized on the Communist-sponsored International Youth Congress in Vienna in June 1952 to get Gyalo out of his hair. His plan was to send Gyalo to Vienna and then have him stay in Beijing, where he could be reeducated in Maoist ideology. A Chinese representative was sent to inform Gyalo of Mao's generous plan to include Mongol, Uighur, and Tibetan people on the Chinese delegation to Vienna as a way of demonstrating China's benevolent policy toward minorities. Gyalo saw Zhang's game, and replied by saying that because he had been away from Tibet for so long he had not been able to visit all of the family properties. He first wanted to effect the land reforms he had been carrying out near Lhasa, and then he would be available to join the delegation to Vienna.

By this time Gyalo was reconciled to the fact that he would fail.[20] As he rationalized to Lhamo Tsering, the Tibetans, particularly the Lhasans, unlike the people of India, Korea, and Indochina, had not been under prolonged periods of foreign occupation. Former conquerors had exercised their control indirectly or transiently. The Tibetan officials therefore had no experience in fighting for freedom. Centuries ago, Tibet had opted for the peaceful pursuit of its religion as the prime objective of its society, leaving its government inexperienced and therefore unprepared to find political solutions at times of crisis. The authorities could only turn to Buddhist *dharma* (teachings) and the Buddhist *sangha* (community), consulting the oracles and the lamas to find a peaceful way out. Furthermore, because of his own long absence from Tibet, he had no political allies or a constituency of his own. There was little understanding of his reforms, which were radical for Tibet and would mean personal losses for the rich and powerful. Some of the Dalai Lama's courtiers also feared his brother would usurp their positions. While some knowledgeable officials understood the need to resist the Chinese, and among ordinary people resentment of the Chinese was rising, effective resistance required arms, money, and educated leadership. These were to be found only in foreign countries, where Tibet's relationships were woefully inadequate.

Gyalo left Lhasa on May 28, 1952, with Lhamo Tsering, ostensibly to visit two family properties at Chayul and Jora in southern Tibet. He told his mother and brother Lobsang of his plans to slip across the Indian border to seek help against the Chinese. He did not inform the Dalai Lama, then only seventeen, so that the young ruler, governing under the heavy scrutiny of Chinese "advisers," would not have to conceal this knowledge from them. The two estates that were the pretext for Gyalo's trip had been granted to his family by Tsarong, the canny old courtier now seeking to preserve his position with the new Chinese rulers. After visiting the estates and implementing his reforms there, Gyalo and Lhamo Tsering secretly crossed the border into Assam, using an escape route that his brother was to take seven years later.

THE U.S. SITS BACK

Despite the Dalai Lama's return to Lhasa and his acceptance of the agreement with China, the U.S. embassy in New Delhi, by that time under

Ambassador Chester Bowles, continued to have "no doubts" that he remained willing to leave Tibet and still opposed the agreement.[21] Their interpretation was that the Dalai Lama and his government were no longer free agents and were gradually succumbing to the pressure created by the Chinese presence. Although Bowles rejected as "practically impossible and politically undesirable" a proposal made by an unidentified Tibetan that the U.S. provide "planes, arms and leadership," he was no less persistent than his predecessor in urging that the U.S. "make at least one final effort by letter or oral messages to encourage the Dalai Lama to resist in ways best known to the Tibetan Government."

Bowles's preferred channel was Takster, by then in regular contact with the State Department. Bowles proposed that the former abbot send his brother a letter reaffirming previous U.S. statements of commitment and include practical suggestions based on his knowledge of the situation in Lhasa.[22] A former advertising magnate, Bowles proposed that the Department send the young ruler small gifts such as the newest photographic equipment and film, which "although small would represent tangible evidence to him of U.S. friendship and would have an effect far out of proportion to their monetary value."

Takster wrote a letter reaffirming the U.S. offer of "full aid and assistance to you when you come out" of Tibet and help in escaping although not to the point of sending a plane to Lhasa. Takster recalled that John M. Allison, who had succeeded Dean Rusk as assistant secretary of state for Far Eastern Affairs, was just as eager as his predecessor to get the Dalai Lama out of Tibet.[23] He said Allison and the CIA seriously considered intercepting the Dalai Lama along his route if he made it out of his capital and flying him to safety. They had asked Takster to determine whether the ice was thick enough for a plane to land on either Lake Yamdroktso, fifty miles south of Lhasa, or Lake Namtso, one hundred miles north. They also planned for him to bring thirty people with him and promised to support a considerably larger retinue in exile in India, Ceylon, or Thailand.

The Dalai Lama replied to these enticements in a letter delivered by Takster to the Department in early 1952.[24] The still hopeful young man said that since the Chinese had not indicated that they planned sudden changes in Tibet or any injury to the Tibetans, it seemed best to treat them in the same correct and careful fashion. He asked his "official friends" in America not to be vexed by his decision, since his policy of defending the integrity of Tibet would not change. The letter instructed Takster to maintain contact with the Americans and not allow misunderstanding to cloud the relationship between the U.S. and Tibet.

In presenting this letter, Takster assured Allison that the Dalai Lama and the Tibetan people were clinging to the hope that "something" could be done after a temporary period of adjustment to the Chinese. Allison reassured Takster that his predecessor Dean Rusk's policy remained in force, but the U.S. understood the Dalai Lama's difficult position against superior Chinese force. He expressed the hope that the fall of Tibet to the Communists "would resemble the tactics of Japanese judo experts who fall in order to rise and gain the final victory." But at Takster's request, Allison agreed not to inflame the situation by official public statements.

Three months later the U.S. intelligence community concluded that there were between 10,000 and 15,000 Chinese troops in Tibet, 5,000 of them in Lhasa. The Washington strategists postulated that, by concentrating these troops in Tibet's few major cities, the Chinese had produced acute food shortages and a consequent growing rebellion. They professed to see a cleverly conceived plan of resistance developing. Takster had delivered a report that people around the Dalai Lama were quietly organizing resistance to the Chinese while appearing to cooperate with them. He spoke of secret new oaths of allegiance to the Dalai Lama, and of the Panchen Lama's supposed intention to make common cause with the Dalai Lama while appearing to serve the Chinese. In retrospect, Takster's sources seem to have been reporting hopes rather than facts, but in the absence of conflicting intelligence the Department regarded Takster's report as "probably true" and saw events going in the right direction without the need to help.[25] It recommended that the U.S. government accept Takster's advice to avoid making public statements about Tibet, which might have adverse effects in India and mislead the incipient Tibetan resistance movement. It should also "refrain from any attempts to communicate with persons in Tibet who are believed to be taking their first steps toward organizing an anti-Communist resistance movement." The U.S. would let things develop naturally.

For the time being, the Dalai Lama was not looking abroad for salva-tion.²⁶ He was trying to make the best of the difficult situation to which he had reluctantly, but voluntarily, returned. After he had acquiesced to the Chinese demand for the dismissal of his two prime ministers in the spring of 1952, he enjoyed an uneasy truce with his overlords. He was able to inaugurate a few of Gyalo's reforms and instructed the Kashag to develop a program of public education to supplement the traditional monastery system. He also abolished the principle of inheritable debts and wrote off all government loans that could not be repaid, thereby lifting heavy burdens off the peasant community.

All this was done with little fanfare. Aware that the reforms would not be popular with the nobility and other vested interests, the Dalai Lama had his requisite decrees imprinted by wooden blocks similar to those used for printing scriptures rather than in the usual way of putting up posters in public places. He hoped this added authority would fore-stall any interference and ensure wider dissemination.²⁷ In his own way, the perceptive pontiff was quietly trying to find ways to institute the more enlightened rule that he knew was long past due, working as best he could within the confines his government had accepted.

Gyalo Forms an Underground

When Gyalo arrived in India he immediately made his way to Dar-jeeling, where he found that his wife had gone to Calcutta to have their second child, a son, Khedroob.²⁸ Gyalo followed her and was subse-quently hospitalized for some weeks with malaria. After he recovered, he turned abroad for help, and on November 15 sent telegrams to Chiang K'ai-shek and to Secretary of State Acheson, by then a lame duck as a result of Dwight Eisenhower's election to the presidency ten days earlier. He asked Chiang and Acheson to support the Tibetans in their efforts to resist China's efforts to absorb their country.²⁹

Gyalo's telegram to Acheson seems to be an amplification of the oral message the Dalai Lama had sent earlier responding to the last-minute appeals sent after his return to Lhasa.³⁰ In it, Gyalo expressed his brother's appreciation for the offers of U.S. assistance as well as his regret that "mistakes had been made," so that the difficult action of denouncing the agreement with Beijing and seeking asylum abroad had not been taken. The continuing proposals from the U.S. that the Dalai Lama come abroad had been thoroughly discussed, but they had concluded it would be too dangerous. If word leaked out, it could mean the irreplaceable loss of the Dalai Lama. This was not a risk the Tibetans were prepared to take. Gyalo then went on to describe the Chinese tactics of subverting the role of the Dalai Lama—military force, forced appointments, bribes, efforts to sow disunity. He explained that the Dalai Lama planned to counter the Chinese by establishing a firm relationship with his people through the measures he was quietly taking to improve their welfare as the first step toward united resistance.

Gyalo ended by outlining a plan for establishing a secret resistance organization inside Tibet, starting with training of Tibetans outside the country who would be sent back to lead and expand local resistance. He proposed that the U.S. government establish a special office for Tibet that would assess events in the country and the potential for resistance. He explained that this was only a sketch of his ideas, which he would outline in detail if Washington was interested. At that time he was not proposing armed resistance, and subsequent American contacts with him for the next few years were limited to debriefings on what his intelligence contacts inside Tibet were providing.

Gyalo's presence and activities soon came to the attention of the Chinese as well as the Indians. Zhang Jingwu, whom Beijing held responsible for ensuring a successful occupation of Lhasa, was still smarting over Gyalo's defection, and he sent several threatening messages by various couriers to induce him to return. The first was delivered by that seasoned courtier, the trader Pandatsang, who like most of the Lhasa old guard had come to an accommodation with the Chinese occupiers. On official instructions he had set up a Tibetan wool market in Kalimpong that summer. Pandatsang told Gyalo that he must return to Lhasa, where Zhang had promised that his "mistakes" would be forgiven. Gyalo refused. The next month a Chinese officer arrived with an official Tibetan delegation en route to Beijing. He said Gyalo could either return to Lhasa, go on with the delegation to Beijing, or remain in India but stay out of politics. The Tibetan government, nervous that they would suffer for his defection, also sent emissaries to press the same alternatives. Gyalo had no problem rejecting them, too.

His Indian hosts were also nervous about Gyalo's residence and activities in the Darjeeling/Kalimpong area, just across the Natu La pass from Tibet. B. K. Kapul, the regional Indian political officer, demanded copies of his cables to Acheson and Chiang and warned him against further political activities as violations of his agreement with Sinha, the Indian mission chief in Lhasa. Gyalo denied he had made any such agreement.[31] He told Kapul to remind Nehru of the promises that he had made through Sinha prior to his departure from Lhasa that he would be free to engage in political activities if he came to India.

Gyalo eventually worked out an accommodation with the Indian officials. Soon after his confrontation with Kapul, the Indian officer told him to expect an "important high level official" coming from New Delhi specially to meet with him. The official arrived in Darjeeling in April of 1953 and turned out to be no less than the director of the Indian Central Intelligence Bureau, B. N. Mullik. Mullik told Gyalo that he was free to carry out political activities from Darjeeling as long as he kept Mullik's own organization informed on what was happening in Tibet.[32] This was the beginning of Gyalo's long association with Mullik, whom he found to be fully aware of the Beijing's aggressive policies.

Later, the intelligence chief would quote Nehru as saying that for a thousand years China had never been able to subdue Tibet, though the Tibetans had often succumbed to Chinese military pressure. Nehru doubted the Chinese would succeed this time, and he was therefore "very keen that the morale of the Tibetans was kept up." Mullik recalled that Nehru instructed him to keep in touch with Gyalo and "all the other Tibetan refugees and help them in every way possible." The prime minister's final comment was that "such contacts would also indirectly help us to prevent any machinations by them from Indian soil against the Chinese."[33] Thus there were limits to his interest in supporting the Tibetans, and Gyalo's hand was not as free as he thought. Both Mullik and his prime minister wanted the Tibetans to challenge the Chinese, but to do it across the border in their own country and not launch crusades from India that might embarrass Nehru in Beijing.

Gyalo understood the sensitive ground rules under which he was going to have to operate in India. He quietly took up residence with his family and began a low-key effort to unite the Tibetan people in the border area that extended under the lee of the Himalayas from Darjeeling into Sikkim and Bhutan. His initial idea was to form an umbrella organization composed of Tibetans who were prepared to put aside the political and regional differences that divided Tibet, publicize the effects of China's occupation, and focus India's attention on the threat posed by a large Chinese army of occupation next door. Gyalo persuaded the former finance official, Shakabpa, to remain in India and join him. (Shakabpa, then in Kalimpong, was understandably apprehensive about returning to Lhasa because of his role in the negotiations with the U.S. the previous year and in the appeal to the UN.) Gyalo also enlisted another member of the old boys' club, Yuthok Shape, who had found life in Lhasa unbearable under the Chinese. He tried unsuccessfully to enlist the radical member of the Pandatsang family, Rapga, but he had his own political agenda. Rapga's more establishment-inclined brother Yangpel also preferred to pursue his own commercial and special political interests rather than join Gyalo's challenges to the old order.

Gyalo, Shakabpa, and Khenchung Lobsang Gyaltsen,[34] a monk who was the Tibetan trade representative in Kalimpong, were the ringleaders. They were popularly known as the Jyin Khen Tsi Sum (the Brother, Khenchung, and Tsipon Shakabpa threesome). Kukula, sister of the crown prince of Sikkim, joined the group, as did a lama from the Kham area named Thonden Rimpoche. Gyalo was able to communicate with members of the Tibetan government through another monastic official, Thubten Sangpo, who was then living in Kalimpong. Sangpo had retained the secret code book[35] he had used to communicate with the Kashag some years before when he was the Tibetan representative to the Chinese Nationalist government in Nanking. Later Phala, the chief of the Dalai Lama's personal staff, sent two monastic officials from Lhasa, Thubten Ninje and Chamba Wangdu. Gyalo put them to work writing pamphlets, which were mimeographed by his younger sister Pema in one of the back rooms at his house on Gandhi Road in Darjeeling.

In 1953, this informal organization began holding small meetings of twenty or thirty to discuss events in Tibet and to organize delegations to lobby Indian officials and members of Parliament in New Delhi. On Tibetan national days, particularly New Year's and the Dalai Lama's birthday, they held rallies and picnics, attracting up to 2,000 people. Gyalo also enlisted the services of an Indian Christian of Tibetan ancestry named Tharchin Babu, who since 1925 had been publishing a Tibetan language magazine, *The Tibetan Mirror,* focused mainly on culture and appearing on an irregular monthly schedule. Gyalo persuaded Tharchin to convert it into a weekly and carry current news. Traders then took the publication into Tibet to let their fellow countrymen know that the rest of the world knew of their plight. When a 1954 flood devastated Gyantse, Tibet's fourth largest city, the Chinese embargoed the news. Gyalo's group organized a Tibetan Welfare Association in Kalimpong to raise money for flour, petition for outside help, and arrange for an article in the *Statesman,* one of India's leading newspapers. The Indian government responded by airdropping medicine in Gyantse and sending the Indian regional officer, Kapul, to Gyantse with 50,000 rupees. The association raised a matching sum to provide flour to the flood victims, a small but effective way of letting the people of Tibet know that the outside world knew and cared about their problems.

The cost of all this was not great, which was fortunate since Gyalo could not contribute funds. Kapul, however, suggested that he take advantage of his position as a member of Tibet's first family to obtain an export permit to send goods into Tibet. Gyalo quickly organized a thriving trade exporting whiskey and tea to the thirsty Chinese occupation troops, the profits of which provided him an income and covered the expenses of his embryonic underground activities inside Tibet. The muleteers also carried pamphlets to sympathizers, urging them to resist the Chinese occupation. They returned with intelligence and provided a covert courier service for other sources on the situation in the capital and central Tibet. Gyalo thus created the essential "ratline" for the flow of propaganda in and intelligence out of Tibet. It was a nice irony that the Chinese army provided partial financing for these operations and was cheated in the bargain. Gyalo ruefully recalls that the muleteers, who shared the Chinese army officers' taste for White Horse whiskey, found a way to tamper with the bottles so they could drink part of the contents. They then topped them up with their own urine and closed the cap. In due course their thirst led to such adulteration of the product that they killed the trade.

Through these openly unobjectionable activities[36] Gyalo had created the means to carry out the mission he left Tibet to accomplish and in a manner that would not force the Indians to take official notice. Lhamo Tsering said that following the flood relief campaign carried out by the Tibetan Welfare Association, Kapul, the initially cautious political officer, indicated to Gyalo that the Indian government would not only countenance, but would support such activities. Gyalo was able to continue his underground contacts and propaganda efforts in central Tibet while keeping his Indian hosts informed on developments there, until his brother was finally forced to flee Lhasa in 1959.

⊘

The government in Lhasa meanwhile was enjoying a period of uneasy calm with the Chinese. Mao's campaigns against "counter-revolutionaries," corrupt cadres, and the bourgeoisie had generally been limited to China proper. The new Chinese constitution adopted the Soviet institutional device of autonomous areas, with one exception. It omitted the nominal right of secession in the Soviet model. This meant the recruitment of minority cadres and traditional local leaders to cooperate in the administration imposed by the Chinese, and in the early years the Chinese cadres sent to local areas generally treated the Khampa and Amdowa people of eastern Tibet with restraint. This helped provide a facade of normality that discouraged active opposition while the Chinese built roads through the eastern border regions to facilitate their control over the rest of Tibet. The Chinese legitimized their occupation with Indian help. In September of 1952 the Indian government had conceded Tibet's foreign relations to China, downgrading its representative to a consul general with the trade agencies in Tibet under his supervision. New Delhi thereby abandoned the concessions inherited from the British, who almost half a century before had imposed their mission in Lhasa in defiance of China's claims to sole authority over Tibet.

The U.K. high commissioner in New Delhi later noted that the active measures the Indian government was taking to improve its strate-gic situation in the border regions belied Nehru's public attitude of "smug acquiescence" to events in Tibet.[37] Nevertheless the show of diplomatic accommodation continued. On April 29, 1954, the Sino-Indian Agreement formally confirmed the new situation in Tibet with India's agreement to withdraw the Indian military escort and training posts in southern Tibet, which at that time were down to three platoons. India also handed over to the Chinese the post and telegraph facilities and rest-houses established by their British predecessors in Tibet. Nehru and his officials had for some time deprecated the importance of these remnant facilities, which he called "symbols of British imperialism." He told his parliament that, although he did not approve of everything about China or what it had done in Tibet, the agreement was "good not only for our country but for the rest of Asia."[38] Hugh Richardson, the former mission chief in Lhasa, later wrote that India's acceptance of "The Tibet Region of China" in the treaty amounted "to countersigna-ture by India of the death warrant of Tibetan independence."

The Dalai Lama contributed to the appearance of an uneasy rap-prochement with the Chinese by accepting an invitation to visit Beijing. He left Lhasa with his family and the Panchen Lama in September of 1954 for what turned out to be a seven-month absence. The Chinese proconsul Zhang Jingwu insisted on accompanying his involuntary ward to the extent of literally linking arms with him so that the younger and more agile Dalai Lama had to drag the cumbersome and physically unfit general through the rugged country along the incomplete roads being built by the Chinese.

In Beijing, he was welcomed with full ceremonial honors by Zhou Enlai and Zhu De, and he had several talks with Mao, who initially impressed him with his assurances that the Seventeen Point Agreement would be implemented only at a pace acceptable to the Tibetans. The young ruler said that "every time I saw Mao, he inspired me again." On one occasion Mao surprised him by speaking favorably of the Lord Bud-dha, praising him for being "anti-caste, anti-corruption, and anti-exploitation."[39] Under this benign treatment the Dalai Lama relaxed and came to enjoy his stay in China. He even came to admire the egali-tarian aspects of Marxist theory, which he respects to this day.[40] He toured extensively and was introduced to grand visitors, including Nikita Khrushchev and Nikolai Bulganin at the fifth anniversary ceremonies for the founding of the People's Republic. He also met Nehru for the first time; the Indian prime minister uttered only a few perfunctory words, obviously uninterested in any discussion of his neighbor's fate or India's role in it. The British envoy was equally circumspect.[41]

By March, 1955, when it was time to leave, Mao delivered a parting message that gave the Dalai Lama a stronger taste of what he envisaged for Tibet. The Great Helmsman provided a tutorial session on how to organize meetings, draw out people's opinions, and make decisions on key issues, which the young ruler found excellent advice and on which he took notes. Mao's final comments, however, provided a chill warning that he fundamentally opposed what his guest stood for. While commending the Dalai Lama on his "good attitude," he declared: "religion is poison. Firstly, it reduces the population, because monks and nuns must stay celibate, and secondly it neglects material progress." The Dalai Lama wrote that when he heard that from Mao, he thought, "you are the destroyer of the Dharma [the Buddhist law of all things] after all."

On his way home he received full confirmation of this. Even while Mao was giving the Dalai Lama the full treatment with his hospitality and promises of better life for Tibet's people, the Chinese had begun a concerted effort to impose their full control and Communist practices on his people, particularly in the Kham and Amdo areas of the border provinces. Their efforts to confiscate weapons, the most highly prized possessions of the Khampas, produced open discontent and sabotage. They turned to taxation, confiscation of large private and monastic properties, and to public humiliations and executions, with the monasteries as particular targets for attack. This began to evoke strong local protests. Khampa and Amdo clan leaders briefed the Dalai Lama's chief of staff, Phala, on their plans to resist the Chinese by force when he passed through their region as part of the official party escorting the Dalai Lama back to Lhasa. The young man was returning to a country on the verge of active rebellion which presented him, as a Buddhist ruler, with moral dilemmas from then on.

CHAPTER 7

The Tibetan Revolt

THE DALAI LAMA returned from Beijing to a relatively peaceful scene in Lhasa. As he remarked in his autobiography, the Chinese, by not interfering with religion in the capital, were hoping that he would be lulled into a false sense of security while they pressed ahead with their program in the countryside, particularly in eastern Tibet. In April 1956 Mao sent a delegation headed by Marshal Chen Yi to inaugurate the Preparatory Committee for the Autonomous Region of Tibet. This fifty-one-man committee, composed primarily of Tibetans under the figurehead chairmanship of the Dalai Lama, was heavily stacked with pro-Chinese members.[1] The Dalai Lama was embarrassed by the pointless and empty discussions that preceded the passage of the committee's predetermined decisions, realizing that the Chinese had made him chairman to lend the appearance of Tibetan authority to their schemes.

Beijing's strategy in Lhasa was temporarily successful in preserving a facade of a peaceful accommodation between the Tibetan establishment and its new masters. Lhasa, after all, had seen conquerors come and go for centuries. It was a different story in the Tibetan regions on the other side of the Yangtze, where the Chinese were imposing their system into the daily lives of the Tibetan populace. Under the cover of the 1954 constitution, autonomous minority regions were to be transformed according to the Communist model at a gradual pace, adopting local forms, recruiting minority cadres, training Han cadres in local ways and cooperating with the "patriotic upper strata." In theory this strategy was designed to promote peaceful relations with the local populace and a smooth transition toward Communism. In practice, it produced a continuing tension between the occupiers and the unwilling subjects whose established ways they were committed to change.

These border areas of the Chinese provinces of Sichuan, Gansu, Qinghai, and Yunnan were inhabited by fractious Tibetan groups who were particularly unsuitable for such social and political engineering.[2] Whether it was their fear of being surrounded by a populace known for its ready resort to violence or simple Han Chinese arrogance toward people they had always regarded as wild, the occupying cadres in this area acted in a brutal and singularly obtuse manner that had begun to backfire by 1956.

Their first targets were the seminomadic Goloks in the Chinese province of Qinghai, where they had been traditionally feared as brigands.[3] Sir Charles Bell described them as people "who trade peaceably for half of the year and rob caravans for the remainder, sending religious offerings to the Dalai Lama in Lhasa every four or five years."[4] Next were the Khampas on both sides of the Yangtze. They were divided into bitterly feuding clans. All were ethnic Tibetans and devoted to the Dalai Lama, but historically their political allegiance to the government in Lhasa had been sporadic. The heavy-handed occupation practices of the Chinese, however, were to cause both the ruggedly individualist Goloks and the clannish Khampas to join local rebellions that were eventually to become a unified movement as resistance spread westward toward the capital.

The first incident of open rebellion occurred in early spring 1956, when an undetermined number of Goloks massacred a Chinese Communist garrison at the town of Dzachuka.⁵ Resentment had accumulated over the occupiers' heavy taxes, interference with their religious practices, food levies, public pillorying, and executions. But what finally set the Goloks on the warpath was a Chinese attempt to confiscate their most highly prized possessions, their personal weapons. There are no confirmed figures, but Chinese casualties were variously estimated between three hundred and nine hundred, with the most frequently cited figures being between eight hundred and fifty and nine hundred. Most reports reaching the U.S. State Department agreed that the revolt at Dzachuka provoked a strong Chinese reaction including air strikes on towns and monasteries.

A second round of hostilities in the summer centered in the Kham area on the eastern side of the Yangtze around the city and monastery of Litang, where the inhabitants had also begun to resist the programs imposed on them. The Chinese brought in reinforcements and increased their air and ground operations against their unruly Khampa subjects in a punitive campaign, committing the classic acts of a rampaging and vengeful army: torture, barbarous executions, public acts of degradation, forced labor, the seizure of private property, the desecration of monasteries, the deportation of men and boys, and finally taking children from their homes for reeducation in China. Chinese settlers took over the property of those who fled this campaign of what would now be called ethnic cleansing. It was the aerial bombing and destruction of the ancient monastery of Litang, built in 1580 and home to 5,000 monks with an arsenal of ancient rifles, that was to become the most frequently cited incident that caused the ordinary people, the monks, and the leaders of Kham to make common cause with the Amdowas and others in eastern Tibet.

From India, Gyalo Thondup continued his efforts to alert the outside world. His Tibetan Welfare Association prepared a document describing the "ruthless attacks by land and air" and the "indiscriminate and cold-blooded bombing" of the towns of Dzachuka and Litang, claiming that more than 4,000 men, women, and children had been killed in Litang alone. This document cited the heavy cost to the Tibetans of China's ambitious construction projects and protested against Chinese interference with religious activities, indoctrination of Tibetan youth, control of education, and heavy taxation. It quoted reports that guerrilla warfare had spread all over east and northeast Tibet, unfortunately repeating an inaccurate report that the Chinese had brought in 100 tanks to Lhasa. It was prepared as an appeal for international support and released to the press.[6] Copies were delivered to Nehru, President Eisenhower, and the prime minister of Pakistan.

The Dalai Lama learned in Lhasa of the bombardment of the Litang monastery, as well as the degrading abuse of monks and nuns and the torture and execution of women and children whose husbands and fathers had joined the resistance movement. He protested directly to the Chinese military commander, Zhang Gwohua, and declared that he intended to write a personal letter to Mao complaining about the troops and cadres.[7] Zhang replied that the Tibetans should expect to be punished if they rejected reforms protecting the masses from exploitation. Despairing of the futility of arguing with Zhang, the shaken Dalai Lama wrote Mao in the remote hope that he would agree that his subordinates were disobeying his own instructions. Mao never acknowledged the appeal or two follow-up letters the young ruler sent later that summer.

In July the Dalai Lama sent a delegation including Ngabo Ngawang Jigme to try to pacify Kham.[8] Ngabo was a strange choice. The Khampas generally regarded him as the man who, as governor of their region, had yielded it without a fight when the Chinese invaded six years earlier, and later as the negotiator of the unpopular Seventeen Point Agreement. The decision to send a mission headed by Ngabo seems to have been made either at the suggestion of the insensitive Chinese or by the Tibetan government as a desperate move to avert open warfare and the increased repression that would certainly follow. Its failure probably surprised no one. There was a brief lull in the fighting, but it was resumed in full force that autumn.

Although the international press had been printing repeated accounts

of the uprisings in eastern Tibet since early May of 1956, it was not until
the following August that Beijing conceded there had been trouble. Dis-
tinguishing between the Chinese-defined Tibetan Autonomous Region
and the border provinces of China where the ethnic Tibetans were in
rebellion, the vice chairman of the Nationalities Affairs Commission,
Liu Geping, declared "there is no rebellion in Tibet."[9] He claimed that
the rebellion in the border region had been instigated by Chinese
Nationalist agents and "a few feudal landlords." Admittedly, military
measures had been taken against the rebels, but Liu denied reports that
insurgents had succeeded in closing the highways.

Nevertheless there was obvious concern in Beijing. In an effort that
was interpreted by New Delhi as a Chinese gesture to quiet Indian fears,
Ragashar Shape, the commander of the Tibetan army and one of the
Dalai Lama's most trusted advisers, was permitted to make a carefully
escorted visit to India in early August.[10] A month later Beijing's proconsul in Lhasa, Zhang Gwohua, told the eighth Communist Party Conference in Beijing that China would introduce reforms cautiously.[11]
Zhang blamed past policies of the "ruling classes of China" for creating
a "very deep gulf between the Tibetan and Chinese nationalities." Making no mention of the recent uprisings, he expressed the hope that a
"very small number of persons who still take an unpatriotic attitude will
soon awaken and return to the motherland and people."

ᴇʍ

Then events from the outside world added a new element to this
scene. During the summer of 1956 the crown prince of Sikkim visited
Lhasa with an invitation to the Dalai Lama to attend the Buddhist
Jyanti celebrations to be held in India later that year to mark the 2,500th
anniversary of Buddha's birth. The political implications of a visit were
obvious. Two years before, the crown prince, who was married to a
Tibetan, had told American officials in Calcutta that on his visit to
Lhasa he had found the Dalai Lama unhappy but resigned to remaining
at his post. Now, he told the newly arrived consul general, R. Borden
Reams, he found the young ruler anxious to leave Tibet, and his advis-

ers believed that his flight could be arranged.[12] He said the Tibetans had already approached the Indian government about asylum but had not received firm enough guarantees. Could His Holiness be assured of asylum elsewhere in addition to financial support?

He also reported on the heavy fighting in Kham, where the Tibetans had captured quantities of Chinese arms but needed another thousand rifles and machine guns to spread the fighting to other parts of Tibet. He suggested that they be delivered through East Pakistan (now Bangladesh) and asked if Tibetan "pilgrims" to Burma and Thailand could be given artillery and antiaircraft training. These reports of armed rebellion came as no surprise. Only two days earlier the consulate had sent a dispatch reporting that "no neutral observer seriously believes the Khampas, Goloks and Litangas will be able to hold out indefinitely against the Chinese. They are short of ammunition and have no fresh sources of supply. While the present rebellion has delayed for a time the integration of this area into the Chinese system, there is no expectation this state of affairs can continue for more than six months to a year."[13]

The consul general equivocated, telling the crown prince that the U.S. government was unlikely to do anything that might jeopardize its relations with the Indian government. Reams asked Washington for guidance. It took Washington some weeks to provide it. On July 24 the Department replied that while it would support the Dalai Lama's request for asylum, he should first seek help from India since the "long range hopes of the Tibetan people" would require its help.[14] There was no reference to the crown prince's request for arms and training for the Tibetans. This was a matter to be negotiated separately with Gyalo Thondup.

The crown prince's invitation to India had come at a fortuitous time for the beleaguered Dalai Lama and those of his advisers who were ready to defy the Chinese.[15] It would permit him to inform Nehru directly that the Chinese had failed to keep their promises, leading to disaffection and revolt. He also could explain in person why he wanted to seek asylum in India, knowing that he had at least a qualified pledge of U.S. support in reserve dating back to 1951.[16] But he also feared that the Chinese would not permit the visit; they had already forced him to decline a visit to Nepal earlier that spring. As expected, the acting Chinese authority, General Fan

Ming, thought it was a poor idea, warning the Dalai Lama that India was a dangerous place.

But in November, just weeks before the Buddhist Jyanti ceremonies were to begin, the Chinese relented. Beijing had apparently taken note of what was happening in Poland and Hungary and decided that the absence of the Dalai Lama from this widely publicized international event would cause adverse commentary about the situation in Tibet. Mao was also pushing his campaign to "let a hundred flowers bloom," his metaphor for nominally allowing dissenting views to be expressed (and thus exposed). General Zhang Jingwu, the senior occupation official, did warn that India was full of spies and reactionaries and if the Dalai Lama tried "to do anything with them," he must realize that "what happened in Hungary and Poland will happen in Tibet."[17] In any event, the Chinese premier, Zhou Enlai, would be visiting India at the same time. He could make sure that both Nehru and the Dalai Lama got the word that China would not tolerate any separatist movements in Tibet.

When the Dalai Lama met with Nehru soon after his arrival in New Delhi on November 25, he outlined in detail the efforts that he had made to accommodate to the Chinese. Nehru had no interest in hearing about China's determination to proceed with communization despite its promises. He had signed away Tibet's independence in the agreement he had made two years earlier with Zhou on the basis of the vaunted Five Principles of Peaceful Coexistence. Having to deal with Beijing's reneging on these same principles was particularly embarrassing when their coauthor, Zhou Enlai, was arriving in New Delhi the next morning. "Somewhat impatiently," the Dalai Lama later recounted, Nehru told him India could not support him and he must return home to work with the Chinese. He did promise he would arrange for the Dalai Lama to meet Zhou.[18]

When they met, it was obvious to the Dalai Lama that Nehru had briefed Zhou on the Tibetan grievances. Zhou was in New Delhi as the first stop on a six-nation tour of Asia. He planned to trade on the reputation he had promoted the year before at Bandung where he had outshone Nehru as the exponent of "peaceful coexistence." The public spectacle of a flight by the world's major Buddhist leader to protest the brutal Chinese occupation of his country would not serve Zhou's image.

But Zhou was also aware of the dangerous challenges to Communist control in Eastern Europe. He and Mao had come up with a carefully crafted formula that permitted Beijing to sympathize with Polish workers and simultaneously criticize Moscow for using Soviet troops to subdue their revolt, while at the same time endorsing Soviet military intervention to smash the "counter-revolutionary rebellion" in Hungary. The distinction drawn by the Chinese was that the Hungarians threatened the unity of the Communist world by trying to withdraw from the Warsaw Pact. Similarly, China would not countenance a direct challenge to the unity of the Chinese empire that Mao was seeking to reestablish.

Zhou tried that formula on the Dalai Lama. He listened closely to the subjugated leader's concerns about the Chinese treatment of his people in eastern Tibet and his observations about the marked difference between the Indian Parliament and the Chinese system. Zhou reassured him that things had improved greatly in China since his visit there two years before. He said that he had heard that the Dalai Lama was thinking about remaining in India and cautioned him that would be a mistake.

Before returning to Beijing a few weeks later, Zhou met again with the Dalai Lama to warn him that the situation in Tibet had deteriorated, indicating that the Chinese were ready to use force to suppress the rebellion. The Dalai Lama replied that his countrymen were resisting unwanted reforms imposed by the Chinese. Zhou countered that Mao had already decided that no reforms would be introduced in Tibet for at least six years and they could be postponed for fifty years if necessary. (Indeed, Mao did disclose such a postponement in a speech on February 27 of the following year, but it was not published until June 18, 1957.[19]) Zhou then urged the Dalai Lama not to visit Kalimpong, an area "full of spies and reactionary elements." Without specifying, the Chinese premier was undoubtedly referring to the Dalai Lama's two older brothers, Takster Rimpoche and Gyalo Thondup, whom he had already met and asked to return to Tibet. They had bluntly told him they had no intention of doing so. Zhou may also have been aware of the rumors that both the U.S. government and the Dalai Lama's brothers were encouraging him to remain in India.

The Dalai Lama had one more session with Nehru, who again urged him to return to Lhasa, reaffirming that he could look for no help from

India. The prime minister at first endorsed Zhou's advice to avoid Kalimpong, but suddenly changed his mind. "India is a free country, after all. You would not be breaking any of her laws," said Nehru, proceeding to arrange for his troublesome guest's travel to the border town with its exile colony. Despite this belated hospitality the Dalai Lama and his brothers felt let down by Nehru.[20] Gyalo Thondup is adamant that Apa Pant, the Indian political officer in Sikkim, had assured him that Nehru would mediate the withdrawal of Chinese troops from Tibet, promising that the Dalai Lama could have his choice of "maharajah's palaces" for asylum if the negotiations failed. But the vulnerable young ruler was being pushed to return to govern under Zhou's lieutenants. Worse, Zhou was fully aware of the Dalai Lama's feelings and was probably aware of his brothers' negotiations with the Americans. The fragile veil of accommodation had been torn.

When the Dalai Lama accepted Nehru's grudging approval to stop in Kalimpong he must have felt a sense of déjà vu. It had been six years since he had passed a winter sitting just across the border deciding whether to cross and seek asylum. Then he had been alone with only his mother and a few of his advisers urging him to leave. Now he would be spending time with two additional proponents of asylum and resistance, his older brothers, Gyalo Thondup and Takster Rimpoche. While briefing his brother on the U.S. pledges of political support, Gyalo carefully avoided mention of the training that the CIA was beginning to provide and the arms aid due later.[21] Telling the Dalai Lama would have meant asking him to condone violence, but Gyalo kept Phala fully informed. This concrete evidence of U.S. interest strengthened the arguments of those urging the Dalai Lama to serve his people by remaining outside of Tibet and seeking foreign support against the Chinese.

It had taken some years for both Gyalo and the U.S. government to arrive at this point of active participation in supporting armed resistance inside Tibet. While he had been organizing the informal Tibetan Relief Association from 1952 to 1956, Gyalo had also been receiving emissaries from the resistance movement in eastern Tibet seeking arms from abroad. The first was an Amdo leader, Gonthang Tsultrim, who operated in the Labrang area about a hundred miles from Lanzhou in the

Chinese border province of Gansu. He came to Darjeeling in 1955 to see Gyalo. The following year a Khampa monk named Gyatotsang came as representative of an insurgent force then mustering in Litang, which became the nucleus of the nationwide movement later mobilized by the best known resistance leader, his uncle, Gompo Tashi. Thondup stressed that neither he nor the central government took the initiative in organizing these homegrown rebellions. They had arisen spontaneously in response to Chinese policies and outright atrocities.

Thondup felt that he had no alternative but to approach foreign sources for the material assistance that these local leaders were seeking.[22] He was under no illusion that these untrained and unorganized groups would have to be able to expel huge numbers of Chinese. To think of a military victory over the People's Liberation Army, he said, would have been "naive." He did think that an effective show of resistance might help to mobilize international public opinion and stimulate countries like India to pressure the Chinese to act more moderately in Tibet. He emphasized that this was a popular rebellion and not a cause supported by the Lhasa nobility, who were meanwhile still accepting official allowances from the Chinese. Even his sister and her husband, Phuntso Tashi, sent their servants each month to receive their allotment of Chinese silver dollars. It was therefore ironic that the Chinese claimed that the revolt had been instigated by reactionaries, when it was the nobility, the ruling lamas, and the officials of the old guard who had accommodated themselves to the Chinese occupiers and only belatedly joined the rebellion and fled Tibet.

During this period the Indians were interested only in supporting intelligence in Tibet, but representatives of the Chinese Nationalist government first showed up on Thondup's doorstep in 1952, shortly after he arrived in India, offering to back paramilitary operations in Tibet. Thondup decided that allying himself with the Nationalists would only validate Beijing's claims that the resistance movement was a foreign creation. In any event, he knew the Nationalists would turn to Washington for whatever assistance they might provide the Tibetans, and he might just as well go to them directly to avoid the political baggage that would come from the Taiwan connection. Now it was time for the Americans to finally make their mark on the roof of the world.

CHAPTER 8

The CIA Joins the War

F ROM ITS INAUGURATION IN 1953 as the unpopular Korean War was winding down, the Eisenhower administration had been seeking to challenge communism by other means than direct and costly military confrontation. Eisenhower gave the CIA its first civilian director, Allen Dulles, who had unprecedented access to the White House and to his brother, the secretary of state. Covert action against communism attained an importance among the CIA's missions that would not be equaled until the Reagan administration in the eighties. The rebellion in Tibet was tailor-made for a covert action program designed to challenge communist consolidation in what was still regarded as Moscow's mirror image in the Far

East.[1] If Americans had known about it, they certainly would have supported it. In 1951, 60 percent favored the bombing of China even though that could have expanded the Korean War. During the middle of the decade, 92 percent opposed allowing the Communists to take the Chinese seat in the United Nations.[2]

From 1952 to 1955, however, the Tibetan resistance was still isolated and not sufficiently well organized to justify covert operational support. The little that the U.S. government knew of Tibet came out of Sikkim and from isolated reports by Gyalo's underground,[3] which was located in central Tibet, mainly in Lhasa, where the prevailing mood was one of accommodation. Then reports of resistance to Chinese actions along the Yangtze River border in 1956 indicated that more active U.S. involvement was warranted. In Washington the zeal for an activist program remained strong. When Gyalo came to the consulate in Calcutta seeking aid, he now was welcomed. CIA operatives met that summer with Gyalo Thondup and his brother Takster Rimpoche and agreed to train a pilot group of six Khampas in guerrilla warfare and radio communications. These men would be parachuted back into Tibet to provide updated and regular reports on the insurgent movement that was taking shape on its own in both eastern and central Tibet. On the basis of these radio reports, CIA would determine whether and what kind of additional assistance would be justified. If they found groups engaged in ongoing resistance operations, they would be able to train the leaders and urge them to use guerrilla tactics rather than fighting pitched battles against the numerically superior Chinese army.

The initial group of six, all from the Litang area of Kham, were selected by Thondup, Takster, Shakabpa, and Gyadutsang, who were the only ones privy to the plans, on the recommendations of the emerging Khampa leader Gompo Tashi.[4] The six were brought out secretly from Tibet and flown to Saipan in December. There CIA officers, aided by Takster and his Mongolian monk retainer (acting as advisers and interpreters), trained them in communications, guerrilla tactics, intelligence collection and reporting, and the use of infantry small arms up to 60 mm mortars and 57 mm recoilless rifles.

The CIA had come to this point of active involvement after several years of searching for ways to challenge the Chinese Communists' consolidation of their control. The increasing evidence of a mounting homegrown resistance effort along the upper Yangtze, coupled with requests for support from credible emissaries, seemed a fortuitous opportunity.[5] Furthermore, the CIA's China mission in the Philippines had just been closed down after a series of unsuccessful operations to threaten the Communists' hold on the mainland. The CIA's Far Eastern Division was ready to take on a new challenge.[6]

Sam Halpern, a Far East Division officer and later executive officer to Desmond FitzGerald when he was CIA Deputy Director for Operations, recalls that the impetus for the Tibet operations on a policy level came directly from John Foster Dulles in the State Department and Undersecretary Herbert Hoover Jr.[7] The primary objective, Halpern said, had little to do with aiding the Tibetans: It was to impede and harass the Chinese Communists. He added that this same policy motivated the CIA program to help the rebel Indonesian colonels in their efforts to overthrow Sukarno in 1958 when he became too tolerant of the Communists in his country. The provenance and impetus for both programs was the same, pressure from the State Department to keep the Communists off balance in Asia. Thomas Parrott, Allen Dulles's liaison officer with the National Security Council, recalled that on one occasion when he reported to the CIA chief that the State Department "had no objection" to a proposed operation, his boss said that was "not good enough. I want to hear that State wants the Agency to do this, as we do these things only at the behest of the Department and other members of the National Security Council."[8] This bureaucratic propriety was characteristic of a man who combined a great zest for action with a lawyer's sense of observing the norms of the National Security establishment to protect his agency.

The decision to support the Tibetan resistance was made in the summer of 1956 before the limits on outside support for insurrections in countries under the effective military control of Communist forces were demonstrated that autumn in Hungary. In the following year Frank Wisner, the CIA operations chief who was consumed by remorse at his inability to help the Hungarian rebels, adamantly insisted that, when the first six Tibetans were sent back to their country after training, their mission must be limited to intelligence collection. Wisner may only have wanted to establish a record in the cable traffic that would not leave CIA open to charges similar to those that had been levied against the agency of having aroused false expectations in Hungary. But he also had a strong sense of personal responsibility and never again wanted to walk away from clients who had been encouraged to achieve impossible objectives.[9] Whether Wisner imposed the limitations out of a sense of personal guilt or bureaucratic prudence, it was nevertheless apparent from the training given the Tibetans that the Far East Division of CIA was ready to undertake a full program of support if the initial teams found it warranted by the situation on the ground and the capabilities of their comrades.[10]

ᦉ

By the time that the Dalai Lama reached Kalimpong in early February 1957, the first group had already begun training in Saipan.[11] The twenty-one-year-old ruler may well not have known the details of the paramilitary support embodied in the new U.S. commitment, but Gyalo had assured him that those negotiating with him had pledged full support for the resistance until Tibet gained its independence. Gyalo is still adamant that the word used in negotiations with the Americans was "independence," not "autonomy" or "self-determination." Whatever the actual words, they were set in an uncertain future, and the Dalai Lama was again confronted with the moral dilemma of how best to serve the immediate interests of his people.

In Kalimpong he stayed in the same house that his predecessor had occupied when he had been forced to seek asylum in India some forty years earlier. The perplexed young man heard out the impassioned arguments of those closest to him, his older brothers Gyalo and Takster, and his closest personal adviser, Phala. They urged him to remain in India. His former prime minister Lukhangwa, whom the Chinese had compelled him to dismiss, added his arguments against trying to govern under what they both now knew was not to be a benign occupation.

Even the controversial Ngabo Ngawang Jigme, who had made his own decision to accommodate to the Chinese, was also in Kalimpong and gave some surprising advice. He told the Dalai Lama that if he could come up with a concrete plan for promoting Tibetan independence from abroad, it might be worthwhile for him to stay in India. But with only the supposition of foreign support, Ngabo told the Dalai Lama he had no alternative but to return to Tibet.[12]

As he had done five years earlier when confronted with this dilemma, the Dalai Lama sought the counsel of the state oracles. When the oracles again divined that he should return, Lukhangwa responded with an old Tibetan adage: "When men become desperate they consult the gods. And when the gods become desperate, they tell lies."[13] But the Dalai Lama decided that it was his duty to return to his country, and in March 1957 began the trek across to the pass leading back to Lhasa.

When he reached Lhasa on April 1, things still seemed normal on the surface. The Chinese had apparently decided to let up on the pressure in the capital. Zhou Enlai, who three months earlier had returned to Beijing from India, reportedly dejected by his talks with Nehru, admitted that he had heard rumors that U.S. agents were urging the Dalai Lama not to return to Tibet.[14] While Zhou said that China would be obliged to use force to suppress any uprising, as the Russians had in Hungary, he and Mao apparently decided it was time to make a show of moderation. On February 27, in a secret speech, Mao admitted that many people in China had been "delighted" when the Hungarian uprising took place and had hoped that "something similar" would happen in China. One of the "contradictions" requiring new methods for consolidating Communist control was the situation in Tibet. He said that the problem of Han chauvinism, with its disrespect for minorities occupying 50 or 60 percent of China's land, must be resolved. He laid down a policy of conciliation but set its bounds. "If you [Tibetans] want to agitate for independence, then agitate; you want independence, I don't want [you to have] independence. . . . As for reform, the seventeen points [of the 1951 agreement] stipulate that reforms be made; but the reforms need your agreement. If you don't [want] reform, then we won't have any. If in the next few years you don't [want] reforms, then we won't have any. This is the way that we have spoken to them [the Tibetans] just now. There'll be no reform under the second five-year-plan, in the third five-year-plan we will see what you think; if you say, reform, then we will reform; if you say no reform, then we'll continue not to reform. Why such a hurry?"[15]

This was followed by a series of conciliatory moves.[16] In April, Zhang Gwohua, Tibet's military overlord, announced that the reforms of the Second Five-Year Plan were being postponed. Then some troops and political cadres were withdrawn and some public works projects were canceled, particularly in Lhasa. The Chinese, however, did not relax their efforts at imposing political control over the Tibetan government and military control over the countryside, where the rebellion was spreading. The effects of military suppression in the countryside were clearly visible from Lhasa: Outside the city, several thousand lay and monastic refugees were encamped on the plains. These were common people who with their local leaders had been pushed westward by Chinese efforts to stamp out resistance in their native areas of Kham and Amdo on the eastern border. The growing number of refugees outside Lhasa indicated that it was probably too late for the Chinese to resolve the "contradictions" in their policies on Tibet.

GOMPO TASHI'S UNDERGROUND

By December 1956, a fifty-one-year-old trader from Litang, where the Chinese had bombed the people and monastery that summer, had decided that it was time to organize a unified resistance. His full name was Gompo Tashi Andrugtsang, and he was uniquely qualified for his task. Gompo came from a family well known for its support of the Tibetan religion and its institutions. As a successful trader he had amassed a sizable fortune by Tibetan standards. He had traveled throughout Tibet and into Nepal on business, so he knew the people and terrain. Gompo also enjoyed a good reputation among those leaders of the Tibetan government loyal to the Dalai Lama and opposed to the Chinese measures that reduced his influence and authority.

Although he was one of the few Tibetans capable of assembling a national resistance organization based in central Tibet, Gompo suffered from some disadvantages. His contacts in Kham were primarily in the Litang area, and as a trader his influence among the local chieftains was limited. These chieftains and their tribes constituted a powerful social group within the distinctive culture of the upper Yangtze border region. In their eyes, traders like Gompo were allied with the forces of modernization that threatened their traditional way of life—a classic conflict between established territorial lords and a rising merchant class. While many of these clannish chieftains initially tried to accommodate themselves to the new rulers in Beijing as they had with their predecessors, they and their followers were repaid by being among those first exposed to Communist programs; hence, they were among the earliest to rebel. When they took to the hills with the common people of Kham and Amdo, they were slowly pushed in small groups toward Lhasa, where they found Gompo taking charge of a national resistance effort. The tribal leaders, however, resented Gompo as socially inferior and a late-comer to the revolt. His access to the Lhasa government and the potential sources of foreign support brought them into his organization only reluctantly. These rivalries and suspicions were to be a serious handicap to the Tibetan resistance movement in the coming years.

Nevertheless it was Gompo and his organization that the CIA came to know and support.[17] Gompo had kept Phala well informed on the growing resistance movement. Phala, who was one of those closest to the trapped ruler, made it clear that the Dalai Lama's moral objections to violence prevented him from responding to the unrealistic pleas of his rebellious subjects for arms from the Tibetan government or endorsing their use of force to rebel. Gompo, disappointed but understanding his sovereign's dilemma, decided he must proceed on his own to convert the efforts of the clannish eastern Tibetans and their homegrown Army of the National Defenders of the Faith into a truly national movement. The canny Khampa trader devised a stratagem to attract these local resistance leaders and provide the cover for a meeting, which he would use to mobilize them for national objectives. He proposed a special religious ritual of gifts and prayers for the long life of the Dalai Lama, who agreed to accept the honor. The Tibetan cabinet, important members of the government, and representatives of the people agreed to present the Dalai Lama a golden throne as a gift at the ceremony.

Tibetans contributed money and personal jewelry, and the throne was built in several weeks by 49 goldsmiths, 5 silversmiths, 19 engravers, 8 tailors, 6 painters, 3 blacksmiths, and 3 welders, in addition to 30 general assistants. It was presented to the Dalai Lama on July 4, 1957, at a ceremony attended by thousands. The throne itself was removed to his palace, where the Dalai Lama expected to occupy it when receiving the people in an annual audience. While it was destined to serve this purpose for only a very short time, the organizational effort involved in its creation was the start of Gompo's effort to launch the nationwide resistance movement. (Long after the movement was crushed, the throne still sits in the assembly hall of the Dalai Lama's summer palace, the Norbulingka, the one place among the public buildings in Lhasa that still contains an image of the present Dalai Lama. This image appears in a large mural that includes all fourteen Dalai Lamas. He is depicted as he was when he occupied this palace as a young man, surrounded by his family—including his two older brothers, who were the first to defy the Chinese occupiers—all of them looking from the back wall toward the throne that was to become a symbol of the resistance.)

Throughout the summer and fall of 1957 the now thoroughly aroused Khampas and their Amdowa comrades attacked and fought the Chinese occupation forces. These attacks produced an ascending spiral of reprisals and counterattacks, despite the measures taken by Mao and his colleagues to reduce the more obvious features of their occupation and delay the resented policies of communization. These palliative steps had been taken too late to head off growing resistance in eastern Tibet, where previous Chinese actions had aroused a rebellion impervious to soothing pronouncements by Beijing. The pattern of attacks and harsh retaliation sent a flow of refugees to central Tibet and turned what had been a local uprising near the border into a national insurrection.

Building on the organizational nucleus formed the previous summer under the cover of the Golden Throne project, Gompo called a meeting of resistance leaders at his house in Lhasa early in 1958. Using the slogan "all *tsampa* [the barley flour staple of the Tibetan diet] eaters must stand together," he challenged the chiefs of the two dozen local Khampa and Amdowa groups composing the Army of the National Defenders of the Faith to unite in a nationwide resistance. He had no troops of his own, but he could provide leadership to this loosely organized group of insurgent leaders now dispossessed from their home base. He enjoyed high repute among the three great monasteries of the Dalai Lama's sect, and monks constituted more than half of the resistance force. Most of all, he had access to Gyalo Thondup, not only the brother of the person that the force was organized to protect, but the man who was the channel to the CIA with its promise of the arms. With only a few exceptions, they agreed to join forces in the united movement Gompo sought, making their pledge before a photograph of the Dalai Lama in the prayer room of the Litang trader's house. This was the beginning of the Chushi Gangdruk organization,[18] named after the four rivers and six mountains of eastern Tibet, homeland of most of the resistance leaders.[19]

Gompo conveyed this decision to the Dalai Lama through Phala. Although Phala was a monk, he supported the resistance, including the use of violence, and encouraged Gompo's organizational efforts. Since 1952, the Dalai Lama's eldest brother Takster had been keeping Phala informed of his negotiations with the State Department and CIA, using the secret code Phala had given him. Gyalo Thondup likewise had briefed Phala on the U.S. government's 1956 offers to help the Dalai Lama in exile and the CIA's training of teams to be airdropped into Tibet.[20] The secret couriers from Thondup's resistance effort in India also reported to Phala. Phala thus served as the intermediary between Gompo and the other resistance leaders and as a buffer to protect the Dalai Lama from acknowledging or endorsing activities involving violence. He was to continue to act as his ruler's eyes and ears to the resistance until 1959 when he organized the Dalai Lama's escape from Lhasa. He was truly "the man who kept the secrets."

The CIA and the
National Volunteer Defense Army

It was while this resistance was gathering force in distant Lhasa that I met my first Tibetans. On an early winter day in 1958, I was asked to give a lecture on Sino-Soviet relations to a group of "Asians" at one of the CIA's nearby covert sites. Accordingly, I arrived to give the standard semiacademic presentation that I usually made to visiting foreign officers. But the audience was a surprise. I first met a pleasant young man named Lobsang Samtem, who was introduced to me as a brother of the Dalai Lama. He in turn presented eight smiling compatriots who were being trained to return to their country to fight with the resistance.

It was apparent that a lecture on Sino-Soviet relations would be as relevant to their concerns as a discourse on the War of the Roses. I scrapped the prepared lecture and dove in to give what I hoped was a useful exposition of how their fight was related to the free world's stand against communism. It was a poor speech, but the Tibetans were polite and welcoming. They asked me to stay on and help them celebrate their New Year's Day. The trainee guerrillas cooked Tibetan dumplings called *mo-mos,* and we drank lots of American beer, since none of their native barley beer, called *chang,* was available. A colleague with a taste for theatricals put on a Japanese kimono and danced as "Madame Fifi." The Tibetans were slightly bewildered, but they loved it, and they reciprocated with their native dances. The shuffling two-step I had learned at the tea dances of the Cedar Rapids Country Club hardly seemed appropriate, so I joined these friendly and open men in their hearty stomping.

It was a rather surrealistic day, but I agreed to develop a political program that would enable these naturally articulate men to explain their objectives to their countrymen when they returned, help enlist more recruits in the resistance movement, and make their grievances and goals known to the rest of the world. It was the beginning of seven of the most satisfying, although at times the most painful, years of my life. I had stumbled into the CIA's support operations as they were gaining momentum. Two teams had completed their training on Saipan and

Palanquin carrying the Dalai Lama back to Lhasa after he decided to try governing under the new Chinese rulers.

Dalai Lama's camp near Phari Dzong on the return trip to Lhasa, 1951.

Dalai Lama's retinue returning to Lhasa, 1951.

The new era arrives in Lhasa, Chinese troops entering the capital in the autumn of 1951.

Lhasa residents returning home after a Chinese Communist political rally held to promote acceptance of their occupation, 1951.

The Dalai Lama and the Panchen Lama visit Tibet's new overlords, Mao Zedong, Zhou Enlai, and Liu Shaoqi, in their capital on Tibetan New Year's Day, 1955.

LEFT: Gyalo Thondup (left) with Sinha, the Indian mission chief, Lhasa, 1952.

BELOW: From left to right: Lhamo Tsering, Gyalo's lifetime friend and resistance partner, with the Indian Mission Chief, a Tibetan official named Pemba Rimshi, and the Dalai Lama's brother-in-law, Phuntso Tashi, Lhasa, 1952. Lhamo Tsering accompanied Gyalo on his flight to India later that spring and served his government until shortly before his death in 1999.

The Dalai Lama's older brother, Gyalo Thondup, near the Tibetan border on flight to India in 1952 to enlist international interest and sympathy for Tibet's struggle to preserve its identity.

Thubten Jigme Norbu, who fled abroad in 1951 after refusing Chinese offers to collaborate with them at the expense of his younger brother, the Dalai Lama.

Gompo Tashi Andrutsang (1905-1964), who united and led his country's resistance against the Chinese under the banner of the Volunteer Freedom Fighters for Religious and Political Resistance.

Members of the Volunteer Freedom Fighters display weapon captured in 1958 from the Chinese near Tsetang, the legendar birthplace of the Tibetan people, one hundred miles southeas of Lhasa.

A group of volunteer freedom fighters in Lhoka.

ABOVE: Lhuntse Dzong where the Dalai Lama paused on his flight to India to set up a temporary government to establish his claim to authority even though he had left Lhasa.

LEFT: Soldiers in front of the Volunteer Freedom Fighters flag, 1959.

BOTTOM LEFT: Tibetan resistance fighters, 1958.

ABOVE: The Dalai Lama, finding it impossible to reach an agreement with the Chinese and fearing further violence, flees to India in March 1959.

ABOVE: The Dalai Lama at the Indian border, April 1959.

RIGHT: The Dalai Lama's reluctant but generous host, Prime Minister Jawaharlal Nehru.

had been parachuted into Tibet the previous September. In addition to their instruction in guerrilla warfare and tactics and the use of small arms, they had learned how to operate the RS-1 hand-generated crystal radio transmitter and receiver, and to use the radio signal plans, telecodes, and one-time encoding and decoding pads that each team carried to convey intelligence from the rebel areas, transmit requests for specific assistance, and guide the planes to their airdrop delivery sites.[21]

This pioneer work in devising a telecode system to describe items that were not in the Tibetan vocabulary and in writing intelligible messages in a language that is frequently imprecise was done on Saipan by CIA officers working with the Dalai Lama's brother Takster and Geshe Wangel, the Kalmuk monk who had first introduced U.S. officers to the Dalai Lama's family in Kalimpong in 1951. After returning from Saipan in 1957, Geshe frequently left his monastery in New Jersey to train other members of the Tibetan resistance in the special grammar of message-writing and to teach them how to translate the messages from the teams when they were received in Washington. This dedicated man abhorred violence, yet accepted its use for a rightful cause. The sight of him walking down Wisconsin Avenue in northwest Washington wearing his red robe and gray fedora was a memorable one.

The first team, consisting of two men, Athar and Lhotse, were dropped onto dunes formed by the receding flood waters of the Tsangpo (upper Brahmaputra) River south of Lhasa. The officer responsible for planning air operations in the Far East noted that the site had been picked by the CIA's chief cartographer, who was forced to work with old British maps[22] dating from the 1904 Younghusband invasion. The plane used on these first drops was a B-17[23] flown by Polish and Czech expatriates[24] trained by the CIA. Both planes and crews were chosen to provide deniability; B-17s were by then available for charter on the open market. These brave and skilled pilots, like their successors over the next four years, delivered the men on target.

The mission of Athar and Lhotse was to make their way to Lhasa and give Gompo Tashi a message for Phala that the U.S. government would provide assistance to the resistance movement if the Dalai Lama would solicit it.[25] The State Department had asked for this reaffirmation, and

Gompo duly transmitted the request. The Dalai Lama, even less inclined to accede to Washington than he had been to the earlier requests from his countrymen, refused. The State Department nevertheless agreed to proceed with the support operations, since its intelligence reports confirmed that the Tibetans were carrying out active resistance efforts on their own. Gompo Tashi took over the direction of Athar and Lhotse, parading them before his forces as evidence of U.S. support.

The second team[26] dropped in the autumn of 1957 was sent to establish contact with the resistance groups then operating in team leader Wangdu Gyatotsang's home area near Litang in the Chinese province of Sichuan. Wangdu was the brother of the man who had come to Gyalo Thondup two years earlier in India seeking aid for the resistance forces then being organized in Kham by their uncle Gompo Tashi. Wangdu and two of his team mates were dropped nine miles from their hometown, which they found had been occupied by the Chinese army. (The fourth member of the team, who couldn't handle the jump, was dispatched overland, but he was killed on his way to join the others.) The team was able to establish contact with Wangdu's third brother, who was in command of a unit at a Tibetan guerrilla base nearby. This force came under attack and Wangdu's two teammates were killed. The three had been able to operate as a team despite the frictions of social status and different clan membership that had become apparent during their training on Saipan. These frictions were one of the first glimpses CIA was to have of the divisions among these isolated local cultures of eastern Tibet and their alienation from Lhasa, something that handicapped the formation of a regional, let alone a national, struggle.

Wangdu escaped and made his way to the resistance headquarters then assembling in central Tibet five hundred miles away. He got there after the first arms drop had been made in July 1958. He was angry that the U.S. had not made similar drops to his colleagues in Kham, but he came to accept that making what would have had to be blind drops after his radio operator was killed ruled them out. He then went to India, where he continued to work with the resistance movement until he was killed sixteen years later by Nepalese troops in an ambush on the border with Tibet.[27] His mission in Kham had ended in tragedy, but the mere presence of the team had raised the prospect of additional U.S. support. This probably caused the scattered local resistance groups in Kham to band together to fight the Chinese using their traditional massed strategy. While this was politically helpful, the concentrations made the Tibetans easier targets for the Chinese and eventually led to their retreat toward Lhasa. It also whetted their appetite for more U.S. assistance.

∞

In the spring of 1958, some months after the first CIA trained team had established contact with him, Gompo Tashi took his men into the field to begin action against the Chinese.[28] Word of Gompo's mobilization of men, horses, and equipment soon reached the Chinese, who reacted by putting pressure on the Tibetan government to suppress the insurrection. The politically captive officials issued the requested proclamations forbidding anyone to join or support the resistance movement. Gompo, in a bold move in late April 1958, called three hundred followers to a planning session in Lhasa, this time using the cover of a Buddhist celebration. Ostensibly, he and his group were collecting funds to perform religious rites and paint holy statues. A divination process, similar to the ones performed to decide whether the Dalai Lama should return to Lhasa, was carried out at a meeting of the principal leaders of the Chushi Gangdruk, now joined by two officers of the Khadang regiment of the Tibetan army.[29] Two alternatives were offered: to remain in Lhasa and challenge the Chinese when the need arose to protect the Dalai Lama, or to assume the initiative by leaving Lhasa to challenge the Chinese army. These were written on two slips of paper, which were enclosed in two balls of *tsampa* dough. These in turn were placed inside a cup that was spun clockwise in front of a statue of the Buddha. The ball with the second choice fell out. That decided the strategy: Only the time and place to initiate action in the field remained to be fixed.

The Chinese shortly thereafter began a census of the Khampa and Amdowa refugees who were living in a tent city on the outskirts of Lhasa. The census was preparatory to the issuance of identity cards, which would be required for continued residence in the capital. Fearing that the census might be followed by mass arrests, the inhabitants began moving out of Lhasa. Like the earlier decrees requiring the Khampas and Amdowas to turn in their rifles, these moves toward population control only served to feed the rebellion. Tibetans from the central and other regions also took note of what was happening to their country.

Gompo decided that the time had come for him to get out of Lhasa and lead the unified resistance movement into military operations. He wrote the Dalai Lama and his two tutors, explaining that the "Chinese oppression was mounting and they were no longer prepared to submit to it." He was leaving to accept the repeated requests from the resistance leaders that he join the now reinforced Chushi Gangdruk at its field headquarters at Trigu Thang, in Lhoka, the region a few days' travel south of Lhasa. There the new organization proclaimed the formation of the Volunteer Freedom Fighters for Religious and Political Resistance (VFF) under Gompo's leadership. This was done at a cavalry parade, with incense burning, the ceremonial display of a photograph of the Dalai Lama, and the unfurling of a new flag incorporating the sword with the traditional Tibetan thunderbolt and the Buddhist lotus. These unsophisticated warriors, displaying a surprising sense of either history or propaganda, recorded their parade on movie cameras. They preserved the film and later made it available to both CIA and commercial TV producers.

The new national resistance army claimed to have 5,000 volunteers.[30] Its new name reflected the fact that, although its forces were predominately from the east—the land of the Chushi Gangdruk—they were now operating in central Tibet. They needed local support, and they now had patronage within the Lhasa government. The astute Phala may have suggested that a Khampa name was hardly appropriate for a national movement, and Gompo's vision of a pan-Tibet organization now prevailed. More recruits were joining up, and a twenty-seven-point code of conduct was imposed. This code, along with a report of the VFF's objectives, was sent to both arms of the Tibetan governing structure, the Kashag in Lhasa and the abbots of the principal monasteries.

Within the monasteries the monks were prepared to lend their support to a movement dedicated to the preservation of their faith. One monk, who was at the influential Sera monastery on the outskirts of

Lhasa, recalls that he was able to use his office to provide cover for those guerrilla leaders whose duties required them to come in and out of the capital. As the man in charge of funerary rites he included their names among the dead so that the Chinese would strike them from their watch lists.[31] The Chinese overlords were quite aware of the threat that was gathering momentum in Lhoka and demanded that the Tibetan government take steps to quell it. The Kashag responded with a pro forma demand that Gompo appear before the provincial government to explain his actions, but he had no intention of putting himself within the range of the Chinese.

Shortly after the proclamation of the VVF, Gompo relocated its headquarters to a site farther east, but still in the Lhoka region south of the Tsangpo River, roughly one hundred and twenty miles north of the Indian border. By this time Athar, one of the men dropped in the area south of Lhasa the previous September, had made his way back to India where he was coordinating the first drop of arms that CIA was planning to make to Gompo's organization.[32]

But Gompo had decided not to wait and set off with seven hundred and fifty men for the government armory at Shanggaden Chokhor, where he hoped to seize additional arms. This armory is located in the mountainous region roughly one hundred and fifty miles west of Lhasa and thirty miles north of Tashilumpo, the seat of the Panchen Lama. The Chinese lay in ambush at a place called Nyemo, approximately halfway to the group's destination. A fierce three-day battle took place in late August of 1958, in which the Tibetans killed approximately two hundred and wounded an unknown number of Chinese, while suffering forty dead, sixty-eight wounded, and the loss of about fifty mules and horses.[33]

Gompo and his men were then able to move on to Shanggaden Chokhor, where officials at first made a show of refusing to yield anything from the government armory, acting, they said, under orders from the Chinese-controlled Tibetan government in Lhasa. One of Gompo's company commanders said this show of resistance was part of a deal Gompo had made with the local officials. Three of the monks who secretly supported the resistance were ostensibly taken hostage to demonstrate to the Chinese that a genuine raid had taken place and the armory had been compelled to yield to superior force.[34] The monks were released that same evening, and Gompo's men went off to distribute weapons and ammunition from the armory.[35] With these arms he was ready to make his way north. There they attacked the Chinese at the Damshung airfield north of Lhasa, along the Tibet-Qinghai highway, a principal supply route for the Chinese. In late October the volunteer army engaged a vastly superior number of Chinese troops in a series of battles in which the Tibetans claimed lopsided victories in terms of casualties, hundreds against Chinese losses in the thousands. In one of these fierce battles, Gompo Tashi suffered multiple wounds that were to lead to his death six years later. The wounded warrior was nevertheless able to retain command of his troops and start moving them east across the barren 15,000-foot Chang Tang Plateau.

     ℛ

The winter storms had begun and the snow was knee deep, but the guerrillas kept moving until they reached Chakra Pembar in northwestern Kham in early December. On the way, five officers and one hundred and twenty men deserted when a former guerrilla, who had escaped after being captured by the Chinese, brought back reports that the Chinese were bringing in more reinforcements to eradicate every Khampa in the area. At Chakra Pembar, Gompo was in friendly and relatively safe territory where he could regroup. He then made a joint attack to cut the Sichuan-Lhasa highway using his regulars, new recruits from the area, and men from the force that had been left behind in Lhoka. The target was Po Tamo, a town built on this vital supply route by the Chinese. The Lhoka force did not reach Po Tamo in time, but Gompo's forces fought a fortnight's battle, again with disproportionately small losses.

In an ambush in the same area, four hundred locals with the aid of twenty-nine of Gompo's men again claimed heavy Chinese casualties and destroyed a number of trucks. At a meeting with about seventy local leaders, Gompo's appeal for new recruits added several thousand new men, and a friendly governor turned over one hundred rifles and 50,000 rounds of ammunition, along with rice and other supplies from Chinese stocks. These reinforcements of men and supplies permitted Gompo to continue operations in this area until the end of the following February, when the Chinese finally brought in airplanes and began machine gunning the men from the air. Gompo said his men "were simply not equipped to resist this kind of warfare," and they began plans to relocate.

The force that had remained behind in Lhoka had also expanded and was claiming control of a larger portion of this area. In January 1959 they laid siege to the Chinese garrison at Tsetang and neutralized it. This was a significant victory. Legend says that the Tibetan race began centuries ago in a Tsetang cave when the patron deity of Tibet, Chenrezi, then in the form of a monkey, consorted with a she-devil and produced six children. They multiplied thanks to Chenrezi's gift of the "golden grain" of barley. In addition to its symbolic importance, Tsetang is a mere two days from the gates of Lhasa. This indicated the strength of the challenge to the Chinese by the Volunteer Freedom Fighters. By early 1959 the rebels were in effective control of large pockets of central Tibet, and the Chinese were definitely under siege.

☙

When Gompo Tashi left his Lhoka headquarters to campaign in the north,[36] Lhotse, the second man and radio operator who had been dropped with Athar the previous autumn, remained behind to receive the CIA airdrops that his partner Athar had gone to India to coordinate. The first of these drops was made in July of 1958, a month after Gompo had departed. Lhotse had arranged for the arms to be delivered to the freedom fighters' headquarters for distribution to the unarmed. By the time the second drop was made on February 22, 1959, Athar had rejoined Lhotse. Lhamo Tsering's records show that these two drops contained 403 Lee Enfield rifles, 60 hand grenades, 20 machine guns, and 26,000 rounds of ammunition.[37]

Given the number of volunteers that had assembled in Lhoka by the autumn of 1958, the arms supplied in these two drops did not make an appreciable difference to the outcome of the resistance in the Lhoka region in 1958 and 1959. Gompo Tashi had fought his battles in the north with the arms he seized on his own and the airdropped weapons themselves became a source of dispute. The number airdropped in July of 1958 simply could not match the demand from the large number of volunteers that had assembled in Lhoka by late summer. There were twenty-eight different groups—the freedom fighters were not as cohesive as they had seemed on the parade ground—and several leaders laid claim to weapons, arguing that they needed them to participate in Gompo's offensive along the Sichuan-Lhasa highway. The first drop contained a relatively small amount of Indian rupees for the expenses of Athar and Lhotse. Gyalo later reported that the size of the sum was exaggerated among the rebel recruits, leading to jealousy. Athar and Lhotse had not been able to distribute the weapons in the second drop before operations from their base were overtaken by the tumultuous events in Lhasa. These arms were carried out by the freedom fighters when they were forced to seek refuge in India.

Nevertheless the spigot had been opened and the commitment held to supply arms and trained men to resistance forces in Tibet when justified by reliable intelligence reports. The airdrop made in July 1958 was the first of more than thirty during the following three years. They operated with crews and aircraft under the aegis of the CIA's proprietary company, Civil Air Transport. Parachute dispatch officers were mainly "smoke jumpers" recruited in Montana from the U.S. Forest Service, alternating between their regular job of putting out fires and keeping them alive in Tibet.[38] They came to be known as the "Missoula Mafia."

The first seven of these flights used C-118 aircraft. None of these earlier flights was detected or attacked by the Chinese despite the long flights over hostile territory for several hours.[39] In the four years from 1957 to 1961, only one crew reported hostile fire, and even that apparently came only from small arms. One pilot reported a near miss with a mountain peak of more than 25,000 feet that was not on his navigational chart. The crews also reported winds of more than one hundred miles an hour that blew them hundreds of miles off course so they could not return to their staging base in Thailand.[40] The configuration of the C-118s also presented problems that resulted in two near misses. A crew member was knocked unconscious by a loose static line, and on another occasion the same man came close to being accidentally forced out of the plane while making a drop over Tibet.

The problems of operating at extreme altitudes and weather conditions threatened the safety of the crews, and the capacity of the C-118s was limited to 12,000 pounds. In a personal telephone call, the CIA's deputy director, General Charles P. Cabell, asked his old Air Force colleague General Curtis LeMay to provide new and much larger C-130 cargo planes. Cabell felt the increased safety of the crews would more than compensate for the loss of the fig leaf of deniability resulting from using an official military plane. LeMay readily granted the request, and, starting in 1959, all drops of men and equipment were made from C-130s with their USAF markings removed. The C-130s enabled the CIA eventually to double the loads to more than 25,000 pounds, sometimes three nights in a row.[41] More than 500,000 pounds—250 tons—of equipment, arms, ammunition, radios, medical supplies, and other military gear, as well as hand-operated printing presses, were dropped by the CIA to the Tibetan resistance forces from 1957 to 1961.[42]

By 1958 the CIA had thus undertaken a full-scale commitment to support the Tibetan resistance. The State Department fully supported the operation, and the Defense Department gave equally full cooperation. When it became apparent early in 1958 that the trainees were getting sick in the lower altitudes of the eastern seacoast site where they were being trained, the Pentagon offered the use of the deactivated Camp Hale near Leadville, Colorado, where the U.S. Tenth Mountain Division trained during World War II. The command at Fort Carson at Colorado Springs readily turned to the task of building the required barracks and arranging for troops to provide security for the site. By Memorial Day, 1958, the second group of trainees was relocated to Camp Hale,[43] where Tibetan resistance training was conducted for the next six years.

This impressive demonstration of cooperation was typical of the generation of World War II veterans then in government. They felt they were carrying out operations literally designed to avoid World War III. Within the CIA, the prototype of this new operations man, with the zest and ability to make the machinery of the U.S. government respond to the new activist policy, was the newly appointed chief of the Operations Directorate's Far East Division, Desmond FitzGerald.[44]

As an army captain serving as a U.S. liaison officer to a Chinese battalion in Burma from 1943 to 1945, FitzGerald had come to appreciate the fighting qualities of the ordinary Chinese soldier when properly led. However, he had also come away with a poor opinion of Chiang K'ai-shek because of the generalissimo's shabby treatment of FitzGerald's field commander, General Joseph Stilwell, whose legendary loyalty and identification with his men FitzGerald admired. FitzGerald's disdain for Chiang was reinforced by the consistently unsuccessful and often irresponsible Chinese Nationalist operations on the mainland, which it was his job to support while he was chief of the CIA China mission in Japan and later the Philippines, until it closed down with his endorsement in 1956. He was equally disillusioned with the daring but unproductive U.S. paramilitary operations behind the lines in Korea and the feckless efforts to oust President Sukarno of Indonesia in 1957 and 1958. After some months as a staff chief in the Operations Directorate, during which he had demonstrated his personal loyalty to his ailing friend Frank Wisner, FitzGerald was ready to take on a new challenge as the man in charge of CIA's operations in the Far East.

The rugged Tibetans appealed to both FitzGerald's romantic spirit and his belief that insurgencies initiated by local people fighting for their own land and beliefs were the only effective way to challenge Chinese Communist expansion in Asia. The Khampa fighters asked only for the means of carrying on their own fight to preserve an ancient culture and religion. To him they seemed like worthy and natural recipients for both paramilitary and political assistance. William Colby said, "The Tibet operations were Dez's baby all the way."[45]

By 1958, the two persons in the CIA chain of command above FitzGerald and below Director Allen Dulles were Richard Bissell, the newly appointed director of operations and his deputy, Richard Helms. Bissell, as a newcomer to the operations world, was prepared to defer to his creative and capable chief of Far East operations. Helms was primarily interested in what he considered was CIA's proper business of intelligence collection rather than the covert political operations that George

Kennan had levied on the CIA ten years before. Dulles was attracted by FitzGerald's imagination and sense of daring, backed by his credentials as a fellow Wall Street lawyer and his impeccable social connections, coupled with his ability to get things done. He was therefore prepared to support FitzGerald and protect him within the little group in the executive branch that decided national security policy and its implementation.[46] FitzGerald thus had a free hand to call on the resources of both the Defense and State Departments. He assembled a group of experienced officers whom he had vetted during the previous five years, observing them in various paramilitary programs in Korea, Thailand, and China. Although at times arrogant, and always unmistakably a Boston Brahmin, FitzGerald commanded the allegiance of a diverse but tight little group, and he reciprocated their loyalty and dedication to a cause in which they all came to believe. All of the elements for full support of the Tibetan resistance movement were thus in place.

In describing FitzGerald's role it would be misleading to leave the impression that he was merely a gifted and dashing operator or a cavalier dilettante. He was a responsible man who questioned the moral issues and objectives of the operations conceived and conducted by his division. He, too, had been deeply affected by the frustrations felt by many CIA officers over what had—and had not—happened in Hungary. In this context, he could not avoid questioning whether the U.S. government was doing the Tibetans a favor by providing assistance, and he reminded at least one of his colleagues that the CIA was dropping human beings and "not confetti" out of planes over Tibet.[47] He was ultimately convinced by intelligence reports that the Tibetans had undertaken their resistance on their own initiative, that they would continue it with or without U.S. support, and that the moral path lay in providing them with reliable modern arms and equipment to replace the inadequate weapons they were using in their unequal battle against the well-armed Chinese forces.

❧

Throughout this period of looming confrontation, Beijing seemed strangely blind to the effect of its uncertain policies. In accordance with the declarations made both by Mao and by the Chinese overlord Zhang Gwohua that "reforms" would not be carried out for at least six years, large numbers of Chinese officials were withdrawn in 1957. Since no reforms were imminent their presence was no longer necessary. But there was no corresponding reduction of the Chinese military in Tibet except from Lhasa. More significantly, as far as the growing insurrection was concerned, there was no promise to postpone the reforms in the areas of inner Tibet—the Chinese provinces of Qinghai, Sichuan, and Gansu—where half or more of the total number of ethnic Tibetans lived.[48]

Throughout 1957 and 1958 local Chinese cadres continued to impose the programs that Mao had promised to postpone. In Gyantse, in central Tibet, the traditional right of local chieftains to levy corvée—roadwork as a form of taxation—on those of their tenants who were being trained by the Chinese as students or cadres to carry out the communization process, was abolished in December 1957. This looked like the forerunner of an attack on the upper strata using the techniques of class warfare that the Chinese had carefully avoided. Then the lamas of the Amdo region were publicly attacked for the first time in the autumn of 1958. Around the same time, the monks stopped receiving rents from the lands that had once belonged to the monasteries but had been reformed into cooperatives. At the same time the Chinese began a propaganda campaign denouncing old superstitions, taboos, customs, and other "religious nonsense designed to deceive the people."[49] While there had been isolated attacks on monks, this was the beginning of a full-scale campaign targeted specifically on monks as "counter-revolutionaries." It was also to produce a swelling of the ranks of the resistance.

These policies may have been a reflection of the upheavals in China proper where the "Great Leap Forward" had been inaugurated with great fanfare in the spring and summer of 1958. Promulgated by Mao as an alternative to the Soviet development strategy, this new approach was based on the mass mobilization programs used in the war years against the Japanese. This program also transferred considerable political power from the central government to local cadres. Technicians were replaced by political agitators. This seemed to fit the pattern of what was occurring in the sensitive rural areas of Tibet, particularly in the already aroused eastern region.

This disregard of consequences was matched by the political and psychological campaign to "liberate" Taiwan that Mao inaugurated that summer, shelling the off-shore islands and proclaiming a twelve-mile limit in the Taiwan straits. Secretary Dulles countered with a declaration that the U.S. would continue to recognize a three-mile limit and would use force if necessary to defend Taiwan. Khrushchev's belated support of his Chinese ally only earned Mao's growing contempt. Although both China and the U.S. backed down later that autumn, this crisis paralleled the political mobilization of the countryside. It may have diverted Beijing's attention to what was occurring in its unruly new colony, or at least have caused Mao to hesitate about engaging in an all-out military campaign on his western border when he might have to use his forces on his eastern coast. In any event, Mao's campaign did nothing to lessen the ardor in Washington to do whatever was possible to thwart China's expansionist ambitions.

The other principals reacted characteristically to the growing rebellion in Tibet. The British continued to dismiss the reports of insurrection and disclaim interest in the situation.[50] Nehru showed Beijing that India still maintained an interest in events in Tibet by forcing the Chinese to receive him in southern Tibet; they had canceled a scheduled trip to Lhasa, claiming that they could not guarantee his safety there. Nehru meanwhile sent what seemed to be a signal to Washington that India might not object to U.S. aid to the Tibetans. An Indian Home Office official showed the U.S. consul general in Calcutta a letter from an unidentified Tibetan reporting on the fighting across the border and stressing the insurgents' need for arms; the official said he thought the U.S. government might be interested in the arms appeal.[51] The Chinese Nationalists, meanwhile, turned down a suggestion from one of their most sympathetic supporters, Assistant Secretary Walter S. Robertson, that "it might help the dissidents in Tibet if President Chiang were to renounce Chinese claims to sovereignty over Tibet."[52] If there was one thing that Mao and Chiang agreed on, it was that Tibet was part of China. Even as a dispossessed landlord, the Chinese Nationalist president was not going to agree to any diminution of the Chinese empire. If the orphans were to receive any help, it could only come from the U.S.

CHAPTER 9

The Dalai Lama Leaves Tibet

EARLY IN January of 1959, three of Gompo Tashi's commanders attacked and overran Tengchen, a Chinese fortress in Kham, some two hundred miles east of Lhasa. Gompo's forces had already been strengthened by volunteers, and the victory attracted even more. The invigorated forces went on to challenge the Chinese in a series of fierce battles north of the Tibet-Sichuan highway until aerial attacks stopped their offensive. Realizing that he could not take on sizable Chinese forces, Gompo changed tactics.[1] After the Tibetan New Year late in February, he moved south in Kham to reorganize the resistance movement into small guerrilla units that would concentrate on cutting the road and other communications of the occupying forces with China proper. At a war council in late February 1959 he and his commanders also decided that it was no longer safe for him to remain in the Kham area exposing his substantial army of veteran troops. Gompo therefore began filtering his men into central Tibet to operate in small units against the Chinese forces guarding their main supply route.

Gompo's successes attracted keen attention in intelligence channels if not yet in the international press. Debriefings of his men who were able to make their way into India disclosed that their comrades controlled the area between the Brahmaputra River and the border.[2] The British High Commission in New Delhi had similarly reported that, while the Indian authorities were playing down reports of the Khampa revolt, their own reports confirmed the uprising was gathering force in the Brahmaputra basin region.[3] The Chinese Nationalist government with its customary hyperbole hailed the Tibetan resistance as part of a "general revolt in the vast Chinese hinterland . . . comprising about 60 percent of the mainland."[4] Jigme Dorje, the prime minister of Bhutan, told the press that "trouble was brewing in Tibet" and warned that the Bhutan militia would repel any rebels trying to cross the border. This show of concern was undoubtedly made for the benefit of the Chinese in an effort to buy protection, since he had allowed the Khampa leaders to transit his country.[5]

In Washington, planning was moving forward for an ambitious program of increased support. While only one of the Tibetan radio teams was still operating in the early spring of 1959, it was in a position that seemed to be ideal to serve as a base for future airdrops. The Chinese economy was beginning to founder following the first year of Mao's disastrous Great Leap Forward, and the Tibetan guerrillas seemed well positioned to place additional burdens on their stretched military forces. John L. Hart, the officer then in charge of CIA's China operations, described the Tibet program as "sui generis."[6] There was, he said, something so "special" about Tibet that no opposition arose within the U.S. government to whatever CIA proposed in support of the resistance. He recalled a certain sense of romance attached to the Dalai Lama and his cause, a "Shangri-la factor" that permitted free range in sustaining operations as long as they harassed the Chinese Communists and by extension the Soviet Union, the monolithic nature of the communist empire then being an article of faith in Washington.

Everything was fair game, and in those freewheeling days most approvals were given orally and few records of operational details were kept. The State Department posed no opposition, and the Pentagon "fell all over themselves to be helpful," Hart recalled. He summed it up as "the perfect operation. No one, neither the U.S. for whom any fall-out sensitivities were remote, or the Tibetans who were already fighting, had anything to lose. Quite the contrary, they both had everything to gain."

LAST DAYS IN LHASA

After denying approval to the operations in which Gompo Tashi and the other resistance leaders were engaged, the Dalai Lama withdrew to the nearby Drepung and Sera monasteries[7] to immerse himself in studies for his final monastic examinations. He refused the demand of the Chinese political commissar, General Tan Guansen, to order out the Tibetan army against the resistance, pointing out that the soldiers would take the opportunity to join their rebelling fellow countrymen. He did acquiesce in Tan's demand to revoke the Tibetan citizenship of his two brothers, Takster and Gyalo, who were attracting international attention to the resistance. He agreed to do this because he felt they were safe abroad. It was one more conciliatory gesture in the hope of heading off a military confrontation with the Chinese.

On March 5, 1959, he left Tibet's most revered religious structure, the 1,300-year-old Jokhang, where he had spent the past four days celebrating the Great Prayer Festival of Monlam and being examined on classical Buddhist logic, canon law, philosophy, and metaphysics. He passed with flying colors. The now fully accredited reincarnate lama then made—for what may have been his last time—the traditional splendid procession that incorporated, as he described it, "the full pageantry of more than one thousand years of uninterrupted civilization" back to his summer palace, the Norbulingka.[8] He noted an unprecedented number of pilgrims circumambulating the Jokhang and an air of expectancy "as if everyone knew that something momentous was about to happen."9

Momentous events were about to happen. Once back at the Norbulingka, he had to face the command theatrical performance that he had agreed to attend at the Chinese military camp on the outskirts of Lhasa. He had further accepted the condition that he leave behind his usual twenty-five armed bodyguards. His host, the political commissar of Lhasa, General Tan Guansen, had stipulated that only two or three unarmed Tibetan guards were to be permitted to cross the Stone Bridge into the Chinese camp, which was resented and feared by the Lhasans as an eyesore and a symbol of repression. He knew his people would dislike his undertaking such an unprecedented venture, but he planned to go quietly and without public notice. It was impossible, however, to preserve secrecy about this semifurtive entry into the jaws of the dragon by a revered leader whose every public move attracted venerating crowds. This was particularly true at this time when the pilgrims who had come to Lhasa to celebrate the Monlam festival were still there. They had inflated the population of the capital to over 100,000, three times its normal size, and it could be expected that enormous crowds would turn out for any move of their leader from his palace, especially in the direction of the hated Chinese army camp.

In what turned out to be a fateful decision, the Dalai Lama's officials decided to issue a public warning that special traffic restrictions would be in force the day the Dalai Lama was to make his visit to the camp. No one would be allowed on the road beyond the bridge leading to the camp. While intended to head off a dangerous confrontation, it had exactly the reverse effect. Rumors quickly spread through the swollen and aroused population of Lhasa that the Chinese intended to kidnap their leader. When the Dalai Lama awakened on the day of the visit he found the Norbulingka grounds, a pleasant wooded park covering a few acres less than two miles from the center of Lhasa, surrounded by a crowd of an estimated 30,000. They were determined to prevent him from keeping his appointment with the Chinese.

There then followed a week of frantic communications between the Dalai Lama,10 desperate to find a way out of fulfilling an engagement that would surely provoke his militantly protective supporters into bloodshed, and an increasingly infuriated Tan. The Dalai Lama warned that the Chinese would take military action, but failed to persuade the crowds to disperse. General Tan wrote him three times inviting him to take refuge in the Chinese camp for his own safety. To buy time, the Dalai Lama diplomatically replied each time expressing his embarrassment that the uproar created by his misguided people prevented him from visiting the general's headquarters. He was now caught in a web of events, few of his making or liking, among supporters who would surely be killed if he remained in the Norbulingka, a resistance effort that he was morally unable to endorse, and an unyielding occupier with whom he could no longer find an accommodation.

On the morning of March 17 the Dalai Lama and his cabinet made one final effort to head off destruction of the Norbulingka and a massacre of its unyielding protectors. In a letter to Ngabo Ngawang Jigme, their cabinet colleague who had been sent to Tan's camp some days earlier to explain the explosive situation, they admitted that their defenders were acting unwisely under the stress of emotion, but there was still hope that the crowds could be persuaded to end their protective siege of the palace. They asked Ngabo to find a way of conveying the Dalai Lama to the Chinese camp by somehow evading the crowd. This last desperate effort to placate the infuriated General Tan was smuggled to Ngabo, who sent a brief acknowledgment promising a detailed answer.

That afternoon two mortar shells, presumably from the nearby Chinese camp, landed in the marsh outside the north gate of the Norbulingka. The Dalai Lama realized that time to negotiate with the Chinese generals had expired. He would have to leave Lhasa lest his own people make sacrificial targets of themselves to preserve his own office, which they prized so dearly.[11]

That same evening the invaluable Phala helped put together an escape party, just as he had nine years earlier when he and his charge were fleeing from an impending but then unknown peril. Now the danger was present and real. The party was picked by Phala, the four Kashag members still present, and the highest monastic official in the government, Chikyab Khembo Gadgrang. While all those close to the Dalai

Lama wanted to accompany him, the party had to be limited to the smallest possible number to slip out of the Norbulingka undetected by both the Tibetan protectors and the potential Chinese captors. In addition to Phala, the four ministers present in the compound made the cut, leaving behind Ngabo to continue his ambiguous relationship with the Chinese.[12] The party was completed by the Dalai Lama's mother, elder sister, youngest brother, and the two tutors who had accompanied him on his similar flight to Yatung in 1950, along with a small number of personal officials and his bodyguard, commanded by his brother-in-law. It was still a sizable number. To pass through the crowd, its elected leaders were informed of the escape plot and sworn to secrecy.

Late that night the Dalai Lama went to the chapel in his small palace and left a scarf on the altar as a symbol of farewell. Wearing a soldier's uniform and fur cap, carrying a rifle, but without his glasses, he accompanied Phala, his other senior abbot, his brother-in-law, and two soldiers out of the Norbulingka gate. The Tibetan guards were told that the senior abbot was making an inspection tour of the perimeter. The Dalai Lama thus passed undetected through the crowd to the bank of a tributary of the Brahmaputra, less than a quarter of a mile away. They crossed in traditional round coracles and were reunited on the south bank of the river with the Dalai Lama's family and other members of the party. Thirty Khampa soldiers and their leaders from the forces alerted by Phala were also waiting with ponies.

The following morning the party crossed Che-la, a high mountain pass, on its way toward the Brahmaputra, the last physical barrier before the mountainous and roadless Lhoka area. Ten miles from the foot of the southern side of the pass they crossed the river by ferry under the cover of a sandstorm they considered heaven-sent. A welcoming party of Khampa soldiers and volunteers wearing the yellow and white armbands of the Volunteer Army meant they were now in territory controlled by the resistance. The escape party, which by then had grown to about one hundred people, separated into small groups. They were protected by unseen resistance bands covering their flanks as they passed through the mountains.

When the party was nearing Chenye, approximately one hundred miles south of Lhasa, they heard Voice of America broadcasts reporting that Lhasa was in a state of unrest and the whereabouts of the Dalai Lama was unknown. Soon thereafter the fleeing ruler received word by courier that the Norbulingka had been shelled forty-eight hours after his flight, but before the Chinese realized he was gone. It was apparent that the Chinese had fired on the palace in the belief that the Dalai Lama was still there. Then they turned their guns on the rebelling Lhasans, marking an end to any Chinese efforts at accommodation.

Even so, the Dalai Lama clung to the hope of establishing a temporary government in southern Tibet from which to negotiate with the Chinese, as he had done from Yatung nine years earlier. Before moving on to search for a haven within Tibet, he met with resistance leaders. Here again he had to confront his fundamental moral dilemma between means and ends. He wrote that he "very much admired their courage and their determination to carry on the grim battle they had started for our freedom, culture and religion."[13] He thanked them for their strength and bravery, and more personally, for their protection. He apologized for the government proclamations denouncing the resistance fighters as reactionaries and bandits, and explained they had been dictated by the Chinese. He admitted that "by then he could not in honesty advise them to avoid violence. In order to fight, they had sacrificed their homes and all the comforts and benefits of a peaceful life. Now they could see no alternative but to go on fighting, and I had none to offer."

While en route he had also written Gompo Tashi a letter conferring on him the rank of general for his leadership "with unshakable determination to resist the Chinese occupation army for the great national cause of defending the freedom of Tibet."[14] The previously ambivalent young monk now noted that "the present situation calls for a continuance of your brave struggle with the same determination and courage."

Asylum in India

Two days later the party heard the news that the Chinese had announced the dissolution of the Tibetan government.[15] A State Council Order dated March 28 portrayed the Dalai Lama as still loyal to the Chinese; his replacement, the Panchen Lama, was described as temporary. Despite Mao and Zhou's earlier assurance to respect Tibetan customs, "democratic reforms" were now to be introduced, and the lower-level Chinese administrative organs abolished in 1957 were to be restored. The order blamed the "upper strata" rebels for choosing their own extinction and accused the "reactionaries" of having abrogated the 1951 Seventeen Point Agreement, which implied that Beijing now considered it null and void. It also referred to Kalimpong as the "command center" of the rebellion, foreshadowing charges of Indian collaboration.

This declaration by the Chinese made the establishment of a temporary government a political necessity for the Dalai Lama lest his people believe he had acquiesced in the Chinese order. He therefore announced the formation of his own Tibetan government with full religious rites and ordered it to be proclaimed throughout Tibet. These ceremonies, which were attended by more than a thousand people, were held at Lhuntse Dzong, a resistance stronghold approximately sixty miles from the Indian border. Like the formal establishment of the Volunteer Freedom Fighters and the epic journey itself, this consecration of a new government was filmed in color by one of the radio operators trained by the CIA. Whether history or propaganda was uppermost in their minds as the cameras turned, the guerrillas passed the film to the Dalai Lama's government-in-exile, which in turn made it available to the international media.

After the ceremonies, the Dalai Lama met with his advisers and reviewed the continuing reports of Chinese troop movements into the area. They realized that as long as the Dalai Lama remained in Tibet the Chinese would hunt him down. The Dalai Lama and his advisers finally decided they had no choice but to seek asylum in India.

One of Phala's last acts before leaving Lhasa had been to send Taikhang Gomo, a junior government official, to notify the Indian consul general, a Major Thapur, that the Dalai Lama was leaving Lhasa to join with the Khampa resistance fighters and might have to flee to India.[16] Phala also asked Thapur to inform Nehru and his officials, which the Indian major agreed to do by telegraph in code. Soon afterward, in New Delhi, Gyalo Thondup approached Nehru to request asylum for his younger brother if it should appear necessary. Nehru replied at once, "Of course, Mr. Thondup."[17]

In Washington, meanwhile, CIA Director Dulles had briefed the National Security Council on the revolt in Lhasa, which, despite the endorsements his agents had been unable to obtain the year before, he said "the Lama supported."[18] He attributed the cause to the Tibetan people's efforts to thwart Chinese plans to kidnap the Dalai Lama. According to his account the Chinese had first tried a policy of leniency but had been subsequently "obliged to take strong measures." A small group of officials in Washington, including the president, had been following the Dalai Lama's journey through messages sent by the two CIA-trained radio operators dropped the previous summer.[19] The operators, who had radio communication only with the CIA in Washington, had joined the escape party outside Lhasa when it met its escorts from the resistance forces. It was therefore some days after the Dalai Lama was on his way that the CIA learned of his flight. After the meeting at Lhunste Dzong, at which the Dalai Lama decided he had no choice but to leave Tibet, the team sent a message asking that a formal request for asylum be forwarded to the Indian government. The message arrived in Washington at midnight on March 28, 1959, a Saturday night. Desmond FitzGerald immediately ordered it forwarded to New Delhi for action, feeling sufficiently certain of the collective intention of the U.S. government to lend its full resources toward preserving the Dalai Lama and his cause. FitzGerald approved the action without waking those within the Washington hierarchy whose coordination would usually have been sought on such an extraordinary request for action. Nehru's full and unhesitating assent was received that same morning, at 6 A.M. Washington time.[20]

The last message from the team reported that the Dalai Lama and his party had safely crossed the Indian border on March 31 and would arrive in Tawang in India's North East Frontier Agency within three days. After describing the continuing shelling of the populace in Lhasa, the drafters of the radio message from the Dalai Lama's party asked Washington to "inform the world of the suffering of the Tibetan people."[21] But it was the Chinese Communists on April 2 who were the first to break the news of the Dalai Lama's arrival in India, charging in a broadcast from Beijing that he had reached there "under duress by rebellious elements."[22]

✑

While his grant of asylum had been spontaneous and unqualified, the Dalai Lama's arrival forced Nehru to confront the personally and politically embarrassing problem of the Chinese presence in Tibet. For nine years he had been juggling the harsh facts of an increasingly oppressive occupation in Tibet against his public advocacy of China as a worthy cosponsor of peaceful coexistence. Five years earlier he had tried to wash his hands of the messy problem of the Tibetans' claim to independence by recognizing China's sovereignty. But Tibet's unwilling subjects refused to accept it. Their early resistance in the remote border regions could be ignored, but now the use of superior force by shelling an armed populace— right on the doorstep of the Indian consulate—and the Dalai Lama's dramatic flight for his life were front page news in the Indian and the international press.

As a leader in India's long and arduous struggle for its own independence against a foreign power, Nehru sympathized with the aspirations of subject peoples. While his country had finally been granted its independence in a peaceful turnover of authority, it had come only after decades of resistance and was accompanied by ugly internecine bloodletting. As a Kashmiri Brahman he had an additional sense of identity with remote and neighboring mountain people who had preserved their cultural integrity against alien invaders over the centuries (this had been demonstrated by his offer to Gyalo back in 1949 to protect Tibet's cultural treasures). He was also well aware of the significance of the world's premier Buddhist coming to reside in the land of Buddha's birth. He must also have felt some discomfort that it was he who had pushed the Dalai Lama back to his country two years before with assurances of the benevolence of his Chinese overlords, which had proven to be unfounded. He was also aware, however, of India's limited capabilities should it want to provide any effective military assistance to its northern neighbor. He was presiding over an overpopulated, underfed, and undeveloped nation. Its military budget, which it could ill afford, was overwhelmingly devoted to preparing for a war with Pakistan, not China, particularly not on behalf of legatee semidependents from whom India had been trying to divest any responsibility for the past twelve years.

Nehru had to find a way to defend himself against the inevitable domestic criticism of his past policies, which had accepted China's takeover of this long-established buffer and India's inability to do little more than provide hospitality to the prime casualty of the situation. He also had to handle this defense in a manner that would preserve his options with the Chinese, with whom he wanted and felt obliged to preserve at least the facade of peaceful coexistence. The Cold War had arrived on his doorstep in the person of the Dalai Lama. Although Nehru wriggled hard to keep aloof, the welcome provided to the Dalai Lama and his entourage, and the hospitality subsequently shown to the Tibetan refugees, reflected well on him and his people. His initial statements in Parliament on March 23 tried to play down what was happening in Lhasa as an internal affair. The U.S. embassy noted, however, that "by announcing that his government had put the Chinese on notice to safeguard Indian personnel and property in Lhasa and by expressing a pious hope for the safety of the Dalai Lama, Nehru had revealed some slight shift from his previous Pollyanna attitude."[23]

A statement issued by the Chinese embassy in New Delhi five days later accused India of permitting the rebels to base their command center in Kalimpong and criticized the Indian Parliament of acting improperly by discussing events in Tibet. In a strong extemporaneous reply, Nehru recalled that Zhou Enlai had already assured him that Tibet was not a province of China, "but was autonomous and the Chinese Communists intended that it remains so."[24] Nehru then cited the geographic, economic, cultural, and religious ties between India and Tibet, and described the fighting in Lhasa, saying "Indian sympathies go out to the Tibetans." He denied the Chinese charges that Kalimpong was a center for the revolt, although a few days later in a follow-up debate he admitted that he had been told "there were more spies in Kalimpong than the rest of the inhabitants."[25]

Nehru did not cite some of Kalimpong's more colorful residents. Adrian Conan Doyle had spent considerable time there attempting a spiritualist reunion with his late father, the great mystery writer. There was also an exiled Burmese prince who regularly tried to murder his servants, and a White Russian mystic named Roerich who was the "Dear Guru" to whom the former U.S. Vice President Henry Wallace had addressed a letter seeking advice. However, when Prince Peter of Greece and Denmark spoke out three weeks later against India's passive policy on Tibet, he and his White Russian wife were expelled. Long resident in Kalimpong, the prince was an anthropologist who published his studies of the Tibetans and regional hill tribes. This and his friendship with Gyalo Thondup led to suspicions that he was a spy. Thondup, a frequent tennis partner, dismissed this as nonsense. He noted that the prince's interest in Tibet was limited to measuring their skulls, 7,000 of them so far, as part of his encyclopedic study of Himalayan polyandry. (After his banishment from India to Denmark, Prince Peter took an active role on behalf of Tibetan refugee children.)

On April 3, Nehru confirmed to a cheering Parliament that the Dalai Lama and a party of eighty officials, members of his family and bodyguards, had crossed into Indian territory three days earlier and had been granted asylum. He said that the young Tibetan ruler was "quite healthy" and would receive "respectful treatment." Two days later the prime minister held a press conference at which the U.S. embassy felt he made it clear that his position concerning events in Tibet was based upon a "mixture of frustration, anger and prudence."[26] His anger and frustration were evident in his questioning of Chinese charges that the Dalai Lama had fled his country under duress, and his pointed repetition of the statements Zhou Enlai had made to him two years earlier that China regarded Tibet as autonomous. The prudential element in his position was demonstrated by his reaffirmation of the great importance he placed on retaining friendly ties between India and China "even though they might differ greatly."

THE DALAI LAMA IN EXILE

P. N. Menon, the former Indian Consul General in Lhasa, had been waiting at Bomdila in India's Northeast Frontier to greet the Dalai Lama when he arrived there after a difficult ten-mile journey by pony from the Tibetan border. Menon had been sent from New Delhi to lay out the ground rules for the Tibetan ruler's political activities in India. Menon expressed Nehru's view that internal autonomy, not independence, should be Tibet's goal and recommended that at his first press conference on Indian soil the Dalai Lama should make only a very brief statement, mainly giving thanks for asylum in India. The Dalai Lama vigorously rejected Menon's counsel, reminding Menon that he had followed Nehru's advice in 1957—and look what had happened. Tibetans now were fighting and dying for complete freedom and independence, he said, and he was determined to struggle for the same goal regardless of the Indian government's attitude.

His own press statement, already drafted, would cite the spontaneous uprising in Lhasa, the Tibetans' peaceful approach to the Chinese Communists, his own escape, the establishment of a free Tibetan government, and would stress that he was in India to oppose the Chinese Communists and appeal to the free countries of the world for support and recognition. When Menon urged the Dalai Lama not to issue such an uncompromising statement, he replied that he hoped the Indian government was not sticking to the disproved line of autonomy but would give him and his people their active support. The resolute young Tibetan ruler then threatened to seek asylum elsewhere if the Indian government found his presence in India embarrassing.[27]

When a shaken Menon cabled this information to his ministry, he was told to let the Dalai Lama speak out except for the establishment of a Tibetan government-in-exile, the termination of the Seventeen Point Agreement, and the three embarrassing letters he had sent to General Tan from the Norbulingka. After further negotiation they arrived at a compromise, allowing the Dalai Lama to issue a full statement of the grievances underlying the rebellion and his own flight. He would avoid reference to a free Tibetan government and the controversial letters and would not specifically denounce the 1951 agreement.

When the Dalai Lama arrived a week later in the tea plantation community of Tezpur in the Indian state of Assam, he was met by some seventy-five correspondents and photographers. He took the highly unusual step of issuing the statement in his own name. While adhering to the agreement not to make declamatory statements on topics the Indians wished him to avoid, his statement was adroitly drafted to get his points across. He spoke of the Tibetan people's strong desire for independence—without demanding that India support such status. He delineated the efforts of his government to adhere to the Seventeen Point Agreement, which they had accepted under duress—without repudiating it at that time. These issues, along with the question of recognition of the free government, were reserved for his meeting with Nehru five days later. He felt he had twice mistakenly accepted Chinese promises of autonomy, once in 1951, and again at Nehru's advice in 1957, and he was unwilling to accept what his people would view as a betrayal for the third time. Three days later, before his meeting with Nehru, the Dalai Lama took full responsibility for his statement, saying, "I stand by it." He felt compelled to make such a forthright public pronouncement to challenge a Chinese news release, which was contending that the impersonal literary style of his statement was not Tibetan at all, insinuating that it had been engineered, along with the revolt itself, by Britain and India, no less.[28]

Nehru and the Dalai Lama met on April 24 in Mussoorie, a hill town in Kipling's *Kim* territory seventy-five miles south of the Tibetan border, where the Tibetan was the guest at the mansion of the Indian industrialist G. D. Birla. A few days before, the prime minister had told a questioner in Parliament who inquired about the distinguished new refugee's political rights that "political activities are not carried on from one country with regard to another." It was not surprising that the two were unable to reconcile their views. Nehru's policy was to work for restoring Tibet's autonomy, while the Dalai Lama remained adamant that he had no alternative but to struggle for independence. (Years later, the Dalai Lama seemed willing to negotiate a settlement envisioning his return to Tibet under some form of autonomy, but it was both psychologically and politically impossible for him even to contemplate such a possibility at that time.) To let Nehru attempt to broker another agreement permitting him to return to Lhasa under yet another Chinese guarantee of autonomy would have destroyed his credibility as a political leader and violated his feelings of gratitude toward his people, who had risked and given their lives to protect him. The two leaders could only agree to disagree on this critical issue.

A White House briefing note for President Eisenhower on this meeting reported that, although the Dalai Lama appeared to be following Nehru's advice to refrain from making public statements, the reorganization of his official staff indicated that he intended "to direct covert political activities from India,"[29] a phrase that presumably referred to the Dalai Lama's intention to function as the head of a government-in-exile even though it might not receive Indian or international recognition.

Nehru later told U.S. Ambassador Ellsworth Bunker that he had warned the Dalai Lama not to expect India to go to war over Tibet, and that the Dalai Lama accepted it. Nor could India supply arms, he said, as this would be tantamount to going to war. He said that the Chinese had mistakenly thought that they could bully India into giving up the Dalai Lama, and what now was going on between China and India was a "moral jiu-jitsu"[30] game in which the defender's trick was to let the attacker knock himself out. Nehru agreed with Bunker that the Chinese would continue to apply repressive tactics, but he believed they would encounter resistance from the Tibetans in the form of guerrilla warfare for a long time.[31]

Nehru also reported to the British high commissioner Malcolm MacDonald that only two checks existed on the Chinese in Tibet. The first was the presence in India of the Dalai Lama, whom they wanted back in Tibet to legitimize their conquest. (The Chinese line was that the Dalai Lama had been kidnapped and taken to India.[32]) The other was the opinion of nonaligned Asian governments and peoples, particularly India. MacDonald commented that Nehru "felt these cards no higher than jacks." But Nehru was more frank with MacDonald than with Bunker.[33] A memo of his conversation with the British high commissioner noted that Nehru had made four important points not made to the U.S. ambassador: the Dalai Lama had never protested the long denial of Tibet's autonomy to the Chinese; the Chinese would ultimately crush all Tibetan armed resistance; the Dalai Lama wanted fighting to cease in Tibet but passive resistance to continue; and the Dalai Lama did not intend to set up a government-in-exile and was not thinking of appealing to the United Nations.

In discussing with his U.S. embassy counterpart the talks that their chiefs had had with the Indian prime minister, one of MacDonald's officers omitted these supplementary points. The High Commission suggested that the Foreign Office exercise the same discreet editing if they passed along MacDonald's account of his talk with Nehru to the U.S. embassy in London, excusing such lack of candor on grounds of preserving a diplomatic confidence. The Foreign Office did give "the cousins" a bowdlerized version of what Nehru told MacDonald, embellishing it with the statement that the Dalai Lama had voluntarily suggested that he had no other plans than to meditate on Tibet's plight and did not expect the Indians to make war or supply arms—much to Nehru's relief.[34] All this cutting and pasting may well have reflected the wishful thinking of both the Indians and the British that they would not have to take a stand or debate the issue with the Americans, whom they would expect to take a more activist position.

On May 22 the U.S. embassy felt the time had come to make an assessment because it believed Nehru's press conference the previous week probably represented the Indian government's last public pronouncements on Tibet for the present.[35] The Dalai Lama's reluctant but steadfast host had said that diplomatic exchanges with China had come to a standstill, that India's main current concern with Tibet was the large number of refugees, and that the Dalai Lama, despite security measures, was free to do as he liked, although Nehru had pointed out to him the need to function wisely and with restraint. His presence in India, Nehru conceded, did create a certain strain in relations with China. The obviously resigned prime minister concluded that, whatever jurists might say about the legal status of Tibet, the issue was one of power politics.

The embassy matched the prime minister's equanimity, commenting that the Indian government, "lacking legal grounds on which to voice objections and military power to threaten the Chinese, had probably gone as far as it could, given the realities and its basic policy of non-alignment, in letting the Chinese know how it felt about their action in Tibet." It noted that although it sought to maintain a correct official posture, the Indian high command had nevertheless encouraged a full expression of popular feeling on Tibet through the press, the political parties, and committees on Tibet. Bunker, who was later called upon to perform difficult diplomatic maneuvering as Lyndon Johnson's ambassador during the Vietnam war, had some appreciation of the performance he was witnessing. His host was balancing his belief in India's special relationship with China, his desire to avoid involvement in the Cold War, and his willingness to tolerate a relatively broad range of free expression and political activity by the Tibetans. This juggling act would collapse when Chinese troops crossed India's northern borders in force three years later.

✍

The Dalai Lama finally spoke out on matters that his hosts had tried to persuade him to remain silent about. On June 20 he held a press conference at his residence in Mussoorie declaring that Tibet had been virtually independent, "enjoying and exercising all rights of sovereignty, whether internal or external" and therefore the Chinese armies had committed aggression.[36] To support his argument, he noted that the structure of the terms and conditions of the "so-called" agreement of 1951 showed that it was a pact between two sovereign states. In any event it was invalid because it had been signed under duress and subsequently violated by the Chinese. He needed to make these points if he was to appeal to the United Nations, an option he kept open.

While expressing appreciation for Nehru's "unfailing kindness and consideration" he pointedly noted that he had put aside the failure of his Chinese overlords to live up to their promises and returned to Tibet in 1957 on Nehru's advice. Again the Chinese had not honored the assurances they had made, resulting in a spontaneous revolt. He then went on to emphasize that he and his government had not been opposed to necessary reforms in the economic, social, and political system prevailing in Tibet. He explained that they had "no desire to disguise the fact that ours is an ancient society and we must introduce immediate changes in the interests of the people of Tibet." It had been his "earnest desire" that the system of land tenure be radically changed by the state acquisition of large landed estates, on payment of compensation, for distribution among the tillers of the soil. His Chinese overlords, however, had "put every obstacle in the way of carrying out this just and reasonable reform." His brother Gyalo Thondup, who was sitting behind him on the platform when he made these statements, must have felt some sense of bitter vindication. He had advocated just such land reforms as a preemptive measure seven years before and had felt forced to flee Tibet when Chinese occupation officials, who had their own plans, and Tibetan aristocrats, unwilling to give up their traditional perquisites, combined to prevent his younger brother from introducing them.

The Dalai Lama now had made all but one of the points that he had originally planned when he sought asylum two months before. The final one concerned recognition of the government he had established on his way into exile, and that delicate matter was handled in response to a question. He declared that "wherever I am accompanied by my Government, the Tibetan people will recognize such as the Government of Tibet." While this formula never earned him the recognition of any foreign government, the Dalai Lama, with tacit Indian acquiescence and support, was able to function essentially as head of a government-in-exile thereafter. He also kept his options open concerning an appeal to the UN, "in case Tibet is not satisfied with the terms of the peaceful settlement" he was asking the Chinese to make with him. Through persistence and good will by both parties, the Dalai Lama and his hosts had arrived at an accommodation permitting him to settle in India and undertake the long political battle to preserve the identity of his country.

CHAPTER 10

Washington Reacts to the Revolt

THE DALAI LAMA'S departure from Lhasa achieved what had been an objective of American policy for almost a decade. Like many answered prayers, the results were not quite what had been anticipated. His unexpected arrival on the doorstep of the international community forced the Eisenhower administration to face several critical issues. As long as the central figure of Tibet's tragedy had remained isolated in Lhasa, Washington had no plan for Tibet in the sense of a coordinated schedule of events designed to fulfill specific policy objectives. James Critchfield, who became chief of CIA's Near East Division in 1959, said his counterpart Desmond FitzGerald in the Far East Division was calling the shots for Tibet, but that operations were essentially "run by the seat of our pants."[1] The formal process of formulating and coordinating U.S. policy decisions, he noted, did not emerge until after the failure of the Bay of Pigs adventure in Cuba two years later.

Now Washington was confronted with these questions: What should be the status accorded the Dalai Lama and his self-proclaimed government? Whether and how should Tibet's case against China be presented to the United Nations? What should be the rationale and means for continuing to support the Tibetan resistance?

When the international press learned on March 23, 1959, that the Dalai Lama had escaped from Lhasa to an unknown destination, all that the Department of State's spokesman, Joseph W. Reap, would say was that the Department had "reliable" reports that a revolt was in progress in Tibet and had been underway since 1950.[2] He was unable to say whether the Department considered Tibet an independent country. He said he assumed it was, but he would "have to look into that."

At the next day's press briefing Reap denied the U.S. was considering supplying arms to the Tibetan rebels, though in fact it already was by CIA airdrop. Further, he said it would be illegal for the Chinese Nationalist government to divert U.S. military equipment to the rebels. Secretary of State Dulles was in Walter Reed hospital dying of cancer, so the following day the press turned to President Eisenhower. He replied noncommittally that the United States did not know enough about what was going on in Tibet to draw a conclusion.

By the next morning Chiang K'ai-shek's government had issued a pledge of self-determination to the Tibetans when the Nationalists regained the mainland. While Chiang's pledge was like promising someone the right to rent or buy a house you hoped to reclaim from well-established occupants, it was a long way from the days when his government was quibbling over the validity of a few Tibetan passports. Reap commended the Nationalist government's statement to the attention of the news-hungry journalists. He also said the United States had "never recognized or condoned" the "so-called" 1951 agreement between Tibet and China. Reap promised a statement on the U.S. position concerning Tibet later that day, but when it came from Acting Secretary

Christian Herter it was less forthcoming than Chiang's. Herter merely said he was "deeply shocked" by reports of the "ruthless suppression of human liberties," and voiced "sadness" at the suffering of the Tibetans.[3] These lofty sentiments did not include any mention of the U.S. government's view on Tibet's political status, let alone a pledge of support for the Dalai Lama's cause of independence and freedom.

Clearly, Washington was not going to be stampeded into any premature commitments until it knew that the Dalai Lama was safely in India and learned what his reception would be there and how the rest of the world reacted. The final official statement on Tibet was included as part of the State Department's daily press briefing on March 28.[4] It pointed to Beijing's admission that Tibetan resistance to Communist rule had been widespread since 1958 and was continuing, involving by Beijing's own count at least 20,000 "patriots" and the entire Tibetan army. Reap's statement moved one cautious step beyond Herter's by denouncing China's intention of destroying the "historical autonomy of the Tibetan people." But there was again no statement of what the U.S. planned to do nor any pledge of support for the "proud and brave Tibetan people," who were being deprived of "their cherished religious and political autonomy" by the "barbarous intervention of the Chinese imperialists."

✌

For years, one of the principal benefits State Department and CIA officers had expected when the Dalai Lama finally sought asylum was dramatic evidence, particularly to his fellow Asians, of the basically aggressive nature of Chinese Communism. The proclamation of the Five Principles of Peaceful Coexistence by Nehru and Zhou Enlai in 1954, followed by Zhou's bravura performance at the Bandung Conference of nonaligned nations the next year, had given added weight to Washington's objective of demonstrating the shallowness of China's dedication to the concept of peaceful coexistence. They expected that by living and traveling abroad, particularly to the Buddhist countries of Asia, the Dalai Lama would act as a symbol and constant reminder of the danger of trusting Beijing's professions of peaceful intent.

When news of the Dalai Lama's safe arrival in India was flashed around the world, the initial Asian reaction was all that the U.S. government could wish for. A State Department Intelligence Information Brief dated April 14 reported that the non-Communist press in Asia "had universally condemned Communist China's suppression of the Tibetan uprising in forceful terms, which leaves little doubt that the Asian impact of Tibetan developments will far exceed that of the Russian intervention in Hungary . . . "[5] This was attributed to the fact that both the Tibetans and the Chinese were Asians and Buddhists and to the absence of any Western involvement that would otherwise cause the Tibetan revolt to be belittled as another Cold War exercise.

Eisenhower's psychological strategy group, the Operations Coordinating Board (OCB), viewed the Tibetan revolt "as a windfall for the U.S." and pressed for the U.S. government to "keep the rebellion going as long as possible and give it maximum emphasis in all public information media."[6] In a memorandum written two days before the Dalai Lama's escape into India was known, the board's staff representative, Colonel Edwin F. Black, who was apparently not privy to the tightly held message traffic from the escape party, argued that it was in the U.S. government's interest to help the Dalai Lama escape and assist the establishment of a Tibetan government-in-exile in some country other than India where Nehru might "want the whole affair hushed up as soon as possible."

But less fervid counsel prevailed. The U.S. government adopted a policy dubbed by the press, and later used by the OCB, of "strategic silence." This strategy recognized that U.S. interests were best served by avoiding any appearance of exploiting the tragic situation for Cold War advantage. The Chinese Communists were already being castigated satisfactorily by the Asians themselves without further need for encouragement from Washington. Moreover, the Dalai Lama was neither readily accessible nor disposed to turn himself into a traveling road show as a victim of Chinese aggression. For his personal and his hosts' protection against journalists and other sources of political or actual physical danger, the Indians ensured that he lived a very private life. Malcolm MacDonald noted that "rarely was a king so hedged not only by divinity, but by platoons of security police."[7]

This policy of strategic silence seemed well advised at that point in view of the spontaneous denunciations of the Chinese by commentators throughout the world.[8] At a National Security Council meeting on April 23, Defense Secretary Neil H. McElroy expressed concern that the U.S. government was not doing enough to keep the Tibetan situation on the front pages. Herter replied by counseling caution that the government not be seen to be stimulating reactions against the Chinese. Rather, Washington should "covertly assist the Asian peoples themselves to keep the Tibetan action prominently before the world."[9] Allen Dulles "promised to get to work on this problem immediately." But apparently the CIA did not move quickly enough to satisfy the OCB psychological warriors. In a memorandum for discussion on June 3, Colonel Black noted that Tibet had disappeared from the world press, and that even the Chinese Communists seemed to have recognized they had nothing to gain from continuing their denunciations of India. "It looks like Red China agrees with the United States that the best way to hush up the Tibetan Revolt is to pursue a policy of 'strategic silence,'" Black said.[10] He proposed that one way to keep the issue before the world would be to get the Dalai Lama out of India "so that he can present his case to the world uninhibited by Nehru's fears of the Chinese Communists' anger."

While it was still uncertain where the Dalai Lama would settle in exile and what the prospects for resistance were, there was no reason for the administration to drop its "strategic silence." While Senator Mike Mansfield had proposed that the U.S. recognize any government established by the Dalai Lama, other leading Democrats warned against hasty U.S. moves that might diminish the benefits of exposing the ruthlessness of communism and its hostility to religion by any effort "to give a Cold War twist to the situation."[11] Washington needed to know how long the new Asian interest in Tibet could be sustained, whether it could be effectively mobilized to aid the Dalai Lama, and what the U.S. government could and should do about maintaining its support for the resistance.

⁊

The revolt in Lhasa also presented the Chinese Nationalist government with a painful dilemma. The Nationalists had a single-minded commitment to liberate China from Communist rule. Toward this supreme goal, they had vowed to support any uprising on the mainland. This posed two problems: the distances exceeded Chiang's capabilities, and the uprising in Tibet was directed not only against the Communists but Chinese rule of any kind. But if the Nationalists, who called themselves the Government of the Republic of China (GRC), failed to aid the Tibetan resistance now that it had erupted, their claim to be the legitimate rulers of a recovered mainland would lose even more of its already shaken credibility.

Chiang had therefore lost no time in broadcasting his message promising that his government on Taiwan would "assist the Tibetan people to realize their own aspirations in accordance with the principle of self-determination." But his pledge was carefully hedged with the proviso that he would make good on it "as soon as the puppet Communist regime on the mainland is overthrown and the people of Tibet are once again free to express their will."[12]

Vice-President Chen Cheng followed with a press release claiming the Nationalists had maintained close contact with the Tibetan anti-Communist organizations since 1957 and "not only in Tibet, but also in such provinces as Kansu, Chinghai, Szechuan and Sinkiang," and that uprisings there had been launched under Nationalist direction.[13] Both claims fudged the facts. The Nationalists had tried unsuccessfully to foment revolts among the Moslem population in Qinghai, but they had nothing to do either with starting the Tibetan revolt or keeping the resistance going. Furthermore it was obvious from Chen's statements that, although Chiang might have promised self-determination for Tibet at some future date, for the present time his government had not given up its claim to the four provinces that included the Amdo and Kham areas whose inhabitants had contested Chinese Nationalist rule as vigorously as they had the Communists. Chen conceded that, because of the distance, the volume of Nationalist aid had been inadequate, but promised that the Taipei government would "do its utmost and surmount all difficulties to provide them [the Tibetan rebels] support on a large scale."

Washington had been watching this display of Nationalist fervor with some concern, fearing that it would tend to blur the spontaneous nature of the Tibetan uprising and lend credibility to Beijing's charges that it had been instigated by the Nationalists. The embassy in Taipei was asked to convey these concerns and urge the Nationalists to proceed cautiously with any appeal to the United Nations until legal questions about Tibet's status could be resolved and diplomatic support could be obtained.[14]

In private, the Nationalists were far less eager to support the Tibetan fight for independence. When Assistant Secretary Walter Robertson renewed his earlier suggestion, this time to Ambassador George Yeh in Washington, that it would be a great help if the Nationalists would publicly renounce their claims to Tibet, this old-line Nationalist diplomat demurred, citing the Constitution of the Republic of China.[15] Yeh also made the point that of 4 million Tibetan people, only about 1.2 million lived in "Tibet proper" and the rest were residents of the Chinese provinces along the Yangtze headwaters. The Nationalists were as obdurate as their successors on this centuries-old territorial issue. Returning to Chiang's March 26 statement, which similarly deferred action on the promised right of self-determination until after the Nationalists recovered the mainland, Robertson goaded further. He said that such postponement of promised benefits left the impression that the Nationalists were imposing self-limitations on their authority to speak as the government of the whole of China, and this position was therefore a weak and undesirable one. "Our own view, of course is that the Nationalist Government represents the whole of China and therefore can take and announce a position regarding a part of mainland China at any time without having to await recovery of the mainland." Yeh scurried away from this hot potato saying he would report the U.S. views to Taipei.

In Taipei, Foreign Minister Huang told Ambassador Everett Drumright that if the Dalai Lama were to proclaim an autonomous government (which Nehru was then promoting) the Nationalists would give it public support. But if he were to proclaim a separate, independent government, the best Taiwan could offer would be covert moral support. When Drumright informed him that Washington wanted "to keep alive the plight of the Tibetan people and our anxiety to help [them] as much as possible,"[16] Huang confirmed that his government could not aid the Tibetans directly, but he reiterated the hope that the Nationalists could participate in any program of U.S. aid to the Tibetan resistance.

Chiang K'ai-shek was less ready than his ministers to admit his government's inability to intervene on the mainland. He expressed his strong displeasure to Robertson's newly appointed successor, J. Graham Parsons, about what he viewed as the failure of the U.S. to cooperate with him in exploiting the uprising.[17] Chiang insisted that the government of the Republic of China must play a role if it was to justify its mission, and he proposed to undertake guerrilla warfare on the mainland, whether or not the U.S. approved.

According to Lhamo Tsering, the Nationalists had airdropped a radio team in 1950 to a local Tibetan tribal chieftain named Dorje Basang in the Truchu area of the Aba Autonomous Region of Sichuan.[18] This team was unable to organize operations, and the team leader escaped into India and was returned to Taiwan. This was the Nationalists' last direct involvement in Tibetan resistance activities, although they had later dropped men and supplies to Moslem dissidents in the northeastern Amdo region.

Much to the Nationalist government's displeasure, the U.S. government never joined in any program with Taipei to support the Tibetan rebels.[19] This did not discourage the Chiang government from later undertaking activities that frequently crossed with U.S. objectives in Tibet. These principally took the form of backing Tibetans who disagreed with officials of the Dalai Lama's exile government, principally Gyalo Thondup. Years later, Nationalist President Li Teng-hui asked Thondup to convey his apologies to the Dalai Lama for the dissension stirred up by agents of Taipei's Tibet and Mongolian Affairs Commission as late as the midnineties.[20]

But when the climactic moment arrived in 1959, the Nationalists' action, or lack of it, belied their public bombast. They were forced to sit on the sidelines, which was fortunate. Their ineffective but sure to be noticed efforts would have only validated the Communist claims that the rebellion had been instigated from the outside.

SUPPORT FOR THE RESISTANCE

In its last message to the CIA in Washington just before the Dalai Lama crossed into India, the radio team accompanying him urgently requested that the U.S. "help us as soon as possible and send us weapons for 30,000 men by airplane."[21] Although support of this magnitude had never been contemplated by Washington, plans for additional support were already in motion when the Lhasa revolt broke out. Further airdrops were scheduled that spring to the freedom fighters' headquarters at Lhoka in southern Tibet. Tibetans trained at the CIA site in Colorado were also ready to be parachuted back into Tibet to help receive the supply airdrops and train the volunteers in guerrilla warfare.[22] After they had seen the Dalai Lama safely to the Indian border, the freedom fighters' escort party returned to Lhoka, where Gompo Tashi was en route to rejoin the main body of his troops. He had already been instructed by the CIA to regroup his forces to receive the forthcoming supplies.

In a memorandum dated April 1, 1959, before the Dalai Lama's arrival in India had been announced, Allen Dulles informed the president that plans were being made by the CIA "within existing policy authorizations . . . in light of the recent upsurge of Tibetan resistance and the flight of the Dalai Lama toward India, which have resulted in a complete break between the legitimate Tibetan authorities and the Chinese Communist government."[23] But these plans had to be scrapped almost immediately. The Chinese were mounting a massive drive to eradicate the resistance strongholds between Lhasa and the Indian border. On April 4, one of Gompo Tashi's supply convoys was taken unawares by the arrival of Chinese soldiers from Lhasa. Gompo's men reported three hundred truckloads of troops. Greatly outnumbered by the Chinese and forced to retreat, the Tibetans abandoned their supplies,[24] a serious setback to Gompo's forces. Within the next two weeks the original freedom fighter stronghold at Tsetang and several other principal bases had fallen to the Chinese. On April 14, the Chinese had captured the rebels' main base at Tsona near the Indian border. Shortly thereafter Gompo and his commanders decided their instructions to remain in Lhoka were outdated and they had no choice but to disregard them.

On April 20, Allen Dulles called the chairman of the Joint Chiefs, General Nathan Twining, to tell him that he had bad news about Tibet—"the resistance boys had been badly trapped."[25] He said that the Chinese had waged a more effective war than anticipated and were using more air power than either the U.S. or the Tibetans had expected. When a sympathetic Twining asked if there was anything the Joint Chiefs could do to help the beleaguered Tibetans, Dulles said that Twining and his service colleagues had already been helping "a great deal," but he knew of nothing more they could do at that time. He told Twining that the Tibetans had asked the CIA to postpone the scheduled airdrops in southern Tibet because they had lost the area where we were going to make the drop. Twining asked whether the embattled resistance forces were going to get out of Tibet safely. Dulles said he didn't know whether the Indians would permit them across the border, but in any case "they won't be much good to us if they are in India."

Three days later Dulles briefed the full National Security Council on the bleak situation.[26] He said that the latest messages indicated that the "dissidents or the patriots had been severely beaten by the Chinese Communists." He also noted the "rather pathetic quality of the messages." The patriots had no food and no ammunition and were requesting our intercession with the Indian government to permit their passage into India. The CIA director said that "of course we would do all that we could to help them but it was a difficult situation." The Chinese Communists had made very effective use of aircraft and of battle-tested veterans of the Korean War. He concluded that it looked as though the rebel forces in the Kham area "had been pretty well knocked into pieces," and the same was probably true of the rebel forces in the Lhasa area. A week later he was back with an equally gloomy assessment—that Gompo Tashi's resistance organization had disintegrated under the Chinese mop-up operations. Dulles noted that the rebels had made the initial mistake of fighting in large groups, although from now on they would "probably discover that the essence of guerrilla warfare consists of fighting in small bands."

Thomas Parrott, Allen Dulles's aide who acted as secretary for the NSC Special Group, recalled that the principals were very sympathetic to the Tibetans and did not criticize the CIA operations supporting them. Members of both houses of Congress urged full support for the Tibetan resistance forces. On April 17, Senator Hubert Humphrey, Minnesota Democrat and a leader of the liberals in Congress, asked the State Department about the possibility of "supporting guerilla military action against the Peiping regime on the grounds that the Tibetan revolt symbolizes the feeling of the Mongolian and Moslem minorities in Mainland China."[27] In response, the Department cited only the logistical difficulties of providing such aid, which would require Indian cooperation. On May 20, the State Department's director of South Asian Affairs reassured Representative Stuyvesant Wainwright that "the Department received with an open mind any CIA proposals designed to exploit the situation in our national interest" and "the Department was not imposing any policy restrictions which would inhibit CIA from support of the Tibetan resistance movement."[28]

Similarly, when serving as the Tibetan Task Force's political officer, I showed the usually reserved Senator William Fulbright the motion pictures taken by the radio operator accompanying the Dalai Lama on his escape.[29] He asked, "What do you expect me to do about this?" When I replied that the CIA sought support for its program to aid the remnants of the resistance in Tibet, the laconic senator said, "All right." In those days, this was sufficient to constitute endorsement by the Senate Foreign Relations Committee, which he chaired.

There seemed therefore to be no objection within either the executive or legislative branches of government. The logistical capabilities for dropping increased loads of supplies and men into Tibet had been greatly improved. The Tibetans had completed their training at Camp Hale and were ready to return home and put it into practice. But all this had to be put on hold until the CIA could determine whether the disorganized nature of the resistance groups still warranted the risks to the Tibetans who would be dropped and to those receiving them, as well as to the Americans making these dangerous deliveries. This reassessment continued through the summer of 1959.

❧

On the diplomatic front, Washington continued its public silence but engaged in private communication with the Dalai Lama soon after his arrival in India. On April 23, he sent a message through Gyalo Thondup requesting U.S. recognition of his government-in-exile. The Department temporized, assuring him that his request for recognition was receiving "immediate and close study" and his affairs were receiving the personal attention of both the president and the secretary of state. In the meantime, he was asked to delay any public request for recognition until after he had determined that it would meet "with a warm response on the part of other nations, including Asian nations, since if such a request were not generally acceded to, his cause would receive a severe setback."

In forwarding this message for the president's approval, the Department indicated that it was seriously considering the merits of recognition.[30] If the U.S. were joined by a substantial number of nations, including those in Asia, it would be "a most helpful step from the free world point of view." On the other hand, the Department wanted to avoid creating the impression that the U.S. was trying to exploit Tibet's plight for Cold War purposes. It noted that India's opposition to recognition of a government-in-exile on their soil was critical. "We cannot of course allow the future decision as to our course of action to rest in India's hands, but we must take into account world opinion, including especially that of other states," the message said.

Among those first approached were the Nationalist Chinese, who reacted as expected by equivocating on recognition, and the British, who danced around the issue throughout the summer by questioning whether Tibet qualified as a "state" entitled to a hearing at the United Nations. In a memorandum dated August 26, the Foreign Office official responsible for Tibetan affairs noted that "we have not so far had to commit ourselves on the question whether the Dalai Lama and his entourage are recognized by us as a Government-in-Exile and we hope to avoid having to do so." He went on to conclude that if, however, the U.K. were forced to declare itself it would have to go along with Nehru's opposition.[31]

Even before the waffling British had made their decision, the State Department discovered little enthusiasm in the international community for recognizing the Dalai Lama's government. In a memo dated

June 16, the Department noted that unless the U.S. responded positively to the Dalai Lama's appeal for support, Nehru's policy of autonomy "may well prevail,"[32] and this "would mean the destruction of the Dalai Lama as an effective symbol of resistance to Chinese Communist political and cultural tyranny." It recommended that without granting recognition, "we should convincingly assure him that he is regarded by the U.S. Government as the rightful leader of the Tibetan people in their struggle against oppression, and to this end we are prepared to support him financially if he is forced to leave India and to help him find asylum elsewhere." If Washington couldn't deliver to the Dalai Lama the political status he sought, it could at least pay to house him and his staff.

Two days later a message was passed orally to a representative of the Dalai Lama "in strictest confidence," informing him that he would not receive the diplomatic recognition he wanted.[33] The officer tried to sugar the pill by including the assurance that his request had received the personal attention of the president and secretary of state. He spoke of "the admiration of the United States Government and people for the courageous struggle against the Communist tyranny waged by the Tibetan people," and expressed America's regard for him as "the rightful leader of the Tibetan people in their struggle against oppression." As for the United Nations, he was told that Washington would continue to oppose Communist China's membership, and that if he decided to take his case there, Washington would do "whatever it appropriately could." He was urged to tour the capitals of countries that might support him at the UN, but not to break with Nehru. However, if he was forced to leave India, the U.S. would "assist in supporting him and an appropriate entourage." It was Eisenhower himself who insisted on the use of qualifying words at various points of the message to the Dalai Lama, to ensure that America's support would not be open-ended.[34]

Not surprisingly, the message was not received well by either the Dalai Lama or Gyalo Thondup, who objected to its oral delivery. While the Department professed to not being able to explain their reaction, it most likely arose from the two brothers' recollections of earlier commitments they had never received in writing. To forestall the Tibetans refusing to take any future action unless the U.S. put it in writing, Eisenhower signed a letter on July 6 confirming the commitments, and this letter was transmitted to the Dalai Lama at Mussoorie "by safe hand." Although the Dalai Lama had failed to obtain Washington's recognition of his government-in-exile, he now had a written assurance of the U.S. government's personal and political support at the highest level.

This did not mean that a common strategy had been completely worked out between Washington and the Dalai Lama. Although Eisenhower's message included reference to the desirability of the Dalai Lama making a tour[35] to foreign capitals expected to be friendly to any appeal he might make to the UN, Washington seemed more interested in such a tour than he was. Dramatizing his plight as a victim of Communist aggression had been one of the objectives of the various offers made over most of the past decade to induce him to seek asylum abroad. But he still had to have some place that would accept him on tour. By July 30, when Allen Dulles briefed the NSC on the Dalai Lama's plans, he noted that the U.S. had put out feelers to Buddhist countries about welcoming the Dalai Lama, but no country had been receptive, probably because they were reluctant to alienate Communist China, and most had Buddhist sects different from the Dalai Lama's own. What was once seen as an opportunity now was couched in terms of a problem.

CHAPTER 11

Tibet in International Diplomacy

D ESPITE THE FLAGGING international enthusiasm for the Tibetan cause, Washington began in the summer of 1959 to make good on its pledges to support the Dalai Lama in making an appeal to the United Nations. The embassy in New Delhi warned the Department not to expect much help from the Indians as Nehru had made it clear that he did not think the United Nations was qualified to deal with the Tibet situation as long as Communist China was not a member. When asked if he had reconciled himself to doing nothing to help the Tibetans, the prime minister had said, "I have not reconciled myself to this position or a hundred or thousand other positions, but I do not pretend to have the authority or power to change the shape of the world."¹ But the embassy concluded that although the Indian government would not favor a UN debate on Tibet, it was unlikely to take any extreme measures that might cause the Dalai Lama to withdraw an appeal or prevent him from travelling to New York to present his case. In fact, the embassy suggested that the ambivalent Nehru "might even secretly welcome some show of world concern re Chinese Communist expansionism."² But the embassy itself seemed to regard a UN debate more as a duty to be performed than an opportunity it would have sought out. This lack of enthusiasm came from the top. Ambassador Ellsworth Bunker told his British counterpart, Malcolm MacDonald, of a disagreement between the State Department's South Asian specialists, who opposed raising Tibet's problems at the UN, and the Far Eastern Affairs colleagues who favored it. "Unfortunately the latter school of thought won,"³ Bunker said. MacDonald found it "a pity" that Bunker had been on leave when this debate was underway in Washington.

Whatever the reservations of the South Asia wallahs, they were overwhelmed at a July 28 meeting chaired by Robert Murphy, the State Department's third ranking officer. Murphy's long-established reputation as a high-level troubleshooter with unchallenged connections was founded on his wartime service as President Roosevelt's personal representative and General Eisenhower's political adviser threading his way through quarreling French factions to line up support for the Allied invasion of North Africa. He later coordinated American diplomacy with Allied military operations during the reconquest of Europe, served as the first postwar ambassador to Japan, helped to negotiate the Korean armistice agreement, served at the United Nations, and was celebrated as one of the few American career diplomats to appear on the cover of *Time* magazine. This formidable diplomatic activist had taken a strong interest in Tibet and was determined to see his government live up to the commitments it had made to the Dalai Lama and his cause. Murphy and his successor, U. Alexis Johnson, had as their special assistant a foreign service officer of the old school, Joseph Scott, whose sense of honor and obligation also served the Tibetans well.

The strategy meeting chaired by Murphy decided to tell the Dalai

Lama that the U.S. government wanted to do whatever it could to assist him in a public appeal to the UN. The embassy was instructed to urge the Dalai Lama to appeal while the issue was alive and to do so in terms of suffering and denial of human rights, which UN members would find easier to support than charges of aggression. This would avoid frightening off potential supporters who might be uncertain about Tibet's legal status or unwilling to confront the Chinese Communists directly. If he took the initiative in appealing to the UN, Washington promised to pressure other countries to invite him to visit their countries to publicize his case. Recognition of his government-in-exile was deferred for the time being, but the embassy was to let him know that "the matter might usefully be reexamined following the contemplated UN action."[4]

Despite the definitive rebuffs that the British had given over the previous decade to repeated efforts by the State Department to enlist their support for the Tibetans, Washington was still not ready to give up on "the cousins." Murphy and his colleagues decided to ask their wartime ally to help them persuade the Japanese to take the lead in sponsoring a resolution at the UN. This initiative never got off the ground. The British continued to punt, and the Japanese shied away because public sentiment favored softening the government's harsh line against the Chinese Communists. Secretary Herter finally accepted the British advice that "on balance it was far better that the Asians take the lead,"[5] a position that Ambassador Lodge similarly espoused.[6] This did not mean any diminution in Washington's efforts to ensure that the Tibetans got a hearing. The steadfast Murphy made a point of emphasizing the U.S. resolve to the minister at the British embassy, Viscount Hood. While agreeing on the necessity of Asian support, especially of the Buddhist countries, Murphy stressed that "the U.S. did not wish to appear remiss or lukewarm because of the human issues involved. If the Dalai Lama asked for our assistance in his travels, we would wish to be helpful and, if he comes to New York, we would feel obliged to give support there."[7] Two days later the Department sent a circular cable to all the U.S. embassies in the Buddhist countries of Asia plus Karachi, Manila, Jakarta, Ankara, and Kuala Lumpur seeking statements supporting the

Dalai Lama's appeal and cosponsors in putting Tibet's appeal on the Assembly's agenda. The Dalai Lama, said the cable, "deserves an opportunity to state his case; otherwise it will appear that his appeal is being met with indifference and Tibet's cause will suffer a serious setback."[8]

The Dalai Lama left his mountain refuge in early September to come to New Delhi and solicit Nehru's support for his appeal. He made little headway. During two long days of discussion[9] the Indian prime minister argued that there was even less chance of countries going to war with China to rescue Tibet than there had been of them fighting Russia to save Hungary. Finally, the prime minister warned the Tibetan ruler that he could not count on Indian support, particularly for any resolution that might question Chinese suzerainty over Tibet, which India had already recognized. He did give his young guest some tactical advice, warning that he would have to produce reliable evidence if he was going to base his appeal on Chinese violations of human rights, because the evidence produced by refugees was generally regarded as suspect. Nehru's final dash of cold water was his reminder that the UN had condemned countries such as South Africa for violating human rights but had obtained no practical results. The Dalai Lama remained resolute and told the prime minister that he would press his appeal. He felt neither he nor his country had anything to lose.

The Dalai Lama then met with the American chargé d'affaires, Winthrop G. Brown to inform him of the generally bleak results of his meetings with the prime minister.[10] Brown offered no new plans or initiatives. But in Washington, enthusiasm for action was running high, and Brown was immediately instructed to seek a further interview with the Dalai Lama to make several points to him before he returned to Mussoorie.[11] Brown was to assure him that the U.S. government was consulting with friendly governments to obtain sponsorship of a Tibetan item on the Assembly's agenda and it would "welcome" him discussing his appeal with Asian missions in New Delhi. He should cable UN Secretary General Dag Hammarskjöld along the lines of his recent public appeal with the request that he circulate it to UN members. Again he was to be advised that an appeal based on the suppression of human rights would win more votes than a charge of aggression.

Brown was also to suggest that the Dalai Lama would advance his cause by a personal appearance at the UN but he should burn no bridges with his Indian hosts lest that threaten his residence there.

Finally, Brown was to reassure the Dalai Lama that the U.S. remained "strongly" opposed to Communist China's admission to the UN and was firmly convinced that any effort to seat Beijing would fail. The message closed with an uncharacteristically emotional instruction to Brown. Should he be approached by his diplomatic colleagues in New Delhi, he was to "stress the U.S. Government's belief that the UN cannot afford to ignore the plight of the Tibetans as victims of brutal suppression by alien military power. For the UN to turn its back on the Tibetans would compound their tragedy." Furthermore the U.S. government did "not accept the idea that the Tibetans would be better off if the appeal by their authentic spokesman, the Dalai Lama, were to be ignored." The cable ended with the final jab recalling that "the well-intentioned advice of India in 1950 that the UN should keep hands off while the Tibetans and Chicoms worked out a peaceful settlement only ended in the present deep suffering of the Tibetan people."

Brown had his marching orders, as did His Holiness the Dalai Lama.

✃

Washington's show of support for the Tibetans was made against the background of one of the more dramatic developments of the Cold War. The dispute between Nikita Khrushchev and Mao Zedong over both ideology and objectives had been brewing since Khrushchev's secret speech in 1956 denouncing Stalin's autocracy, promulgating the doctrine of peaceful coexistence, and admitting the possibility of achieving socialism by peaceful means. Mao's concern over the consequences of Khrushchev's pronouncements in Eastern Europe and the implications for his own style of governance had caused him to respond in 1958 with a show of belligerence in foreign affairs and a domestic program to advance Communism according to a unique Chinese model of mass mobilization called the Great Leap Forward. Mao's innovations met with Soviet sneers, reciprocated by Beijing's scorn for the Soviet premier's visit to the U.S. as part of his program of peaceful coexistence with Western democracies.

The revolt in Tibet in March 1959 and the armed clashes between the Chinese and the Indians on the Tibet frontier later that summer became issues in this increasingly nasty and public donnybrook between the two leaders of the Communist world. Mao's role in both of these events had not pleased Moscow, which was courting Nehru as one of the founders of peaceful coexistence that had become a dead cause in Beijing. This was particularly true in the late summer of 1959, when Khrushchev was off to promote his adopted passion for this doctrine in Washington.

Although Khrushchev had supported the Chinese efforts to suppress the Tibetan revolt, earlier that summer he blamed the Chinese for creating the conditions that provoked the rebellion. This was apparent in the report that the ideological guardian of the Soviet Communist party, Mikhail Suslov, prepared on the "differences which emerged"[12] during Khrushchev's stormy visit to Beijing, which took place immediately after his meeting at Camp David with Eisenhower. Suslov linked the serious deterioration in relations between China and India to the "counterrevolutionary rebellion" in Tibet. He acknowledged that "reactionary circles of India to some extent were involved in this rebellion. However," Suslov continued, "the rebellion would not have taken place had one [Mao] implemented timely democratic reforms and appropriate measures to improve the economy and culture" that took into account the "historic specifics of Tibet and had been duly vigilant with regard to reactionary elements." He noted that "unfortunately the Chinese comrades" had not drawn the "appropriate conclusions from the warnings" of the Soviet party's Central Committee. He did make it clear that Moscow was not quarrelling with China's right to "put down decisively" the revolt and that Moscow would support Beijing's "claim with justification that the issue of Tibet is a domestic affair." But the fact remained that ill-advised Chinese policy had allowed it to erupt in the first place.

Furthermore, Suslov charged, the Chinese had played into the hands of the "imperialists" who were exploiting "the Tibet question" to undermine communist influence in southeast Asia. In contrast to Nehru who "behaved with reserve," Mao had launched a propaganda campaign that concentrated its fire on the Indian leader. Suslov could only explain this as part of a scheme by Mao to cause Nehru's downfall and his succession by a pro-Western government, which would hasten a revolution in India.[13] This in turn would discredit Khrushchev's pursuit of peaceful coexistence, particularly with parliamentary socialist countries like Nehru's. Mao's objective had been further advanced by the clashes between the Chinese and Indian troops on the Tibetan border beginning in August. Suslov declined to fix blame for these incidents, but he pointed out that again they served the purposes of the "imperialists" by giving them a further excuse to "raise an uproar about 'the aggression of Red China,'" and for harmful attacks on Nehru that injured his political position. He then cited the statement issued by TASS on September 9 calling on India and China to "settle their frontier incident" and "thwart efforts to divide the Asian states and intensify the Cold War just before the exchange of visits between Soviet Premier Khrushchev and President Eisenhower."[14] The exasperated ideologist noted that this statement was followed by another border clash and an unproductive exchange of charges between Moscow and Beijing. Suslov could only conclude that "the Chinese comrades could correctly assess neither their own mistakes committed in their relations with India, nor the measures taken by the CC CPSU [Soviet Communist party] for regulation of the Sino-Indian conflict." When Khrushchev had made these points to Mao, "the Chinese comrades reacted . . . painfully."

There is little evidence that Washington was prepared to make any efforts during Khrushchev's visit late in September to exploit the growing dissension between him and Mao. When the NSC met on September 10 to discuss tactics for promoting Tibet's appeal to the UN, Allen Dulles cited the "ugly mood" of the Chinese Communist leaders because of the failure of Mao's Great Leap Forward.[15] He suggested no course of action that would take Sino-Soviet differences into account. A few days later Assistant Secretary Graham Parsons wrote Secretary Herter that "in the context of the Khrushchev visit our failure to take an initiative on Tibet will throw doubt on our ability to exert leadership among free peoples," and would "be likely to add further to the concern already felt among Asian states that we may be softening in our willingness to oppose communism."[16]

When Khrushchev and Eisenhower held their three days of meetings at Camp David, there is no record that there was any discussion of the Soviet premier's growing differences with his Chinese counterpart, particularly their obviously differing views on the continuing conflict on the Tibetan-Indian border, nor any mention at all of the situation in Tibet.[17] Parsons's concerns that the U.S. not appear to be failing the Tibetans as a consequence of the new era of détente were not addressed, postponed to be considered either after or independently of the Soviet premier's visit.

Khrushchev left Washington on September 28 and went immediately to China to reiterate his doctrine of "peaceful coexistence." In separate statements, Herter and his undersecretary Douglas Dillon finally made some effort to exploit the apparent differences between Moscow and Beijing by declaring that the USSR must be held responsible for the actions of the Chinese and other members of the Soviet bloc.[18] Khrushchev immediately sent a letter to Eisenhower denying this thesis and reaffirming his support for China's claim to Taiwan.[19] The Chinese reacted with similar vigor, denouncing this "psychological attack" designed to "distort relations between the USSR and China and to cast doubt on the sovereignty of China."[20]

☙

Even while preparing for the epochal Camp David Summit, the Department had been busy lining up sponsors for the Tibetans at the UN. The Irish and the Malayans had agreed to take the lead. It was a fortuitous combination. Malaya had fought and subdued a Communist insurgency, and Ireland was a champion of underdogs facing religious persecution and of the independence movements sweeping Asia and Africa. The British Foreign Office, however, continued to try to head off action by the UN. But on September 17, Prime Minister Harold Macmillan decided to swallow hard and accept the reluctant conclusion of the Foreign Office that Britain would have to support inscription of a resolution.[21] He noted that "from the point of view of domestic opinion the Government would be in a difficult position" if it did not support at least giving the Tibetans a hearing. Lloyd, in his address to the General Assembly, accordingly noted that "over Tibet, we have been greatly grieved to hear accounts of massive repression there by Communist China, of the suppression of ancient liberties, and ruthless assaults upon the historic life of a sturdy and friendly people."[22]

Lloyd, obviously hoping that would be enough, made one last try at a meeting with Secretary Herter and his French colleague Maurice Couve de Murville to keep Tibet off the agenda.[23] The British foreign secretary suggested that it "would open the way to discussion in the UN of subjects like Oman, Nyasaland, Ulster and perhaps even segregation in the United States." (The empire might be dwindling, but its representatives were required to deploy all available arguments in its defense.) According to the Foreign Office, the noncombative Herter agreed that the great powers had been wise not to intervene in disputes between India and China and not to convert Tibet into a Cold War issue. But in view of the promises made to the Dalai Lama about a UN appeal, Washington would have to work for something more than just some references to Tibet in the General Debate. The State Department account of this meeting records a more vigorous defense by Herter for obtaining a hearing of the Dalai Lama's case at the UN.[24]

On September 22 the Foreign Office finally caved and instructed the U.K. representative to support inscription of a resolution on Tibet.[25] The British concession came during a frenzy of activity by Washington to invigorate action at the UN, where the enthusiasm of Lodge's U.S. delegation was apparently limited. The stalwart Parsons expressed his indignant surprise that "despite the decisions reached at the highest levels in this Government and the assurances which this Government has given to the Dalai Lama,"[26] Lodge's UN mission had suggested that the Department seriously consider dropping the idea of a resolution on Tibet. Parsons insisted that Lodge "at once be instructed that the decision to seek inscription of the item in conjunction with other interested states is firm and that [U.S. mission to the UN] should assume the necessary leadership to ensure the successful handling of the case." Ambassador MacArthur in Tokyo was urged to use his "most persuasive manner" to urge the Japanese to vote at least for inscription.[27] Ambassador Bunker was instructed to tell Nehru of the importance Washington attached to the Indian attitude toward inscription and again assure him that the U.S. did not wish to make Tibet a Cold War issue.[28]

ERNEST GROSS,
COUNSEL TO THE TIBETANS

It was to take three more weeks of intense diplomatic maneuvering before the Assembly would vote on whether even to hold a debate on Tibet. During that time Gyalo Thondup arrived in New York to press his brother's case. To ensure that the Tibetans worked the UN corridors with maximum effectiveness, Robert Murphy arranged for former Ambassador Ernest Gross to advise Thondup on the tactics for obtaining a hearing. Gross had been the deputy U.S. representative at the UN in 1950, when Tibet's previous appeal had been shelved at the urging of the Indians. Since then he had joined an international law firm in New York and acted as personal counsel to two successive UN secretaries general, Trygve Lie and the incumbent Dag Hammarskjöld. Gross knew the ropes at the UN better than any American lawyer or diplomat.

This did not make him immune from attack by the China Lobby, an amorphous but powerful group ranging from distinguished public to sometimes shadowy figures.[29] Among the best known were the California publisher and senator William Knowland, Henry Luce, son of American missionaries to China and founding chief of the Time-Life empire, Anna Chennault, the attractive Chinese widow of the World War II Flying Tiger General, and Lowell Thomas, the self-appointed spokesman for Tibet. Others were former diplomats, missionaries, and businessmen. They all backed Chiang's dream of returning to the China mainland and his single-minded readiness to challenge any threat to diminution of the territory he no longer controlled. Some of the lobby members sat on the American Emergency Committee for Tibetan Refugees, and they advised Thondup not to use Gross's services because as secretary of the World Council of Churches he had signed—but not drafted—a report favoring U.S. recognition of Communist China. This put Thondup in a difficult situation as the committee was providing aid to the Tibetan refugees as well as trying to advance their political agenda. Thondup, who was very familiar with this agenda, discounted their advice. Gross was able to persuade the representative of the committee that he personally strongly opposed recognition of Mao's government and this particular tempest in a teapot subsided, though Chiang's representatives continued to play a generally unhelpful role regarding the Tibetan appeal.

Murphy was characteristically out ahead of his colleagues. He had not coordinated with Lodge when he arranged for Gross to serve as Thondup's counsel, and turf warfare broke out when an irate Lodge called Herter on October 6 to complain that he had been left out of the loop. Herter, trying to find a middle position between the activist Murphy and his protocol-conscious UN ambassador, told Lodge "that we didn't want a resolution recognizing the independence or sovereignty [of Tibet] but rather a slap on the wrist. In view of the Hungarian thing, however, this should not be passed up completely."[30] He went on to say he had told the Irish that "our feeling was this was a serious enough offense to human rights that it should not go unnoticed." However, "all we wanted to do was to have this thing come in as mild a resolution as possible."

Lodge was also annoyed over procedure. He complained that it was Gross, rather than he, who had been instructed to persuade the Tibetans to drop the idea that the Dalai Lama make his appeal in person at the UN. The Department had found little enthusiasm among its allies for such an appearance. The Tibetans had never been enthusiastic about the idea that had originated in Washington so Thondup had agreed to abandon the project.[31] When Herter explained that Gross had already handled this matter, the Old Boston envoy agreed that Gross was a "good man." But Lodge was never a person to be assuaged easily and called Herter two days later complaining that it was not clear what Gross was supposed to advise Thondup and his colleagues about. Herter told him that "we are now stuck with Gross's employment and it was now a question of our finding our way through the maze a bit."[32] In any case, he informed Lodge, Eisenhower had already written the Dalai Lama promising to do everything possible to bring his case before the UN.[33]

When Lodge met with Thondup and Gross later that same day he had become either more resigned or more relaxed. He reported that Thondup "makes an extremely favorable impression and is an excellent spokesman for the Tibetan cause."[34] Lodge seemed reassured that he was not dealing with a zealot, but someone who "recognizes the importance of not seeking action on a basis (i.e. charges of aggression) which would fail to receive necessary support and could then be exploited by the Chicoms and others against the Tibetans." From that time on, the team of Thondup, Gross, and Lodge's UN mission functioned in surprising accord, given the basic differences among the personalities involved: the purposeful Thondup, who had been instructed to claim independence for Tibet; the pragmatic Gross, who was energetically serving both his Tibetan client and the more limited interests of the U.S. government; and Lodge and his mission, who placed great weight on procedure and status.

Gross, following the American line, first attempted to convince Thondup that the Dalai Lama's appeal should be based on human rights violations and not on reviving the charges of aggression that were unsuccessfully laid in 1950.[35] Thondup stubbornly argued that the Dalai Lama believed independence was an essential goal for inspiring the struggle of the Tibetan people. If the question were not raised, the Chinese Communists would use the failure of the United Nations to discuss it as propaganda to persuade the Tibetan people that further resistance would be useless.

Gross had made his own delegate count and warned Thondup he could find very little support for a resolution based on the sovereignty of Tibet. He advised that the realities of the situation dictated a campaign centered on the theme that "our plea concerns not land, but people," and he warned Thondup there was no point in "knocking at a locked door" because the net result might be no resolution at all. On the other hand, if the Tibetans obtained a large show of support for their human rights case, they could always move on later to the political question of sovereignty and recognition. After expressing disappointment over the unpleasant facts confronting them, Thondup and his deputy Tsipon Shakabpa accepted Gross's advice. Thondup was a realist, and he could truthfully tell the hard-liners at home that he had made their case force-fully and yielded only when it looked hopeless. When Lodge echoed this same advice, Thondup had already been well primed for it by Gross.

While the CIA had hired a public relations firm to help the Tibetans publicize their case, Gross preferred to use his own extensive contacts in the establishment.[36] He had already been in contact with the Luce pub-lications and the *New York Times,* and this old pro was also preparing a list of UN delegations and their individual political priorities, so that he and Thondup could lobby for their support. Gross would also take on the responsibility of presenting the Tibetan position to Hammarskjöld, where his personal relationship would assure him of a sympathetic hear-ing. As for an appearance by the Dalai Lama, the lawyer-diplomat sug-gested it might be more appropriate for the Tibetan leader to appear before the UN Human Rights Commission at its session the following March. While Gross may have been following the Department's advice, it seems more likely that his own soundings told him that a request for such an unprecedented personal appearance would inevitably prompt an acrimonious debate, and that it might well lead to an embarrassing rejection of the Dalai Lama's pleas.

❧

One week later the General Assembly voted to debate "The Question of Tibet" as proposed by Ireland and Malaya.[37] Finally, the Tibetans were at least to obtain a hearing. As they had reluctantly promised, the British voted for inscription, while the French abstained, fearful that the prece-dent might admit a debate on Algeria, which Paris claimed was as much a part of France as Beijing claimed Tibet was part of China. India was listed as "not voting." The head of the Soviet delegation, Vasily Kuznet-zov, broke Moscow's reserve to denounce "the sponsors of the Tibetan question resolution, and especially the State Department of the United States who have launched a malicious and slanderous campaign against the great Chinese people and their Government to frustrate or at least impede the process of creating relations between states that has recently commenced."[38]

This was the least Khrushchev could deliver in public for his Chinese comrades while not repudiating the new "Spirit of Camp David" he had established with Eisenhower a fortnight before. The Russians had in fact attempted to derail the initiative by more classic diplomatic means in private.[39] Kuznetzov had approached the British ambassador, Pierson Dixon, suggesting they both urge Aiken to drop the question. Dixon told Kuznetzov that although Britain had already been trying to discourage inscription, there was widespread sympathy for the Tibetan people and in any case Britain was in no position to seek to dictate to the Irish. He then slipped away from this discussion, expressing the British desire to see Tibet's problems considered in a "non-political way" and the hope that Moscow would approach the question in the same spirit. Kuznetzov said he would do his best but added that he was not afraid to fight and would undoubtedly have to say "hard things" in the Assembly on Tibet.

On October 21, after two days of debate, the General Assembly voted 45 to 9, with 26 abstentions, to approve a resolution that noted "that the fundamental human rights and freedoms to which the Tibetan people, like all others, are entitled include the right to civil and religious liberty for all without distinction." It also noted Tibet's cultural and religious heritage and its traditional autonomy, expressed "grave concern at reports . . . that the fundamental human rights and freedoms of the people of Tibet have been forcibly denied them," and deplored "the effect of these events in increasing international tensions." The resolution made no mention of who was depriving the Tibetans of their rights or of their independence. Even references to "freedom" had been finessed into the vaguer concept of "freedoms." These omissions and evasions had been carefully and painfully crafted by the Irish after marathon sessions with the other delegations to carry what the traffic would bear.

But even these equivocations and a direct, last minute appeal by U.S. Ambassador John Hay Whitney in London to Selwyn Lloyd could not bring the British around.[40] They offered only to instruct their representative to make a strong speech at the end of the debate to "make clear their abhorrence of the Tibetan situation" and, with strange logic, "to avoid as far as possible influencing other votes." In the vote they were counted among the abstainers, along with the French and Tibet's fellow

Asian Buddhists, Burma, Cambodia, and Ceylon. It was hardly the definitive victory for which the Tibetans or their American supporters had hoped and worked.

WASHINGTON STIFFENS ITS SUPPORT

Despite this less than full show of support by the UN, Murphy was still committed to backing the Tibetans to the hilt. He was also a political realist. He readily saw the merit of his deputy Graham Parsons's argument that, if the U.S. took the lead in recognizing the Dalai Lama's government-in-exile and only a few countries followed, the Tibetan ruler would be seen as an American puppet. "This would almost certainly damage the prestige and influence he now enjoys as one of Asia's most revered leaders and would hamper his activities on behalf of the Tibetan people."[41] Parsons no doubt based his bleak assessment of the prospects for recognition on the hesitant behavior at the UN of those who might otherwise have been expected to be Tibet's natural supporters among the countries of Western Europe and Asia. "Nonetheless," Parsons argued, the U.S. must "take a stand conforming to our historic position as a supporter of the principle of the self-determination of peoples," because without an expression of American sympathy the resistance movement would lose heart.

This combination of political expediency and moral argument apparently persuaded Herter to make the policy decision that the United States would support "the right of the Tibetan people to have the determining voice in their political destiny" and to do so in public. This would mean informing not only the Dalai Lama but the fainthearted British and Indians as well as the adamant Chinese Nationalists.[42]

When Thondup called on Murphy for a post-UN stocktaking session on October 29 he was in for a pleasant surprise.[43] He opened by making his expected bids for diplomatic help to encourage recognition of his brother's government-in-exile and for financial and military assistance to continue the resistance against the Chinese. Murphy assured Thondup of the president's personal sympathy for the Tibetan cause and the "great importance" the U.S. government attached to keeping it alive. Thondup philosophically accepted the UN action as a good start. Murphy suggested that the Dalai Lama consider visiting other countries to educate them on the situation in Tibet. He then told Thondup that the U.S. had traditionally stood for the self-determination of peoples and believed this principle should also apply to the Tibetans. The usually politically keen Thondup apparently missed the significance of Murphy's statement and merely expressed his appreciation. Murphy let this pass and went on to ask Thondup to what use he intended putting the arms he was requesting. Thondup replied that the arms supplies would help keep alive the hopes of the Tibetan resistance groups still operating to the north, east, and west of Lhasa.

Murphy closed the meeting by repeating the U.S. support for the Tibetan people's right to self-determination. He asked Thondup to keep this position confidential until it had been communicated to the Dalai Lama, after which the British and Chinese Nationalist governments would be also informed. Thondup was apparently still not fully aware of the step forward that this declaration represented in U.S. policy and again expressed polite appreciation to Murphy.

By the time Thondup met with Parsons two days later he had obviously been briefed by Gross and realized the importance of what Murphy had said and its implications for U.S. policy. (Gross told me some years later that even though the State Department was not prepared to declare itself publicly in favor of Tibetan independence, it was willing to use self-determination as a euphemism for the Tibetans' right to declare independence themselves.[44]) Thondup told Parsons that he had not fully understood the significance of what Murphy had said, but he was sure that the Tibetan people would be very grateful for a public declaration by the U.S. supporting their right to self-determination. What worried him was that if the U.S. consulted foreign governments beforehand they might oppose it, and that India in particular might try to stop it. Parsons assured him that, although the U.S. might consider delaying the announcement at the request of one of those consulted, "we would not give them a veto power. We would listen to their views but expect to carry out our own decision."[45]

Undoubtedly coached by Shakabpa, who remembered his previous difficulties in pinning down the Americans, Thondup sent Murphy a
memorandum of their conversation a few days later, trying to push him
further by asking him to confirm his statements of support. He included
the statement that "Mr. Murphy made it clear that it was the intention
of the Government of the United States to issue a declaration clearly stating that the people of Tibet are entitled to the right of self-determination
and that the Government of the United States would take such measures
as may be found necessary to enable the Tibetans to exercise that
right."[46] In a reply drafted by Parsons, Murphy "regretted that he could
not confirm all aspects of Thondup's note" and gave a leaner version that
specifically did not include a promise to "take such measures as may be
found necessary . . . "[47]

While Thondup could not have known it, his version was in accord
with the policy Herter had expressed privately two weeks earlier. The
secretary had told his staff that the U.S. would "be prepared to consider
appropriate assistance" to the Tibetans to determine their own destiny
"should a change in the situation make this practicable."[48] The tough
fight to win the very lean UN resolution they obtained may have caused
Murphy not to hold Herter to his surprisingly forward position. As an
old hand at diplomatic maneuvering, he would not have wanted to foreclose his options in dealing with a shifting political situation. It may
have been simply a matter of not wanting to have words put into his
mouth, least of all by a newcomer to the game. But there was no doubt
that even Murphy's edited statement represented a real diplomatic
advance for the Tibetans. Ambassador Bunker was instructed to deliver
to the Dalai Lama an official letter signed by him confirming the
Department's intention to make the promised public statement of support for Tibetan self-determination,[49] of which the governments of the
Republic of China, the U.K., and India had already been informed.[50]

When Parsons briefed George Yeh, the Chinese Nationalist ambassador, on the policy shift, he headed off the envoy's anticipated objections by citing Chiang's own statement of March 26 promising the
Tibetans the right to determine their own political future when the
Nationalists regained the mainland.[51] The letter to the Dalai Lama reaf-

firming Washington's decision to announce its support for the Tibetans' right to self-determination had also cited Chiang's promise.[52] (A State Department staff summary of this correspondence did contain the hedge that the new position did not "necessarily commit us [the U.S. government] to ultimate recognition of Tibetan independence."[53]) Yeh, surprisingly, merely asked for Chiang's statement to be mentioned in the press announcement of the new policy and for advance notice before the announcement was made. The British, for all their fluttering over the status of their former wards, also reacted in an equally matter-of-fact way. The Far Eastern Department's chief told the U.S. embassy officer who came to brief him that British policy had emphasized Tibetan autonomy under Chinese suzerainty, and therefore was "perhaps also a kind of recognition of self-determination in accord with British practice of extending measures of self-government to British colonies in preparation for further self-determination when they became ready for it."[54]

When Thondup returned from the UN via London, he was offered an appointment with Selwyn Lloyd, a definite upgrade from his reception en route to New York when he met with the foreign secretary's deputy, Lord Lansdowne, who received him because the Foreign Office felt an audience with Lloyd "might give him the wrong impression." Whether the British were suffering from a guilty conscience for their failure to vote for the Tibet resolution or were impressed by the way Thondup had been received in Washington, it was clear that his stock in London had risen.

By the time the statement supporting Tibetan self-determination was publicly released two months later, the Chinese Nationalists were having second thoughts.[55] They expressed disappointment at not having been consulted—which of course they had been—"insofar as the subject matter concerns the status of a part of the Chinese territory." But their real objection was that the statement referred to Tibet as "an autonomous *country* [author's italics] under the suzerainty of China." The Department dismissed their objections by pointing out that they had been shown the statement weeks before and had raised no complaints. In any event, U.S. support for the right of the Tibetans to determine their own form of government was now a matter of public record.

Eisenhower in India

While Washington was moving toward a more forthright position on Tibet, the Dalai Lama's Indian hosts were still trying to limit his political activities. Even though his own Old Guard advisers were not enthusiastic about his travel abroad, the Tibetan ruler had requested a meeting with Eisenhower during the historic first U.S. presidential visit to India in December of 1959. The State Department strongly endorsed it, but when Bunker pressed the Indian government to permit this public testimonial of U.S. goodwill, it refused. Indian Foreign Secretary Dutt argued to Bunker that such a controversial meeting "could cast a cloud on the whole visit," would raise Chinese suspicions, and add fuel to their "insulting" charge that the Indian government was being pressured by Washington to encourage the resistance in Tibet.[56] Nehru, while prepared to receive one of China's foremost opponents, was obviously not ready to provide the stage for an event of political theater intended to demonstrate his guest's sympathy for the victims of the country with which India was still trying to find an accommodation.

Bunker had made his request when Washington's relations with India were strained by some uncharacteristically awkward remarks Herter had made at a news conference on November 12.[57] Herter noted that the U.S. government "had not taken any sides at all" in the border dispute precipitated by Chinese incursions from Tibet into disputed areas along India's eastern and western frontiers. Piling insult on injury, he loftily presumed the Indian claims were valid but still had no "objective reading" on which to base his presumption. Half an hour after the news conference, the Department hurriedly issued a statement in Herter's name condemning China's use of force to resolve the border dispute and explaining that he had been addressing himself only to the "legalities" of the matter. This must have been cold comfort to Nehru, who had received little support from the U.S. beyond a letter from Eisenhower in September assuring him that he "fully appreciated the problems" of China's frontier incursions.[58] Nehru must have found it ironic that the senior foreign affairs official of a government urging him to take a more aggressive position against

Chinese aggression in Tibet was citing mere "legalities" in describing China's probes against his own country. In this strained atmosphere, it was evident that Washington believed this was not the time for the U.S. government to be exerting pressure on Nehru about Tibet, and Bunker recommended dropping the request for Nehru's agreement to a meeting between Eisenhower and the Dalai Lama.

Such a meeting, between the leader of the free world and the newly dispossessed victim of Communist aggression, against the rich backdrop of the world's largest neutralist country, would have been one of the more colorful and symbolic events of the decade. The psychological and propaganda value of publicizing the Dalai Lama as a victim of Communist aggression had been a principal objective of the eight-year program to persuade the Dalai Lama to leave his country. But when the small committee of professionals assembled by Gross to maintain the momentum of the UN resolution met in late November, they were unaware that no such meeting was in the cards.

The best-known member of this Tibetan "kitchen cabinet" was C. D. Jackson, a senior officer of the Luce journalistic empire. Jackson was also close to Eisenhower, having served under him in psychological warfare operations during World War II and having worked for his presidential campaign.[59] Jackson had managed the organization responsible for operating Radio Free Europe and dedicated himself to the cause of liberating Eastern Europe from Communism. His consequent frustration over the tragic consequence of the Hungarian revolt had driven him to even more vigorous support of similar causes. He was therefore ready to lend his personal support and considerable prestige to the Tibetan cause. So was another member of the group, Earl Newsom, a well-known public relations man for the New York establishment. When I met with the "kitchen cabinet" in the bar at the club on top of Number 1 Rockefeller Plaza, Newsom recalled that his father, a Presbyterian minister, used to open his meetings with his vestry by asking "are we plotting for or against the good of the Lord?" In this case, Newsom declared, there can be no question, "so let's get busy plotting." Jackson was adamant that the president must meet with America's unacknowledged protégé and offered to have *Life,* then the world's premier magazine of photojournalism, send a team to India to cover this historic event. As one of Eisenhower's close advisers on the U.S. government's psychological warfare program, he proposed that he call the president's press secretary, James Hagerty, to insist on the meeting.[60]

This was heady stuff for a junior case officer, and I was slightly uneasy about the enthusiasm I had unleashed as we sat there "plotting" together. I suggested that Jackson first call his close friend—and my boss—Allen Dulles. Jackson immediately put a call through to the CIA director and opened the conversation by inquiring if "there was still a testicular policy down there on the Potomac?" He then proceeded to lay out his proposal to enlist Hagerty's services in persuading "Ike" to meet with "this Dalai Lama fellow" by telling him that he is "one of the guys wearing a white hat" in the struggle against the Communists. (Eisenhower was reported to be a great fan of Zane Grey westerns.) Dulles, replying with his characteristic Santa Claus–like ho-ho-ho's, expressed great appreciation for Jackson's efforts but stressed that he would take the responsibility for referring Jackson's proposal to the White House. As soon as the meeting was over I called Desmond FitzGerald to tell him of this exchange. He was amused, but told me to get back to Washington and be at his office by 8:30 the next morning to await a certain call from "the boss," who was sure to be exercised by this unauthorized aid volunteered by one of his high-voltage friends. The call came on the button. Des defended his officer for having fulfilled his mission of obtaining publicity for the Tibetans, and Dulles finally agreed that I had done what "a good case officer should"—but warned against any further contacts with one of his friends without his prior approval. There were no further meetings of the "kitchen cabinet."

The Tibetans' only contact with the visiting U.S. president was therefore peripheral and indirect. On December 13, Gompo Tashi, then in India recovering from wounds, delivered to the U.S. embassy for the president "one Khampa sword by which we fought our enemy, as well as the enemy of the world, the Chinese Communists," a Tibetan charm box, a Khampa warrior's outfit, and a letter appealing for continuing advice and support. Since the resistance leader had not established contact with the embassy through channels giving him official status, the

Department advised the embassy that its oral acknowledgment of the letter and gifts were sufficient.[61]

In fact, the Dalai Lama was not to meet any American president until thirty-two years later. At first this was a matter of protocol imposed by the Tibetans: the Dalai Lama refused to be received anywhere except as a chief of state. Later the obstacle was U.S. policy: Eisenhower's National Security Council Special Group had suggested that if the president couldn't meet the Dalai Lama in India, it would still be useful for the young leader to come to the U.S. even without an appearance before the UN.[62] Washington, however, was not willing to take on the anticipated howls from Taiwan if it received him as an official visitor. When the problem was bucked to the CIA, it asked Gross to find a private group to sponsor a visit. He had found the National Council of Christians and Jews readily willing to invite the Dalai Lama to address American notables at the historic Cooper Union in New York.[63]

Arrangements to hold this conference late in the spring of 1960 were accordingly completed at a series of meetings at Rumplemayer's Cafe facing Central Park, where the head of the council liked the chocolate sundaes. Herter also asked for a half-hour's informal visit with the president, but all these plans collapsed when the Dalai Lama was persuaded that it would be inappropriate for his first visit abroad to be a private one. He acted on the advice of his tradition-bound secular and monastic officials, who feared that travel under anything less than full official status would jeopardize his claim to be chief of an independent state and cost him his unique dual authority. The result was that he did not travel abroad at all to publicize Tibet's plight at the time when public awareness of Chinese aggression was still fresh. (Not until seven years later did he make his first visit outside India, and that was to Japan and Thailand, where he was received as a religious leader only.)

These patterns were to hold for years. The Dalai Lama's nervous but generous Indian hosts came to accept him and the government-in-exile that they had helped him set up in their country. Although the site of his unrecognized government was a politically safe distance from the Indian capital, it was geographically and psychologically close to Tibet. The international community accorded him lesser recognition, but he nevertheless succeeded in establishing a continuing claim on its attention and conscience by his unique moral character and his own extraordinary skills. The U.S. government mostly lived up to its commitments. It provided the promised subsidy for him and his entourage. It made a genuine effort to win a public hearing of his case at the United Nations. It supported his countrymen's efforts to maintain their resistance against the Chinese. Finally, it had given him and his people a public pledge of more explicit political support than previously conferred. This was not the recognition of independence that the Dalai Lama sought, but it was a surprisingly bold action for that time. And if it struggled in the diplomatic sphere, the United States showed no sign of hesitation when it came to the secret war for Tibet—at least for now.

CHAPTER 12

Operations at
High Altitudes

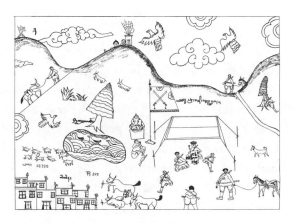

T HE U.S. GOVERNMENT'S difficulties
in winning political support for the
Tibetans did not cause any reduction
in its efforts to train and equip Tibet's own
resistance forces; if anything, it made them
more vigorous.

The rationale for continuing these operations, even after the Dalai Lama had fled to
India, was that continuing resistance would validate his claim to the attention of the international community. U.S. geopolitical interests
would be served by forcing Mao to divert his
already stretched resources to counter guerrillas in a remote and rebellious area. It was also
U.S. policy at that time to contest wherever possible Communist control of China. In
December, 1959, Robert Murphy authorized

informing the Chinese Nationalist government that its program of developing resistance forces inside China would have full U.S. support. The Nationalists planned to train 3,000 special forces to participate in efforts to "restore freedom to the mainland by political means."[1]

While the CIA's support to the Tibetan resistance was a separate program, kept carefully compartmentalized from activities conducted with the Nationalists, it shared the objective of changing the regime in Beijing. Unlike the operations contemplated with Chiang's intelligence organization, the Tibet program was already in place and organized. A resistance movement did not have to be created—it was already in action. Furthermore, it had already demonstrated that it could seriously contest the Chinese army. But if the resistance was to be sustained, more men had to be trained as guerrillas and more arms were needed. The CIA had the site to provide the training in how to use the arms it now had the capability to deliver inside Tibet.

For more than a year before the diplomatic campaign reached its climax at the UN, a training center in Colorado had been functioning to provide instructors, leaders, and communicators for the kind of guerrilla warfare the Tibetans would have to fight if they were to survive as a people. Far distant in miles and spirit from the bureaucracy of Washington, this unique camp was staffed by veterans of earlier CIA paramilitary programs in Southeast Asia, and favorites of Desmond FitzGerald, who regarded this as very much his program.[2] While many of the instructors had some misgivings about the worthiness of the people they had tried to help in previous programs, they had few doubts about the Tibetans. A unique mutual respect sprang up between the instructors and the men they were training to serve what became a common cause. In the simplistic ethos of the operational world of that era, the CIA men viewed their Tibetan pupils as Oriental versions of self-reliant, straight-shooting American frontiersmen who were under attack and seeking only the means to fight for their own way of life. There was even a fanciful myth that some of the CIA officers who worked with the Tibetans converted to Buddhism and sought solace in the prayers they learned from their charges.[3] It's a nice picture, but it didn't happen. The instructors came to have a high regard for these men and their religion, but they didn't become novices.

Located in the Colorado mountains at the site of the former head-quarters of the wartime Tenth Mountain Division, Camp Hale reproduced the conditions in which the Tibetans' comrades were fighting half a world away. The valley between the passes leading to Aspen on the west, with the Vail ridge to its back, lay at an altitude of 10,000 feet and had many of the physical features of eastern Tibet. The Tibetan trainees called the camp "Dumra" (after *dumra,* the Tibetan word for "garden") and their instructors *ghegen,* which is the Tibetan word for "teacher." None of the instructors spoke Tibetan at the start of the seven years that the camp served as a base, but "Mr. Bruce," a DePauw graduate and former marine officer, later received university language instruction and practice in the field. His ability to communicate directly with the Tibetans was a great asset. But the primary job of day to day interpretation was carried out by young Tibetans who had been sent to Darjeeling by Gyalo Thondup for training in English. They made an immeasurable contribution to the successful functioning of the camp by interpreting not only the words but the different cultures of the *ghegen* and the trainees to each other. With their unpronounceable names, the Tibetans became individuals to their instructors by the random assignment of American nicknames. In their turn, the instructors, a varied group, each with his own specialty, were known only by their own first names in accordance with standard intelligence practice.

"Mr. Tom," a young former airborne sergeant and veteran paramilitary officer, ran the camp with a firm hand that earned him the respect of both his colleagues and the trainees. Thinlay Paljor, one of the young interpreters, said they appreciated his "genuine sympathy for the Tibetan cause."[4] He was assisted by "Mr. Zeke," a former professional football player from the Pennsylvania mining country, who had established his credentials in earlier paramilitary operations in southeast Asia. The Tibetans thought him to be a "man of not many words, with a short temper but with an open good heart." The most colorful of this crew was "Mr. Tony," who prided himself on his reputation for toughness and a lack of sentimentality similar to Kurtz in Conrad's *Heart of Darkness,* "but who was very popular with the men who [ironically] thought him very active and jovial." "Mr. Ray," the communications instructor, had served as a radio operator on merchant ships making the dangerous Murmansk run taking supplies to Russia during World War II. After the war he graduated from St. John's College in Annapolis, Maryland, which based its curriculum on the Great Books and endowed him with a sense of pride as a classical scholar. "Mr. Al," the "log"—logistics specialist—fussed over getting the right clothes, food, and weapons for "the boys." These men, who were the backbone of the staff, had been carefully selected by "Mr. Mac." He had trained the first group in Saipan two years before and identified closely with them and their cause, a feeling the Tibetans reciprocated.[5]

In the early days the instructors took turns cooking for the entire group. His colleagues recall with great amusement the sight of Zeke the former lineman running from his classroom to the kitchen to rescue a batch of almost-incinerated brownies that he was making from a U.S. Army cookbook designed to serve one hundred soldiers. "Mr. Ray" cooked breakfasts at 5:30 A.M. with Tibetans who mumbled their prayers as they prepared and dished out eggs, toast, and oatmeal. One rule was never to complain about the food, scrupulously adhered to after a medical technician returned to Washington because one of the instructors criticized his spaghetti sauce. The "medic's" successor, "Mr. Harry," was no chef, but he willingly took his turn while he ministered to the surprisingly few injuries sustained by the trainees during their rigorous instruction, administered penicillin for those suffering from congenital VD and taught courses in field first aid.[6] The days were long and there were frequent night exercises. On free evenings the staff ran training films, occasionally showing new movies, and most often the trainees' favorites, *The Bridge on the River Kwai* or *The Treasure of the Sierra Madre*.

Both the trainees and their instructors lived in no-frill army barracks, with the Tibetans grouping themselves into the teams that had chosen to be dropped together into Tibet. In consultation with the instructors, they generally sought each other out, first for their common regional ties, and then for personal compatibility and complementary skills. Although they lived at close quarters, there seemed to be a remarkable absence of friction, and if there was any dissension among them, the Tibetans kept it to themselves.

The instructors had individual cubicles within one barracks that in many ways resembled a picturesque POW camp. It offered little privacy and a minimum of comfort. This created petty annoyances and complaints about those who slammed or left open the double doors into the drafty barracks, snored, talked in their sleep, or neglected to move along their laundry in the washing machine. Reveille call each morning was sounded by tapes of Japanese popular songs, repetition of which soon became irritating. Likewise the oft-told war stories of past operations in Asia grew stale. Tensions understandably erupted among these independent-minded men with strong personalities and diverse interests, usually after a few of the *ghegen* broke out to drive over the road to visit the Cloud City Bar in Leadville, despite the frequent hazards of bad weather.

But otherwise the atmosphere was generally remarkably congenial, and the training somehow worked because both Tibetans and Americans believed in what they were doing. Thinlay Paljor recalled that when he first arrived at Dumra he thought it would be like a concentration camp, but he said he came to have fond memories of the place where "we, the Tibetans and the American instructors, all lived as one large family." The unique harmony that existed in this military monastery, among the guerrilla trainees chanting mantras between and even during classes, the CIA instructors who had found a cause they could enthusiastically support, and the physically beautiful and isolated valley, prompted its inhabitants to regard it as a latter-day Shangri-la. Its mission, however, was not peaceful meditation but preparing its graduates for their duty of resisting a vastly superior enemy occupation of their homeland.

The most time-consuming part of the program was teaching the prospective guerrillas how to encrypt, send, and receive Morse code at fifteen to twenty words per minute from inside Tibet by radio. This course lasted approximately three months. A telecode book had been created that translated words or phrases into numbered code groups. These numbers were encrypted by a one-time pad that made it impossible for messages to be read if intercepted. The brighter students were picked as radio operators, while the poorer students cheerfully cranked the hand generators, a rhythm familiar to anyone used to turning prayer wheels. For seventeen years, this training facilitated the link between Washington and the Roof of the World.

The barracks classes also taught map-reading, techniques for organizing secure intelligence and underground networks to observe and report enemy locations and troop movements, and finding directions by compass and by the stars, which many students could do better than their instructors. By the spring of 1959 the men were able to work from the first accurate maps of their country ever made, a product of overflight photography. I was Mr. Ken, the political *ghegen.* Lacking only my dissertation to earn a Ph.D. in political science from Stanford, I was also known as "Dr. Zhivago." (This was an in-house joke; it was the name that I had claimed when asking a United Airlines stewardess to refrigerate some measles vaccine that I was bringing to the camp for the trainees.) I offered a rudimentary course in the history of communism and propaganda techniques, supplemented by practical instruction in the use of a portable mimeograph for producing leaflets and booklets to enlist local support and recruits.

Not surprisingly, these men from a society built around religious instruction and artistic portrayal of the scriptures turned out to be natural propagandists for a cause in which they believed to the point of being ready to give their lives. On free evenings, the few monk artists were surrounded by volunteers as they colored in their drawings of the injustices and injuries they had suffered from the Chinese.[7] Others turned out the resistance creed on the mimeograph machines. But my experiment in "nation building," which I foisted off on my good-natured colleague, "Mr. Joe," was a failure. Using the dialogues in Plato's *Republic,* the trainees were asked to define justice and good government in the free Tibet for which they were fighting. But for them, dialectical discourse was properly confined to religious matters and the monasteries. They were willing to defer to the Dalai Lama and the learned monks for the kind of government they wanted. We dropped the course.

The training was directed toward indoctrinating these men in the necessity of fighting as guerrillas. On the firing ranges "Mr. Bill," a young New Englander fresh from serving with the U.S. Army in Korea, taught the use of a variety of ordnance, including the British Enfield, which was in common use in eastern Tibet, the U.S. Springfield, and the U.S. M-1 Garand. Enfields were sent in the initial airdrops in 1958 and early 1959 because they were readily available, would not provide evidence of their U.S. origin, and were familiar to the Tibetans. In the autumn of 1959 the CIA began dropping M-1s because their superior firepower outweighed the other considerations.

The trainees were also taught to fire 57 mm and 75 mm recoilless rifles, 60 mm and 81 mm mortars, and handguns. They repeatedly practiced the procedure for selecting a secure drop zone and illuminating it with the classic "T" so it could be spotted from the air. Several hundred acres of mountainous terrain were suited for frequent field exercises, practicing what they had learned from another young former army man, an Oklahoman named "Mr. Roy." He rehearsed them in using map and compass, laying ambush sites, and selecting drop zones and receiving drops from the airplanes, for which the Tibetans had coined the word *namdu,* meaning "sky boat." The field exercises were held throughout the year in all weathers, similar to what the trainees could expect when they returned home.

All this was then possible in splendid isolation. The camp was guarded at the only point at which it was accessible by road. Signs were posted along the perimeter warning that it was a U.S. government weapons-testing area. This generated the local legend that it was an atomic test zone,[8] which was deliberately reinforced by strenuous denials and occasional (conventional) explosions to discourage casual mountain hikers. "Mr. John," who had set up the camp with the cooperation of the Department of Defense, had located the site well. The trainees needed to leave this self-contained reproduction of their homeland only for an airfield to make the three parachute jumps from airplanes that were part of their training. For this they had been well prepared by "Mr. Jack," a former smoke jumper with the U.S. Forest Service in Montana, who was the model of the self-sufficient Marlboro man of action but few words. He personally felled and stripped the trees to build the platform from which the men made their practice jumps. An especially close bond grew between him and the trainees, whom he and some of the other instructors accompanied on their qualifying jumps.

Even today there remains a camaraderie between those men now living in India and Nepal who were trained at Dumra and their American *ghegen.*[9] It may have been this strong bond and shared sense of purpose that caused them, and perhaps the trainees, to underestimate the enormously adverse odds they faced when they returned to Tibet to carry out their dangerous missions.

OPERATIONS RESUME INSIDE TIBET

By the time the Dalai Lama had fled to India in the summer of 1959 and the resistance was under concentrated attack, the Dumra graduates were ready to take their expertise back to their comrades and serve as conduits for arms and supplies. The matching air capability to carry out such missions was also available. The question was whether the situation of the resistance forces inside Tibet still warranted such operations. By mid-April Gompo Tashi and the main body of his organization had fought a series of battles in an attempt to reestablish a headquarters at Tsona in southern Tibet about thirty miles from the Bhutan border.[10] Finding themselves overwhelmed by Chinese troops and air power, they decided to make their way to India. At the border they received and rejected the request from CIA headquarters to remain in Tibet and wait for arms to be dropped.[11] After they crossed the border into Tawang, the commanders met with Gompo and decided that rather than laying down their arms they would try to obtain a pocket of land inside Tibet, and from there reunite the resistance forces for guerrilla operations.[12] This plan was thwarted when Indian army troops surrounded the meeting site and seized the Tibetans' arms.

Gompo Tashi had brought with him information about the men he had recruited and left behind to conduct guerrilla operations in the territory northeast of his now overrun headquarters in Tibet. He advised that the local resistance forces could conduct ambushes along the Sichuan-Lhasa highway and disrupt traffic along this major supply route for the Chinese army. Gyalo Thondup was informed by his underground that similar resistance pockets were holding out along the other principal Chinese supply route, the highway northwest of Lhasa to Qinghai. But both needed help from Washington. The policymakers were receptive—

diplomatic support for Tibet at the UN would be hollow if the resistance folded—and the CIA was ready and eager to support the guerrillas. Such operations develop their own momentum, which makes them hard to stop. So plans went ahead to dispatch teams into the areas where the resistance was still alive and to follow them with arms drops if justified.

On September 19, 1959, nine men who had been trained at Camp Hale, all but one of them Khampas, were dropped around Ringtso near Lake Namtso in the high plains region roughly two hundred miles northwest of Lhasa.[13] Refugees had reported that a local resistance leader named Natsang Phurpo had a force there of 4,000 men. The nine men were given two radio sets, code books, signal plans, backup radio equipment, maps, compasses, binoculars, and Tibetan clothing. Because this was a "blind" drop to an unknown reception, they carried M-1 rifles and Sten submachine guns. Their mission was to persuade Phurpo and his men to attack Chinese trucks transporting borax from the local mines. When the team arrived where Phurpo had last been reported operating, they discovered that the Chinese army, tipped off by a traitor among Phurpo's forces, had been alerted to the presence of the guerrillas and attacked and dispersed them.

The team members had no choice but to make their way to India. They buried their radio and trekked three hundred and fifty miles across the northern plain to the Mustang area of Nepal. It took them eight weeks. These resourceful and hardy men survived by shooting the wild animals that live in this nomad area. When they arrived in Mustang, where a mixture of Tibetan resistance veterans and old-time Khampa bandits had sought refuge, they contacted their leaders in Darjeeling, who instructed them to come ahead and report on the details of their mission's failure and their heroic escape. Within weeks they were again brought out of India in secret, flown across the Pacific for the second time to Dumra in Colorado, and there debriefed and prepared for a new assignment.

In the same September moon phase, three other teams totaling eighteen men were dropped in the Pembar area, where Gompo Tashi had left behind a budding resistance force the previous spring. Pembar is in Khampa territory, more than two hundred miles northeast of Lhasa, in the mountains south of the Amdo region of ethnic Tibet. It had become a gathering place for resistance fighters who had been forced out of their homes farther east in Kham. A local lama, who was also a resistance leader, had provided an updated assessment on the resistance potential to Lhamo Tsering in Darjeeling. The teams were to confirm the presence of these forces and encourage them to undertake an organized guerrilla campaign in the Pembar area.

Their primary mission was to gain control over the Shotalasum area, of which Pembar is the center. The Chinese had been unable to assert their authority over this mountainous region between the northern and southern branches of the Sichuan-Lhasa highway, and resistance forces had successfully attacked Chinese military installations there. By setting up pockets of resistance the guerrillas could establish bases from which they could harass and interdict supply convoys and troop transports, cutting the Chinese supply route to central Tibet and hampering the army's efforts to suppress the rebellion.

Two of the teams were composed of Khampas from Litang, Markam, and Dêgê, three of the principal Khampa towns of the Yangtze River border area where the revolt had begun three years before. The mission of the first team of seven men was to train the Pembar resistance in guerrilla tactics and receive the arms drops, which began a month later. The second team of six Khampas was at first ordered to proceed to Zayul in southeastern Kham near the Burmese border, but their instructions were later rescinded and they were ordered to stay at Pembar to assist in the reception of the arms drops.

The first arms drop delivered 126 pallets of cargo, which included 370 M-1 rifles, 192 rounds of ammunition per rifle, 4 machine guns with 1,000 rounds of ammunition, and 2 radio sets. The following month a second drop contained much the same, plus three recoilless rifles and 150 rounds. A third delivery made during the next full moon dropped 226 pallets: 800 rifles, 20 cases of hand grenades, 113 carbines, and 200 cases of ammunition, each containing 10,000 bullets. The last drops were made on January 6, 1960, when three planes dropped 657 pallets of arms and equipment. These included, in addition to the arms, 30 cases of medicine, 12 cases of food, and, by request, a mimeograph machine and a box of propaganda booklets.[14]

The pilots making the drops reported that the drop-zone sites were located exactly at the map coordinates that the Dumra-trained teams had reported in their radio messages and were illuminated with textbook "T" bonfires. They also reported that the resistance fighters had assembled two hundred mules to receive the equipment, turning the area into a vast military encampment.[15] The Dumra graduates instructed the local warriors in the tactics of guerrilla warfare and reaffirmed the increasingly urgent instructions from the CIA to disperse. In principle, the advice was sound. But it was based on the assumption that the resistance fighters were free to fight as guerrillas. In fact, they traveled with families and herds they could not abandon. In retrospect, the only way these men could have survived as guerrillas would have been to abandon their defenseless dependents and move in small bands to remote mountain outposts as soon as they were armed with the airdropped weapons. In practice, that kind of dispersal was not possible. Besides, there was always the lure of more drops from this inexhaustible arms warehouse in the sky.

The Chinese, alerted by the flights, soon located what had become a fixed campsite. Within a month after the last supply drop, the Chinese called in troops and air power for a massive campaign to disperse and destroy this concentration of resistance forces. By the late spring of 1960 the entire force of fighters, families, and animals had been either killed or scattered. Of the thirteen men of the two Dumra teams who had vainly tried to persuade their comrades to fight like guerrillas, five made it to India some months later by following the Brahmaputra River into the North East Frontier Agency.

The third team dropped to Pembar was composed of five men, three from the Amdo plateau of northern Tibet and two from central Tibet. All had been trained at Dumra. They had been instructed to make their way from the Pembar drop zone to the southern part of Amdo to verify reports of active resistance groups, and they soon confirmed the presence of sizable resistance groups that needed arms. The largest concentration was in the Sudeh area in the southwestern part of the Amdo region, where a group of Amdo leaders had been joined by Khampa groups fleeing the Chinese army. They agreed to attack convoys on the Qinghai-Lhasa highway—a major artery for supplying the Chinese troops in Lhasa—once they had the necessary arms and equipment. They accepted the team's radio operator, Nasar Tashi Tsering, a fellow Amdo who could call for and obtain delivery of the needed arms, as their leader.

Their principal encampment was at Nira Tsogeng,[16] just south of the 18,000-foot Thangla Pass, and on December 13 they received the first of eight arms drops. Two planes dropped 290 pallets, which included 1,680 rifles and 368,800 rounds of ammunition. On January 10, 1960, two planes again flew to the area, but only one was able to make a drop of 140 pallets containing more arms. Five days later four planes arrived, again with arms and other supplies. Thus more than 4,000 resistance fighters had been armed.

On the last overflight, three teams totaling sixteen men were parachuted into the area. These included six of the nine members of the team that had been dropped to Ringtso, returned to Colorado, and now were being parachuted back into their homeland a second time. Gompo Tashi's nephew, Ngawang Phuljung, who was one of these men, had been sent to act as the leader for the three teams composed of classmates at Dumra. Their mission was to persuade the armed resistance forces to break up into small guerrilla groups and begin attacks to close the northern highway to Lhasa.

But the disastrous pattern of Pembar prevailed. The encampment took on permanence, the potential guerrillas were encumbered with dependents and herds numbering about 30,000 animals, and the area did not provide sufficient cover and sustenance for them to disperse and survive. In vain, the teams from Dumra exhorted their comrades to break up and relocate in scattered areas. Like Pembar, the assumption that this was feasible now seems unrealistic. The Chinese did not wait long. On February 22, 1960, they began an air bombardment and encircling land operation, and within six months after the first drops the Chinese were able to decimate and scatter this force. Many of the fighters fled across the desolate northern plain to Ladakh, most to die on the way for lack of fresh water. The Chinese used cavalry and tanks to pursue the radio teams but they escaped, most of them only to die of thirst after sending a final message reporting the destruction of the encamp-

ment. One man surrendered out of sheer exhaustion and was imprisoned in Lhasa, where he remained after his release in 1979.

Only one Dumra man, a radio operator, escaped and made his way to
India. He was later dispatched back to Metok in the Bemako area of
southern Tibet opposite the North East Frontier Agency, where a remnant of Gompo's Chushi Gangdruk force had established a base. This
group requested arms, and a drop was being considered when the Chi-
nese-Indian border skirmishes turned into a full-scale war in 1962.
When the retreating Indian soldiers destroyed the bridges across the
Brahmaputra, this operation was shelved.

A final team of seven was dropped to the Markam area of Kham on
the western side of the Yangtze in the early spring of 1961. It was led by a
man in his twenties named Yeshe Wangyal, the son of a local Khampa
chieftain and guerrilla leader in the Markam area. At Dumra, Yeshe
Wangyal was known by the instructors as "Tim" and was regarded as one
of the most intelligent and gifted of the Tibetans. He had a natural
instinct for guerrilla warfare and firmly believed in a unified Tibet, artic-
ulated in the propaganda pamphlets he learned to produce at Dumra.
These pamphlets, written in the beautiful script of the educated Tibetan,
were reproduced in quantity by the CIA print shop and taken by the
trainees at their own request when they were parachuted into Tibet.

Tim was the Renaissance man of Dumra, as well as the acknowledged
leader among his Tibetan comrades. They called him "Phuba Pon," a title
of respect accorded to him as his father's son. He had been one of those
dropped into Ringtso sixteen months earlier, where he and his teammates
discovered that the resistance force they had been sent to support had been
rounded up by the Chinese. After their hazardous escape to Nepal, Tim
had returned to Dumra, and was then sent back across the Pacific to a staging area in southeast Asia, whence he was to be dispatched on another
mission into the Kham area. Hours before they were to board the plane
taking them to the drop zone, Tim and his teammates calmly but firmly
announced that they had decided not to go on the mission. They
objected that they were being sent to an area unknown to them, where
they would have no contacts. Tim had obviously learned a painful lesson
from his earlier experience of dropping into an unfamiliar area with an

uncertain reception. Their instinct was sounder than those who were dispatching them. To us the Tibetan resistance was homogenous, and we were
still ignorant of how local and personal were the loyalties of the resistance
forces, even within their own regions. There ensued prolonged and emotional arguments, not all of them honest on the side of us *ghegen,* who
saw cancellation of the mission as a personal failure and a threat to continuance of the whole program. But Tim and his mates remained
adamant. The mission was scratched. It was a painful experience for
both the team and its teachers. They were right, and we were wrong.

After some months at another holding area in the Pacific, Tim volunteered to lead his team back into the Markam area, which he knew.[17] No
pressure had been exerted by the *ghegen* on these men to undertake
another mission. However, they must have felt a deep sense of obligation
to themselves, to Gyalo Thondup and Gompo Tashi, who had selected
them for training at Dumra, and in Tim's case to his father. Tim had
received information from Gyalo Thondup that his father was still alive
and fighting. He wanted to join him, especially since he now had the
means to obtain arms for his father's resistance group. The other members of his team were three Khampas and three men from central Tibet.
Their immediate mission was to find and join Tim's father and two other
resistance leaders from the Markam area, Mepa Pon and Dakpa Lama.

Among those on the mission was a former medical student and soldier in the Tibetan army, Nyemo Bhusang, whose regiment had taken
part in the revolt in Lhasa by lying in the street to block the Dalai Lama's
passage to the Chinese army camp. Fifty members of the regiment had
subsequently made their way to the resistance stronghold in southern
Tibet, where they took part in the skirmishes with the Chinese. Those
who finally reached India surrendered their arms. After five months
working as a paramedic on a refugee road gang in Sikkim, Bhusang was
recruited for training at Dumra and given the nickname of "Ken." Tim
picked him for the team.

The seven Tibetans were dropped by faint moonlight on a mild late
winter night near a small village called Gojo in the Markam area of
Kham. The ground was dusted lightly with snow, which the team considered a good omen because white is an auspicious color in Tibet. Ken

said that he and the rest of the team were euphoric at finally embarking on the mission for which they had been trained at Dumra. They also took heart from the fact that some of the plane's crew disdained parachutes, which meant that they had shared the risk of being killed if the plane crashed.

After hiding their parachutes and supplies in small rock shelters that local nomads use for their animals, the team set off to reconnoiter the area. They found that Tim had made an error in identifying the drop site, which was farther from the town of Markam than he had remembered. They traveled through the sparsely populated mountains for two nights until they reached a meadow on the other side of a mountain from Markam. At dawn they saw three cow sheds, where they rested because one of the team had been injured in the drop. If they encountered either a Chinese or a Tibetan police patrol, they would say they were from a road construction camp, seek information for contacting the local Chinese road construction commander, and inquire about the three "bandits" reported to be in the area—that is, Tim's father, Mepa Pon, and Dakpa Lama.

While the others rested, Tim and two other members of the team met three Tibetan herdsmen. The team members planned to ask the herdsmen if they had seen any Chinese patrols or "bandits." If they were friendly, Tim would try to buy food. One of the herdsmen turned out to be a former servant of Tim's father. At first he refused to accept Tim as the son of his former employer because Tim was supposed to be in India. When Tim asked him if he and his companions had heard the plane two nights before, they grumpily said they had, and that it had caused them much trouble by disturbing their herds. The herdsmen then said that Tim's father had been killed months ago and the other two guerrilla leaders were hiding in the dense woodland covering much of this Yangtze valley area. But the guerrillas meant trouble to these frightened herdsmen, who refused to sell them food and ordered them to leave or be reported to the Chinese.

The undaunted Tim had a nephew living about fifteen miles away, and he was able to meet with him early in the morning a few days later. The nephew said the two other leaders, Mepa Pon and Dakpa Lama, were expected that night to obtain food. He volunteered to set up a meeting for Tim two days later. Tim and Ken subsequently went to meet the two leaders, who were accompanied by six bodyguards, while the rest of Tim's team stayed hidden. Mepa Pon confirmed that Tim's father had been killed and said that he had assumed leadership of the group, which consisted of approximately eighty people, including women, children, and elders. Tim promised arms, ammunition, and funds from the U.S. government. Mepa Pon was definitely interested. Ken, with three members of his team and six of Mepa Pon's men, then returned to the drop zone, where they retrieved the equipment from the cache of stone huts.

On the way back with the weapons they found Chinese pamphlets warning all resistance forces that they were vastly outnumbered by 60,000 Chinese troops in the area. They also discovered that the Chinese controlled the local village. Their worries increased when Tim and the two other teammates failed to meet them at their rendezvous sites, but four days later they had a happy but tearful reunion with Tim and their two other comrades, who had been forced by aggressive patrolling Chinese to dodge the appointed rendezvous. They then took stock of what they realized was a desperate situation.

Despite the almost equal split between four Khampas and three men from central Tibet, the team made all their decisions by consensus. The "*tsampa* eaters" were standing together. They wanted to fight the Chinese, but they had been instructed by the CIA officers who planned their mission to make their way out to India if they found the Chinese presence overwhelming. There were to be no more quixotic stands against unbeatable odds. The team decided that, even if the claim of 60,000 men was exaggerated, the Chinese exercised sufficient control to make the prospect of challenging them unrealistic. They therefore had two options, both of which were made more difficult because they had by then joined forces with Mepa Pon's group of fighters and dependents. The first alternative was to head south to India, about one hundred and fifty miles away, across a major pass and several rivers. They could use the rubber boat that had been dropped with them, though that would mean repeated trips to ferry all of their new comrades. They also knew that their route to India was heavily patrolled by Chinese troops under orders to seal the border. The alternative was to follow the route through the nomad plains, with which Tim had become familiar on his ill-fated earlier mission. But that would be a rigorous trek, their passage slowed by the dependents.

The team opted for the second route because they were less likely to encounter Chinese patrols. Tim and Ken then told Mepa Pon and Dakpa Lama of their plan, offering to take along the noncombatants. They would move slowly and live off the abundant wild animals. The local leaders agreed, and the entire group set out, heading to the north on their way to India by the route of Tim's earlier escape.

They ran into Chinese almost immediately and fought nine battles evading them. The first of the Dumra men, "Colin," was killed in the second encounter. By now only about forty of the Mepa Pon/Dakpa Lama force were still able to fight. They and the remaining six members of the team were exhausted and starving. Ken recalled that he felt no fear, not because he was brave, but because "human beings lose fear when they are desperate." On the previous evening they had bought a yak from a local nomad. The starving men killed and ate the yak, drinking its blood for strength, with none of the regret they normally would have felt about taking life.

The rejuvenated group then settled in for the night in a small forest on a mountainside, which they thought would be safe from the Chinese. But at 6 A.M. the Chinese appeared in force. It was early summer, three months since they had been dropped less than one hundred miles to the south. They soon realized there would be no escape: all would be killed or captured. Ken took small clay charms that had been blessed by the Dalai Lama and ground them into powder, which he gave to the other team members. The six men then took positions a few feet from each other and began firing at the Chinese. Although slightly frightened, once Ken started firing he began to enjoy it, even found it quite "intoxicating" as thousands of bullets were fired at them by the Chinese without hitting them. He felt protected by the holy charm, but by midmorning when he crawled toward "Aaron" and "Luke," he found both dead. They were both from Litang and had been inseparable since they joined the original Chushi Gangdruk some years before. Now they had joined each other in death by taking the cyanide capsules that had been included at their request in the packs dropped with them. They preferred death to capture.

At noon the Chinese overran the decimated band. Ken was knocked unconscious with his cyanide pill in his mouth. The lethal capsule was apparently removed by one of his captors. He awakened to find himself along with fifteen or twenty survivors of the Mepa Pon/Dakpa Lama group under guard by Chinese troops. He was brought tea by one of the women who had surrendered the day before. She told him that Tim and the other two members of the team were still alive when he was captured, but she had no idea of their fate. Ken was later told that their bodies had been carried away on the back of a yak.

Ken was taken with the other survivors to a Chinese army camp near Markham. He was denounced as an American spy, which made him a prize of war worthy of being sent to a military prison camp near Lhasa and held with Tibetan government officials and members of the nobility. In the trauma Ken lost his voice, but his captors sent him to a hospital where he was treated with acupuncture. When he regained the power of speech he was interrogated under torture. After seven days he admitted that his initial story of having come from India was false. In subsequent sessions of torture and interrogation he was finally forced to tell the whole story of his training in the United States, who had sent him there, the route by which he had gone from India to Colorado, the names of his instructors, the number and identities of those who had been with him at Dumra, what they had been taught there, and finally, the objectives of the U.S. government in supporting the Tibetan resistance. Contrary to their usual propaganda practice, the Chinese never released the details, especially of the foreign involvement. Facing the threat of a Nationalist invasion of a weakened China during this third year of bitter famine throughout China, it apparently did not serve Mao's purposes to publicize the extent of U.S. government support for resistance to his rule.

Ken was held in this prison from 1961 until 1964, when he was moved to a second prison. There he met Tashi, a servant of Gompo Tashi's who had been captured in northern Tibet, and Yeshe, the man who had surrendered at Nira Tsogeng. In the second prison were twelve Tibetans accused of being American spies, and there they were held until their release with twenty-one officials and nobles in 1979. Ken had been held for eighteen years without trial.

Ken was allowed to leave Tibet for India and subsequently went to work for the security department of the Dalai Lama's government at Dharamsala, where he lives today. Since his capture, he has suffered from a persistent rash that would seem easily explained by these traumatic events, but Ken believes it to be the result of the cyanide pill he had in his mouth when the Chinese knocked him unconscious with a rifle butt. When asked if he felt guilty as the only survivor, Ken said that when he was in prison under torture he felt that those who had died were the lucky ones. But now he feels happy to be alive and has no sense of guilt. Despite his miserable life as a consequence of his experience with the Americans, Ken greeted me with great affection as one of *ghegen*s from Dumra and spoke warmly of the U.S. efforts on behalf of the Tibetans when we reunited in Dharamsala in October of 1996.

ℭℭ

The fall of this last team of valiant volunteers marked the end of the CIA's active involvement in air operations in Tibet. The record had been dismal. Of the forty-nine men dropped into Tibet since 1957, only twelve survived. Ten had escaped after arduous and dangerous treks to India. One had surrendered and one had been captured, and both of them served long prison terms. The other thirty-seven had been killed in greatly unequal battles against Chinese air power and overpowering numbers on the ground, coupled with an unforgiving climate and the absence of a safe haven in which to establish a secure base.[18]

Looking back on these operations thirty-six years later, Lhamo Tsering, who along with Gyalo Thondup had selected these men and helped plan their missions, attributed their failure to several factors.[19] The resistance fighters would not or could not accept the advice of the trained teams to fight as guerrillas and instead took on the Chinese in frontal attacks. The resistance operated in infertile countryside that could barely feed its own people let alone a guerrilla force. The Chinese, by control of both the air and the ground, could locate and annihilate the resistance groups. There was also no communication among the different operational areas.

Mao himself had confronted many of the same problems in 1928 when he had tried to establish a base in Jinggangshan, a remote mountainous area astride the Hunan-Jiangxi border.[20] In his report, "The Struggle in the Jinggang Mountains," he cited homesickness among forces who found the Jinggangshan area "a poor and lonely place"; exhaustion; the inability of the area to support the number of Red Army troops; and their consequent eagerness to break out of the trap by embarking on a military expedition against superior Nationalist forces. The result was a disastrous defeat in August of 1928. Over thirty years later the Tibetans rebelling against a now all-powerful Mao were to suffer a similar fate.

Lhamo Tsering's criticism of the CIA's failure to provide equipment for the groups to communicate with each other, share intelligence, and coordinate their movements is valid. The equipment was withheld lest the Chinese monitor the transmissions; the CIA believed the Tibetans would not observe proper communications security. In retrospect, the advantages of giving this equipment to the resistance fighters would now seem to have outweighed the possible risks.

Sometime after the loss of Tim's team, Lhamo Tsering acquired a Chinese army document noting that it took twenty bullets for a Chinese soldier to kill one Tibetan guerrilla while the Tibetans used one bullet to kill one Chinese. He also noted that the Tibetans used up or destroyed all of their supplies before surrendering, while the Chinese frequently abandoned their supplies when they felt themselves outnumbered, thereby providing the resistance with a local source of weapons. The Tibetans did seem capable of functioning successfully as guerrillas on occasion.

Lhamo Tsering still believed that the resistance mission of preventing or at least slowing down Chinese control in central Tibet was realistic and achievable, but only if these men had been able to reorganize themselves in time. Their downfall came from their natural preference for great encampments, similar to the medieval-style tournament gatherings they once had known. And they were facing what in retrospect seem to have been insurmountable disadvantages. The achievement of dropping men, arms, and equipment into the middle of a hostile, isolated, and physically forbidding area was a brilliant technical and logistical success. The Tibetans surely had played their part bravely. But the concept of sustaining a large-scale guerrilla movement by air in Tibet had proven a painful failure.

CHAPTER 13

Mustang and Washington

I N EARLY 1960 the CIA air operations supporting the resistance in the Kham and Amdo regions were at their height, and optimism both in Washington and among the Tibetan leadership in India about the prospects for maintaining the resistance remained high. The Chinese had not yet launched the blitzkriegs that were to decimate and disperse the resistance concentrations in the east. Gyalo Thondup kept his brother the Dalai Lama informed of the general terms of the CIA support, as it was no longer possible to preserve the screen of his official ignorance. While he was never asked to give his blessing to these operations (which necessarily involved violence), the Dalai Lama had little choice. For the tens of thousands of

Tibetans who had fled their homeland as he had, and for those they left behind with only hopes for his return, the Dalai Lama defined Tibet. He was asking the world to help him regain what had been lost, and here were his people fighting for the same thing. He could only tacitly accept these operations as the necessary price of the fight for independence.[1]

Early in February, Allen Dulles briefed President Eisenhower on the current operations and requested his approval for the continuation of the program.[2] The president had taken a keen interest in these operations, as he had in all covert paramilitary operations developed as alternatives to a full military challenge to communism. But Eisenhower the soldier was fully aware of the risks and questioned whether continuing the resistance might not result in even more brutal reprisals by the Chinese. Desmond FitzGerald replied that "there could be no greater brutality than had been experienced in Tibet in the past." Eisenhower then turned to Herter to ask if he favored continuation of these operations. The secretary, who had been willing to settle for a mere "slap on the wrist" for the Chinese at the UN, now seemed more combative. He voted to continue the operations because "not only would continued successful resistance by the Tibetans prove to be a serious harassment to the Chinese Communists but it would serve to keep the spark alive in the entire area." The results in the long run, he argued, could "mean much to the free world apart from humanitarian considerations for the Tibetans." The president gave his approval, apparently convinced by the unanimous support of his national security advisers and their arguments that the moral balance favored the U.S. continuing its support to the Tibetan freedom fighters.

Herter's argument that forcing the Chinese to combat a continuing resistance effort would cause trouble for the regime was particularly relevant in 1960. Although complete intelligence was not available for several years, there were ample indications that Mao's regime was vulnerable. The consequences of Mao's disastrous Great Leap Forward were becoming apparent in the famine that would eventually starve at least 20 million Chinese to death in the name of his egalitarian and collectivist ideology. The governing elite was still digesting the fall from grace of the revolutionary hero, Marshal Peng Dehuai.[3] Khrushchev, in a vote of no-confidence, had terminated Soviet aid to the Chinese nuclear program. While Mao had the power to crush the Tibetans, their continuing insurrection must have been particularly worrisome during this time of political instability.

Washington was therefore receptive when the CIA received a proposal from Gyalo Thondup early in 1960 to revive the resistance movement inside Tibet. He acted on behalf of the resistance leader, Gompo Tashi, who had taken refuge in Darjeeling after fleeing, wounded, with his resistance forces in 1959. Several thousand of his men were working on road gangs in Sikkim or elsewhere along the Indian border, but they were ready to return to the fight. Gompo proposed that they regroup to operate inside Tibet opposite the Mustang kingdom in Nepal.[4]

Mustang, a territorial enclave of several hundred square miles extending north into Tibet some three hundred and fifty miles southwest of Lhasa, is an area of extremes both in remoteness and in topography.[5] Bounded on the south by two of the world's highest mountain ranges, Annapurna and Dhaulagiri, it is bisected by the Kali Gandaki river, which flows through one of the world's deepest canyons. Its capital, Lo Mantang, is situated roughly twenty miles from the Tibetan border on a plateau 13,000 feet high. There the twenty-fourth King of Lo, a man of Tibetan ancestry and Buddhist faith, reigned under the nominal rule of the Gurkha kings in Kathmandu, with whom his ancestor had sided in the 1855 war between Tibet and Nepal. By 1960 the king of Mustang recognized Nepal's nominal authority only by sending gifts of no great value each year to the palace in Kathmandu. The Nepalese government made little effort to exercise any control beyond posting a small cantonment of lonely and miserable soldiers at Jomosom, twenty miles south of the sketchily defined border between Mustang and Nepal. They also discouraged casual travel in this area, which had become sensitive because of China's presence in Tibet. While the great ranges isolated Mustang from Nepal on the south, the less precipitous slopes and passes on the northern border made Tibet relatively accessible to the men who formed the body of Gompo Tashi's forces.

Gompo Tashi had become familiar with Mustang on the trips that he had made as a pilgrim and trader to western Tibet in former years. Even then he had marked it as an area that would lend itself to guerrilla operations. At a meeting with CIA operations officers in early spring, Gompo, accompanied by Gyalo Thondup and Lhamo Tsering, proposed that members of the resistance force be reunited and establish a base in Mustang, from which they would send small guerrilla units into Tibet. While the CIA officers fully appreciated the advantage of using Mao's own classic tactic of a secure base offering a safe haven for retreat, the U.S. government could not approve establishing a base even in such a remote region without permission from the Nepalese government. Political and security reasons ruled out asking Kathmandu for permission.

A compromise was therefore agreed upon.[6] Twenty-one hundred men in good physical condition and literate in Tibetan would be recruited from the scattered forces of the National Volunteer Freedom Fighters that had fought under Gompo in central Tibet. Most were veterans of the Chushi Gangdruk, the original eastern Tibet resistance group, now joined by members of the much smaller Mimang Tsongdu resistance movement from central Tibet. This meant that approximately 70 percent of the force came from Kham, 25 percent from Amdo, and 5 percent from central Tibet. They were to make their way in contingents of three hundred to Mustang, from where they would set out to find permanent sites across the border inside Tibet, where they would operate as guerrilla units. The practice of the resistance fighters in eastern Tibet, who had concentrated their forces in fixed locations with disastrous consequences, was not to be repeated. Only after the first three hundred had found an area inside Tibet from which they could disperse and live as guerrillas would the next increment be sent to Mustang to repeat the process. Eventually seven groups would operate independently from separate sites in the area south of the Brahmaputra River parallel to the Lhasa-Xinjiang highway. The CIA agreed to drop arms, trained leaders, and supplies to these sites as long as there was no public disclosure. This last point was critical, and it was agreed that the scheme would be abandoned if word of these operations leaked to the press.[7]

Gompo Tashi selected twenty-six men to be sent for training at Dumra, including Lobsang Champa, a leader from Litang, who was designated by both Gompo and CIA to be the leader of the Mustang force when he returned from Colorado. Gompo then named Gyen Yeshe, a

Khampa monk from Batang, to lead an advance party to Mustang. There he was to make local contacts and arrange the logistics for temporarily supplying each reinforcement until they moved to their destinations inside Tibet. It was to be an orderly procedure to take place over the next several months, ensuring that no more than three hundred men would be in Mustang at any one time. The plan sounded good on the drawing board. Gyen Yeshe had performed well when Gompo had gone off to fight the Chinese in Kham two years earlier and left him in charge of the main resistance force in central Tibet. He was generally accepted by the men, even though the majority of them came from other parts of Kham that were traditionally jealous and even antagonistic toward people from Gyen Yeshe's hometown of Batang. Gyen Yeshe accordingly set off in late spring. Among his seven-man party were two radio operators trained at Dumra who reported their safe arrival in Mustang in June. The resuscitation of Gompo's army in a new location, conducting complementary operations to what remained of the beleaguered resistance in the east, seemed well underway when things started to go wrong.

The first setback had no direct connection with Tibet. On May 1, 1960, in what was to become an international Mayday situation, a U-2 high altitude photo reconnaissance plane flown by an American pilot under contract to the CIA was brought down by a rocket 1,300 miles inside the Soviet Union.[8] Although the Russians had known about and protested these flights from their inception, they had chosen not to publicize their own embarrassment over their inability (until that moment) to shoot down these high-flying intruders. Neither did they have any physical evidence of the flights upon which to base a complaint. Eisenhower, aware of the sensitivity of the U-2 flights, insisted on personally approving each one only after convincing himself that the information would warrant the embarrassment if the flights were discovered. He had agreed to this mission at the CIA's insistence that this would be the last chance to photograph the construction of the first Soviet intercontinental missile. The destruction of this plane, whose U.S. connection was at first formally denied by the White House, could not have come at a worse time. Eisenhower was preparing for a summit meeting in Paris with Khrushchev that had been years in the making. It turned into the political disaster Eisenhower had always feared following a series of White House miscalculations set up by the canny Russians, who did not announce for six days that the pilot had been captured alive. In the interim Washington issued a series of cover stories that were all revealed to be false when a gleeful Khrushchev produced both the wreckage and the pilot. Eisenhower, hoping to deflate the matter, decided to admit publicly that the flights had been flown under his authority. After demanding and not receiving an apology, Khrushchev stormed out of the summit, and the "Spirit of Camp David" was dead. One consequence was the president's decision to order a stand-down on intelligence operations of a provocative nature. Covert flights over unfriendly territory would require waivers, and these were not easily granted, particularly ones to launch a substantial new guerrilla army. This decision, a consequence of events thousands of miles away, was to have repercussions in the distant Himalayan kingdom of Mustang.

The suspension of overflights had no immediate effect on the plans for the Mustang operations, which had already been set into motion. Gyen Yeshe was on his way to the Nepali valley to prepare for the secret arrival of the initial contingent then being recruited. The twenty-six men selected to be commanders of the force to be built over the coming months were on their way to Dumra for training. According to the plan, it would be some months before the first groups would have made their way into Tibet. By then it was expected that the ban on overflights would be either eased or lifted.

The new ground rules did make the principal American requirement in agreeing to drop supplies to the men from Mustang—that they were to move into the isolated kingdom without public notice—even more critical. This condition turned out to be unrealistic. The first group of recruits proudly told their comrades on the road gangs about where they were going and what they were going to do there. The word spread quickly through these tight communities of dedicated but frustrated men. Soon large numbers of former guerrillas turned up in Darjeeling to volunteer for the Mustang force. Lhamo Tsering asked Gompo Tashi to send men to Sikkim to stem the deluge of recruits. The hereditary ruler of Sikkim, the *choegyal,* sent an angry protest to Gyalo. The Tibetan workers were repairing his kingdom's roads as a public works project at Indian expense, and he thought they were being wooed away by a massive recruiting drive. These belated efforts were in vain.

On August 1, the *Statesman,* one of India's leading dailies based in Calcutta, began a series of articles with headlines reading Mysterious Exodus from Sikkim: Khampas Leaving in Hundreds; amplified two days later by Tibetan Exodus Continues: Even Persuasion Fails to Change Their Minds; and finally on August 13, 2,700 Tibetans Leave from India. The accounts were accurate. From CIA headquarters urgent and angry messages were sent to Thondup demanding that the flow of men to Mustang be stopped and threatening to cancel the agreement to supply the growing force. But Thondup was powerless to block these determined men as they left their families to make their way by bus, or on foot, through the jungles of southern Nepal. By early autumn Gyen Yeshe was overwhelmed with more than 2,000 recruits ready to fight, but in need of food and arms.

The CIA thus found itself stuck with a sizable problem and no ready solutions. What was supposed to have been a covert operation was now an open secret throughout the Himalayas. The plan calling for a series of carefully contained movements on a tightly controlled schedule was now irrelevant. Instead of groups of three hundred, there were seven times that number to be fed, housed, and employed immediately. While the plan had been to supply small groups by air only inside Tibet, the potential guerrilla army massed in Nepal was not prepared to move unless it received the arms—and they could only come by air. But the flights had been grounded in deference to Eisenhower's ban on provocative intelligence operations, and it was too soon to ask for an exception, especially for flights that might call additional attention to this unplanned concentration of no longer secret resistance forces.

Thus, the winter of 1960/61 was a frustrating one for both the Tibetans and the CIA officers directing their operations. Gyen Yeshe sent messages pleading for support, including one poignant account of the men being forced to boil their leather shoelaces for soup. Washington found it hard to believe the numbers involved, so Yeshe buttressed his pleas for food and arms with photographs of 2,000 men massed in front of his headquarters. Funds were eventually provided for food, but resentment among the local populace had already erupted against the Tibetan intruders, who bought or took what they needed.

However urgent the food problem, the pressure for a quick solution for political reasons was less critical. The king of Mustang's Tibetan ancestry put him in the Dalai Lama's camp, although his genuine sympathy was mixed with apprehension about the large group of tough Khampa warriors who had become uninvited residents of his kingdom. In any case, even if he wanted to do anything about these new residents, he commanded no troops of his own. He was therefore not an important factor, nor was the Nepalese government. While concerned about occasional border incursions by the Chinese, Kathmandu was not prepared to assemble the forces required to expel a group of this size from such a remote region. It was easier for the Nepalese to ignore their presence and simply deny access to any enterprising journalist or trekker who might try to make his way to the inaccessible Mustang plateau.

The Chinese, after one incursion into Mustang in hot pursuit of fleeing Tibetan guerrillas before Yeshe's forces mushroomed,[9] also seemed disinclined to bother much. The CIA was to learn later from documents captured in 1961 by the Mustang guerrillas that, in addition to a shortage of military spare parts, the Chinese were concerned about the morale of their own troops, who were suffering from the consequences of Mao's Great Leap Forward. These documents revealed that two-thirds of the infantrymen in the People's Liberation Army had never seen action, and that most of their company commanders were veterans but had not been leaders in the Korean War. Service in Tibet must have been doubly difficult for these demoralized troops, and commanders undoubtedly had little heart for search and destroy missions in the rugged canyons of the Kali Gandaki. Furthermore, Zhou Enlai had visited Kathmandu to court the Nepalese government. A scrap with Tibetans inside Nepal was not on Beijing's list of priorities when its resources were already pinched.

The stalemate between Washington and Mustang continued throughout the autumn of 1960. The CIA repeatedly asked Gyen Yeshe to send back as many of these unwanted volunteers as possible, but it was not prepared to abandon this potential capability to mount an organized resistance inside Tibet. Like the airdrop operations in eastern Tibet, the Mustang force had taken on a life of its own, and it was a capability that was not to be easily abandoned. It was then a few months before the November presidential elections, and decisions on major operations such as these were put on hold. Desmond FitzGerald later reported with great satisfaction to us anxious colleagues that, at a White House meeting he attended on election day, Eisenhower had said that if Nixon were elected the CIA could be assured that its operations in Tibet would continue.[10] The ban on overflights would apparently be lifted as long as they took place inside Tibet. He could not, of course, speak for Kennedy.

KENNEDY TAKES UP THE CAUSE

When Allen Dulles met with John F. Kennedy in December 1960 he found the president-elect ready to continue backing the Tibetan resistance. This is not surprising. James Thomson, who served under Kennedy as the NSC's China officer, noted that the political climate of that period "was not one that encouraged China policy innovation at the White House."[11] The election margin had been too narrow. The Republican opposition was ready to look for signs of supposed appeasement, and the ugly memories of the "who-lost-China?" debate were still fresh. The new secretary of state, Dean Rusk, said some years later that he had found President Kennedy "uninterested in any changes in China policy" because it was "one of those things where there was no opportunity to get anywhere because of the attitude of Peking and, therefore, he'd prefer not to stir it up."[12]

Moreover, support of a resistance movement already in the field appealed to the activist Kennedy administration. As the man in charge of Asia policy at the State Department under Truman, Rusk had urged the Dalai Lama to flee Tibet in 1951, and he was thoroughly receptive to the CIA's support for the Tibetan rebels when briefed on it as incoming secretary in 1960.[13] McGeorge Bundy, when asked some years later about how he as the president's national security adviser viewed the operations in Tibet, said they "sounded like the things we were and ought to have been doing at that time."[14] After all, their leader had at his inauguration pledged the country to "bear any burden, pay any price" in the defense of freedom, and as one Cold War historian has noted, Kennedy's people made "Eisenhower's crew seem pikers by comparison"[15]—with one notable and outspoken exception. The chief dissenter was the new ambassador to India, John Kenneth Galbraith. This distinguished Harvard economist and author made no secret of his long friendship with the president and his family. He took great delight in sending off witty and frequently biting critiques of various U.S. foreign programs, using his privileged diplomatic channel to the president. His unique style of diplomatic reporting amused Kennedy, who shared his dispatches with his NSC staff for their entertainment and sometimes irritation. During the next year Galbraith was to make full use of the Harvard connection to send telegrams in his distinctive prose, supplementing them by visits to Washington to urge the president to terminate the agency's support for the Mustang force. His predecessor Bunker and his staff had never matched Washington's enthusiasm for the Tibetan operations, but they had been good bureaucratic soldiers and carried out orders from headquarters. That was not Galbraith's style.

The new ambassador had been briefed on the CIA's covert operations in India on March 29, 1961, two weeks after Kennedy had approved an airdrop to the Mustang contingent inside Tibet. He took an instant dislike to the whole thing, which he characterized as a "particularly insane enterprise" where "planes dropped weapons, ammunition and other supplies for dissident and deeply unhygienic tribesmen who had once roamed over the neighboring Tibetan countryside and who now relieve their boredom with raids back into the territory from which they had been extruded."[16] When Galbraith returned to Washington in May, he was able to prevail in his efforts to terminate all covert operations in India itself, most of which were directed against the Indian Communist party. He was even more vociferous in his opposition to the Mustang operations, arguing that some accident might befall one of the CIA airdrops, which would involve India and compromise the work of his embassy in the same way that a U-2 overflight turned into a diplomatic disaster for Soviet-American relations.

But the administration and indeed Kennedy himself were still suffering from the previous month's humiliation at Cuba's Bay of Pigs. Kennedy was by then concerned about the threat of a Communist takeover in Laos, and this concern would increase over the vulnerability of the government of South Vietnam. Kennedy had seen no evidence that Mao was relaxing his hostility toward the U.S. The Tibetan guerrillas represented the kind of unconventional force that he had long advocated as an alternative to the Dulles-Eisenhower nuclear doctrine of massive retaliation. He therefore did not yield to his articulate and persistent ambassador.[17] The CIA's support for Mustang, now already well underway, would continue, as would the ambassador's opposition.

The CIA had put the operations at Mustang back on track early in 1961, soon after Kennedy's inauguration. The Tibetan volunteers had been organized into sixteen companies of one hundred each, with men drawn from various cities, tribes, and areas to break up the natural preference of the Tibetans to cluster in hometown units that tended to encourage ancient feuds and rivalries. Their rigorous daily training schedule would have gladdened the hearts of the Dumra instructors. The men were now looking for missions.

By early spring, authorization had been obtained from the new White House team to provide arms for seven companies to establish bases across the border. Reinforcements and replacements would be sent from Mustang as needed. On March 15, 1961, the planes flew from their base in Thailand to make the first airdrop of arms and trained radio operators, enough to outfit and staff four companies. The parachute drop was made to a site inside Tibet south of the Brahmaputra River opposite Mustang.[18]

The arms and the men were retrieved without incident and taken out of Tibet and back to Gyen Yeshe's headquarters, which was about fifteen miles south of the capital of Mustang and twenty-five miles from the Tibetan border. There Gyen Yeshe decided to split the arms among eight companies. His strategy was to send units of forty to fifty men down from the Mustang plateau onto the Brahmaputra floodplain, where they would attack isolated Chinese military camps and travel along the Lhasa-Xinjiang highway creating disruption along this major supply route.[19]

The prime operating season was from August through April when the Brahmaputra was fordable. According to Lhamo Tsering, Gyalo

Thondup's operations chief, these attacks were sufficiently effective to force the Chinese to post one division in the area and to divert traffic for western Tibet to the Qinghai-Xinjiang highway three hundred kilometers to the north.[20] The guerrilla units would operate for two to three weeks inside Tibet and then return to their base at Mustang for replacements and resupply. Ngadruk, one of the commanders of these units, said that the raiders included men from other companies in a further effort to break up the old clannish spirit that was part of the original Chushi Gangdruk organization.

By then Gyen Yeshe had converted his role as chief of the advance party into that of permanent commander of the entire force at Mustang. He had dealt with the unexpected deluge of recruits and imposed discipline among what could have become an unruly mob. He also still enjoyed the confidence of Gompo Tashi. The intended field commander, Lobsang Champa, had been sent for training at Dumra the previous summer with the men selected as company commanders, but all had been stranded there as a consequence of the U-2 incident and the publicity over the unexpected flood of recruits. Although Lobsang Champa still had the CIA's full support, Gyen Yeshi refused to yield command. When Lobsang Champa finally returned that summer, making his way to Mustang on foot through the jungle like the recruits, the CIA ordered he be given command of the five hundred men at what was now the Mustang base camp. This Solomonic solution did not resolve the problems among a command already divided by old regional loyalties and rivalries. Gyen Yeshe's action in demoting his potential rival even further did not help. The CIA's protégé ended up as commander of only one company of a hundred men, a position he had little choice but to accept.[21]

While the first drop had been made with the understanding that the men would use the arms to establish themselves inside Tibet, their reluctance to give up their safe haven in Nepal was not surprising. This was to be a running controversy between the CIA and Gyen Yeshe that was never resolved. The Mustang commander continued to request the arms that had been promised for the three additional companies. But in response to Galbraith's continuing protests, Kennedy agreed that all future drops had to be made with Indian approval.

The question then became what constituted Indian approval. In November 1960 Indian Foreign Secretary Dutt had called Ambassador Bunker's attention to an Indian government white paper covering March to October of 1960 in which India had protested repeated Chinese violations of Indian airspace. The Chinese denied that any of their planes had flown over Indian territory but alleged that American planes based on Taiwan had been dropping arms, agents, and equipment to the Tibetans. Dutt went on to tell Bunker that "of course he did not know" whether the U.S. had dropped supplies in Tibet, but he wished to inform the ambassador that the Indians were planning to take vigorous action to shoot down any planes violating Indian territory. He therefore hoped that if the U.S. was planning future airdrops it would not fly over Indian territory. Bunker commented that he believed that Dutt's statement indicated while the Indian government was "not averse to aid being rendered to the Tibetans," they were fearful it would "greatly weaken the Indian position vis-a-vis the Chinese Communists, lend color to Chinese assertions that the rebellion was instigated by the U.S., pull the rug from under severe critics of the Chinese in the Indian press and parliament, and turn public opinion against the U.S., all things the Nehru Government was anxious to avoid."[22]

In responding to Kennedy's new requirement, the CIA countered that it would be impossible for either Nehru or his intelligence chief to give explicit approval for such flights. Eisenhower's bitter experience in acknowledging his approval of the U-2 flights the year before had provided a persuasive argument against breaching the tradition of shielding chief executives. In addition to the impression that Bunker had obtained from the foreign secretary a few months before, the CIA had other indications that U.S. aid to the Tibetans had India's tacit approval. As a precaution, however, the flight route to the Mustang area was planned to ensure that the planes would be over Indian territory for only a matter of minutes.[23]

Using these arguments, the CIA asked for enough flights to complete the arming of all seven companies through Mustang. The National Security Council's Special Group debated the request throughout the summer of 1961. By this time the remaining company commanders had

returned from Dumra, and the raids on Chinese installations and convoys were continuing. The results of one raid gave dramatic support to
the CIA request.

In October 1961 a party led by a Dumra alumnus named Ragra
attacked a convoy carrying a Chinese assistant regimental commander.
This Chinese officer and all of the members of the convoy were killed,
and the commander's pouch was captured intact containing more than
1,600 classified documents.[24] Among this intelligence gold mine were
twenty-nine issues of the *Bulletin of Activities of the General Political
Department of the People's Liberation Army.* These and other documents
contained in the pouch provided firsthand intelligence on the serious problems of governance that had grown out of the Great Leap Forward. They
described famine conditions and their effect on the morale of troops who
knew how their own families were suffering at home. The People's Militia, listed in Pentagon order of battle estimates as part of China's military
forces, was revealed not only to be an empty asset, but in some cases to
be participants in uprisings against the government they had been
formed to protect. The documents also acknowledged the continuing
stalemate with the United States, the necessity to accept the fact that it
would be "temporarily" impossible for China to regain control of Taiwan,
and the strained relationship with the Soviet Union, from whom Beijing
could expect no help if attacked with nuclear weapons.

This dramatic intelligence haul arrived in Washington at a critical
time in the policy debate over whether the U.S. should continue to support the resistance force at Mustang. Ambassador Galbraith had
renewed his efforts to end this support and close out the operations. In
a message on November 30, 1961, to Under Secretary of State for Economic Affairs George Ball, Galbraith cited the unsuccessful and "insulting" dialogue he had exchanged with Ball's colleagues Alexis Johnson
and McGeorge Bundy in his efforts to win over the president to his
point of view. The unyielding ambassador repeated his arguments that
the Mustang force had been unable to fulfill any of the objectives that
had been the rationale for its creation. The operations that covered "a
few square miles on an incredibly vast area" had made no dent in keeping the Chinese from consolidating their hold on Tibet. Further, the

world had taken little or no notice of this effort to maintain a show of resistance against Chinese aggression there. Finally, the relative value of the intelligence yield was questioned. The irate ambassador concluded that "the truth is that the operation continues because it got started." In a postscript to Ball, who was moving up to the undersecretary position the next day, he added, "I am very serious about this. Do get it under control."[25]

Galbraith and Ball had been codirectors of the U.S. Strategic Bombing Survey in 1945, which had concluded that the Allied bombings of Germany in World War II had been only marginally successful in reducing military production and not cost effective in the use of manpower. This pair of distinguished skeptics were to reunite in a dogged and articulate campaign maintained over the next year to disband the Mustang force, which they considered to be another unproductive effort. In November 1961, however, Washington overruled the ambassador's objections. Allen Dulles had been able to take the captured documents, along with the bloodstained pouch of their dead owner, for a dramatic appearance before the Special Group, one of his last before his retirement that month. This dramatic "evidence of effectiveness" in the intelligence payoff of these operations, coupled with the protection afforded by the restricted flight path to Mustang and Washington's reluctance to give up an existing capability against an uncertain enemy were sufficient to win the president's approval for resumption of the airdrops.

A second drop for the three remaining companies was accordingly made inside Tibet on December 10, 1961. But as he had done with the equipment dropped earlier, Gyen Yeshe divided the newly arrived matériel among six companies, retaining all of the seventeen pistols for his personal armory.[26] The arms were sufficient to equip only about half the number of potential guerrillas at Mustang. This was all the policymakers were willing to approve as the debate continued in Washington about the utility of the Mustang operations when set against the political problems they posed. They were sufficient to permit periodic raids to harass the Chinese along the highway and in their camps south of the Brahmaputra along a three-hundred-and-fifty-mile front inside Tibet.

But the Mustang force was basically in a holding pattern. Some of the men were now armed for action, but no one was willing to commit them to a full-scale effort against the Chinese, had the Mustangers been willing to undertake one. Almost a year later, even after the Chinese were looming on the Indian border, Allen Dulles's successor, John A. McCone, met on November 10, 1962, with Secretary Rusk to discuss policy. McCone noted that he had gathered from discussions among the Special Group that there was some doubt that the U.S. government "really wished to pursue the original 1958 objective of freeing Tibet of the Chinese Communist occupation." If there was an inclination to change this policy, he wanted to know it promptly. He cited the varying policy directions that were coming out of different offices within the State Department and from Ambassador Galbraith in New Delhi. This had caused him to conclude that "we were not operating on a policy line but were acting from day to day in a manner considered best by an individual of the State Department."²⁷ This feeling of operating in a policy vacuum was shared by those of us at the working level.

McCone's initiative produced a decision within a week by the Special Group to put a hold on active operations until a program of "contingency planning" initiated by the CIA had been worked out. Such planning was overtaken a few days later when the Indians turned to the U.S. after the Chinese poured over their northern frontier to trounce the outgunned and outmanned Indian army on the Tibetan border. After a year of temporizing the Tibetans were to become assets again rather than problems.

DIPLOMATIC MOVES

The government-in-exile did not do all its campaigning in the field. On the first anniversary of the revolt, the Dalai Lama announced he was preparing a new constitutional and economic structure.²⁸ The charter would embody many of the reforms, primarily the redistribution of state and church land and the accompanying traditional governing structure, that his brother had tried to persuade the old guard in Lhasa to accept in 1952. This was a first step toward demonstrating the

Tibetans' will to claim self-determination as promised in the Herter declaration. Washington endorsed such enlightened "nation building," and Ernest Gross was asked to advise in drafting the document. Predictably it was criticized as premature by Chiang K'ai-shek and privately dismissed in the British Foreign Office as "romantic moonshine or deliberate propaganda."[29] The Tibet the British had known was not congenial to reform constitutions.

But some Indian veterans of the independence movement felt otherwise. In April of 1960 a group of prominent Indians, including J. P. Narayan, J. J. Singh, and Purshottam Trikamdas were enlisted to host an Afro-Asian Conference on Tibet and against colonialism in Asia and Africa. Delegates from nineteen Asian and African countries met in New Delhi and unanimously adopted a resolution supporting the Tibetan people's right to self-determination. While none of the delegates were official representatives of their governments, several of their governments expressed sympathy for the convention. (India, preparing for a visit by Zhou Enlai, did not.) In the autumn Singh and Trikamdas accompanied Thondup to New York to line up Afro-Asian support for a UN resolution supporting self-determination for Tibet. They managed to introduce the resolution but it became a casualty of both the regular session, which got bogged down late in 1960, and the rump session the following spring.

Thondup did have the satisfaction of being received for the first time by an American secretary of state. The lame duck Christian Herter saw him and suggested that his brother could keep his cause alive by abandoning his demand to be received abroad as a head of state and travel abroad as a "great religious leader."[30] Herter's undersecretary for political affairs, Livingston T. Merchant, repeated this advice and reaffirmed that the U.S. was "devoted" to the principle of self-determination and was "convinced" that it was applicable to Tibet. The events in Tibet "had not been a one-time episode which could be pushed aside and forgotten as time went on," and the U.S. would do its "utmost" to ensure that the UN was aware of its concern.[31]

While Herter and Merchant were unable to translate their good intentions into action before they left office, their successors were equally committed. The new undersecretary, Chester Bowles, wrote the new UN representative, Adlai Stevenson, on March 17, 1961, that he had been studying the U.S. government's relations with the Dalai Lama in terms of Washington's long-term objectives. He had concluded that the U.S. had "much to gain in the long haul by finding ways to live up to our commitments to the Tibetans." He promised that "in the near future, we shall be putting forward to the President an action program for Tibet, which is independent of our UN stance and which embodies this conclusion." Bowles was obviously prepared to push for action without regard for diplomatic niceties. The reserved and eloquent Stevenson replied that he understood and shared Bowles's "concern over the developments in that strange and far-off land and . . . thoroughly agreed that Tibet is not an item we should pass over lightly."[32] The Bay of Pigs maelstrom then intervened, and the Tibet resolution got lost for that session. But even this painful event did not seem to lessen the new secretary's enthusiasm for the Tibetan cause. On May 30, Rusk wrote the Dalai Lama pledging that the U.S. intended "to continue to focus the attention of world opinion on the tragic plight of Tibet and on your struggle for the inalienable rights of your people. The American people look forward to the day when the people of Tibet will enjoy freedom in peace."[33] When Thondup came to Washington later that year, Kennedy sent similar unspecified, but enthusiastic, pledges through his aide Michael Forrestal to the Dalai Lama of U.S. support for the Tibetan cause.[34]

Six months later the Tibetans reached what was to be the high-water mark in their claim for international recognition, On December 20, 1961, the General Assembly, with 56 yeas, 11 nays, and 29 abstentions, renewed "its call for the cessation of practices which deprive the Tibetan people of their fundamental human rights and freedoms, including their right to self-determination." The lobbying efforts by Thondup, Gross, Singh, and Trikamdas had obviously paid off, and the new administration had delivered on the pledges it and its predecessors had made.

Even the British finally came off the fence and voted for the resolution, presumably on the orders of the new foreign secretary, Lord

Home, who had become impatient with his staff's petty arguments and excuses. One Whitehall aide had suggested that a UN resolution supporting Tibet's independence might make the lot of the Tibetans even harder. Home dismissed this with a curt, handwritten marginal note, "It could hardly be worse."[35]

CHAPTER 14

The Indians
Join the Fight

རྫོང་ཆེན་རི་གནམ་སྐྱ་ལྷག་སྐར་འབའ་ལྷས་སྲིད་དུ་ཚེ་མེ་འབར། ...
ཉིས་ཀྱི་མང་རྒྱབ་མཚོ། འདྱར་ལྷ་གཉིས་གནས།

T HE YEAR 1962 was to mark a significant
change in both the content and mode
of the U.S. support for the Tibetan
resistance. It was no longer to be primarily a
U.S. effort. The Indians, who during the past
fifteen years had resisted persuasion and all other
efforts to involve them actively in opposing the
Chinese occupation of their northern neighbor, now became major partners. These dramatic shifts in roles were consequences of the
border war between India and China, from
which Beijing walked away after humiliating
the Indians on the battlefield and undermining Nehru's claims to international leadership
of the Third World.

Although Nehru had projected himself
throughout the fifties as the leader of the

nonaligned movement and the chief exponent of the Five Principles of Peaceful Coexistence (Panch Sheel), he was the leader of a country that had been founded on strong nationalist principles and was still moved by the emotional cry of *swaraj*—self-rule. India had also inherited the British policy of fostering an autonomous and semi-independent Tibet as a physical and political buffer against the Chinese. Its complex prime minister was also a realist who recognized the need to balance his country's limited capabilities against its strategic challenges.

While Nehru had felt powerless to check the Chinese in Tibet by military means, his intelligence chief Mullik said the prime minister believed it was even more important that "India's frontiers must be guarded."[1] He therefore promptly sanctioned the creation of a staff within the newly established external intelligence service to collect information from Tibet and China. In addition, the prime minister, always suspicious of the military, gave control of all border operations to Mullik, an authority the intelligence chief retained from 1951 until October of 1959.[2] The Indian army was excluded from the Himalayan border area; its primary mission was defending the nation against Pakistan. Under this curious bureaucratic structure, the actual defense of the North East Frontier Agency was entrusted to the Assam Rifles, a paramilitary force under the minister of External Affairs.[3] Using his unique authority Mullik had by 1959 created sixty-seven check posts along the frontier, manned by a staff of 1,334 employees trained in Tibetan and Chinese and capable of intercepting and decoding Chinese communications in southern Tibet.[4] While competent to determine what was happening in their immediate sector, these border watch and intelligence collection posts were also symbols of India's sovereignty on the Himalayan frontier. Stretched along a 2,000-mile border, they were few and far between. The administration of these remote territories by the civil authorities and their paramilitary colleagues, backed by the regular army in rear areas, was likewise loose and relaxed. Mullik had built an impressive corps of a new breed of officers knowledgeable in the language and customs of the ethnic areas in which they served, but as a border defense they were mere pins on the map.

During the decade these posts were being developed, Nehru and Zhou Enlai had been sparring over the delineation of the border, which now had become an issue only when the Chinese filled what had been a power vacuum in Tibet. There were two areas of dispute. In the far west between Kashmir and Tibet, the Chinese had built a road across the Aksai Chin (Desert of White Stones). This bleak 17,000-foot plateau, which took its name from the saline encrustation on its rocky floor, could not support human or even animal life. The Indians learned about this road, which ran across territory they claimed but did not watch over, in 1957, two years after it was built. In the east they were more watchful, even aggressively so. The Indians had established posts up to, and in some cases a few miles along and north of, the McMahon Line drawn at the Simla Conference of 1914. This boundary had been accepted by the British and Tibetans but not by the Chinese. The British had made no serious effort to enforce the boundary until the final years of World War II, but it was really their Indian successors, aroused by the Chinese Communist occupation of Tibet, who tried to make the McMahon Line binding.

There were no real confrontations with the Chinese until after the 1959 revolt in Lhasa, whereupon aggressive patrolling by both sides produced both casualties and fierce debate in the Indian Parliament. This left Nehru little political room for maneuver. In April 1960 Nehru, his pride and political reputation at stake, refused Zhou's offer to trade recognition of the McMahon Line for India's acceptance of Chinese occupation of the Aksai Chin. When they met later that year in Washington, Secretary Herter made no comment on the relatively attractive package deal his guest had turned down, but he did suggest to the proud Indian that he "keep talking" with the Chinese. Nehru replied that he was prepared to make minor revisions in the frontier with Tibet but nothing on the scale apparently envisaged by the Chinese. The haughty Kashmiri Brahman then made the gratuitous statement that "Southeast Asia is full of Chinese, whereas India has only about 10,000, mostly in Calcutta and mostly shoemakers and laundrymen." He added that Ho Chi Minh "had congratulated him on having so few Chinese and had indicated his dislike of them."[5] The spirit embodied in the popular slogan chanted by the India crowds in the mid-fifties, *Hindee Chinee bhai bhai* (Indians and Chinese are brothers), had obviously become a relic of the past.

The proud prime minister's intelligence chief was always ready to back up Nehru's demands. In September 1961 the Central Intelligence Bureau (CIB), acting in its extraordinary role as the authority for border operations, forwarded a policy paper to the General Staff concluding that the Chinese would not occupy land in the disputed regions if they encountered Indian troops. The CIB paper recommended an expanded forward strategy establishing new posts right up to the border in those regions "wherever there is a gap."[6] Even thirty years after the event, General Palit, then director of Military Operations for the General Staff, found it "inconceivable that a civilian intelligence organization should have made recommendations concerning military operations." But the CIB proposals were to become Palit's marching orders.

Under great pressure from Parliament, Nehru met on November 2, 1961, with his defense chiefs to discuss Chinese incursions in Ladakh. His intelligence chief assured him that the Chinese would not dare to challenge "even a dozen soldiers" placed in Ladakh, despite the military commanders' warning that the expanded operations would exceed their capabilities. The Indian army was nevertheless ordered to "plug the holes" along both frontiers.[7] These orders were based on the assumption that the Chinese would not attack and perhaps on the unconscious premise left over from the "Whitehall dependency" that the West would bail out India if its existence were threatened.

Throughout the buildup to the October 1962 crisis on the eastern border, the U.S. had maintained a business-as-usual attitude. The Tibetan resistance forces at Mustang were utilizing the arms dropped to them the year before to conduct raids from their Nepalese stronghold along a two-hundred-and-fifty-mile sector inside Tibet. In Washington the debate fueled by Ambassador Galbraith's continuing objections and Undersecretary Ball's reservations continued over the utility of the Mustang operations and whether the Indian government tacitly approved this support that the U.S. government was giving to the Tibetans. At that time Washington had little appreciation of the "forward policy" that Nehru and his brash advisers had adopted to defy the Chinese to challenge the occupation of land in the disputed border regions.[8] There was consequently no consideration by either the proponents or the critics of the operation at Mustang that the Indians might view the Tibetan guerrillas as filling one of the gaps beyond their capabilities in the line they were seeking to establish in their venturesome challenges to the Chinese on the northern border.

While Indian public attention during the summer of 1962 was focused on the barren plateaus of the western sector, a new crisis was brewing in the east at a place called Thagla Ridge in the Himalayas at the point where Tibet, Bhutan, and the Indian North East Frontier Agency meet. Early in June the Indian ministry of External Affairs gave its blessing after the fact to a small outpost recently established by the Indian army below the ridge, which the army's own maps showed as Chinese territory. Approval was granted either by mistake or as part of the policy of asserting rights to all land claimed by India, despite New Delhi's understanding with Beijing three years earlier not to change positions in this disputed area.

Three months after the Thagla Ridge outpost was emplaced, a Chinese party of about sixty men moved down into the valley and took up positions dominating it. A junior Indian officer at the Thagla post reported that the Chinese force numbered about six hundred, apparently hoping his exaggerated report would bring the army to his aid. He was right. Brushing aside the enormous logistical difficulties of taking ammunition and supplies to troops located at altitudes more than 13,000 feet six days' march from the nearest road head, New Delhi decided to challenge the Chinese. The arrogant Defense minister V. K. Krishna Menon, who had no personal military experience and was best known abroad for his discursive speeches at the United Nations, acted while Nehru was away at a Commonwealth conference in London and gave orders on September 9 to evict the Chinese.[9]

Troop movements on both sides led to clashes during the next few weeks with minor casualties. The Indian high command, ignoring the misgivings of the local commanders, sent troops first through the jungles and then onto the steep mountain trails to reinforce the exposed outpost. On October 4, New Delhi sent the Chief of the General Staff, General B. M. Kaul, a favorite of Nehru, to take charge of the operation. The Indian press heralded him as head of a "special task force created to oust the Chinese"[10] by all means. Kaul, a charismatic but hyperactive officer with little combat experience, took up his new post with great fanfare. He immediately set off for the front on a forced march, during part of which he had to be carried by a Tibetan porter more acclimated to the high altitude. The dashing general also could not have realized that his opponents were operating under new orders sent to China's border forces on October 6: "If the Indian Army attacks . . . don't just repulse them, hit back ruthlessly so that it hurts."[11]

Once Kaul reached the scene of the impending confrontation below Thagla Ridge, he "was able clearly to discern the tactical absurdity of the project and the almost total absence of logistics to support it, should it ever be undertaken."[12] The general and his government were still operating under the premise that the Chinese when confronted would not attack. He could only hope this premise would hold, unlikely as it appeared when he actually surveyed the scene. Kaul immediately sent off the first messages describing the situation as seen firsthand by a senior commander. Kaul's discoveries, however sobering, did not lead him to propose that the hapless mission be abandoned.

It was too late for the Indians to back down even if they had wanted to. At dawn on October 10, as Kaul prepared to launch his attack, the Chinese beat him to the punch and began to move in force into the Namka Chu valley below the Thagla Ridge. In this first clash, the Indians lost six killed, eleven wounded, and fourteen missing out of the two platoons involved. The Chinese were now present in overwhelming numbers, obviously prepared to use whatever force was necessary to drive out the pushy Indians, not only from the few miles of disputed boundary land, but farther down into the Brahmaputra valley if they chose. The illusion that the Chinese would not resist because of domestic economic difficulties or political problems with the Russians, or for some even more remote reason such as remnant feelings for the era of peaceful coexistence, was shattered in one morning.

Kaul, five years later, wrote of his epiphany in the mountain valley: "Frankly speaking, I had now fully understood all of the implications of our predicament."[13] He decided that the only hope of saving the situation was to fly to New Delhi and win Nehru's permission to postpone the eviction operation, which was patently hopeless now that the Chinese had finally called the Indians' bluff and done so with impressive force. After Kaul presented his bleak assessment to his still unconvinced colleagues and a noncommittal Nehru, he offered his own recommendations. There are several versions of what he proposed, ranging from pulling back the brigade confronting the Chinese to seeking speedy assistance from the United States.[14] Nehru and his reluctant generals rejected Kaul's solutions but did agree that the operation would have to be postponed. They were adamant, however, that the unfortunate brigade must remain in place even if it was not to attack the Chinese again. To withdraw now was politically unacceptable so soon after the Indian public had been geared up to celebrate a victory.

No official document and certainly no public announcement ever spelled out India's unspoken decision to back off quietly in the hope that the Chinese would be satisfied with having made their point. But the possibility that Beijing might have accepted a standoff became hypothetical after Nehru made some offhand remarks the next day at the airport leaving for a short business-as-usual visit to Ceylon. Goaded by reporters seeking to learn what orders had been given to the troops facing the Chinese, Nehru impulsively assured them that "our instructions are to free our territory." Pointing out the difficulties of terrain and the enemy's numerical superiority, he added, however, that the date was "entirely for the Army" to decide. The Indian press omitted these qualifying additions and heard only a call to battle, which it welcomed with great acclaim. The prime minister's remarks were interpreted abroad in the same way—and not just by the Western press (the *New York Herald Tribune*'s editorial was entitled Nehru Declares War on China), but more ominously in Beijing. The *People's Daily* reported that Nehru had "openly and formally authorized the Indian military to attack China's Tibet region at any time."[15]

Four days after Nehru's unfortunate remarks and their distorted coverage, the Chinese Military Affairs Commission decided to implement a plan of counterattack drawn up a year before by Marshal Liu Bocheng.[16] The ill-fated Indian Seventh Brigade, many of its 6,000 men wearing summer uniforms and carrying only fifty rounds of ammunition, could only sit helplessly in their disadvantageous position while the Chinese in the mountains above massed a force of 10,000 well-equipped veterans acclimated to the altitude and terrain by service in Tibet. The attack came on October 20. Four days later the Seventh Brigade had ceased to exist. Its members were either dead, wounded, captured, or in humiliating retreat through Bhutan and the North East Frontier Agency.

After a week the Chinese halted their advance. The Indian government and people, unchastened by this painful demonstration of Chinese military superiority, were galvanized into an unprecedented show of national unity and defiance. Nehru was finally forced by parliamentary criticism to fire Menon, but Indian preparations to challenge the Chinese continued. The volatile Kaul returned to the lists after hospitalization for pulmonary edema and exhaustion. Palit describes how "riding on a high, [Kaul] had struck a Rommel-like pose"[17] for the cameramen and described, with dramatic embellishments, how he would deal with the Chinese. Yet later that same afternoon Kaul complained privately to Palit's wife of the odds against his mission succeeding.

Unfortunately Kaul decided to make his stand at Walong in the eastern North East Frontier area. He launched an attack on November 14, choosing the date because it was Nehru's birthday. His forces met seasoned Chinese troops, veterans of the Korean War, who inflicted a decisive defeat on the Indians with casualties in the hundreds, and missing, including prisoners, in the thousands.[18] Kaul sent off a frantic message to New Delhi proposing that India "get such foreign armed forces to come to our aid as are willing," without which it would be impossible to stem the tide of the pursuing Chinese. When the army chief flew off to the North East Frontier Agency to steady the obviously rattled Kaul and organize the defense of the force still in place below Thagla, he found that the local commanders had already decided to withdraw. The Indian army was on the run and India was in a state of near panic. Nehru then sent a personal appeal to President Kennedy for help to meet what was widely feared as an imminent Chinese invasion.

THE HARRIMAN MISSION

Throughout the crisis in the Himalayas, Washington had been preoccupied with graver matters closer to home. Ordinarily the prospect of Chinese spilling across the Himalayas would have reawakened memories of the hordes that came across the Yalu into Korea a decade before and would have made it the "flap" of the moment in Washington. But the Seventh Brigade's collapse happened on the first day of the U.S. naval quarantine set up to press Khrushchev into removing the nuclear missiles the Russians had introduced into Cuba that summer. While the Indians were fleeing from the Chinese who were coming over the mountains from Tibet, Washington and the rest of the world were grappling with the real possibility that the U.S. might feel forced to invade Cuba, which could provoke a retaliatory nuclear attack on the United States. For the first time the possibility that Washington might be a target seemed real. Emergency evacuation and relocation sites in the Appalachians were a more immediate concern than the crisis shaping up in the Himalayas half a world away. Galbraith noted in his journal that for a week he "had a considerable war on my hands without a single telegram, letter, telephone call or other communication of guidance."[19] On October 28, Washington and the world breathed a sigh of relief when the Russians agreed to withdraw their missiles. The next day the White House immediately turned toward India and responded generously to the Indian request for the weapons and equipment that had been lost or never arrived at Thagla Ridge. Within four days U.S. Air Force C-130 aircraft were landing in Calcutta with arms and ammunition.

On November 19, Kennedy responded even more speedily to Nehru's "desperate" call for help[20] after the debacle at Walong by offering to send a high-level mission to assess what the U.S. could do to help fill India's needs. That same day the Chinese announced they would begin observing a cease-fire and withdraw their troops from India by December 1. The president, however, proposed to Galbraith that he suggest to Nehru that "even under the changed circumstances the team would be useful as a tangible gesture of US support."[21] Both Galbraith and Nehru accepted the offer immediately, and the mission headed by one of America's most distinguished politicians and diplomats, Averell Harriman, was on its way the next day. It included Paul Nitze, the assistant secretary of defense for International Security Affairs, Roger Hilsman, who had led an OSS guerrilla unit behind the lines in Burma during World War II and was then the head of the State Department's Intelligence and Research Bureau, and what Hilsman described as "a half-dozen staff experts."[22] The plane was a windowless KC-135 jet tanker converted for passenger use by the installation of eight portable bunks and twenty portable seats. Despite its lack of amenities, a seat on the plane was a prized possession. As chief of the CIA Tibetan Task Force, I got one near the back. James Critchfield, chief of the CIA's Near East operations, recalled that he was traveling abroad at the time and received a call from Richard Helms, then the chief of CIA's clandestine operations. Helms told Critchfield to get himself to New Delhi and link up with the Harriman mission, which Helms described as the "hottest ticket in town."[23]

During the discussions on the eighteen-hour flight to New Delhi, Carl Kaysen, a Harvard economist serving as National Security Council deputy for military affairs, favored seeing the border conflict turn into a full war between the Indians and the Chinese. Nitze argued that settling for a de facto cease-fire would give the Indians an opportunity to regroup and rebuild their strength. Harriman sided with Nitze. When the mission arrived in New Delhi Galbraith took them immediately to see Nehru. It turned out to be an extremely awkward meeting. Hilsman described Nehru as a tired old man, "reluctant to admit that he had been wrong in courting the Communist Bloc or to ask for American aid."[24] His colleagues were not too proud, and $120 million worth of U.S. and British aid was eventually provided to resupply the Indian military.[25] His intelligence chief was also ready to accept the assistance of the CIA.

Among those on the Harriman mission was Critchfield's CIA counterpart chief of Far East Operations, Desmond FitzGerald. FitzGerald had assets to offer—the Tibetans then being trained in Colorado—and he and Mullik were in many ways natural soul mates. Although Mullik was an untouchable and FitzGerald was a Boston Brahmin, both enjoyed access to the leaders of their respective countries. Mullik was one of Nehru's closest confidants,[26] and FitzGerald dined with the Kennedys in Georgetown. Both had a disdain for the regular military and its chain of command, preferring the irregular operations and bush warfare that FitzGerald had known in Burma. Mullik had become familiar with the tribal area for which Nehru had given him responsibility in the fifties. They shared a high regard for the Tibetans, whom Mullik had long known and quietly supported. But FitzGerald was to take an unaccustomed backseat on this trip. Galbraith regarded him as the "most sanguinary, imaginative and personable architect of covert operations in CIA history. Also the most irresponsible."[27] Years later he recalled with a delicious chuckle how he had made sure that someone kept a close eye and rein on this "dangerous" man when he was in New Delhi.[28] The imperious ambassador had a closer rapport with the more reserved Critchfield, whom he enlisted to deal with the Indian service. Des was kept busy with the formal meetings with Indian officialdom and the Tibetans while Critchfield negotiated with Mullik.[29]

In an analysis of the Sino-Indian conflict for Rusk, Hilsman had noted that the "continued strengthening of the Indian defensive position and possible disruption of Chinese supply lines through guerrilla activities are the primary means of denying this area to Peiping's political-military penetration, short of escalating the conflict into a major war."[30] This was the strategy generally accepted at that time by both the Americans and the Indians. The bulk of the military hardware to be provided by Washington and London would go to restock and beef up the badly battered Indian military establishment. CIA would develop an on-the-ground intelligence collection capability to determine Chinese strengths and weaknesses inside Tibet, to be exploited by guerrilla action. The Tibetans who would carry out these missions would be trained at Camp Hale, which had been in a holding pattern for some months while the future of the Tibet program was being debated. CIA would also continue its support to the force that had come into being under its parentage at Mustang. FitzGerald was delighted to have found vindication for his efforts in having kept these two capabilities viable. In a separate program negotiated by Critchfield, CIA would provide logistical and training support to the paramilitary force then being created by Mullik to guard India's northern border. Unlike the Mustang force, whose direction was to be shared with the Indians, Mullik's new creature was to be solely under Indian direction. Having agreed to take on these new programs aimed at providing the Indians with an increased sense of security about their northern frontier—and a hazy objective of exploiting some undefined opportunity to change the situation in Tibet—the mission departed.

The Tibetans provided the manpower for all these programs. Eighteen months earlier, when Galbraith was being briefed in Washington on CIA's support to the Tibetan resistance operations, he had walked out, saying this program reminded him of "the Rover Boys at loose ends."[31] Now the Tibetans had become assets, and the support that CIA had been giving became the basis for a shared program with the Indians, although the U.S. and Indian objectives were not identical. The U.S. supported the Tibetan resistance primarily as a means of challenging Chinese aggression, mixed with a small element of Wilsonian idealism as part of the Cold War struggle. For Mullik, these hardy mountaineers represented an immediate capability for guarding the vulnerable northern frontier and a potential force for attaining an independent Tibet, which he felt was India's only long-term guarantee of security in the Himalayas. The Tibetans had little choice but to accept the support of both countries in the hope of using it for their own more immediate objective of reestablishing an independent Tibet.

Ↄ

The Chinese, having made the point that it was they, not the Indians, who could call the shots along the disputed border whenever they wanted, proceeded to implement their unilateral cease-fire. Early in December of 1962 they began pulling back. The military equipment left behind by the retreating Indian troops was returned—cleaned, polished, and inventoried by the Chinese.[32] This included even a few American automatic rifles, still in their packing crates, that had been part of the early U.S. shipments sent in response to Nehru's first request for help six weeks before. While the Indians regarded these moves as efforts to humiliate them, they were in no position to challenge the Chinese, and the Indian army subsequently remained well back of the disputed areas. Nehru continued, however, to hedge on Zhou Enlai's proposals to negotiate firm boundaries, which have not been formally demarcated over three decades later.[33]

The devastating defeat that the Chinese had inflicted on the Indians served Mao's purposes in demonstrating how a leader of the communist world should act, in contrast to Khrushchev's retreat from Cuba. It also made Mao's point that in a pinch Nehru would turn to the Western democracies. It did not achieve the next stage he had predicted to Khrushchev two years earlier, a popular repudiation of Nehru and a revolution in India. But it had rid him of what must always have been a chafing relationship. Mao had never liked sharing the joint leadership of the former colonial countries of Asia.[34] The British chargé in Beijing, four months after the Chinese had declared their unilateral cease-fire, discounted the possibility of further Chinese Communist military actions against the Indians, reasoning that the Chinese were in a "very priggish mood, because of their inherent overweening sense of moral superiority"[35] and also because they had gained their objective of exposing India's weakness and humbling Nehru.

During the October crisis Khrushchev had dropped the neutralist position he had taken two years previously when the border confrontations were still minor. As his ships edged toward the U.S. naval blockade and a nuclear war loomed, the Soviet premier could not afford to continue his spat with Mao. Accordingly he sent a letter to Nehru warning him that he was embarking on a "very dangerous path" in his boundary dispute with the Chinese, and *Pravda* saw "reactionary circles" inside India fanning the conflict as part of a plot to set "these great powers China and India at loggerheads, as well as undermining the Soviet Union's friendship with fraternal China and friendly India." Once the Cuba crisis was over, Khrushchev reverted to his earlier position of neutrality. According to a CIA report, a Soviet diplomat said that it was impossible to understand why the Chinese had advanced against India at that time. (Apparently Moscow had accepted the Indian version of the boundary issues.) The Russian said that the Chinese moves were "as inscrutable to the Soviet observer as they are to the West," noting that this "was not the first and probably will not be the last surprise Peiping has in store for Moscow."[36] He confided that Moscow had tried to discourage the Chinese from "such adventures," but it had only limited means to coerce the Chinese. According to him, the Russians had pointed out to the Chinese that an attack on India would result in US military aid to India and that "it was preferable for the Russians to supply India with limited amounts of weapons rather than have the Indians accept much larger shipments from the West." While Moscow had suspended its plans during the October crisis to provide MIG fighters to the Indians, they were delivered after the Sino-Soviet quarrel grew more open the following year.

Washington was equally perplexed by Mao's moves. His ability, however, to withdraw his troops from the land they had taken from the Indians in spite of Nehru's rejection of their cease-fire proposal, earned him "grudging admiration." Hilsman quotes one Kennedy aide, referring to the Chinese movements in and out of India, as saying: "There is no doubt who is in control over there. Can you imagine the difficulty we would have with the Pentagon in pulling back and giving up territory that had cost that many casualties, no matter how great the political end it served?"[37] Some months later, Kennedy noted that China, which in all probability would soon have nuclear weapons, with "weak countries around it, seven hundred million people, a Stalinist internal regime, nuclear power, and a government determined on war as a means of bringing about its ultimate success, would be potentially a more dangerous situation than any we have faced since the end of the Second (World) War." He added that "it may take some years, maybe a decade, before they become a full-fledged nuclear power, but we are going to be around in the 1970's, and we would like to take some steps now which would lessen that prospect that a future president might have to deal with."[38]

No option was foreclosed. In a meeting in September 1963 with Chiang Ching-kuo, the son and political heir of Nationalist China's deceased leader Chiang K'ai-shek, Kennedy made it clear that the U.S. would do anything to weaken the power of the Chinese Communists who "pose a tremendous danger to world peace."[39] The U.S., however, would not back "losing operations" such as the 1961 Bay of Pigs invasion, which in retrospect he realized was based more on hope than on realistic appraisals. In the same conversation, however, he did ask Chiang if he thought it would be possible to airlift three to five hundred men to distant Chinese atomic installations such as the one at Baotou without the planes being shot down.[40] Chiang said that he had already discussed this with CIA, and "they had indicated that such an operation would be feasible." Such drastic measures were not attempted, and Kennedy searched for more conventional means.[41] In a speech given by Hilsman on December 13, but vetted by Kennedy himself before his assassination, the administration signaled that it was time to recognize that the Chinese Communist government was here to stay, and that the U.S. was willing to find an accommodation if China would be less hostile. But in the meantime this did not mean that the U.S. would abandon its present policies of countering any aggressive actions undertaken by Beijing.

This left the Tibetans with Washington supporting them in their battle against Chinese occupation and India goaded by the Chinese threat into becoming a major partner. The immediate effect was a quantum jump in aid to the Tibetan resistance, but the Tibetan freedom movement began to undergo an involuntary change. Instead of focusing on fighting for their own independence, the Tibetans became defenders of their host's borders. They were welcome recruits in parallel but not identical causes, but they had to prevent their ultimate goal of freedom from being submerged by the immediate objectives of their new Indian partners. Their survival depended on successfully juggling these differing priorities and kaleidoscopic policies of their principal patrons, the Indians and the Americans, who were making their own adjustments to the shifting balances of the Cold War. But despite their relatively recent entry into such grand geopolitical games, the Tibetans were to accomplish it.

CHAPTER 15

Operations in a New Era

ཨ་རོ་དགུར་ ཧྲུང་ད་ཕག་བཞིན་ཤེས་པའི་རི།

རིམ་ཆ་བཞིན་ ལྒོ་དོ་མོ་ཆེམ་གླུང་ལེམས་མམ་ཐམ་དགབ་ི་བཀོ་ལྡང་ད་ ཟ་རྣམ་ལ་སར་ལམས་ཆེག་ ཧུ་ཆེམ་ཆ་དྲུང་དུ་སྟོ་ཟམ་ག་ལྡང་པ་ལས་ ཐ་ག །

BEFORE HIS ELECTION, Kennedy had read and been impressed by Mao's writings on combining political and guerrilla tactics to win what the Communists and the Third World called wars of "national liberation." Khrushchev had also given a speech just before Kennedy's inauguration pledging Soviet support for such "sacred" national insurgencies, and the new president read it as a declaration of war against his plans for a new and more cooperative era in U.S. relations with the developing world. Henry Kissinger now believes that Kennedy misinterpreted the speech, and that Khrushchev really was aiming at his ideological enemies in Beijing.[1] But whatever the motives of the

Soviet leader, they represented one more challenge that the activists in the Kennedy administration were eager to take on.

Once in office, Kennedy's official response was to upgrade the Special Forces training program at Fort Bragg, North Carolina, and establish a special counterinsurgency committee in Washington under General Maxwell Taylor. To stress his interest, he placed his brother Robert Kennedy on the interdepartmental group as his representative. Even the disaster at the Bay of Pigs in Cuba did not diminish the Kennedys' enthusiasm for unconventional warfare, a buzzword of those days. In the lofty chambers of the Old State Department Building next to the White House, senior officials energetically expounded their newly acquired or resurrected wartime expertise on how to fight wars in the jungles and the mountains of the Third World. They met under the aegis of Averell Harriman, known affectionately as "the crocodile"[2] by his badgered but admiring colleagues in the State Department, where he did not tolerate fools gladly and pursued his bureaucratic prey with great determination. It was easy to arouse wholehearted support for using this newly developed expertise to help the Indians, to say nothing of the appealing thought of using Mao's own concepts of guerrilla warfare against his troops in Tibet. Although Washington did not appreciate the historic irony at the time, Mao was already preoccupied by the preservation of his own doctrines and the course of the revolution he had fathered.

The new Tibetan-manned Special Frontier Force (SFF), which Mullik had created on his own, received Washington's full endorsement.[3] It embodied the boldness and innovation of the New Frontier and the new administration's desire to meet the challenges of the Cold War in new ways. The organization was popularly known as Establishment 22, a name it got from its commander, a highly respected retired Indian, Major General Uban, who had commanded the Indian Twenty-second Mountain Regiment during World War II. When word got around, Tibetan refugees effectively repeated the stampede to Mustang two years earlier. This time the destination for the frontier road gangs was the old British hill town of Dehra Dun. From there they were transported to the SFF home base in the first range of the Himalayas, one hundred and twenty kilometers from the Tibetan border.

The Tibetans initially signed on to regain the independence of their country, but it was to become a continuing matter of dispute how their service under the command of the Indians would contribute to that fundamental objective. Gyalo Thondup said that until 1962 the Indians had consistently rejected his appeals to train Tibetans as resistance fighters inside Tibet. This attitude changed dramatically, however, after the border defeats and the arrival of U.S. military aid.[4] The refugees from the Tibetan resistance had suddenly become valuable assets instead of troublesome relocation problems. Thondup was summoned to New Delhi, where he worked out an agreement with Mullik of the Central Intelligence Bureau and K. L. Mehta of the External Affairs ministry to encourage Tibetans to join SFF. They wanted 6,000 troops but eventually trained a force twice that size.

Thondup said the original agreement called for these men to be used only inside Tibet—presumably to organize resistance activities there—and not merely to defend India's borders or perform other missions for the Indians. Mullik may have made such an agreement in good faith. In his memoirs he said that he was convinced that Nehru himself was "preparing for the day when it would be possible for India to reestablish Tibet in an semi-independent if not independent status."[5] Furthermore, in 1962, war with China, previously unthinkable, now had become a possibility. If it broke out, the Tibetans would then be in the front lines of a war waged in their own country. In practice, however, this ultimate goal was to remain distant and secondary to the protection of India's borders, since the frontier force was authorized to act only on the Indian side of the frontier and not to cross into Tibet for the purpose of challenging the Chinese.

Nevertheless, the training of SFF was consonant with missions behind enemy lines, which kept the hope of fighting for independence alive. The men, who were eventually joined by two companies of Tibetan women, were given six months of basic training identical to the Indian army's. Then they were given supplemental training by CIA and Indian instructors in commando tactics, guerrilla warfare techniques, sabotage, and the use of explosives.[6] These willing recruits became highly proficient in the use of light arms, learned rock climbing, and made five required parachute jumps, which qualified them for paratroopers' wings. The Indians now had their own special unit of Green Berets (they wore red), and they were Tibetans.

These gung ho troops did go into Tibet, but not to fight a war for independence. Instead, the Indians used them as scouts because they were able to survive the extraordinary terrain and high altitude that the Indian soldier found too difficult. Organized in companies of 123 men and commanded by Tibetan officers, they operated from bases along the frontier from the Kashmir border, where two companies set up a base on the Siachen Glacier, to the eastern Himalayan peaks that separated Tibet from the North East Frontier Agency. From these bases they conducted cross-border reconnaissance operations to place sensors for detecting nuclear and missile tests and devices for intercepting Chinese military communications.[7]

The Indians now had the border defense capability long sought by Mullik and built on the motivation of its members to regain their own homeland. The Tibetans were engaged in an endeavor far more to their liking than building roads—and one that gave them the feeling that they were preparing for the day when they could fight the Chinese for their independence. In the meantime they were repaying the Indians for their hospitality. In case of war with China, the Indian government was said to have a secret plan to win Tibet's independence with the Special Frontier Force in the lead.[8] The Indians never said as much to their Tibetan troops, but the illusion that they were preparing for their own war kept them going.

The U.S. provided light arms and instructors for this clone of the Green Berets. American interests were served by the firsthand intelligence gathered by the force as well as the prospects for the rebirth of the resistance movement. Moreover, the cooperation broke down old barriers between the U.S. government and the previously aloof Indians. Like the Indians, the Americans, however, saw the force as potential rather than actual combatants for the long-term cause of Tibetan independence.

While the SFF was being organized and trained, CIA made another attempt to determine the role of the forces based in Mustang, now that their maintenance and use was to be a shared concern with the Indians. In early summer 1963 CIA officers held a meeting in the field with the Mustang commander, Gyen Yeshe.[9] The guerrilla leader, now in unchallenged command of the force's sixteen companies spread along the upper Kali Gandaki valley, brought five of his company commanders with him. One was the man who had led the raid that captured the bag of classified Chinese documents. The other four were Camp Hale alumni, one of whom was the agency protégé, Lobsang Champa, who had by then become reconciled to a subsidiary role under Gyen Yeshe.

The meeting reopened the debate on the CIA's insistence that the guerrillas relocate inside Tibet before the agency would agree to more air drops. Gyen Yeshe and his men again cited the chicken-and-egg argument that with the weapons dropped so far, he had been able to arm only half the men in his companies, and they could not leave their safe haven in Mustang until they were fully equipped to engage the Chinese. The CIA representatives cited the political problems that prevented the Tibetans from establishing their permanent operating base inside Nepal. It would be difficult, if not impossible, to obtain Washington's approval for further arms drops until the guerrillas relocated across the border. After several days of grim but mutually respectful debate, prolonged discussions among the commanders, and lengthy private prayer sessions by Gyen Yeshe, the Tibetans submitted a compromise proposal. Four groups would operate inside Tibet and three in Nepal. Gyen Yeshe made it clear that he was not trying to evade the dangers of operating inside Tibet, declaring that he would be with one of the groups inside his homeland. The other leaders, however, said that they would reserve their decision until they had returned to Mustang and discussed it with their colleagues. They subsequently reported that they had been unable to find locations for viable bases inside Tibet, although they would send out extended reconnaissance and raiding parties from Mustang, which they did. The issue of their mission remained unresolved.

The strategy session with the Mustang leaders was part of a set of reviews of its programs in both Tibet and China that CIA was conducting that summer. A stocktaking session was held at Camp Hale concerning the future mission of the 133 Tibetans who were there being

Tibetan cavalry crossing the plateau close to a town.

C-130B flying a relief mission over the Andes in Peru, 1964. These were the type of planes used to drop men and arms into Tibet.

Site of Camp Hale, Colorado, wartime home of the U.S. 10th Mountain Division, called "Dumra" (garden) by the Tibetans being trained there in guerrilla warfare by the CIA.

The compound at Camp Hale. INSET: Sign to discourage visitors at Camp Hale.

A staff meeting at Dumra with four of the "gheghens" (instructors), known to the trainees as (from left to right): "Misters Tom, Ken, Ray, and Zeke," 1959.

Lessons at Camp Hale. "Mr. Ken" teaches world history.

Gyan Yeshe and Lhamo Tsering (fourth and fifth from left) with six of the guerrilla commanders at the pass overlooking Tibet in the early days of the operation at Mustang.

Yeshi Wangyal, "Tim," the leader of the ill-fated team dropped into Markham in 1961.

Wangdu and his lieutenants at their Mustang headquarters, 1969. Wangdu (wearing sunglasses), "Bill," one of the Cornell cadre and an interpreter at Camp Hale, and Lhamo Tsering, are the three men standing on the right.

Wangdu (his back to the camera), the leader of the Tibetan guerrillas who operated in Tibet from a stronghold in the Mustang peninsula of northern Nepal, receiving King Birendra who had come to greet his uninvited guests on Tibetan New Year's Day. Lhamo Tsering used this photograph in his defense when the Nepalese government later claimed that it had objected to the guerrillas' presence in Nepal.

The first class of the Cornell Cadre at their house in Ithaca, New York, with program coordinator Norman J. Meiklejohn. At Cornell University they were trained to act as administrative staff for the exile government's relations with the Indians and Americans.

The Dalai Lama with Ernest Gross who represented the Tibetans in their appeals to the United Nations and who kept their case before the international community.

The only portrait of the Fourteenth Dalai Lama presently on public view in Lhasa. With his family in the mural to the left, they are looking at the Golden Throne in the Assembly Hall of the Norbulingka.

The Dalai Lama's family. Norbu and Gyalo are to their mother's left and Lobsang Samten is in front of Norbu.

Lhasa officials and foreign dignitaries share the view of the Golden Throne. Hugh Richardson, the former British Resident Agent in Lhasa is the one wearing the black hat.

The Dalai Lama with the author and his wife, Andy, in Dharamsala, 1995.

Gyalo Thondup and the author with "Mark" (Tashi Choedhar) one of the interpreters at Camp Hale and one of the Cornell Cadre, in New Delhi, 1995.

The author introduces his son, John, to "Roger" (Ngadruk), one of the guerrilla commanders and a Dumra alumnus at a reunion in Darjeeling thirty-five years later.

trained in intelligence collection, communications, and guerilla tactics. It was decided that they would be best utilized in creating an in-depth intelligence capability inside Tibet, which would determine whether resistance that justified support was still alive there. This emphasis on intelligence as a primary mission caused one senior officer who had witnessed several generations of Tibetan programs come and go to remark caustically that the program managers had "reinvented the wheel." A parallel effort to help build a long-term program around the Dalai Lama to heighten a sense of nation among his refugee constituency and to keep his cause before the international community was also prescribed. William Colby, who had succeeded Desmond FitzGerald as chief of CIA's Far East Operations, included these conclusions in a report to the Special Group in September 1963. He noted that the agency review of its operations in China and Tibet had shown that these activities were "not especially productive" and that "the responsible operators have come to the conclusion that probably a change of approach is indicated. This would restrict targets to those of real significance, and would provide sufficient agent forces to accomplish the objective." He warned that "sizeable losses would have to be anticipated."[10]

Although "sizeable losses" probably referred to the casualties that could be anticipated should the U.S. government decide to support the ambitious operations in China proper that were being promoted by the Chinese Nationalist government, there was little enthusiasm for initiating any new major challenge to the Chinese in Tibet. But Washington still wanted a substantial Tibet program. In early 1964 the Special Group approved a new program, with a healthy price tag of $1,735,000, which was "to keep the political concept of an autonomous Tibet alive within Tibet and among foreign nations, principally India, and to build a capability for resistance against possible political developments inside Communist China."[11] The new program endorsed the emphasis on intelligence collection and political action recommended in the agency reviews. The monthly subsidy of $15,000 initiated in 1959 to maintain the Dalai Lama and his entourage as a political force active in India with representation abroad was to be continued. Although the role of the Mustang force remained hazy, there was no consideration of dismantling it.

It had now become part of Washington's stake in the Tibet situation and the U.S. commitment to stand with the Indians. The $500,000 annual subsidy was continued, but the Mustang leaders were urged to reassign part of their unarmed men to India for further training.

By early winter 1964 one of the more demonstrable symbols of the new era of Indian collaboration, a Combined Operations Center, had been established in New Delhi.[12] It would assume direction of the 133 Tibetans who had been trained at Camp Hale and of the guerrilla operations based at Mustang, but not the command over SFF, which was exercised solely by the Indians. In principle, there was an equal division of command and responsibility among the three members of the center. The U.S. underwrote the costs of the operations, trained the agents, provided the radios and other gear, and contributed operational guidance and its presumed expertise. The Tibetans provided the manpower for the missions. But the Indians controlled the territory and thereby the operations. There was mutual respect among the participants, and the center worked surprisingly well.

From the beginning the center was forced to confront the chronic problem of defining what role the Mustang force should play in relation to the SFF operations and the overall objectives of the three member parties. The center was further plagued by the fact that its control over the Mustang operations was neither tight nor tidy. The Indians tended to defer to the U.S. godfathers who had created this force. The Americans were nevertheless aware that, in using Gyen Yeshe's army, they had to take account of India's sensitivities concerning Nepal and China. Gyalo Thondup tried to call the shots for the Tibetans, but as a one-man foreign minister, intelligence chief, and political adviser to his brother, he had no time to spend at Mustang. Gyalo's operations chief, Lhamo Tsering, was tied down in New Delhi and could only make the arduous and time-consuming journey to Mustang when emergencies demanded it. All this meant that Gyen Yeshe and his predominately Khampa army were left free to sort out their endemic quarrels while planning and carrying out missions. Combined Operations, meanwhile, attempted to define what these missions should be.

The consequences of this remote control were demonstrated early in the summer of 1964 in one of those bizarre episodes that seem to spawn in the remote Himalayan atmosphere. George Patterson, the Scottish missionary and volunteer advocate of the Khampas, had dropped out of operations after 1951, when he had served as an intermediary in the U.S. government's unsuccessful efforts to persuade the Dalai Lama to seek asylum abroad. For a decade he had remained in India as a British correspondent covering events in Tibet and the other Himalayan kingdoms, then had left after several arguments with the Indian government. In 1964 he returned, determined to put the Khampa resistance on the world's television screens.[13]

Under the guise of promoting a Himalayan confederation and producing a television program on the plight of Tibetans exiled in Nepal, Patterson made his way to an area north and west of Kathmandu that was known to harbor Khampa guerrillas. Accompanied by a British producer and a cameraman, he was able to establish contact with a Khampa named Tendar who led one of the guerrilla groups operating as an outpost of Gyen Yeshe's main force. Tendar's group was located sixty miles and several peaks to the west of Gyen Yeshe's headquarters. Using documents signed by two former officials of the old Tibetan government, Patterson convinced Tendar and his men that the cause of the Dalai Lama would be served by filming Tendar's group ambushing a Chinese convoy along the Lhasa-Xinjiang highway. The film would be shown on television worldwide, providing evidence of active resistance to Chinese rule in Tibet.

These men needed little encouragement; ambushes were their stock in trade. Within three days of his arrival Patterson and his companions were being led by twenty Khampa guerrillas across a 20,000-foot pass to a ravine inside Tibet. That was the site that had been chosen to lay the ambush for a convoy moving along the highway. Early in the morning two days later, four Chinese trucks were ambushed in a fifteen-minute action photographed by the cameraman from a protected position above the valley. The trucks were either destroyed or disabled, and the eight Chinese soldiers in them were killed. The Tibetans suffered one casualty, a fifty-two-year-old Khampa who had been left for dead but miraculously made his way back to the guerrilla base three days later.

Tendar, meanwhile, notified Gyen Yeshe's headquarters that the ambush laid on for the benefit of television had been successfully carried out. He had tried to obtain advance approval from his chief, but by the time the courier arrived in Mustang, it was too late to stop the ambush even if Gyen Yeshe had wanted to. In due course Gyen Yeshe informed Combined Operations of the staged raid. His message, in the rudimentary language used in such communications, was received with great consternation. Combined Operations feared that making such a public spectacle of a small raid might provoke a violent reaction from the Chinese. At the very least, it would force the Nepalese to take official note of the Khampa presence, to which until then they had turned a blind eye. As it turned out the worries were unfounded. The film was not shown on British television for three years. But the whole episode nevertheless demonstrated the tenuous control that the principals had over what happened on the ground in those isolated valleys and mountainsides in Nepal.

The actions of any guerrilla group are unpredictable. It must of necessity operate on its own, and this was particularly true of the isolated Mustang force. It was composed of men who came from a tradition that only accepted firsthand governance, when it accepted governance at all. They had not asked Lhasa's permission or endorsement when they began their revolt against the Chinese. By this time most of them had been making their own operational decisions for almost a decade as a matter of survival. Their natural inclination toward unilateral action was compounded by the fact that the Tibetans had more immediate objectives that were not shared by their partners. They had begun their insurgency with the single-minded objective of ridding Tibet of the Chinese. They had little interest in delaying their actions to serve some future Indian strategic interest or even more remote U.S. objective. Lines of command, as well as the less-than-perfect convergence of plans, were as distant between Mustang and New Delhi in 1964 as they had been between Kham and Lhasa when the Tibet revolt began in the previous decade.

The Patterson escapade caused heated discussions within Combined Operations.[14] The Americans complained that no one had any control over Gyen Yeshe and urged that he should be removed from command. Gyalo Thondup was reluctant to do this because Gyen Yeshe had been selected by Gompo Tashi, who had died that fall after several years of medical treatment of the wounds he had suffered in battle in 1958. In his will he named Gyalo, "a man deeply devoted to the cause of Tibet," as his successor in carrying on the freedom movement. It was no time for Gyalo to turn out Gompo's designated guerrilla leader. The Indians, although greatly annoyed, still wanted to preserve the Mustang capability and were willing to defer to Gyalo, giving him stern orders to bring his recalcitrant fellow countrymen under some control. The Americans thus were persuaded not to jeopardize an operation over an issue of tribal command that they only hazily understood, despite their heavy investment in Mustang. The decision about command at Mustang was postponed.

But the problem was aggravated by the persistent fact that more than half of the men at Mustang had still not been armed. It had been four years since the last airdrops to Mustang, and Gyen Yeshe's requests for weapons were understandably becoming more insistent. In response to a questionnaire from Combined Operations, he said that he had a total of 1,865 men, of whom 1,707 were fully trained and able to use arms. The previous two drops made in 1961 had provided arms for seven of the sixteen companies into which these men were organized and ready to fight once they had weapons. The U.S. decided to make one further drop, this time with Indian endorsement. In May 1965 the third and last drop was made, this one in Mustang rather than Tibet. The drop included 250 rifles, 1,000 grenades, 6 mortars, 36 Bren guns, 42 Sten guns, 6 57 mm recoilless rifles, 75 handguns, and 72,000 rounds of ammunition.[15]

Despite the problems of communication and command demonstrated by the unauthorized ambush made by a unit operating on its own some distance from Gyen Yeshe's headquarters, Combined Operations decided that it was necessary to disperse the Mustang forces. The anticipated publicity over the made-for-television ambush and the increasing notice that the Nepalese were being forced to take of their difficult squatters increased the political vulnerability of their occupation of the Mustang valley. Under constant harassment, the Chinese might decide that the high political and military cost of a sweep into Mustang would be worth ridding themselves of this challenge to their control of western Tibet.

Gyen Yeshe was accordingly instructed to send some of his forces to western Nepal, opposite Purang inside Tibet near Lake Manasarowar. Others were to be sent to an area near Panch Pokhari, northeast of Kathmandu. The men sent from Mustang to reconnoiter the proposed relocation site in the west reported it could not provide logistical support for a permanent operating base. The area around Manasarowar might be sacred but it was barren and would sustain no sizeable force. The party at Panch Pokhari, however, found that the local populace spoke Tibetan and food supplies were available. One hundred men were therefore dispatched, though only fifty stayed on because of the difficulty in getting guns through the Nepalese checkpoints to the relocation sites.

Since relocation turned out to be no solution, business at Mustang continued as usual.[16] The Johnson administration was by this time preoccupied with Vietnam. From a policy point of view there was no disposition to drop challenges to the Chinese elsewhere. Raiding parties continued to go into Tibet from August through April, when the Tsangpo River was fordable. They were supplied with a special version of their staple diet of barley (*tsampa*) enriched with vitamins and nutrient supplements. This cereal had been developed with the help of the Kellogg Company by the CIA Tibetan Task Force's team doctor, Edward "Manny" Gunn, who had taken on the problem of finding a ration that would provide the energy the guerrillas needed to operate in these extremes of altitude and temperature. By 1963, loads of "Khampa *tsampa*" were being shipped to the Roof of the World.

Meanwhile the Chinese were building up their presence, increasing the cost in casualties to the Mustang raiders, however well fortified they may have been by their Battle Creek rations. Gyen Yeshe's leadership was coming under increasing criticism from company commanders, who accused him of misappropriating funds. It was becoming apparent that the Mustang force was not a long-term capability.

While dealing with the problems of the Mustang force, the Combined Operations Center was also actively engaged in its other designated responsibility of dispatching the men trained in Colorado on their intelligence/fact-finding missions inside Tibet. The men were taken to one of the old camps of the famed big game hunter Jim Corbett. Although the

Tibetans were no sissies, in Colorado they had become accustomed to the relatively more luxurious U.S. Army-style barracks and food. They were therefore soon ready to leave this more spartan outpost in the Kumaon Hills, where the rations were more like what they would have to depend on inside Tibet. There was a Hobson's choice of sleeping quarters— inside buildings that had acquired a substantial rat population while being used for grain storage, or outside where snakes coiled around the trees. Fortunately the snakes were diverted in their eating habits by the abundance of local vermin, but most of the Tibetans—and the visiting Combined Operations officers—chose to share the former granaries with the rats.

From the camp small teams were guided to the frontier by knowledgeable Indian veterans of the CIB's border posts.[17] Starting in early 1964 and continuing for the next three years, twenty-five teams were sent into Tibet.[18] They were dispatched along the entire border, but mostly in central and western Tibet. The results were mixed, but generally disappointing. One team was able to survive and send reports for over two years from an area south of the Brahmaputra and north of Mount Everest. One lasted for seven months, another for two months, in small cities south of Shigatse. Others were forced to return within weeks, unable to find a safe base inside Tibet or even obtain food. They found little support among the local people, who feared their presence and wanted nothing to do with inciting resistance unless the teams could deliver sufficient support to overcome the omnipresent Chinese. They could not.

In the course of the operations four men were arrested. Another was captured and doubled. The deception was immediately detected because he used his real name instead of the prearranged code name in transmitting his messages by radio. Combined Operations radioed false information to the double agent until it was decided that this feckless game would only permit the Chinese to identify the location of the base transmitter. By 1967 it had become evident that the risks were not worth the scattered and peripheral intelligence to which these teams had access or their limited ability to organize resistance. Their missions were therefore ended and they were called back to India. The Tibetans had performed valiantly, but it is impossible to follow Mao's tactic of merging with the local population—"swimming with the fish," he called it—when the fish live in a sparsely populated and easily patrolled aquarium.

THE NEW POLITICAL ERA

The Indian government's readiness to utilize the Tibetans openly as part of their military defense carried over to the political arena. In 1963, on the fourth anniversary of the revolt, the Indian government made no effort to discourage the Dalai Lama from promulgating a new constitution for an independent Tibet. When Beijing protested, the Indians would have none of it. The Chinese alleged that five years earlier the Indian government had "engineered and supported the rebellious activities of the reactionary clique of the upper social strata in Tibet." The Indian External Affairs ministry rejected this as "false and malicious," declaring the revolt the "spontaneous and inevitable" reaction of a suppressed people. It concluded with the observation that China's charges belied its professions of wanting to live in peace with its neighbors.[19] The Five Principles of Peaceful Coexistence had obviously been buried on the Tibetan border.

India gave its tacit approval to the new Tibet offices opened by Gyalo Thondup in New York and Geneva during the spring of 1964. The suggestion came from Ernest Gross, who had come to be accepted by the Dalai Lama and his inner cabinet as a valued foreign adviser on international affairs. With the U.S. State Department's acquiescence, Gross had proposed that the Tibetans establish these offices under the guise of promoting Tibetan handicrafts and publicizing the Tibetan cause. Thondup readily recognized that they would provide the Dalai Lama with unofficial representation and an on-the-scene presence in the two principal cities where Tibet's international status would be discussed— New York, as the headquarters of the UN, and Geneva, as its center for refugees and the nascent human rights movement. These offices were part of the long-term political package approved by the Special Group, and Thondup was granted an annual budget of $150,000 to run them.

The Indian government, without any official announcement, agreed to provide the necessary certificates of identity and reentry permits to the personnel staffing the offices. As their first representative in New York, the Tibetans named former foreign minister Thupten Tharpa Liushar, who in 1951 had carried Ambassador Henderson's letter offering assistance to the Dalai Lama. Another old hand, Thupten Woyden Phala, was sent to Geneva. This top monastic official had been the resistance leaders' confidential contact with the Dalai Lama, often bringing him messages he did not want to hear. Now Phala's primary responsibility was humanitarian: to arrange for the resettlement of the 1,000 Tibetans, including one hundred orphans, that the Dalai Lama had agreed to send to Switzerland. While grateful for the goodwill involved, the Tibetan leader sent these people abroad with reluctance, fearing further scattering of the Tibetan diaspora. In New York, Liushar took an active role in the negotiations for the continuing Tibetan appeals to the United Nations. Later an office was opened in London. The State Department, while reaffirming that the U.S. did not recognize Tibet as an "independent entity," noted that the U.S. did believe that the Tibetan people had the right of self-determination and the right to such representation. The embassy in New Delhi was also instructed to tell the Indian government, if asked, that the Department had been aware of the Dalai Lama's plan to open the offices and had no objection.[20] Thus, the Tibetan presence was established abroad, and these offices in New York, Geneva, and London operate today.

Gyalo Thondup immediately found himself overwhelmed by the demand for English-speaking Tibetans for these intelligence and diplomatic activities. The handful of Tibetans who had been to college were already fully engaged. The teenage Tibetans tutored in English at prep schools in Darjeeling and Kalimpong had served ably as interpreters at Dumra, but their knowledge was limited.

The situation harked back to previous ill-fated efforts by Britain's Indian civil service to foster the training of young Tibetans in English and other skills needed in the outside world. The British had been stopped by the old guard in Lhasa, which felt threatened by the introduction of dangerous foreign learning and modern ideas. So few were sent abroad that the careers of most can be traced. In 1912, four young Tibetans were sent to Rugby, the historic boys' school in England. The youngest went on to study electrical engineering at an English university and had a distinguished career in Tibet as a district magistrate and engineer; one was killed during World War I while serving with an Indian battalion; and the other two became middle-level monastic and civil officials respectively. The British Mission School, opened in 1923 in Gyantse, lasted only two years until the thirteenth Dalai Lama turned against its sponsors. Robert Ford, the British radio operator captured in 1950 by the Chinese when they invaded Kham, met two of its graduates, who had turned out well. One, described by Ford as "probably the best educated man in Kham,"[21] was governor of Markam, a district of the upper Yangtze, where he was known as a progressive official. The other was a well-regarded provincial finance minister. A 1944 venture to train thirty-three "old family" children and ten commoners lasted only one year, until it was closed under pressure from conservative monastic officials.

But twenty years later Tibet was in a dire predicament. It needed modern skills and contacts in the wider world. When I proposed that the CIA put together a crash course in basic English composition and speech, and international relations, William Colby enthusiastically approved. Known in the agency as a dedicated "nation builder," Colby believed that the CIA should be making such educational investments in the future. The Special Group agreed, and $45,000 was set aside for the annual expenses of this training. Ernest Gross formed the customary committee of distinguished persons to lend their names to a program for training young civil servants for the Dalai Lama. A retired U.S. foreign service officer, Norman J. Meiklejohn, worked with Cornell University to design a course of one academic year combining the rudiments of anthropology, world history, contemporary politics, and elementary governmental organization, with heavy doses of English composition.

A house was rented near the Cornell campus with a political science graduate student in residence, and the first group arrived from India in the autumn of 1964. Most were young men from ordinary Tibetan families who had been working with Gyalo since they were teenagers. Several were Dumra alumni. Their presence on the Ithaca campus caused a mild but passing sensation. Only one visitor, Timothy Leary, was disappointed. The former Harvard psychologist, then the guru of the LSD movement of the sixties, invited himself to give these exotic students a psychedelic show, which, he assured them, consisted of standard Tibetan temple practices. He raced around a darkened auditorium, chanting and beating drums, and found it hard to believe that none of these citizens of Shangri-la was familiar with the ceremonies he performed. Nor had any of them known anyone able to transmit his body to another location by spiritual exercises, another of Leary's fascinations with Tibetan mysticism.

Two additional groups were brought to Cornell for training during the next two years, generally with satisfying results. While none had received a formal high school or even middle school education in English, the first two groups were highly motivated and shared a great respect for and healthy fear of Gyalo. For its own purposes the university used its prevailing system to grade these students, and none received less than a C. The seventeen graduates of the first two groups were variously assigned and continued to work at least through the midseventies, and some even now, at intelligence installations in India, the Office of Tibet in New York, the Tibetan language section of All-India Radio, the new *Tibet Freedom* magazine, at Tibet House in New Delhi, or in minor posts within the Tibetan government-in-exile at Dharamsala. In later years three of the men were used to establish resettlement projects for the forces at Mustang. The only female within the group is now the Dalai Lama's representative heading the Office of Tibet in London, Mrs. Kesang Y. Takla. The last group of six men seemed to be less motivated, and most ended up going into business for themselves in the United States. The program was terminated in July 1967 due to the Katzenbach strictures against CIA funding of political programs in the U.S., which had resulted from the exposure that year of the agency's backing of the National Student Association. It had by that time provided an able and dedicated cadre to help Gyalo utilize the political and paramilitary support from India and the U.S. while the governing structure at Dharamsala was getting organized.[22]

❧

The art treasures of Tibet stand at the heart of the culture its people were fighting to preserve. By 1963 the religious wall hangings, ceremonial temple objects, and personal jewelry that had been the only things most monastic and lay refugees had to take with them when they escaped from Tibet, were rapidly disappearing at bargain prices to dealers and tourists through the bazaars of India and Nepal. This had been a danger of which Nehru had warned Thondup in 1950 when he urged that the Dalai Lama ship as many of these artifacts as possible to India for safekeeping. At that time the Dalai Lama and his government had been understandably too concerned about the greater problem of losing their country to take Nehru's advice. Thirteen years later it was apparent that although CIA was helping the Tibetans establish their presence in the international community, the artifacts that were the basis for their claim for recognition as a unique and independent culture were being scattered to distant drawing rooms and museums.

The new official Indian attitude of benign tolerance for the Tibetans' political activity, and India's willingness to recognize the refugees' distinctive cultural identity, suggested that the Indian government would not oppose opening a small museum of Tibetan art in New Delhi. I also knew that it was the sort of thing that would appeal to Desmond FitzGerald. It lay within the tradition he knew from his father, who had supported the expeditions to Mongolia by the Museum of Natural History forty years earlier. As a psychological warrior he also recognized the political value of a museum displaying Tibet's culture in the Indian capital. He readily approved a grant to Thondup of a modest, but adequate, sum to purchase a representative collection of Tibetan religious art before it all disappeared abroad.

Thondup made judicious purchases of the best available *thangkas*, the distinctive wall hangings of Tibet, representing its six major schools of religious painting. He rented a large Indian bungalow on one of the streets near the diplomatic enclaves. To cover the walls, my wife and I bought up the entire supply of the hand-loomed yellow cotton in the Indian Cottage Industries store. The colorful *thangkas* looked handsome, and the museum was an artistic success. More important, this collection of ancient paintings could be viewed in one place where the world would see them as symbols of a culture that was being lost.

Thondup was fully aware of the political implications of being permitted to open this institution. It gave the Tibetans the standing then accorded to the principal Indian princely states, which maintained consularlike installations called Houses in New Delhi. The Indians seemed quite willing to accord this status, and Tibet House was formally opened on October 26, 1965, by Education Minister M. C. Chagla, and the late prime minister's daughter, Indira Gandhi, who was then Information minister. Chagla used the occasion to loft what seemed to be a trial balloon hinting at the withdrawal of Indian recognition of China's suzerainty over Tibet.[23] He noted that India had recognized this status on the condition that the autonomy of Tibet would be preserved. Now "we recognize how wrong we were. Tibet's autonomy no longer exists. Its culture has been driven out . . . [therefore] the conditions under which we recognized China's suzerainty no longer exist." This elicited a surprising reaction from the usually hawkish Indian press, which argued for caution in making any such basic shift in policy, and this apparently caused the government to back away.

But the Tibetans now had a publicly recognized presence in the Indian capital. Tibet House was later replaced by an attractive permanent structure, which remains a major attraction for scholars and tourists. Like the creation of the Cornell cadre, Tibet House was one of the more lasting tangible contributions that CIA made to the Tibetans.

FADING SUPPORT AT THE UNITED NATIONS

India's support for Tibet did not extend to the United Nations. In the spring of 1964, at their first meeting following Nehru's death, Prime Minister Lal Bahadur Shastri told Thondup that India would vote for a UN resolution on Tibet for the first time. But the resolution itself would have to be cast in terms of human rights violations, he warned, and not endorse self-determination for Tibet. Y. D. Gundevia, the foreign ministry's senior civil servant, later urged Thondup to settle for this half-a-loaf resolution as part of a gradual policy of increasing Indian support for Tibet.[24] He suggested that the following year India might be able to express stronger public support by becoming a cosponsor.

The British meanwhile had reluctantly decided that they had little choice but to vote for a human rights resolution on Tibet. Not to do so, the Foreign Office argued, would "annoy both the Americans and the Indians."[25] This resigned attitude of pallid support was in line with comments made by Lord Home to Lord Mountbatten a year earlier. Mountbatten, Britain's last viceroy in India, had received a letter from the Dalai Lama and forwarded it to the foreign secretary, who felt obliged to reply to the Tibetans although "there is little anyone can do for the poor things."[26]

The U.S., however, told Thondup that any resolution that did not include an appeal for self-determination "might be viewed as an indication of a decline in international concern with this issue as well as an acquiescence in the Chinese domination of Tibet."[27] If Thondup was willing to settle for a weaker resolution in order to ensure a favorable Indian vote, the Department counseled that he make sure it was seen as an Asian initiative. But the Asians were drifting away even from their earlier half-hearted support. Only the Philippines agreed to act as a cosponsor, along with Nicaragua and El Salvador, which hardly made it an "Asian initiative." Ernest Gross, who was still determinedly representing the Tibetans, believed that Manila was probably aroused by fear of China, which had just exploded its first nuclear bomb.[28] Inscribed on the UN agenda for 1964, Tibet was not debated. When Tibet came up the next year, Thondup had to settle for a resolution calling for an end to "practices which deprive the Tibetan people of the human rights and fundamental freedoms [this word was made plural after prolonged negotiation] which they have always enjoyed." The U.S. went along merely to get something passed, and the Tibetans took what comfort they could from finally winning an Indian vote. It was the last time the General Assembly would act on Tibet's complaint. China, despite the turmoil of the Cultural Revolution that Mao was soon to unleash on his own people, had moved from being an outsider in the Cold War to a powerful player, and Tibet was becoming a worthy but expendable casualty.

MOSCOW REENTERS THE GAME

Khrushchev's forced retirement in October 1964 had not resolved the bitter ideological feud between his successors and Mao,[29] and Moscow was still willing to exploit their differences even in China's backyard. About that time the Soviet secret service began negotiations with Gyalo Thondup about supporting the Tibetan guerrillas in their efforts to drive the Chinese out of Tibet. This curious episode of Cold War intrigue began in the summer of 1964 when T. N. Kaul, India's pro-Russian ambassador in Moscow, asked Thondup why he looked only to the Americans for help. Why not the Russians? suggested Kaul. Thondup observed that this seemed a futile exercise, since he had always seen Moscow support Beijing at the UN. Kaul suggested that Thondup ignore past history. The Dalai Lama's brother accordingly approached the chief of the TASS bureau in New Delhi, a man named Markov, thereby beginning extraordinary negotiations that were to last for three years.

As Thondup recalls,[30] Markov introduced him to a small group of senior KGB officials who said that they had come to New Delhi to meet with him at the instruction of their chief Alexandr Paniushkin, the head of the KGB First Chief Directorate. He had been the Soviet ambassador to China from 1939 to 1945 in the days of Chiang K'ai-shek, and then served as ambassador to Washington from 1947 to 1952 as the Cold War began. He returned to China as ambassador from 1952 to 1953, when Stalin was completing the Soviet sacking of Manchurian industry, an early portent of the already serious differences between the two great Communist powers. Paniushkin must have taken some relish in 1964 at the thought of challenging not only the Chinese Communists but also the Americans and the Chinese Nationalists all at one go in Tibet.

When Thondup expressed his skepticism about Soviet intentions, Paniushkin's representatives countered with an offer to support the Tibetans on "everything." They promised money, arms, and training to the Tibetan resistance fighters at a training center to be established in Tashkent. The trainees would come as tourists to Eastern Europe, whence they would be smuggled into the Soviet Union and on to

Tashkent. The Russians later amended this offer and said the Tibetans would be flown covertly out of New Delhi's Palam airport as passengers on the Soviet air force planes that were already ferrying military supplies to India. After training in guerrilla warfare they would be infiltrated by way of Pakistan or Afghanistan into Tibet, where the Russians would support their efforts to reinvigorate the resistance movement.

The KGB officials told Thondup that he was naive to count on the Americans, who had been making deals under the table with the Chinese for years in secret talks between their ambassadors in Warsaw. They promised that, unlike his supposedly untrustworthy American allies, Thondup could count on their support—once a Russian gave his word he delivered the goods. Thondup asked the KGB negotiators if they would be willing to discuss these plans with the Indians. He preferred to make this a joint venture because he could not afford to offend his Indian hosts. They rejected that, dismissing the Indians as "useless." They also refused Thondup's other condition that the Soviet Union support Tibet's appeals at the UN. While Moscow was willing to play at covert efforts to challenge the Chinese, it was unwilling to do so in an open international forum.

When the KGB refused to give any overt sign of support, Thondup ended the negotiations, which by then had stretched into 1967. He had his own game plan to explore within the interstices of the Cold War and feared that operations with the Russians would become known to the Chinese and jeopardize any chance of negotiations with Beijing. While he felt that the pragmatic Chinese could well understand Tibetans working with Americans and Indians as natural allies, they would be angered by a collaboration with China's new enemy, and the possibility of coming to any agreement with them would be irrevocably foreclosed.

Thondup finally told Mullik's successor Ramji Kao of the Russian proposals, and the Indian intelligence chief almost "jumped out of his skin." Kao, who had always been highly supportive and a good friend to the Tibetans, warned Thondup that whatever Kaul may have advised him, he should not make common cause with the Russians under any circumstances. Without telling either Kao or the Russians of his own reservations, Thondup backed away. The KGB's ploy died when Thondup retired from Tibetan foreign affairs in 1969.

The Great Game in Central Asia was thus never revived. The limited guarantee for their future that the Tibetans had won from the Indians was to survive as the Americans began preparations to slip away as the rest of the world already had. The orphans of the Cold War had ironically found a home in exile among those who had most wanted to remain aloof from the great struggle.

CHAPTER 16

The U.S. Government Withdraws

B Y 1968 the guerrilla force at Mustang was aging and composed mostly of men who had been fighting and living as partisans in the field since the midfifties, separated from their families. There had been no move to recruit new men since the first rush in 1961 produced surplus volunteers. The remaining 1,800 Tibetans in Mustang, however, continued to be a remarkably well-disciplined force.[1]

Nevertheless, it was generally agreed that although Gyen Yeshe began as a dedicated patriot, he had become a flawed leader. In 1966, complaints reached Gyalo Thondup and the Combined Operations Center in New Delhi about the way he ran the camps like a clan leader in his native Kham, particularly in his disdain for keeping any accounts of the substantial official funds for the Mustang force, and his autocratic style in assigning missions and allocating supplies. The complainants were mostly the officers who had been trained by the CIA in Colorado. Many reported that as the operational role of the Mustang forces diminished, Gyen Yeshe had become occupied by prayer and the care of the extensive collection of antiques that he had amassed from refugees passing through his domain. He did not believe in sharing his authority, or even his counsel, and certainly not control of the funds, with his commanders, particularly those he considered corrupted by foreign theories and practices of administration.

Combined Operations in New Delhi sent Lhamo Tsering to Mustang in 1966 as fact finder and arbiter between the whistle-blowers and their dictatorial commander. Gentle but persistent, Lhamo Tsering established a tenuous truce. The protesting officers offered a token apology for criticizing their chief, and Gyen Yeshe retracted his demand that they accept dismissal from the force. Lhamo Tsering then set up a finance department for receipts and disbursements instead of permitting Gyen Yeshe to pass out funds like a tribal chief.

Lhamo Tsering also inspected the camps and found only half the men armed with weapons, the rest with wooden sticks. The third arms drop had been made in 1965 on condition that it would be the last until Gyen Yeshe was able to position some of his men inside Tibet. But they had been unable to establish bases across the border, and that ended the arms drops. The Mustang force was therefore only partly armed and underemployed. But after Lhamo Tsering returned with photographs of the Mustang bases that the American supporters saw for the first time, they and the Indians were impressed by this evidence of a well-trained and organized force, despite its problems at the top. Combined Operations was reluctant to give up what seemed to be a capability in being. What was needed was a firm hand on the command at Mustang and a definition of its mission.

In 1968 Combined Operations finally confronted the command problem head on. The defiant Gyen Yeshe had closed down the finance department a few months after Lhamo Tsering set it up and again demanded control of the Mustang group's money. In an effort to curb

Gyen Yeshe's excesses, Wangdu Gyatotsang, the nephew of Gompo Tashi, the late leader of the Volunteer Freedom Fighters, had been sent to Mustang as deputy commander. Wangdu had impressive credentials. He was one of the first men trained by the CIA. He had parachuted back into Kham and fought there until the local resistance was overrun. He had then made his way to India by way of his uncle Gompo Tashi's headquarters in southern Tibet. He had spent the next decade working with Gyalo and Lhamo Tsering and had come to be highly regarded by the exile government in Dharamsala. Not surprisingly, Gyen Yeshe took a personal dislike to his new deputy, and their bitter disagreements resulted in a continuing deterioration at Mustang.

In the summer of 1968 Lhamo Tsering was sent back to Mustang in a fact-finding group. He represented Combined Operations, and Phuntso Tashi, the Dalai Lama's brother-in-law, represented his government-in-exile at Dharamsala. There they found Gyen Yeshe characteristically holed up at his headquarters, while his deputy Wangdu was conducting military exercises in the field. After another unsatisfactory meeting between Gyen Yeshe and his challengers (brokered by the fact finders), the delegation returned to India convinced that Gyen Yeshe had to be removed from Mustang if the organization was to survive. The dissension between the commander and his deputy was affecting morale, and most of the men had turned against Gyen Yeshe.

Field operations nevertheless continued. After his arrival at Mustang the year before, Wangdu had established a training center. He began sending groups to harass the Chinese and organize an underground built around whatever presence the Mustang guerrillas could establish inside Tibet. But by this time, 1968, Combined Operations decided that the Chinese had consolidated their military control so firmly in the area of Tibet where the Mustang units operated that further guerrilla actions would be futile. The mission of the Mustang forces was refocused on collecting intelligence and building an underground. Small groups were sent inside Tibet to collect local intelligence on the Chinese, which was forwarded by five radio teams located just over the border inside Nepal. According to Lhamo Tsering they were able to provide intelligence on Chinese military activities along a three-hundred-and-fifty-mile front inside southeastern Tibet.[2] In addition, two teams were dispatched into Tibet to monitor Chinese military traffic moving along the Lhasa-Xinjiang highway, reports of which they radioed to Combined Operations.

In February 1969 Phuntso Tashi used the occasion of the tenth anniversary of the Tibet revolt to request Gyen Yeshe to attend the celebrations in Dharamsala. Once he arrived in New Delhi en route to Dharamsala the recalcitrant guerrilla leader was informed by Gyalo Thondup that he had been removed from his command. Although promised a responsible position in the Dalai Lama's security office at Dharamsala, the proud commander resented what he considered a summary and humiliating dismissal. He certainly had no interest in settling in Dharamsala, where the issue of his accounts was bound to arise. He accordingly slipped out of New Delhi and made his way back to Mustang.

Gyen Yeshe's return was fortuitous. His supporters were planning to hold Lhamo Tsering hostage, blaming him for their leader's removal. But Gyen Yeshe told them to stand down. He said that he had come back only to settle his affairs and was returning to Dharamsala to explain any discrepancies in his accounts. He departed, ostensibly for India, but made it only a few miles down the Kali Gandaki valley to Tukuche. There he made plans to start his own outfit of less than one hundred supporters, primarily from Batang, his hometown in Kham. But he failed to organize this rump guerrilla band and settled temporarily with a small group of followers farther down the valley in Pokhara, the jumping-off outpost to the Mustang peninsula. The dauntless Lhamo Tsering then returned to India to try to salvage what he could from this increasingly embarrassing and unproductive conflict of wills.

But it was too late. The Johnson administration had supported continuance of a full paramilitary and political program for Tibet until the end of its term of office. In the spring of 1968 it had even considered the resupply of arms and ammunition to the Mustang force. But the Combined Operations Center's recognition that summer of the bleak prospects for effective military action by the Mustang guerrillas against the Chinese made this policy support irrelevant. CIA's Near Eastern operations chief, James Critchfield, told the Special Group's successor, the 303 Committee, that "achievements inside Tibet were minimal—

outside more substantial."[3] The deployment of landline wiretap teams to selected priority targets were the only projected new activities within Tibet that were called for in the future program. These did not require the 1,800 men still at Mustang to accomplish them. Early in 1969 the CIA informed Gyalo Thondup it was withdrawing its support for the hapless Mustang force. Thondup was asked to prepare a resettlement plan to be carried out during the following three years. The Tibetans later attributed this to the Nixon administration's plans to establish diplomatic relations with Beijing, but the decision had already been made to abandon Mustang for operational and not geopolitical reasons.

When the CIA gave notice that it was ending its support to the Mustang force, Henry Kissinger had only begun his exploratory moves to establish relations with the Chinese government. China was in the midst of the convulsions caused by Mao's Cultural Revolution, and there was neither any need nor interest in making sacrificial offerings to a giant suffering from self-inflicted wounds. While the moribund talks between U.S. and Chinese negotiators, which had been dragging on for twelve years in Warsaw, had been revived, the subject of Tibet was not raised by either side. The Mustang guerrillas were never a bargaining chip there or elsewhere.[4]

By 1969, the operations at Mustang had been going on for more than eight years, which far exceeded the normal lifetime of most major covert action projects with which I was associated. The principal support within the CIA had come from Desmond FitzGerald's Far East Division. His South Asian counterparts never shared his enthusiasm for his efforts to challenge the Chinese through their backdoor.[5] By 1969 FitzGerald was dead, and the zeal had waned for carrying on what was now seen by many to be an outdated commitment created during a different phase of the Cold War.

Many in Washington remembered the problems created by the presence of Chinese Nationalist soldiers who had retreated into northern Burma in 1949 and remained with the support of the Chiang K'ai-shek government and attendant suspicions of CIA support. Most of these relics of the Chinese civil war had been removed only after two presidents, Eisenhower in 1953 and Kennedy as late as 1961, had put great pressure on the Chinese Nationalist government. Marshall Green, then assistant secretary of state for East Asian affairs, recalled all this and said no one wanted to repeat it.[6]

More important was the recognition that the original mission of the Mustang force had not proven feasible. The guerrillas simply were unable to establish bases inside Tibet from which they could disrupt Chinese supply and communications lines. Furthermore, the Mustang force had been supplanted in many ways by the Special Frontier Force (SFF). This force, rather than Mustang, was going to receive the essential sustaining material and political support over the long term from both the Indians and the U.S. In the unlikely event of a major conflict with China, it would be the SFF and not the aging Mustang guerrillas that would play the major part in any action in Tibet. Its declining mission, coupled with the internal war among its commanders, made it an operational luxury that was difficult to justify in Washington, where it had lost its constituency anyway.

Gyalo Thondup, who felt the U.S. government was reneging on its commitments, remained for the initial bargaining over the termination agreement. He then turned the problem over to the faithful Lhamo Tsering and retired from the active role that he had played for twenty years in Tibetan political life. Thondup had been extraordinarily skillful and effective in obtaining both material and political support from the U.S. government for the Tibetans, and Washington had come to have great regard for his abilities. The Department respected him as a tenacious negotiator who was able to understand, even if he disliked, the practical limits to what the U.S. government could do for Tibet in the international community. Desmond FitzGerald had great admiration for him as a political animal and as a man of action. I once heard him tell Thondup: "Please arrange in your next reincarnation to be the Prime Minister of a country where we can do more to help you." Thondup had never bothered to cultivate support among the traditionalists in the Tibetan exile government at Dharamsala. He had been tolerated not just because he was the Dalai Lama's brother, but because he was one of the few Tibetans who knew how to operate in the wider world, especially in Washington. As proof of that, he had delivered the goods for more than a decade. Now the U.S. had left him in an embarrassing and diminished position, and he decided to bow out. While Thondup was eventually to come out of his self-imposed exile a decade later to negotiate with the Chinese leadership, his departure from the Tibetan political scene in 1969 was the beginning of the end of an era.[7]

It was left to the able, self-effacing, but fiercely loyal Lhamo Tsering to fill the breach, as he had so many times since he first made common cause with Thondup in Nanking twenty years before. This dedicated man was one of the unpublicized heroes of the Tibetan resistance, and his abilities as a quietly effective administrator were now put to the test. He and Wangdu, now the Mustang commander, decided that to preserve morale they would not inform the men of the CIA's withdrawal and would keep the force alive while quietly dismantling it. Wangdu maintained an active training schedule, while Lhamo Tsering initiated various programs to ease the men into other vocations. One of the handful of new recruits, Jamyang Norbu, recounted that when he arrived in Mustang in 1971, military routine and discipline were being maintained, despite rumors that the days of the force were numbered, and the internecine war being waged by Gyen Yeshe's supporters.[8] Wangdu conducted exercises in rock climbing and other commando skills, and the men slept alongside their weapons, ready for action whatever its origin.

The initial plan that Lhamo Tsering worked out with Combined Operations called for the resettlement of five hundred of the Mustang force a year for three years, leaving a rump group of three hundred crack troops as a token resistance force to be supported by the Indians and the U.S. To economize, Lhamo Tsering tried to send another three hundred men to join their fellow countrymen serving with the SFF, but they balked, and only one hundred and twenty agreed to go. He sent others on leave to India to ease pressure on the dwindling Mustang treasury. He started farming projects and a literacy program to provide the demobilized warriors with some elementary tools for coping with life outside the guerrilla camps. Three of the cadre who had been trained at Cornell, Lobsang Tsultrim, Thinlay Paljor, and Wangchuk Tsering, were sent to Nepal to develop projects to provide employment for the former resistance

fighters. These three were able to establish Tibetan carpet-weaving fac-
tories and handicraft centers in Pokhara and Kathmandu, open the
Annapurna Hotel in Pokhara and set up a transport business running
trucks and buses between Pokhara and Kathmandu and taxis in Kathmandu. These enterprises all succeeded. In 1969, the Cornell alumni
arrived with twelve looms. These became the origin of the thriving carpet-weaving business, subsequently developed by Tibetan and Nepalese
entrepreneurs, which is now one of Nepal's principal employers.

The peaceful conversion process did not go unchallenged. A Tibetan
New Year's Day celebration in 1970 ended with the arrest of one of Gyen
Yeshe's supporters for threatening to take armed action against Wangdu
and the Mustang force. An effort by the man's supporters to rescue him
ended in a showdown with the main body of the force loyal to Wangdu.
Two of Gyen Yeshe's supporters refused to surrender and were killed,
while most of the remaining men were arrested. Gyen Yeshe embellished
and publicized the event, which caused a major controversy within the
Tibetan government at Dharamsala.[9] It also was an embarrassment to
those within the Indian government who still supported the force. This
shoot-out was followed by a small group of Gyen Yeshe's men ambushing the three-man Combined Operations courier team. They killed one
of the couriers but failed to get the substantial sum of money the team
was carrying to the Mustang headquarters.

These rearguard actions against disbanding the force prompted the
dispatch of yet another investigating team. In meetings with Lhamo
Tsering, Wangdu, and Gyen Yeshe, both sides agreed to argue their case
before the Tibetan cabinet. Lhamo Tsering proceeded to India and
waited in vain for Gyen Yeshe to appear on the three dates that the cabinet scheduled for the hearings at Dharamsala. The Tibetan government
finally ruled against Gyen Yeshe and made his offenses public. Gyen
Yeshe negotiated Nepalese citizenship for himself and three of his men
in return for his surrender and collaboration. The proud rebel leader
eventually settled in Kathmandu, where he lives as a recluse. Reportedly
remorseful over the way his command ended, he spends his days praying, a discredited casualty of his misuse of the customs of governance
from a different time and place.

☙

Although both the CIA and the Indians had extended the deadline for ending their financial support,[10] and Gyen Yeshe remained relatively quiescent in Kathmandu, Wangdu did not have an easy time closing down the camps. The sponsors reneged on their original proposal to retain a reserve corps of three hundred men and demanded that the entire force be resettled. The company commanders resisted the reassignment of their best and youngest men to the SFF. Resettlement could only reduce the main force gradually. It remained intact with a sizable number of weapons but without a purpose. While the Tibetans are a patient people, trained by their religion to think in terms of eternity, like most human beings they can become volatile when their grievances continue to be frustrated. Both the sponsors and the Nepalese were looking for ways to defuse this situation. The Nepalese acted first, resorting to blunt methods. As funds were drying up and Wangdu was struggling to relocate his reluctant troops, the Nepalese began an anti-Khampa campaign, denouncing the men holding on at Mustang as "Khampa *drokpas*" (the latter word a pejorative term for western Tibetan nomads held in low esteem by the Nepalese). They also publicized local incidents in the Mustang region that they had previously ignored, holding Wangdu personally accountable for failing to keep his troops in line.

Early in 1974 the Nepalese Home minister summoned Wangdu to Kathmandu and demanded that his men surrender their arms. The conventional wisdom among the Tibetans is that the Nepalese were responding to pressure that Mao put on Nepal's King Birendra when he visited Beijing in 1973. (William I. Cargo, then U.S. Ambassador in Kathmandu, said that, although he could not categorically rule out Chinese pressure, the U.S. embassy had no knowledge of it and he is "80 per cent sure" that the embassy would have known.[11] He also said that the Nepalese had never discussed the Mustang situation with him or his staff.) Whatever prompted the Home minister to act, his demand that the veterans give up their arms presented Wangdu with a dilemma. He replied that unless the Nepalese could guarantee a resettlement plan for his men still in the camps, he could not transmit the request because they would use their arms to kill him. At that point the Home minister seems to have understood the problem and asked Wangdu to submit a detailed plan for resettlement.

Wangdu was more adept at training guerrillas than in converting them to pastoral pursuits. He asked Lhamo Tsering to come to Mustang to survey job possibilities for those to be resettled. Combined Operations feared he knew too much to risk capture in what was becoming an increasingly insecure and uncontrolled area, but Lhamo Tsering felt he and Wangdu had the responsibility of resolving the situation. He went to Nepal in March 1974, but while he was staying at the guerrilla-owned Annapurna Hotel in Pokhara, he was arrested by the Nepalese police, who had been alerted by the still vindictive Gyen Yeshe.

After arresting Lhamo Tsering, the Nepalese government issued an ultimatum to Wangdu demanding that his men at Mustang surrender their weapons within ninety days. Wangdu sent a messenger to Dharamsala asking how to respond. After a series of meetings, the Dalai Lama and his government decided that the Mustang force had no choice but to yield to the Nepalese request, but that the men were likely to comply only if ordered by the Dalai Lama himself. Phuntso Tashi, the Dalai Lama's brother-in-law and his chief of security, was therefore sent to Mustang with the fateful message. The Nepalese brought him and Lhamo Tsering to Jomosom, a village near the Mustang camps, but they refused to permit Lhamo Tsering to accompany Phuntso Tashi. They apparently had got wind of a plan for Ragra Jetar, the man who commanded the group that captured the treasure trove of Chinese documents thirteen years earlier, to lead an escape party to free him. Lhamo Tsering had flatly rejected it on the ground that it would only end in the deaths of many men and to no avail. He had earlier rejected a similar proposal after his arrest at Pokhara. He recognized that the days of the guerrilla warriors at Mustang were over, and their problems would not be solved by a Wild West movie rescue.

Phuntso Tashi, accompanied by the Dalai Lama's representative in Nepal, Dhondup Namgyal, then set off on his joyless mission to the camps carrying a tape of the Dalai Lama's voice asking the men to surrender their arms. The Dalai Lama explained in his autobiography that, while he had admired their valor, he had never been in favor of their activities. In any event, they had been organized to fight the Chinese, not the Nepalese, and fighting their hosts would be "senseless" because it would only harm the thousands of other Tibetan refugees in Nepal. He asked them to lay down their arms and reach a peaceful settlement. As the Dalai Lama explained, "The Tibetan struggle needed a long-term approach."[12]

When Phuntso Tashi arrived at Wangdu's headquarters he found the guerrilla leader and his commanders prepared to take on the Nepalese at Jomosom and free Lhamo Tsering in the process. Phuntso Tashi rejected the plan and played the tape made by His Holiness. After hearing it, a bitterly disappointed Wangdu gave up his opposition and permitted the tape to be played at the other camps. On July 23 a group from Wangdu's headquarters surrendered their arms, but only after painful sessions in which two men committed suicide. Soon afterward, men from the other camps packed their belongings and weapons and began a mournful trek south from the last redoubt of the Tibetan resistance. For most it was the end of a cause that had defined the last twenty years of their lives.[13]

Wangdu had meanwhile fled his headquarters with a small group of followers determined to carry on resisting the Chinese. During the next month they zigzagged two hundred miles along the border between Nepal and the Tibetan border to western Nepal, where one of the Dumra-trained satellite Mustang radio reconnaissance teams was located. There Wangdu sent a message to Combined Operations proposing that he reorganize his forces in this isolated area. Combined Operations had no interest in reviving Mustang and ordered him to India.

Wangdu and his group accordingly set out to cross back into Tibet, from where they planned to escape to India across one of the passes on the India-Tibet border. Their plan was foiled when they encountered a large Chinese military force inside Tibet and had to double back into Nepal, where they fell into the trap set by Nepalese troops near Tinker Pass. Wangdu went ahead with a few men, while the majority of his group stayed behind to cover the rear. He was ambushed in a fire fight that lasted only a few hours and was killed.[14] The rear guard fought a long battle with the Nepalese, and some eventually escaped by climbing over cliffs with ropes, using techniques they had learned at Mustang under Wangdu's instruction. They then made their way to India.

By going down fighting, the last Mustang commander ensured his place as a hero of the Tibetan resistance. But the Nepalese, angry and frustrated at years of being used by the Tibetans in a battle not their own, were determined to destroy his legend. They arranged for Gyen Yeshe to fly from Kathmandu to the Tinker Pass battlefield to identify the body of his late rival. The body was then taken to Kathmandu, where it was the centerpiece of a public spectacle held in a downtown park.[15] Wangdu's rifle and personal belongings were also put on display with military objects from the guerrilla camps at Mustang.

Meanwhile Lhamo Tsering had been taken to the Police Training Center in Kathmandu. The police had angrily told him that Wangdu had fled to an unknown destination, but they would release him if it was clear that Wangdu had left Nepal. After they learned of Wangdu's death they interrogated him intensely about his mission. They finally appeared to accept his account that he had been at Mustang trying to organize resettlement and surrender for the guerrillas according to the agreement with their Home minister. The police then promised to release him if he agreed to sign a document agreeing to leave Nepal and do nothing further against Nepalese law. Lhamo Tsering signed the document, but his captors subsequently reneged. Lhamo Tsering believes they did so under Chinese pressure. He cites a strange incident earlier in the spring, when he was taken into custody and the Nepalese asked him to go to Tibet to help implement China's reforms. He understandably had no desire to put himself in the hands of those who had denounced him as a criminal responsible for the resistance. The Nepalese were presumably not surprised when he turned down their offer to promote the new order that the Chinese were installing in his homeland.

For the next five years, Lhamo Tsering was held without charges as a political prisoner until he was put on trial with six Mustang veterans. All had either resisted the Nepalese demands to surrender or had taken a prominent role in the Mustang scene. One was Ragra, who while a hero to CIA as the man responsible for the captured Chinese documents, was undoubtedly looked on less favorably by the Nepalese as the man who had brought the escape plan to Lhamo Tsering while he was held at Jomosom.[16] Two others had been company commanders. One had been captured while attempting to flee from Mustang with Wangdu, and one had been chief of the training group at Mustang. The sixth was the radio operator for a team that had been operating in the area that George Patterson had gone through on his way to photograph the staged ambush in 1964. Wangdu had also sent him with others to Dharamsala for guidance on whether to surrender. Ironically, the Nepalese took him into custody when he returned with the advice they favored.

The 1979 show trial was heard by a special court of representatives from both the Home and Justice ministries and the Nepalese intelligence service. Working from a detailed record of what had transpired at Mustang from 1961 to 1974, they asked Lhamo Tsering how he could argue that he had gone to Mustang in 1974 only to deal with resettlement issues when he had recruited people on Nepalese territory and armed them to carry out activities against Nepal's friendly neighbor. Lhamo Tsering responded that both the king of Nepal and his uncle had visited Mustang. The king had been received by Gyen Yeshe and accepted a horse as a gift. As further evidence of the king's approval, Lhamo Tsering presented a photograph of the king in a friendly pose with Wangdu taken on that occasion. He pointed to the good relations between the Mustang forces, their neighboring police unit, and soldiers garrisoned at nearby Jomosom, with whom they often celebrated Tibetan New Year's Day and other occasions. He also cited the projects of the Mustang guerrillas repairing and constructing bridges and airstrips in the area. Had these been the acts of an unfriendly and illegal force?

The five court-appointed lawyers pointed out that even if the Mustang activities had violated Nepalese law, the Home minister had pledged not to prosecute those who, like the defendants, had surrendered their arms before July 31, 1974. This in effect had meant that they had been given legal exemption for these activities.

The court rejected these arguments and convicted all seven. One who had fought a Nepalese policeman was sentenced to be executed and the others to life in prison. The court did note that the defendants could appeal to the king for a pardon. They did so, but the process proved lengthy and they spent two more years in jail. In 1981, King Birendra responded to an appeal for their release from the Dalai Lama and put them on his birthday amnesty list. The king, aware that delegations from Dharamsala had begun touring Tibet, apparently felt that improved relations between the Dalai Lama's government and Beijing made it politically acceptable to his powerful neighbor to release these last holdovers from the Mustang force. The saga that had begun with such high hopes twenty-one years earlier had come to an end.

✍

While the guerrillas at Mustang were furling their battle flags, their counterparts in the SFF were finally given their chance to engage in combat. The outcome was different, less tragic, but in the end no more helpful to the cause of Tibet's freedom. In November of 1971 the Indian commander ordered approximately 3,000 men of the Special Frontier Force into action in the Chittagong Hill Tracts to aid the East Pakistani insurgents fighting for the independence of what was to become Bangladesh.[17] The Indians, who supported the insurgents, were free to commit the troops because the SFF was purely their creature. Although Mustang had come under the direction of Combined Operations after 1962, the U.S. had no voice in the command of the SFF or how its troops were used. The Tibetan leadership at Dharamsala also had a passive role. Sonam Palden, a member of the force at the time, recalled that when the unit's political officer had visited Dharamsala to confirm that the Tibetans were to go into Pakistan he was given unenthusiastic but tacit approval. In Dharamsala, where there were mixed feelings about using the force to fight except in Tibet, the Security Department punted, telling him: "If the Indians send 1,000 soldiers to Bangladesh, the Tibetans should send four"—another way of saying that the Tibetans should provide the least number they could gracefully deliver. There also may have been those who recalled the days of a decade before when the Pakistanis had aided the Tibetan resistance by permitting the men being sent to Camp Hale to be exfiltrated through what was then East Pakistan and by making the airfield just outside of Dacca available for the flights being made into Tibet.[18] The Tibetans had reasons to feel a sense of obligation to both the Pakistanis and their Indian hosts.

But the men in the force were eager to join the war and show how well they could fight. Their government had agreed, albeit reluctantly, and they couldn't let Dharamsala lose face. Besides, said one of them later, "we'll show the Indians that we Tibetans can fight."[19] Jamyang Norbu, then a young recruit at the disintegrating Mustang camp, agreed that there was no popular criticism of the Indians among the Tibetan exiles for using their people in the war. The Tibetans viewed participation as a training exercise for an eventual war to liberate their own country.[20] They were also proud that their units had saved the royal family of the Chakmas, Tibeto-Burman people who had been made unwilling subjects of East Pakistan when it had been carved out of British India. Pakistani troops were on their way to eliminate them when SFF Tibetans took control of the Chakma homeland.

The Tibetans of the SFF acquitted themselves well and proved their mettle and worth to their Indian hosts. They had blocked the potential escape route of the Pakistani forces into Burma and pinned down a sizable number of Pakistani troops in the Chittagong Hills. They lost fifty-six killed (including Wangdu's "cousin brother," Thondup Gyatotsang) and one hundred and ninety wounded.[21] Their battle was not waged against the enemy for which their force had been created, but it served to keep alive their hope that the next one would be for their own independence. Their record provided a temporary boost to the hopes of the men at Mustang that perhaps their day too would come. Today this prospect has become less of an operating hope and more of a rationale for those who find serving in the SFF a good career. This became especially true after 1971 when the Indians recognized their contribution in the battles that led to the creation of Bangladesh by granting them pay and rations equal to those of their Indian colleagues.

THE DIPLOMATS ALSO STAND DOWN

While the U.S. had begun to defer to the Indians its role as the Tibetans' major military patron, Washington's zeal in pursuing the Tibetans' cause in the diplomatic realm was also beginning to ebb. The

U.S. was assuming more of a maintenance role, rather than taking on any bold new initiatives.

On December 18, 1965, Gyalo Thondup, buoyed by finally having won the vote of the Indians for even a weak UN resolution, made one last effort to win U.S. support for the establishment of a government-in-exile under the Dalai Lama in India. U. Alexis Johnson, then deputy undersecretary of state, temporized. He noted that "Taiwan posed something of a problem . . . not that Taiwan's influence was strong, but it was a factor that we must consider."[22] He would discuss it with his colleagues. Three months later the Department told the embassy that it was "unenthusiastic" about adding "this sensitive item" to the diplomatic agenda it was then pushing with the Indians.[23] The embassy was to let Gyalo down gently, citing the fact that such a change in status might present his Indian hosts with problems and they were being remarkably tolerant of his political activities. Furthermore it might jeopardize the existence of the Tibet offices operating in New York, Geneva, and London. In other words: Don't rock the boat! The embassy reported that he accepted "in apparently good heart."[24]

Action at the United Nations faded out in similar fashion. During the summer of 1968 the dauntless Ernest Gross made one last try for India to sponsor a resolution. He wrote his old friend Chester Bowles, asking him to intervene personally as U.S. ambassador to India. Bowles's staff supported the move—they noted it would be appropriate in International Human Rights Year—but warned that the Indians might not wish to "run afoul of Soviet and East European sensitivity by raising an issue concerning human rights"[25] so soon after the Soviet invasion of Czechoslovakia. The drafters suggested that had the Czech crisis not occurred, the Soviets might have been tempted to drop their previous public opposition to a Tibetan resolution, citing the increase in Soviet propaganda over the past two years on the plight of national minorities oppressed by "Great Han chauvinists." Bowles wrote Gross that the embassy would continue to work on Tibet and "nudge the Indians toward a more active approach."

In September, however, the Indians notified Thondup that they had decided not to cosponsor a resolution. Gross advised his Tibetan clients that he could find no other government willing to act on their behalf now that India would not. With characteristic enthusiasm, Bowles agreed to meet Thondup at Gross's request and wrote his old friend that he felt "very strongly that both the United States and India are ducking their responsibilities regarding the independence of Tibet." The ambassador was ready to have another go at trying to persuade the Indians to cosponsor a resolution, "particularly since it would tend to sharpen the differences between China and India which under present conditions tends to strengthen our own position while presenting the Soviets with a difficult decision." He suggested Gross visit him after the forthcoming election to help. But Bowles's job became a casualty of Nixon's election, and so did any official U.S. interest in keeping the Tibet issue alive at the UN.

It was not until February of 1969, while the U.S. was already withdrawing from the unproductive operation at Mustang, that the architect of the new president's foreign policy started steering a course toward one that would eventually foreclose any role for the Tibetans. Nixon asked Kissinger to create the impression among the Soviets' East European allies that the U.S. was "exploring the possibilities of rapprochement with the Chinese."[26] Kissinger said this was intended to disquiet the Soviets and prod them into helping the U.S. end the war in Vietnam, which was Nixon's electoral pledge and principal preoccupation at the time. Kissinger used the president's request to initiate an interagency study of China policy. This review was to assess the present U.S. relationship with both Beijing and Taiwan, evaluate Chinese Communist intentions in Asia, and assess the costs and risks of alternative U.S. approaches on China.

In March there was a series of clashes between Soviet and Chinese troops on the Manchurian border, which continued throughout the spring. These incidents were accompanied by like clashes in the Chinese-Russian border region in Xinjiang beginning in April. When both the Russians and the North Vietnamese privately expressed their concerns to the U.S. that it not take advantage of the growing Sino-Soviet differences, Nixon's own Metternich saw his opportunity to exploit "the growing obsession of the Soviet leaders with their China problem."[27] Together the two began a series of quiet moves, such as easing minor restrictions on trade and tourism with China and gentle hints, which Kissinger called "visiting cards for the Chinese,"[28] that were left with China's friends in Pakistan and Rumania. These moves culminated in Nixon's historic visit to Beijing in February of 1972 and his talks with Mao Zedong and Zhou Enlai, whom the U.S. had been accustomed to regard for over two decades as arch enemies.

It is an accepted legend among the Tibetans that during these talks the U.S. acceded to Chinese demands to withdraw its support for the Dalai Lama and his political activities in India and abroad. Winston Lord denies this. Later a U.S. ambassador to China, Lord sat in on Nixon's meetings with the Chinese leaders and on all the Kissinger negotiations with the Chinese that led up to and followed the Nixon visit. Lord prepared the briefing books and agenda for all of these meetings, and he recalled no items on the U.S. involvement in Tibet.[29] U.S. subsidies to the Mustang force, to the Dalai Lama, and to his government were not issues in these meetings, he said. Acknowledging that the talks took place twenty-five years ago, Lord said he also could not recall any discussion of Tibet during any of Nixon's or Kissinger's conversations with the Chinese. Kissinger's National Security Council deputy John Holdridge attended the meetings with Zhou and also confirmed that the subject of Tibet did not arise.[30] Neither side, he explained, was interested in raising more controversial subjects in addition to the major differences over Taiwan.

Although Tibet may not have been on the table in the Beijing talks,[31] the era of official U.S. support for the Tibetan cause was over. U.S. policy had come full circle from the days in the early fifties when encouraging Tibetan resistance was part of an overall effort described by Dean Rusk as "doing anything we could to get in the way of the Chinese Communists."[32] Two decades later Kissinger would assure President Nixon that "in plain terms we have become tacit allies" with Mao.[33] The roles of the participants in the Cold War had so shifted that Kissinger reported to his chief: "We are now in the extraordinary situation that, with the exception of the United Kingdom, the People's Republic of China might well be closest to us in its global perceptions."[34]

There was no role for Tibet in Kissinger's new equation, and it was only a matter of time before the CIA, acting at the behest of the State Department, asked Gyalo Thondup to close down Tibet's office in New York.[35] What the Department had once been willing to condone quietly as an unofficial embassy in 1963 was now recalled as something that the Chinese had vigorously protested when it was set up. The Department therefore saw the Tibet Office as a possible impediment to the decision to set up U.S. and Chinese "liaison offices" in Beijing and Washington respectively. Ernest Gross was given the thankless task of delivering the request to close down the New York office, the opening of which had been his own idea. In a heated discussion over lunch in a Lexington Avenue Chinese restaurant, Thondup angrily refused. There was nothing the Tibetans could do about the U.S. government backing down on its military and political support to his people, but they were not going to be put out of business in New York, he declared. "You can put Mr. Thonden [the New York representative] in jail, but we are not going to close down." The office remains open to this day.

Late in the summer of 1974 the U.S. government completed its retreat by cutting off the subsidy that it had been covertly paying the Dalai Lama to maintain himself and his government.[36] Its rationale was that the money was no longer necessary because the Tibetans now were able to attract sufficient public support from India and abroad. The Tibetans regarded this as the final breach of the commitment made to them in 1951, when the U.S. government was trying to persuade the Dalai Lama to leave Tibet, and later reaffirmed in 1959, when he was forced to flee his country. They saw themselves as tools of the Cold War being discarded, now that they no longer served the purposes of the U.S. government. The orphans had no choice but to accept this with quiet resignation while they set about making their own fate.

CHAPTER 17

In Retrospect

THE TIBETANS

In November 1995 I met with the Dalai Lama in his pleasant and spacious bungalow in the old British hill station of Dharamsala in northern India. He had been living in exile for thirty-six years, and I had just retired after forty-four years of service with the CIA. The Cold War that had defined the U.S. government's intense involvement in the affairs of his country was over. It was a sparkling autumn day. His homeland lay on the other side of the mountain ridges above the flower-filled garden, and the only sound was that of an occasional prayer bell in the distance. It could have been a movie set for Shangri-la, but our knowledge of the ugly forces that had placed the Dalai Lama there spoiled that illusion. It was, however, a good time and place to reflect on some of the events that we had both known during the past four decades.

The question that I wanted most to discuss came out of the years I had spent as a CIA case officer working with the Dalai Lama's people in resisting the Chinese occupation of their country. Did we do a good or bad thing in providing this support? I knew he had struggled with the same question as he tried to fulfill the demands of his dual role as both the spiritual model and patriotic leader of his country. Almost four decades earlier he had firmly refused to approve the offers then being made by the U.S. government to provide the arms his supporters requested as they organized their insurgency. In the intervening years there had been indications that his attitude had mellowed, but his basic opposition to violence remained unchanged. This gentle but resolute lama accepted the use of my simple dichotomy to evaluate the consequences of the CIA's aid.[1]

On the good side, he said, this aid raised the morale of those fighting for a cause for which they were prepared to die. It contributed to their ability to control the area south of Lhasa through which he escaped to India in 1959. He had no doubt that the Chinese would have prevented his escape if they had been able to apprehend him. He credited the organized resistance movement and the international attention focused on his successful escape with causing the Chinese to spare the life of Tibet's other religious leader, the Panchen Lama, who survived to challenge the Chinese by refusing to replace the Dalai Lama as temporal ruler of Tibet.[2] Instead, he proclaimed that some day the Dalai Lama would reclaim his golden throne in an independent Tibet.

On the other side of the ledger, the Dalai Lama continued, thousands of lives were lost in the resistance. He ruefully noted that Washington had cut off its support for political and paramilitary programs in 1974. To him, this confirmed that the U.S. government had involved itself in his country's affairs not to help Tibet but only as a Cold War tactic to challenge the Chinese.

But to this uniquely thoughtful person, all human affairs are a complex mix of intentions, actions, and consequences. Some years earlier he told the author Michael Goodman: "The CIA was pursuing a global policy against Communist China, while we were opposing Communist aggression in our country; our basic aims did not clash, so we accepted it [assistance from the CIA]."[3] He also conceded that the Tibetans could not have been expected to endure Chinese killings and hardships without fighting back. "If there is a clear indication that there is no alternative to violence, then violence is permissible." In a speech at Harvard University a few months before our conversation, he noted that, according to the Buddhist viewpoint, result and motivation are more important than method. In the Tibetan resistance against China the method was killing, but the motivation was compassion, and that justified the resort to violence.[4] When I asked if these were still his views, he said yes.

He amplified and qualified his acceptance of the use of violence in extreme situations to serve a justified cause. He noted that although World War II and the Korean War, like all wars, caused a great deal of suffering and destruction, in retrospect they helped "to some extent" to protect democracy, liberty, and freedom. The Korean War prevented the hostile takeover of South Korea, which went on to become a free and prosperous country. He warned, however, that only after violence takes place is it possible to assess its benefits or harm. In Vietnam, the purpose of the U.S. participation was similar to America's worthy participation in World War II and Korea. But the prolonged war almost destroyed Vietnam, and the consequences of the U.S. intervention in the final years of a thirty-year struggle in that country turned into disaster. The lesson seemed to be that, while the motive for using force may be good, the unforeseeable results may be bad. This man, who has been witness and participant in the history of the last half of this century, concluded it was therefore safest to avoid violence whenever possible.[5]

This conclusion is consonant with an interview he gave to the *New York Times* a few years earlier. In contrasting his current situation with the CIA's support for the resistance, he said: "Today, the help and support we receive from the United States is truly out of sympathy and human compassion. In spite of their desire for good relations with China, the Congress of the United States at least supports Tibetan human rights. So this is something really precious, genuine."[6]

∾

The Tibetan most responsible for obtaining the CIA's support for the resistance was Gyalo Thondup, the Dalai Lama's older brother. He frequently suffered from some of the same doubts. He knew that his requests and agreements for assistance could not be approved by his brother. He also personally knew many of the men he sent to us to be trained and sent back into their country. He recognized the great danger and adverse odds they faced. They were the best and the bravest of their generation, and we wept together when they were killed fighting alongside their countrymen.

When we met in India in 1996, we spoke of these men in the context of the commitments made by the U.S. and Indian governments forty years before. Thondup, somber, was haunted by two major questions. Would his country be better off today if the Dalai Lama had not come to India in 1956 to seek asylum, banking on the assurances that it would be granted? He recalled in detail the enticements held out by Apa Pant, the Indian political agent in Lhasa, which he had used in his unsuccessful effort to persuade his brother to come to India to seek asylum then. Should he have made the concomitant agreements with the CIA that initiated the U.S. support for the resistance movement then organizing itself inside Tibet?

In both cases, Thondup felt that he had been let down. Nehru did not make good on the promise of asylum in 1956. Neither did the U.S. government deliver on the promise to support independence for Tibet, and he adamantly insists that its representatives made that promise. Furthermore, the arms eventually delivered to the resistance by the CIA were inadequate. He speculated that the Dalai Lama's futile request to Nehru for asylum and the subsequent CIA arms drops became known to the Chinese, and these challenges to China's authority provided Mao with the excuse to crush the Tibetan resistance. He often wonders whether, if the Dalai Lama had remained in Lhasa and not come to India in 1956, and the CIA had not become involved, the rebellion would have faded and many lives would have been spared.

But Thondup acknowledged that he could not be sure that the Chinese would have moderated their repressive policies in Tibet because Mao was "already drunk with power." He concluded that, with or without promises of U.S. assistance, Gompo Tashi would have been forced by his own people to form the Volunteer Freedom Fighters army and resist the Chinese with whatever arms he could have obtained on his own from local sources and foreign arms traders. Thondup also questioned whether he would have had the right to deny the resistance leaders the access that he had to the U.S. government. These were men literally from the backwoods of Tibet, representing the common people, and they were seeking only the means to fight their own battles. They knew no one in the foreign embassies and consulates, but he did. They looked to him to use his contacts on behalf of a cause that they were initiating to preserve their country and his brother as its leader. He did what was expected of him.

Thondup summed up his revisitation of these old ghosts with a Buddhist-like conclusion: It is premature to talk in terms of good or bad or right or wrong.[7] The consequences of the actions that were put in motion forty years ago are still being played out. "Let's see what happens," he said. Despite his philosophical resignation, the valiant old warrior hasn't given up. He continues, in his characteristically independent style, to seek some political formula acceptable to the Chinese that would permit the Dalai Lama to return to Tibet to serve with dignity and authority, thereby vindicating the sacrifices of the Tibetan people and the lifetime efforts of himself and his brother on their behalf.

ᘒ

Lhamo Tsering, who acted as the chief field officer for the CIA's operations with the Tibetan resistance, was less equivocal. The Tibetans "had the moral strength and the willingness to fight the Chinese, but no means to do so. They desperately needed outside support and assistance and help. The CIA gave them that help."[8] It kept the spirit of resistance alive inside Tibet, and that showed the world the Tibetans were still fighting for their country. "This helped a lot in gaining support for our cause."

Tsering noted that the relationship between the CIA and its Tibetan clients was not all one-sided: The U.S. benefited from the intelligence gathered by the resistance forces. Neither was he totally complimentary. He believed that the agency reneged on an agreement to maintain an elite force of three hundred men in Mustang as a symbol of resistance. He also felt that CIA was unduly rigid in imposing deadlines to complete the resettlement of the Mustang veterans. He graciously conceded, however, that these were "minor points in comparison to all [the U.S. support] that went on before."

Despite his seven years in a Nepali jail, he did not feel the Tibetans were "betrayed" by CIA. "That is the way of politics." He recalled Thondup telling him that there was no contract between the U.S. and the Tibetans, that "things could always change, and today's friends could become tomorrow's enemies and vice versa." Lhamo Tsering therefore had no illusions about the CIA's help. "In fact, it is amazing that CIA helped us as long as it did."

℣

During the last five years, I have talked to several other Tibetan survivors of these operations. All made clear that they were disappointed that the U.S. government stopped sending arms, but none questioned whether we should have provided them in the first place. Several expressed a pragmatic understanding, similar to Lhamo Tsering's, that they had become casualties of a changing world. One of the old Mustang commanders philosophically said the U.S. gave them the guns with the understanding that they would survive on their own as guerrillas. When this proved impossible, it was understandable that the U.S. would withdraw its support.[9] One of the younger Mustang veterans commented that by the time he arrived it had become a spent force of aging warriors, leaving the U.S. little choice but to terminate its support. While some of Thondup's Tibetan critics blamed him for misdirecting or eventually losing the U.S. aid, none suggested he should not have sought it.

Athar, a member of one of the first teams dropped into Tibet in 1957 who later became disaffected with Gyalo Thondup's leadership, still speaks positively of the aid provided by the CIA in response to Gyalo's requests. He recalled that he saw at first hand the great boost to morale that this support gave to the freedom fighters.[10] The guerrillas were particularly impressed that Americans were willing to risk their lives to deliver these weapons "in a war zone" because this provided heartening evidence that they were no longer fighting alone. Athar also credited the U.S. for facilitating the welcome accorded by the Indians to the Dalai Lama in 1959 in response to the messages he was trained to send on the radio provided by the CIA. He concluded: "We have been successful in preserving the Tibetan religious traditions in India: if you feel that has been good, then it also means that the establishment of the Volunteer Freedom Fighters Army was a success and that means that the CIA's support helped us."

This is hardly a comprehensive sample. I talked to only a few of the families of those whose parents or relatives were killed in the revolt. Among Tibetans of the resistance generation, the legacy of U.S. military support seems generally positive. Ken, who spent eighteen years in prison[11] after his capture by the Chinese (who also rounded up his team and killed his teammates) expressed no bitterness. Even more surprising, the son of Tim, the team's leader, shares this same absence of recrimination. This young man, who was only three months old when his father was killed on this tragic mission, recently expressed his family's remembrance and gratitude for "the enormous support by the agency's staff then involved in those days."[12] The only regret of the veterans and their families was that American support was not larger, did not start earlier, and did not last longer.

Lhamo Tsering's son, Tenzing Sonam, has spent several years interviewing former guerrillas for a television documentary. He, too, expected to find some bitterness and some sense of betrayal. But rarely has he encountered a harsh word against the CIA from any of these veterans. He suggested that by native temperament and as Buddhists, Tibetans understand that all situations are essentially transient. When these veterans talked about their encounters with the Americans it was "with fondness and respect."[13] Mostly, he said, they expressed a sense of gratitude for what the CIA had done for them and their cause. Admittedly, these men would be likely to speak respectfully to the son of the man who had been their link to the agency and had spent seven years in prison for serving their cause. But Tibetans are not bashful about saying what they think, and they have expressed remarkably little public resentment about the U.S. military support or the way it was cut off.

THE UNITED STATES

The Dalai Lama is correct that the U.S. government supported the Tibetans primarily because of their role in the Cold War policy of containment. But this motivation had a richer content and background. When the U.S. government first became involved with Tibet in 1951, its commitments contained a measure of the idealism that was part of the Truman Doctrine of assisting free peoples. Although the principal goal was to do anything "to get in the way of the Chinese Communists,"[14] it is also true that Washington believed the Dalai Lama might somehow make good on his claim to an independent Tibet if he could escape the control of the Chinese Communists.

The containment policy that provided the rationale for these commitments was based on the premise that it was necessary to stop communist expansion anywhere. The men who originated the programs to carry out this policy had fought in World War II. They were determined to prevent an even more horrible sequel. As the coffin of Desmond FitzGerald was carried out of the National Cathedral in 1967 the congregation sang James Russell Lowell's hymn "Once to Every Man and Nation Comes the Moment to Decide," which continues, "In the strife of truth and falsehood for the good or evil side." By then, World War III seemed far less imminent, but when FitzGerald and his colleagues decided to intervene on behalf of the Tibetans a decade earlier, the lines were still drawn. None of us doubted that the Tibetans were on the "good" and the Chinese on the "evil" side.

The men FitzGerald chose to carry out this program quickly made common cause with the Tibetans. It was not "their" war they were fighting, it was ours, and we wanted them to win it. As one of those who occasionally reminded himself that these were fellow human beings being killed on both sides, Tibetan and Chinese, I would rationalize my moral misgivings as the necessary sacrifices demanded by the cause of freedom in Tibet. Today some of these precepts and the programs they engendered seem simplistic, but when the U.S. government gave its support it was not merely using the Tibetans as means to an end. We shared common goals.

The arms and training given to the Tibetan resistance was only part of a larger program to back Tibet's claim to the conscience and attention of the international community. This claim was validated by the willingness of the Tibetans to fight for their rights. As long as there was demonstrable resistance inside Tibet, the Tibetans could argue for a hearing at the United Nations. Action at the UN in turn heartened that resistance. In Washington, all the members of the National Security Council accepted the complementary relationship between the political and paramilitary aspects of support for the Tibetans. While both the Dalai Lama and Gyalo Thondup probably understood this, we never discussed it with them in these terms because it would have been difficult for them to accept such a tradeoff. It was an easy equation for us to make, but it was the Tibetans who were making the sacrifices. Moreover, the meager political return they were receiving from the UN must have seemed hardly worth these sacrifices to the Dalai Lama and his brother, who had to justify the sacrifices to themselves and to those for whom they felt responsible.

The Americans who negotiated with Thondup in 1956 probably did make promises to back Tibetan independence—promises that were never honored. The negotiators were for the most part operations officers who may well have been swept up in the optimism of their own plans, not legal experts schooled in the differences among independence, autonomy, and self-determination. The interpreters stumbled over a further problem in the Tibetan language, which at that time had no distinct words for these different concepts. Everyone heard what he wanted to hear.

This ambiguity in language was compounded by imprecision in U.S. policy. Throughout the fifties the State Department wrestled with the question of Tibet's legal status. It finally compromised on recognizing Tibet's independence in fact but not in law. Under this formula, those making the initial commitments to the Tibetans could well have unintentionally promised more than Washington was prepared to deliver. It was only in

1960 that the U.S. government brushed aside the formalistic, but nonetheless active, claims of the Chinese Nationalist government to sovereignty over Tibet and went on record for the rights of the Tibetans to self-determination. The Eisenhower State Department then promoted this concept on behalf of the Tibetans at the UN and instructed the embassy in London to remind the British government that Washington's position was no different from what it had laid out to His Majesty's government in 1950: support for rights of the Tibetans to determine their own destiny, particularly since "Tibet as a practical matter [had been] independent of China from 1914 to the time of the Communist invasion in 1950."[15]

The Department left itself many loopholes. It hedged its forthright statement with the caveat that support for self-determination did not necessarily commit the U.S. to recognize Tibetan independence—only the right of the Tibetans to seek and claim it. Thirty-five years later it backtracked even further when it told Congress that "Historically, the United States has acknowledged Chinese sovereignty over Tibet . . . and since at least 1966, US policy has explicitly recognized the Tibetan Autonomous Region as part of the People's Republic of China."[16] It seems the Tibetans' suspicions were well-founded about the half-loaf of self-determination they were handed in fulfillment of earlier commitments.

These shifts by the U.S. government in its interpretation of Tibet's legal status have compounded the Dalai Lama's chronic problem of being forced to use Western concepts, many of which are inapplicable or irrelevant, to put his case before the world. The legal record that the U.S. government willed to its former protégé is not a totally helpful one. It remains to be seen how well it will serve him in a dialogue with the Chinese, where any solution will have to be based on the unique bilateral relationship that has existed between these two countries throughout history. Classic formulations of international law will not suit the needs of either side.

↩

There is far less to apologize for in the military support given the Tibetans. The Lee Enfield rifles first provided to the resistance fighters were chosen because they were immediately available, they were not identified with the U.S. government, and the untrained recipients were familiar with them. They were dropped by B-17s because the planes were available and their sponsors could deny them. But the old and less reliable Lee Enfields were later replaced by U.S. Army M-1 rifles because Tibetans trained in their use were available to jump into Tibet and could pass along their training to the recipients. C-130s of the U.S. Air Force replaced the hired B-17s because they provided greater safety for the air crews. The U.S. government was willing to risk disclosure to provide the best weapons it had and deliver them by the planes best equipped to drop the maximum loads possible.

The basic flaw was not in the logistics but in the concept of these operations. There is a military adage that generals and armies fight the last war. Many who advocated and planned the U.S. paramilitary operations to support the Tibetans were World War II veterans of raids behind the Japanese lines or parachute jumps into Europe to support the resistance against the Germans. Although the men who trained and dispatched the teams belonged to a later generation, they were strong proponents of this type of guerrilla warfare. There was also a grudging but strong admiration in Washington for the way that Mao had used guerrilla tactics to harass and pin down vastly superior numbers of Japanese and later Chinese Nationalist troops. The idea of using Mao's own tactics against him had great appeal. Supporting a self-generated movement in Tibet at its roots fit what came to be Washington's model of countering communist expansion.

The fit was imperfect. The European resistance movement was only a small part of a greater effort, which succeeded because of the vast manpower and matériel that the Allies delivered to the battlefront. The guerrillas in Burma became irrelevant when the Allies committed major forces to push back the Japanese in the Pacific, island by island, and the United States finally vanquished them with the atomic bomb. The Tibetan resistance forces never really participated in or benefited from a greater military effort. Furthermore, Mao operated from a secure territorial base, first in North China, then in larger areas, which the Tibetans were never able to establish in their own homeland. Operations in Tibet were planned on the mistaken assumption that the resistance forces could and would operate in their homeland as guerrillas. The Tibetans' custom of fighting accompanied by their families and herds, coupled with the absence of a local safe haven, denied them the advantages of successful guerrilla movements.

The Americans who designed and directed the Tibetan operations were not dogmatic. We did suffer from a lack of intelligence regarding the situation inside Tibet. In the fifties neither the CIA nor the State or Defense Departments had any depth of knowledge about the Tibetan people or the topography of their country. Almost none of the officers involved in these operations had ever been to Tibet. Our dealings with the Tibetans had to be conducted either through interpreters or with the few Tibetans who spoke English. Our principal contact was with Gyalo Thondup. He, like the Americans, had little immediate knowledge of the people or conditions of eastern Tibet where the revolt originated. He had left his native Amdo region as a boy and did not know the chieftains or the people of Kham. He was therefore primarily dependent upon information provided by emissaries seeking aid from these areas. It was a primitive and slow intelligence system, dependent on men who made their way to Darjeeling over some of the world's most challenging terrain on treks lasting several weeks. They were untrained observers, and the reports they brought concerning the numbers, conditions, and needs of their colleagues could not be confirmed. The most critical problem was that their information was frequently outdated. The CIA and the other U.S. government agencies had few alternative sources of information.

The other intelligence failure was an underestimation of the Chinese capability and willingness to invest disproportionately large numbers of troops and military aircraft, enough to wipe out the Tibetan resistance. Mao refused to let bands of unruly border tribesmen deny him his dream of reuniting the greater Han empire. The CIA was admittedly surprised at the size of the forces, particularly the air power, that the Chinese deployed to clear the resistance forces out of central Tibet after the Dalai Lama made his successful escape through there in 1959. What proved fatal was this miscalculation of Chinese military capabilities and the degree of their determination to use them, together with the mistaken assumption that the Tibetans would fight as guerrillas. When combined with inadequate or outdated intelligence, the result was that U.S. air crews, taking great risks with considerable skill, delivered large quantities of arms and equipment too late to people who were not able or willing to use them in a manner that might have enabled them to survive.

There was also a certain operational hubris. It was an exciting effort to mount and sustain paramilitary operations that stretched from the reflecting pool in Washington, to the Colorado Rockies, Okinawa and airfields in southeast Asia, all the way to the Roof of the World. Once underway, an operation like this acquires a psychological and bureaucratic momentum that is difficult to stop. Preserving the operation becomes an objective in itself. The accompanying political effort at the United Nations added another extraneous pressure for the military resistance to be seen as succeeding. Hopes for what had become a shared cause, and our pride in the operational structure that had been built to promote it, skewed our judgment. It also was to take most of the U.S. government some years to settle for the more modest goals of supporting and building the elements of a civil society as the limits to what it could contribute to liberating countries from authoritarian rule. We were a long way from that acceptance—and some remain unconvinced today—when we undertook to support the Tibetans in their fight for freedom.

Just as the intentions of the U.S. government in undertaking these operations had been mixed, so were the motivations for ending them. For the U.S., ending its arms support to a no longer active resistance movement did not represent a breach of the commitments made to the Tibetans two decades earlier. From the beginning the U.S. had made its support conditional on the existence of an active resistance inside Tibet. The withdrawal of political support to the Dalai Lama was less justifiable. It no longer served U.S. purposes to support him as a challenge to China, a country we now were courting. He and his cause had become expendable in the new alignments in the Cold War. The Dalai Lama had not approved of the paramilitary support that the U.S. was providing to his cause. He could, however, have regarded it as implying a commitment from which the Americans walked away. This sense of betrayal was reinforced when the U.S. withdrew the support it had also been providing for his political activities.

A few years ago Morton Halperin, a foreign policy scholar, principal of the American Civil Liberties Union, and certainly no fan of covert action, called the U.S. government's support for the Tibetan resistance in the fifties and sixties "a noble operation."[17] It was noble, but it was imperfect. The genuine desire to help a beleaguered people regain their independence was noble and forms the moral basis for their continuing claim on the American conscience to this day. The united and enthusiastic efforts of the entire government to marshal and deliver help to the Tibetans was unprecedented. There were, however, political and geographical limits to America's ability to provide what was needed to achieve the Tibetans' goal of independence. The altruistic motivation in lending this help was always secondary to other objectives. In the end the Tibetans became the worthy but hapless orphans of the Cold War.

Fortunately the story does not end there. After the U.S. government left the Tibetans on their own, they went on to establish their cause in the conscience of the world. This legacy may finally be harvested four decades later if the hopes for a dialogue between the Dalai Lama and the new Chinese leadership raised by Presidents Jiang and Clinton in Beijing in June 1998 are realized.

Both the American people and their government have an extraordinary interest in this situation, which is even more keen today than it was when the U.S. government first became involved in the affairs of this remote country. Skeptics attribute this to Hollywood's rediscovery of Shangri-la and go on to debunk a myth of a land of perfect tranquillity that the Tibetans never claimed. They then conclude that the U.S. interest is unwarranted or at least misplaced. This conclusion is unfair to both the Tibetans, who have fought with valor and integrity for their cause, and to the Americans, who have supported it with a mix of motives and constancy. It is beyond the scope of this book to define Tibet's cultural and religious contributions, which alone attract justified followers. Its aim is to preserve the political record that underlay the obligation that President Clinton felt to represent the Tibetan case before the world in Beijing in the hope of finding a constructive solution that would permit the orphans to come home at last. The realization of this hope would validate the more worthy motives of we who tried to help them achieve this goal over forty years ago. It would also alleviate the guilt some of us feel over our participation in these efforts, which cost others their lives, but which were the prime adventure of our own.

CHAPTER I

1. This is the figure for what the British called "political" Tibet. It does not include "ethnic" Tibet—the areas of Amdo and Kham—part of which lies within the southwestern provinces of China's long disputed upper Yangtze valley. These vast areas are inhabited predominantly by Tibetan people.

2. Fosco Maraini, *Secret Tibet* (New York: Viking Press, 1952), p. 52.

3. Charles Bell, *Portrait of a Dalai Lama* (London: William Collins, 1946; London: Wisdom Publications, 1987.

4. Nicholas was disposed to favor Dorjieff's espousal of the Dalai Lama as he had recently revived an ambitious plan, which had been submitted to his predecessor, for expansion of the Russian Empire. This plan, drafted by another Buryat Mongol, Peter Badmayev, called for bringing parts of the Chinese empire, including Tibet and Mongolia, under Moscow's control by fostering insurrections against the weakened and resented Manchu rulers. Peter Hopkirk, *The Great Game*, New York: Kodansha, 1992, p. 503.

5. India Office, minutes, May 27, 1942, FO 371/31637. The correspondence among Whitehall, the Indian government in New Delhi, and the British ambassador in Nanking during the period April through July 1942 is contained in FO 371/31637 and 31638.

6. Foreign Office, minutes, May 21, 1942, FO 371/31637.

7. Office of Strategic Services (OSS), background report, September 30, 1943, NARA RG 226, E 092, box 200, folder 39.

8. In contrast to the wartime austerity that their colleagues in London and elsewhere were living under, the British mission in Lhasa was enjoying a relatively good existence. In a letter dated September 13, 1942, the political officer reported that the Mission was entertaining "on a grand scale" that week, giving luncheons for the Kashag, the Dalai Lama's father, and "the other elite of Lhasa." At these two affairs thirty guests accompanied by their servants would be fed "6 fatted sheep, one yak, and maunds [an Indian maund was equivalent to 82 pounds] of rice, butter, sugar, etc." FO 371/35754.

9. Described by Rinchen Dolma Taring, a member of the prominent Tsarong family, in her autobiography, *Daughter of Tibet* (London: Wisdom Publications, 1986).

10. One of Tolstoy's later, more ambitious, proposals was the resettlement of a sizable group of Tibetans, with their yaks, in Alaska, presumably under his tutelage. The necessary legislation did not obtain congressional support. Department of State, telegram 3386, April 6, 1962, NARA RG 59, box 2161.

11. "Across Tibet from India to China," *National Geographic Magazine* (August 1946), pp. 169–222.

12. Melvyn C. Goldstein, *A History of Modern Tibet, 1915–1951* (Berkeley, Calif.: University of California Press, 1989).

13. Dalai Lama, *Autobiography* (New York: HarperCollins, 1990), p. 21.

14. Secretary of state to President Roosevelt, memorandum, July 3, 1942, Foreign Relations of the United States (FRUS), China, p. 625.

15. Roosevelt to secretary of state, letter, July 3, 1942, FRUS 1942, China, p. 623.

16. Doris Kearns Goodwin, *No Ordinary Time* (New York: Simon and Schuster, 1994), p. 385.

17. Tolstoy to the Franklin D. Roosevelt Library, letter, September 21, 1970, Roosevelt Library, File 71-496, Gifts.

18. Goldstein, *History of Modern Tibet*, p. 392. The British may have remembered that Suydam Cutting of the American Museum of Natural History had given the Thirteenth Dalai Lama the following gifts, which Cutting lists on page 178 of his book, *The Fire Ox and Other Years* (New York: Charles Scribner's Sons, 1940): "illustrated books on American architecture, a chair with a folding canopy, a self-winding gold wrist watch, silver plated polar bears mounted on agate, an ornamental glass bowl, and a special glass cocktail shaker equipped with a churn, which would never serve him in the ordinary manner, but would be useful for mixing his buttered tea."

19. Gyalo Thondup, telephone interview with the author, March 16, 1995.

20. Tolstoy to Roosevelt Library, letter, September 21, 1970, File 71-496. Three of the tapestries, known as *thangkas,* described by the Dalai Lama in his letter to Roosevelt thanking him for his letter and "tokens of good will" as "depicting the sextet blessed with long existence, the four dutiful brothers (friends) and the eight lucky signs" are held in the Roosevelt Library; the fourth, which was sent by the regent, was apparently lost in transit.

21. President Roosevelt to General William J. Donovan, letter, March 26, 1943, President's Personal File, box 8108, Roosevelt Library.

22. Office of Strategic Services, *Route from India to China Transversed by Captain Tolstoy and Lt. Dolan: Motor Road Possibilities,* report, July 25, 1943, NARA RG 226, E 196, box 226, folder 358.

23. Department of State, memorandum, March 30, 1943, FRUS 1943, China, pp. 624–625.

24. This correspondence between the Department and OSS is contained on pages 624–629 of FRUS 1943, China.

25. The Chinese representative in Lhasa, a Dr. Kung, was aware of Tolstoy's desire to change his itinerary and offered to send a message to Chungking requesting Chiang to ask the Tibetan government to allow him and Dolan to proceed to China. Kung, recognizing the contempt with which his government was held in Lhasa, did confess that he was not at all sure of the Tibetan government's reply to a request from Chiang. As the British Mission chief noted in reporting on this exchange, "Tolstoy had the good sense" to decline Dr. Kung's offer. British Mission to Capt. Ilya Tolstoy, telegram, February 23, 1943, FO 371/35754.

     Tolstoy needed no coaching from his British colleague on Kung's limited influence with the Tibetan government. In the final report on his trip he noted: "When we were at Lhasa bad relations had existed for a long time between Dr. Kung and the Government of Tibet. Both sides gave as the reason an unimportant incident, but the true cause seemed to be that Chungking had instructed Dr. Kung to communicate directly with the Kashag or cabinet of Tibet; and that the Tibetan cabinet refused to treat with him directly, stating that he must communicate with it through the Foreign Office as do the representatives of other foreign nations—Britain and Nepal. The issue having been raised, Chungking would not accept a position which denied her suzerainty over Tibet, and for months prior to our departure from Lhasa Dr. Kung could not communicate with the Government of Tibet." NARA RG 226, E 196, box 226, folder 358.

26. Memorandum to Colonel Donovan, March 12, 1943, NARA RG 226, E 92, box 200, folder 39.

27. British mission, Lhasa, to Sir Basil Gould, political officer, Sikkim, letter, February 28, 1943, enclosure to Indian foreign secretary letter 17, March 23, 1943, FO 371/35755.

28. Ludlow's superiors in New Delhi and London reacted vigorously to what they considered to be the misguided acts of "amateurs." The viceroy reported loftily that he would quickly inform the British representative in Lhasa of "the un-wisdom of his action" and noted that "American enlightenment in matters Tibetan may come in due course, but he would judge it unsound that we from here should attempt to hasten the process." Viceroy to the secretary of state for India, New Delhi, telegram, May 3, 1943, FO 371/35755.

29. In his letter of thanks to the Dalai Lama for the messages and gifts that he had sent through Tolstoy, President Roosevelt noted that "Your Holiness and the people of your Pontificate share with me and the people of America a feeling of reciprocal interest and good-will." He pointed out that "the associates of the

United States in the war which was thrust upon it by the predatory powers of Japan, Germany and Italy and their satellites have now grown to thirty-one countries. Recent events of which your Holiness is no doubt aware have heightened our spirits, strengthened our determination, and demonstrated to the world our unshakable faith." President's Personal File, box 8108, Roosevelt Library.

30. The Tibetans in granting permission to Tolstoy did remind him that he had switched signals on his travel plans after arriving in Lhasa. Tibetan foreign office, letter, February 1943, FRUS 1943, China, p. 622.

31. Aide-mémoire, January 17, 1945, FO 371/46121.

32. FRUS 1943, China, pp. 632–633.

33. Churchill had been vexed with Chiang for some time, particularly since 1942 when the Chinese leader had protested the interning of Gandhi. At that time "the former Naval person" had sent his friend President Roosevelt a message declaring that he had taken "it amiss that Chiang should seek to make difficulties between us and should interfere in matters about which he had proved himself most ill informed which affect our sovereign rights." Churchill went on to suggest that Roosevelt might "remind Chiang that Gandhi was prepared to negotiate with Japan on the basis of a free passage for Japanese troops through India on their way to way to joining hands with Hitler." He noted that the style of Chiang's message "prompted him to say 'cherchez la femme' [Chiang's very political wife]." Churchill to Roosevelt, telegram 128, August 14, 1942, Harry L. Hopkins Collection, Churchill/Harriman file, box 311, Roosevelt Library.

34. Papers as President, Map Room files, box 168, Roosevelt Library.

35. FRUS 1943, China, p. 628.

36. Aide-mémoire, May 15, 1943, FRUS 1943, China, p. 630.

37. FRUS 1943, China, pp. 634–636.

38. John S. Service, Oral History project 1977–1978, pp. 238–239, Harry S. Truman Library. Service was probably referring to Hisao Kimura, a Japanese who spent the war on a hapless intelligence mission for the Japanese military in the Amdo region of northeastern Tibet. He reached Lhasa only after the war ended. He described his spy days in his book *Japanese Agent in Tibet* (London: Serindia Publications, 1990).

39. A War Department memorandum of conversation dated March 13, 1944, cites the president's continuing interest in investigating the possibilities of an overland route over which to supply aid to the Chinese. NARA RG 226, E 92, box 200, folder 39.

40. Tolstoy, OSS interoffice memorandum, January 20, 1944, NARA RG 226, E 190, box 644, folder 0918.

41. OSS memorandum, March 29, 1944, NARA RG 226, E 190, box 644, folder 0918. Tolstoy had apparently not endeared himself to either his OSS colleagues or the Allied China Burma India (CBI) theater headquarters. The fol-

lowing year, patterning his behavior on his Tibet mission, he had unsuccessfully tried to carry out an investigation through north China by tagging along
on the U.S. military political observer group, the Dixie mission, which was
sent to make contact with Mao and his forces in their caves in Yenan and
report on their capabilities. Both the CBI political advisor and the Dixie Mission commander Colonel David D. Barrett, thought Tolstoy "a swell person
to know personally," but they feared his tendency to act on his own. Memorandum, NARA RG 226, E 190, box 712, folder 1318.

42. Memorandum to James Dunn, NARA RG 226, E 190, box 644, folder 918.

43. Allocation of the limited tonnage then being flown over the Hump had by
this time become a matter of bitter controversy between the theater commander, General Stilwell, and General Chennault, the commander of the
Fourteenth Air Force. Robert W. Merry, *Taking on the World* (New York:
Viking, 1996), pp. 128–142.

44. Donovan to James Dunn, memorandum, NARA RG 226, E 190, box 644,
folder 918.

45. Internal OSS memorandum, April 7, 1944, NARA RG 226, E 190, box 644,
folder 918.

46. Tibetan foreign office to Tolstoy, letter, NARA RG 226, E 190, box 644,
folder 918.

47. Robert Ford describes the training of these men and the operation of his station in eastern Tibet in his book *Wind Between the Worlds* (New York: David
McKay Company, 1957).

48. This correspondence is all contained in NARA RG 226, E 190, box 644,
folder 918.

49. Richardson on Tolstoy, December 1, 1949, Report of debriefing of Richardson
by the Office of the U.K. High Commission, Calcutta, FO 371/76317.

Chapter 2

1. Gyalo Thondup, telephone interview with the author, August 8, 1995.

2. Cited by Goldstein, *History of Modern Tibet*, p. 536.

3. Text printed in Goldstein, *History of Modern Tibet*, pp. 538–543.

4. The letter noted that Shen Tsung-lien, who had acted "carefully and pru-
dently" in maintaining good relations between the two countries, was on his
way back to Nanking. It urged that "the Chinese Government honor him in
an appropriate way." Shen was the latest in a line of Chinese representatives
since 1934, when the Chinese sent a representative to Lhasa on a mission of
condolence for the death of the previous Dalai Lama. He presumably set up
shop and stayed on, to the annoyance of the Tibetans. See Goldstein, *History
of Modern Tibet.*

5. Goldstein, *History of Modern Tibet*, pp. 550–552.

6. Gyalo Thondup, interview by author, August 5, 1995.

7. Goldstein, *History of Modern Tibet*, p. 561.

8. Phillips Talbot, interview with the author, June 27, 1994.

9. The correspondence is contained in FRUS 1947, vol. VII, pp. 588–593.

10. British General Staff memo, in Goldstein, *History of Modern Tibet*, p. 549.

11. Department of War, memorandum, March 19, 1947, forwarded via Office of Chinese Affairs, NARA file 893.00 Tibet/3-1947.

12. FRUS 1947, vol. VII, p. 594.

13. FRUS 1947, vol. VII, p. 595.

14. FRUS 1947, vol. VII, p. 602.

15. Yangpel Pandatsang was a member of a maverick family that owned one of the largest and most powerful trading houses in eastern Tibet. His two brothers had organized a rebellion in the thirties against the central government in Lhasa, whose aristocratic officials they despised. The Chinese Communists were to attempt unsuccessfully to persuade them to become collaborators when they invaded their home territory in 1950. Yangpel was the family's more respectable brother who served the government's—and the family's—interests in Lhasa. As governor of the region south of Lhasa he had been one of Tolstoy's first hosts in Tibet in 1942. U.S. embassy, New Delhi, telegram 353, November 21, 1947, FRUS 1947, vol. VII, p. 602.

16. FRUS 1947, vol. VII, pp. 600–602.

17. Tsipon W. D. Shakabpa, *Tibet: A Political History* (New York: Potala Publications, 1988), p. 295.

18. Ibid.

19. British embassy, Nanking, dispatch, May 19, 1948, FO 371/70042.

20. FRUS 1948, vol. V, p. 759.

21. Shakabpa provided a copy of his passport containing both the British and U.S. visas to Goldstein, who printed photocopies of them in his *History of Modern Tibet*, page 587.

22. John F. Kennedy, quoted in Arthur Schlesinger, *A Thousand Days* (Boston: Houghton Mifflin, 1965), p. 828.

23. FRUS 1948, vol. V, pp. 361–362.

24. FRUS 1948, vol. VII, pp. 764–765.

25. FRUS 1948, vol. VII, pp. 766–767.

26. Cable to Stuart and Chinese reply, FRUS 1948, vol. VII, pp. 767–769.

27. FRUS 1948, vol. VII, pp. 770–772.

28. FRUS 1948, vol. VII, pp. 772–773.

29. Memorandum of conversation, August 6, 1948, FRUS 1948, vol. VII, pp. 775–776.

30. FRUS 1948, vol. VII, pp. 779–780.

31. "5 from Tibet Here to Drum up Trade," *New York Times,* August 12, 1948, p. 43, col. 5; *Pathfinder,* 11 August 1948.

32. Henry S. Evans, memorandum, May 3, 1970, Papers of Henry S. Evans, box 1, Hoover Institution on War, Revolution and Peace.

33. FRUS 1948, vol. VII, p. 786.

34. President's Personal File, box 200, Truman Library.

35. Goldstein, *History of Modern Tibet,* p. 607.

Chapter 3

1. Henderson's transfer is described on pages 110–112 of H. W. Brands's biography, *Inside the Cold War* (New York: Oxford University Press, 1991).

2. Brands, *Inside the Cold War,* p. 192.

3. FRUS 1949, vol. IX, p. 1065.

4. Office of Chinese Affairs, memorandum, April 12, 1949, FRUS 1949, vol. IX, pp. 1065–1071.

5. U.S. embassy, New Delhi, to the secretary of state, telegram, April 12, 1949, FRUS 1949, vol. IX, pp. 1071–1073.

6. Gyalo Thondup, interviews with the author, Kalimpong, India, November 10–21, 1995; Dalai Lama, interview with the author, Dharamsala, India, November 18, 1995.

7. FRUS 1949, vol. IX, pp. 1076–1077.

8. FRUS 1949, vol. IX, pp. 1078–1079.

9. FRUS 1949, vol. IX, p. 1080.

10. Lowell Thomas Jr., *Out of This World* (New York: Greystone Press, 1950), p. 30.

11. Thomas, *Out of This World,* p. 238.

12. Richardson on the Thomases, mission report, September 1–15, 1949, FO 371/76315.

13. Thomas, *Out of This World,* p. 239.

14. Robert Trumbull, "Tibet Fears Told by Lowell Thomas," *New York Times,* October 11, 1949, p. 21, col. 1.

15. Thomas, *Out of This World,* p. 311.

16. "Lowell Thomas Back from Tibet," *New York Times,* October 25, 1949, p. 25, col. 7.

17. Dean Acheson and Lowell Thomas, memorandum of conversation, February 17, 1950, Papers of Dean Acheson, Truman Library.

18. *New York Times,* December 2, 1949, p. 16, col. 3.

19. FRUS 1949, vol. IX, pp. 1080–1082.

20. Richardson's advice and Tibetan responses are found in the monthly report of the Indian mission, Lhasa, November 14, 1949, FO 371/76315.

21. FRUS 1949, vol. IX, pp. 1084–1085.

22. Director of the State Department's Office of Chinese Affairs and the British counsel of embassy in Washington, memorandum of conversation, December 21, 1949, FRUS 1949, vol. IX, p. 1095.

23. FRUS 1949, vol. IX, pp. 1096–1097.

24. FRUS 1949, vol. IX, pp. 1092–1093.

25. Nicholas Thacher, interview with the author, June 2, 1994.

26. FRUS [1950], vol. VI, p. 285.

27. U.K. High Commission, New Delhi, telegram 34, January 5, 1950, FO 371/84465; Goldstein, *History of Modern Tibet,* pp. 619–620.

28. U.S. embassy, New Delhi, telegram 44, January 10, 1950, FRUS 1950, vol. VI, p. 272.

29. Harrison E. Salisbury, "Soviet Backs Mao on Formosa Claim," *New York Times,* January 5, 1950, p. 19, col. 1.

30. Gyalo Thondup (interviews, November 1995) described his experiences in China.

31. FRUS 1950, vol. VI, pp. 275–276.

32. "China Not Abandoned by U.S., Says Jessup," *New York Times,* December 20, 1949, p. 25, col. 4.

33. NARA RG 59, 793B.00/1-2050.

34. Indian mission, Lhasa, report, January 15, 1950, FO 371/84453.

35. Dalai Lama, interview.

36. Dean Acheson, *Present at the Creation* (New York: W. W. Norton, 1969), p. 356.

37. Department of State, telegram, January 12, 1950, FRUS 1950, vol. VI, pp. 275–276.

38. Gyalo Thondup, telephone interview with author, August 4, 1995. Thondup provided further details on his meetings with Panikkar and the commitments made by him and Nehru in the November 1995 interviews previously cited.

39. FRUS 1950, vol. VI, pp. 283–285.

40. FRUS 1950, vol. VI, p. 273.

41. Foreign Office to Commonwealth Relations Office, FO 371/84451.

42. U.S. embassy, New Delhi, dispatch 30, January 9, 1950, NARA RG 59, 793B.00/1-950.

43. U.S. embassy, Colombo Ceylon, dispatch 45, January 22, 1950, NARA RG 59, 793B.00/1-2250.

44. Indian mission, Lhasa, monthly reports, January 15, 1950, and February 15, 1950, FO 371/84453.

45. FRUS 1949, vol. IX, pp. 1095–1096.

46. Foreign office, minute, November 10, 1949, FO 371/76317.

47. Foreign office, minute, November 11, 1949, FO 371/76317.

48. FRUS 1950, vol. VI, p. 284.

49. Ministry of Defence to Foreign Office, letter, March 6, 1950, FO 371/84465.

50. Foreign Office to ministry of Defence, letter, February 22, 1950, FO 371/84465.

51. Commonwealth Relations Office to the ministry of Defence, letter, February 16, 1950, FO 371/84465.

52. Ministry of Defence to Foreign Office, letter, April 11, 1950, FO 371/84465.

53. *New York Times*, March 21, 1950, col. 1, p. 8.

54. Thondup, interviews, August 1995.

55. Goldstein, *History of Modern Tibet,* p. 637.

56. Gyalo Thondup, quoted from a BBC monitoring report, FO 371/84456.

57. Foreign Office, minute, May 21, 1950, FO 371/84456.

58. Thondup, interviews, November 1995.

59. FRUS 1950, vol. VI, pp. 331–332.

60. U.S. embassy, New Delhi, telegram 380, FRUS 1950, vol. VI, pp. 331–333.

61. His life in Kham and his relationship with the Pandatsangs are described in two books, *Tragic Destiny* (London: Faber and Faber, 1959) and *God's Fool* (London: Faber and Faber, 1956).

62. Patterson, *God's Fool,* pp. 187–188, and *Tragic Destiny,* pp. 17–18. Patterson also discussed the planned revolt in detail in an interview with the author, Roseland, NJ, January 12, 1995.

63. In forwarding his report of his meeting with Patterson to the High Commission in New Delhi (FO 371/84449), Anderson described only the Chinese threats against Tibet, but made no mention of their more ambitious plans for the conquest of the other Himalayan states and India. In all other respects Anderson's account of the meeting generally jibes with that provided by Patterson in his book, *Tragic Destiny.*

64. Patterson, interview.

65. Foreign Office, minute, September 12, 1950, FO 371/84450.

66. John M. Turner, letter to author, December 12, 1994.

67. Based on his log, copy filed by British foreign office, FO 371/84450.

68. U.S. embassy, New Delhi, telegram, June 3, 1950, 739B.00/6-350, NARA RG 59, NND 822910, box 4226.

69. Ted Gup, "Star Agents," *Washington Post Magazine* (September 7, 1997), pp. 9–13, describes MacKiernan's service as a CIA officer in Xinjiang, his journey, and his murder at the Tibetan border.

70. U.S. embassy, cable 863, June 14, 1950, NARA RG 59, NND 822910, box 4226.

71. FRUS 1950, vol. VI, pp. 364–365.

72. Address to the Indian Council on World Affairs, "Objectives of U.S. Policies toward Asia," *Department of State Bulletin,* April 10, 1950.

73. U.S. embassy, London, cable, June 20, 1950, FRUS 1950, vol. VI, pp. 365–366.

74. *Cold War International History Project Bulletin,* Issues 4 and 5 (fall 1994; spring 1995), Woodrow Wilson International Center for Scholars, Washington, D.C.

75. Harry Rositzke, *The CIA's Secret Operations* (New York: Reader's Digest Press, 1977), p. 173.

76. Department of State cable, July 11, 1950, described in footnote, FRUS 1950, vol. VI, p. 376.

77. U.S. embassy, New Delhi, telegram 96, July 15, 1950, FRUS 1950, vol. VI, pp. 376–378.

78. Department of State, telegram 104, July 22, 1950, FRUS 1950, vol. VI, pp. 386–387.

79. U.S. embassy, New Delhi, telegram 302, August 7, 1950, FRUS 1950, vol. VI, pp. 424–426.

80. U.S. embassy, New Delhi, dispatch 262, August 7, 1950, NARA RG 59, 793B.00/8-750.

81. Robert Trumbull, "Tibet Disaffected as Reds Lie in Wait," *New York Times,* August 20, 1950, p. 5, col. 2.

82. U.S. embassy, New Delhi, telegram 609, September 10, 1950, FRUS 1950, vol. VI, pp. 493–495.

83. Department of State, cable 396, FRUS 1950, vol. VI, p. 503.

84. Foreign office, minute, August 9, 1950, FO 371/84456.

85. U.S. embassy, New Delhi, cable, August 14, 1950, FRUS 1950, vol. VI, pp. 440–441.

86. Henry R. Lieberman, "Tibet Gets Offer for Tie to Peiping," *New York Times* quoting New China News Agency, August 6, 1950, p. 8, col. 1.

87. U.S. embassy, New Delhi, cable, September 10, 1950, FRUS 1950, vol. VI, p. 495.

88. U.S. embassy, New Delhi, cable, October 26, 1950, FRUS 1950, vol. VI, pp. 540–541.

89. U.S. embassy, New Delhi, telegram 996, October 26, 1950, FRUS 1950, vol. VI, p. 541.

90. Goldstein, *History of Modern Tibet,* pp. 698–703.

91. "Advancing Toward Tibet," *New York Times,* October 25, 1950, col. 6, p. 1.

Chapter 4

1. Eric Teichman, *Travels of a Consular Officer in Eastern Tibet* (Cambridge: Cambridge Press, 1922), p. 2.

2. Ford, *Wind Between the Worlds,* p. 47.

3. Edgar Snow, *Red Star over China* (New York: Random House, 1938), p. 193.

4. Ford, *Wind Between the Worlds,* p. 147.

5. Ford, *Wind Between the Worlds,* pp. 135–190.

6. The texts were printed by the *New York Times,* November 3, 1950, p. 6, col. 3.

7. Brands, *Inside the Cold War,* p. 204.

8. U.S. embassy, New Delhi, cable 1052, November 1, 1950, NARA RG 59, NND 822910, Box 4226.

9. U.S. embassy, New Delhi, cable, November 3, 1950, FRUS 1950, vol. VI, p. 551.

10. Nehru, interviewed by Reuters, October 30, 1950, as reported in BBC monitoring report attached to Foreign Office minute analyzing Nehru's remarks, November 2, 1950, FO 371/84457.

11. B. N. Mullik, *The Chinese Betrayal* (Bombay, India: Allied Publishers, 1971), pp. 131–137. Mullik was Nehru's chief of intelligence.

12. War office, memorandum MO2/DO/1040, November 2, 1950, FO 371/84457.

13. Foreign office, telegram 2538, November 10, 1950, FO 371/84454.

14. Jebb to foreign office, telegram, UKUN 1721, November 14, 1950; Jebb to Sir Pierson Dixon, letter, November 15, 1950. Both are filed in FO 371/84454.

15. Beckett's November 17 comments on Jebb's proposal, his letter of November 25 seeking Shawcross's ruling, and the attorney general's reply on November 28, 1950, are all contained in FO 371/84455.

16. Department of State, telegram 713, November 14, 1950, NARA RG 59, NND 822910, box 4226.

17. Ernest Gross, interview with author, New York, NY, November 28, 1994.

18. Department of State, telegram, November 16, 1950, FRUS 1950, vol. VI, pp. 577–578.

19. Acheson, *Present at the Creation,* pp. 471–473.

20. Ibid., pp. 478–485.

21. Robert C. Strong to Oliver E. Clubb, memorandum, January 3, 1951, 793B.00/1-351, NARA RG 59, NND 822910, box 4227, first folder.

22. FRUS 1951, vol. VII, pp. 61–68.

23. The Office of Policy Coordination was created by a National Security Council directive in the summer of 1948, largely in response to the urging of the State Department's policy planning staff chief, George Kennan. It was to conduct covert, rather than merely psychological operations and began under the direction of Frank G. Wisner, an OSS veteran who brought many of his former colleagues into this new organization. Administratively housed in CIA, but supervised by the Department of State and the military, its bureaucratic status remained anomalous until 1952, when it was combined with the foreign intelligence collection component of CIA into the Office of Plans. This became one of the three directorates of the Agency under Gen. Walter Bedell Smith. Michael Warner, *The CIA under Harry Truman* (Washington, D.C.: CIA History Staff, Center for the Study of Intelligence, 1994), pp. xx–xxii.

24. Franklin Lindsay, interview with author, Cambridge, MA, January 31, 1996.

25. Thubten Jigme Norbu (Takster Rimpoche), interview with author, Bloomington, IN, May 16, 1995.

26. Dalai Lama, *Autobiography,* p. 64.

27. Department of State to New Delhi, cable, January 6, 1951, FRUS 1950, vol. VI, p. 618.

28. British embassy, Washington, to Foreign Office, dispatch, November 25, 1950, FO 371/84455.
29. Department of State to British embassy, Washington, aide-mémoire, December 30, 1950, FRUS 1950, vol. VI, pp. 612–613.
30. U.S. embassy, New Delhi, cable 1691, January 12, 1951, FRUS 1951, vol. VII, pp. 1506–1508.
31. Burke described his interviews with Harrer in an article, "The Flight of the Dalai Lama," *Life* (April 23, 1951), pp. 130–142. Burke, sworn to secrecy by Henderson about the embassy conversation with Harrer, honored his pledge.
32. Henderson to Dalai Lama, letter, FRUS 1951, vol. VII, pp. 1610–1612.
33. Department of State, telegram 1633, April 6, 1951, FRUS, vol. VII, p. 1619. Henderson also received full support from the U.S. ambassador in Ceylon, J. C. Satterwaithe, who told him that he was "to be highly commended for the courageous course of action." Satterwaithe to Henderson, Top Secret letter, April 13, 1951, 793B.11/4-1351, NARA RG 59, Ceylon. Commenting on Satterwaithe's letter, the State Department assured him that "Loy's project" had "full Departmental backing." Matthews to Satterwaithe, letter, April 24, 1951, 793B. 11/4–1351, NARA RG 59, Ceylon.
34. U.S. embassy, New Delhi, telegram 2891, May 24, 1951, FRUS 1951, vol. VII, pp. 1682–1685.

CHAPTER 5

1. Phuntso Tashi, interview with author, London, England, November 15, 1996.
2. The Dalai Lama excused Ngabo in a private interview with the author in Dharamsala on November 18, 1995. Takster Rimpoche does not share his younger brother's charitable estimate of Ngabo, whom he described as a self-seeking person who is Tibet's "number one traitor" (interview with the author, May 16, 1995). Phuntso Tashi, who may be indirectly defending his own participation in accepting the agreement, told the author in the November 15 interview that he believed Ngabo was a good man caught between irreconcilable forces. The more charitable interpretation gains support from a report by Shakabpa in early July 1951. He said that Ngabo, then on his way home from Beijing, had sent word that the Tibetan government was not to allow fears for his safety to affect its decision on whether to ratify the agreement. U.S. consulate, Calcutta, telegram 31, FRUS 1951, vol. VII, p. 1735.
3. Attributed to Sambo Rimshi and Phuntso Tashi by Goldstein, *History of Modern Tibet,* p. 770.
4. Jigme Ngabo, the son of Ngabo Ngawang Jigme, interview with author, Washington, DC, March 13, 1996.

Phuntso Tashi confirms that the Chinese promised that if the Dalai Lama returned to Lhasa within three years he would be welcomed and the Chinese would reduce the size of the army. They would establish a Chinese army headquarters in Lhasa, which would include one member of the Kashag; they would retain an army of 3,000 there, which would include 1,000 soldiers as a security guard for the Dalai Lama; and they would provide the funding for these installations. He said that the delegates asked that these points be included in the agreement, but the Chinese refused. Phuntso Tashi, interview.

As for a later determination of the borders, Jigme may be referring to an inconclusive exchange his father apparently had with Zhou Enlai. According to Phuntso Tashi, Ngabo sent a letter to Zhou after the signing of the agreement to propose uniting all of Tibet's traditional provinces, i.e. Kham and Amdo in the east with central and western Tibet. Zhou replied orally through Li Wei-han, saying this would be considered after China controlled Tibet. Zhou said that he realized there had been a historical association of the eastern provinces with the central government in Lhasa, but since the liberation of Kham and Amdo the old grievances with the central government in Beijing had been eliminated and things were much better in these areas.

5. U.S. embassy, New Delhi, telegram 3398, May 29, 1951, FRUS 1951, vol. VII, pp. 1687–1692.

6. Department of State, telegram 2051, June 2, 1951, FRUS 1951, vol. VII, pp. 1693–1695.

7. Thacher, interview.

8. Dean Rusk, telephone interview with author, May 27, 1994.

9. The briefing papers prepared for President Truman by his naval aide contained a digest of Wilkins's report of Chinese pressure on the Tibetan negotiators, and Shakabpa's statements to Wilkins that continued resistance to the Chinese might be dependent on U.S. help in arranging asylum. The president was also kept up to date on Takster's covert departure from India and the Department's subsequent talks with him in Washington. These included the Department's assurances of U.S. support for Tibetan autonomy, as well as a promise of "similar financial assistance for the long-term promotion of resistance by the Tibetan people against the Chinese in case the Dalai Lama leaves Tibet, publicly repudiates the agreement and continues to oppose Communist aggression actively." Although there is no available record of the president's reaction, it is apparent that he was kept well abreast of Tibetan affairs. Briefing papers, October 27, October 30, November 6, November 13, November 21, 1950, and June 12, June 14, July 11, July 13, 1951, Naval Aide to the President file, box 22, Truman Library.

10. U.S. embassy, telegram 3515, June 5, 1951, FRUS 1951, vol. VII, pp. 1701–1702.

11. U.S. embassy, New Delhi, cable 3576, June 11, 1951, FRUS 1951, vol. VII, pp. 1707–1710.

12. Department of State, telegram 2183, June 16, 1955, NARA RG 59, 793B.00/6-1551.

13. U.S. embassy, New Delhi, telegram 3764, June 24, 1951, 793B.00/62451, NARA RG 59, NND 822910, box 4227, first folder, reports this action. In later correspondence the embassy identified Harrer as the third person, besides Liushar and Shakabpa, to whom the letter had been given.

14. Editorial note 35, based on consul general, Calcutta, telegram 1, July 1, 1952, FRUS 1952–1954, vol. XIV, p. 73.

15. U.S. consulate, Calcutta, dispatch 625, June 28, 1951, file 611.93B/6–2851, NARA RG 59, NND 822910, box 4226, first folder.

16. U.S. consulate, Calcutta, dispatch 615, June 25, 1951, NARA RG 59, NND 822910, box 4227.

17. Department of State, telegram 4, July 3, 1951, 793B.00/7-251, NARA RG 59, NND 822910, box 4227, first folder.

18. U.S. consulate, Calcutta, telegram 13, July 3, 1951, FRUS 1951, vol. VII, pp. 1728–1729.

19. Evan M. Wilson, July 18, 1975, Oral History interview collection, Truman Library.

20. Takster Rimpoche, interview. This final week in Calcutta is described by Patterson in *Tragic Destiny,* and by Takster in *Tibet Is My Country* (New York: E. P. Dutton, 1961).

21. Although conveyed to Takster Rimpoche orally, they were reported to the embassy in Department of State telegram 91, July 12, 1951, FRUS 1951, vol. VII, pp. 1748–1749.

22. William O. Douglas, *Beyond the High Himalayas* (Garden City, N.Y.: Doubleday and Co., 1952), pp. 208–210.

23. Takster Rimpoche, interview.

24. Enclosure to New Delhi Dispatch 70, July 11, 1951, FRUS 1951, vol. VII, pp. 1744–1745.

25. Kalimpong to U.S. consulate, Calcutta, telegram, July 12, 1951, enclosure 6 to Dispatch 34 Amconsul, Calcutta, July 21, 1951, NARA RG 59, box 4227, China 1950–1954.

26. U.S. consulate, Calcutta, telegram 47, July 16, 1951, FRUS 1951, vol. VII, p. 175.

27. U.S. embassy, New Delhi, telegram 157, July 12, 1951, FRUS 1951, vol. VII, footnote p. 1749.

28. Takster Rimpoche, interview.

29. Department of State, telegram 107, July 13, 1951, FRUS 1951, vol. VII, pp. 1749–1750.

30. U.S. consulate, Calcutta, telegram 21, July 16, 1951, FRUS 1951, vol. VII, pp. 1753–1754.

31. Patterson, letter to the author, April 2, 1996.

32. Outlined in U.S. consulate, Calcutta, telegram 52, July 17, 1951, FRUS 1951, vol. VII, pp. 1754–1755. There is no available record of a formal Department approval for this plan, but this Calcutta cable indicates that it was proceeding with full U.S. authority.

33. George Patterson, telephone interview with author, March 26–27, 1995.

34. Patterson, interview, January 1995.

35. Pandatsang to U.S. consul general, Calcutta, letter, March 1, 1960, American Emergency Committee for Tibetan Relief (AECTR) file, Hoover Institution on War, Revolution, and Peace.

36. Dean Rusk, telephone interview with author, May 24, 1994.

37. Dalai Lama, interview. The Tibetan ruler may also have been remembering the Tibetan proverb cited by his former prime minister Lukhangwa about the gods lying when they too become desperate, which he had later recalled when the Nechung oracle advised him to remain in Lhasa in 1959. Dalai Lama, *Autobiography,* p. 135.

38. Dalai Lama, *Autobiography*, p. 66.

39. Dalai Lama, interview.

40. U.S. consulate, Calcutta, telegram 114, August 13, 1951, FRUS 1951, vol. VII, pp. 1776–1778.

41. U.S. embassy, New Delhi, telegram 613, August 14, 1951, FRUS 1951, vol. VII, pp. 1786–1787; Department of State, telegram 81, August 15, 1951, FRUS 1951, vol. VII, p. 1790.

42. U.S. consulate, Calcutta, telegram 154, September 10, 1951, printed as a footnote to the embassy's September 12, 1951, cable endorsing it. FRUS 1951, vol. VII, pp. 1803–1804.

43. New Delhi, Airgram 662, 10 September 1951, NARA RG 59, box 4227.

44. Department of State, *United States Policy Concerning the Legal Status of Tibet,* U.S. State Department Historical Division Study No. 403, November 1957, p. 17, NARA RG 59, box 3949.

45. Ibid. The possibility that the U.S. might upgrade its recognition of Tibet's legal status should relations with the Nationalist government change was conveyed to Gyalo at a meeting attended by his wife. The reporting officer noted that Mrs. Thondup was "considered to be a Chinese Nationalist agent," so presumably the Department was willing that the Chiang government know that its acceptance of the legal authority claimed by both Mao and Chiang over Tibet was not immutable.

46. U.S. embassy, New Delhi, telegram 269, July 19, 1951, FRUS 1951, vol. VII, pp. 1757–1758.

47. Aide-mémoire dated December 30, 1950, but delivered January 3, 1951, FRUS 1950, vol. VII, pp. 612–613.

CHAPTER 6

1. Indian mission, Lhasa, report, December 15, 1951, FO 371/99659.
2. Phuntso Tashi recalled this feature of the benevolent policies of the early occupation, "which made everyone [apparently including him and his wife] happy." Phuntso Tashi, interview.
3. Information Office, Embassy of India, Washington, D.C.
4. Indian mission, Lhasa, monthly report, December 1951, FO 371/99659. In his final years, Tsarong demonstrated his underlying loyalty to the Dalai Lama and his country, according to Jamyang Norbu, one of the more militant spokesmen for the Tibetan Youth Congress. In an interview with the author in New York on May 15, 1996, Norbu recalled that Tsarong returned to Lhasa in 1958 from a visit to India when his family and friends were urging him not to return. Tsarong told them that he "couldn't leave that young Lama all alone there." Norbu also recalled that another Tibetan who had remained in Lhasa during the uprising that took place when the Dalai Lama fled in 1959, remembers seeing the old commander-in-chief hunched over one of the Aufschnaiter maps planning operations against the Chinese. He was captured after the Chinese put down the rebellion and imprisoned for a few months in Lhasa, where he was mistreated. The doughty old general apparently retained his good spirits throughout this final ordeal and died in prison the night before he was scheduled to be the defendant in a "struggle session" staged by his captors.
5. Indian mission, Lhasa, report, December 15, 1951, FO 371/99659.
6. Lhamo Tsering, *bTsan rGol rGyal sKyob* (Resisting Oppression and Protecting the Country), Dharamsala, India: Amnye Machen Institute, 1992, vol. I, pp. 117–118.
7. In his November 1995 interviews with the author, Gyalo Thondup said Alo Chondze later had to flee Lhasa for India, where Gyalo used him to write anti-Chinese propaganda. Chondze nevertheless returned to Lhasa in 1959, where the Chinese gave him a job. He lost it after some personal difficulties and was forced to emigrate to Australia. Personality differences seem to have caused Gyalo to think less of Chondze than did the Tibetan resistance leader, Gompo Tashi. In his book, *Four Rivers, Six Ranges, Reminiscences of the Resistance Movement in Tibet* (Dharamsala, India: Information Office of the H.H. Dalai Lama, 1973), p. 42, Gompo notes that he had been impressed by Chondze and had arranged for him to escape when the Chinese imprisoned him in 1956.
8. Lhamo Tsering, *bTsan rGol rGyal sKyob,* p. 123.
9. See Frederick C. Teiwes, "Establishment of the New Regime," in *The Politics*

of China, edited by Roderick MacFarquhar (Cambridge: Cambridge University Press, 1993), pp. 18–20.

10. Indian mission, Lhasa, monthly report, January 15, 1952, FO 371/99659.

11. Indian mission, Lhasa, monthly report, April 16, 1952, FO 371/99659.

12. The participation of both Zhangs is noted in their entries in Donald W. Klein and Anne Clark, *Biographic Dictionary of Chinese Communism* (Cambridge, Mass.: Harvard University Press, 1991).

13. Indian mission, Lhasa, reports for April and May, 1952, FO 371/99659. Dalai Lama, *Autobiography,* pp. 75–77.

14. Indian mission, Lhasa, monthly report, June 16, 1952, FO 371/99659.

15. Even today he runs afoul of the Tibetan government-in-exile at Dharamsala in his single-minded pursuit of frequently controversial policies he considers best for his brother and his country.

16. Tsering, *bTsan rGol rGyal sKyob,* p. 111.

17. In his interviews with the author in November 1995, Gyalo Thondup said that even the prime ministers eventually "thought blue," i.e. conservatively, when the time came to implement his reforms and refused to endorse them. His proposals had an intriguing precedent, which also was part of their undoing in the Tibetan mind. In the eighth century Tison Detsen, one of the great Tibetan kings, made three unsuccessful efforts to divide the wealth of the country among all the people. After his third effort, the king's mother, who disapproved of these experiments, poisoned her son. Charles Bell, in his book *The People of Tibet* (Oxford: Clarendon Press, 1928, p. 13), notes that the law of Karma ordains that as a man sows so shall he reap, both in this life and in future lives. The priesthood thus explained that the king's equalization scheme was doomed to fail: How can there be equal opportunities for all, since each person must start where his good and bad deeds have placed him?

18. Gyalo Thondup's meeting with Zhang. Tsering, *bTsan rGol rGyal sKyob,* pp. 109–111.

19. Thondup, interviews, November 1995.

20. Tsering, *bTsan rGol rGyal sKyob,* pp. 135–140.

21. U.S. embassy, New Delhi, telegram 1749, November 15, 1951, FRUS 1951, vol. VII, pp. 1848–1849.

22. Footnote to embassy telegram 1749, cited at note 21.

23. Takster Rimpoche, interview.

24. Dalai Lama to Allison and Allison's response, memorandum of conversation and footnote, February 13, 1952, FRUS 1952–54, vol. XIV, p. 9.

25. Department of State, memorandum, May 14, 1952, FRUS 1952–1954, vol. XIV, p. 73.

26. On June 24, 1952, the U.S. consulate in Calcutta obtained from the crown prince of Sikkim's sister, Kukula, an oral message from the Dalai Lama reply-

ing to the commitments made to him by the U.S. government the previous year. The Dalai Lama again expressed his appreciation for the U.S. sympathetic attitude toward him and his subjects. He said that when the time was propitious for Tibet's liberation he hoped the U.S. would find it possible to give the Tibetan government [unspecified] material aid and moral support. He reaffirmed that the Tibetan people were not pro-Chinese, but were Tibetans first. Department of State, *United States Policy Concerning . . . Tibet*, p. 18.

27. Dalai Lama, *Autobiography*, page 79.
28. Khedroob carries on the work of both his mother and father managing the Tibetan refugee center in Darjeeling that she established, and his father's political activities as a member of the Tibetan assembly.
29. Tsering, *b Tsan rGol rGyal sKyob*, pp. 154–156.
30. Editorial note, FRUS 1952–1954, vol. XIV, p. 73.
31. In his monthly report for June, 1952, Sinha wrote, "Gyalo assured us that he would not make either Darjeeling or Kalimpong his headquarters and that he would scrupulously avoid involvement in politics." FO 371/99659. In the previously cited interviews in November 1995, and again in a conversation on July 11, 1996, Gyalo Thondup vigorously disputed Sinha's report. On the contrary, he said that when he requested asylum through Sinha, he made it clear that he felt he could no longer serve his brother by remaining in Tibet and wanted to join his wife in Darjeeling to carry on his political activities in support of Tibet from there. He said Sinha shared his anti-Communist sentiments because of his own treatment by the Chinese in Lhasa, sympathized with his efforts, and accordingly sent his request for asylum to Nehru, who replied that same evening, granting him entry to India with no restrictions on his activities. Gyalo had no explanation for Sinha's version except that the Indian official may have been diplomatically papering over the record to protect himself from Chinese charges of complicity. Gyalo discounts a similar version of this event that Lhaso Tsering includes in his book *b Tsan rGol rGyal sKyob* (p. 150) as a misapprehension due to the fact that Lhaso Tsering was not privy to his negotiations with Sinha.
32. Gyalo Thondup, interview with the author, November 1995.
33. Mullik, *The Chinese Betrayal*, pp. 180–181.
34. He was also in charge of the Dalai Lama's treasury, still stored in the stables of the maharajah of Sikkim in Gangtok, where it had been placed in 1951. Tsering, *b Tsan rGol rGyal sKyob*, p. 181, describes efforts made by Tibetan government officials who were collaborating with the Chinese administration to return these funds to Lhasa. Gyaltsen took the position that the treasury represented the legacy of all the Dalai Lamas, and since the present one was not free to make his own decisions, he would not release it. The funds were not used by Gyalo Thondup or his group and were kept intact until the Dalai Lama came into exile in India in 1959.

35. Gyalo Thondup to author, letter, May 20, 1996.

36. The Chinese administration in Lhasa belatedly took note of the activities of the association some years later when it denounced the leading members, Gyalo Thondup, Shakabpa, Khenchung Gyaltsen, Thubten Ninje, Chamba Wangdu, Chamba Tsondu, Alo Chondze, and the former Prime Minister Lukhang as "reactionaries" and revoked their Tibetan citizenship.

37. U.K. High Commission, New Delhi, dispatch 266, November 9, 1953, FO 371/105626.

38. U.K. High Commission, telegram 63, May 20, 1954, FO 371/110647. Nehru's justification fits with the strategy he outlined to Bowles three years earlier. In a private conversation on November 7, 1951, the prime minister emphasized that he was in no way blind to the potential dangers that might develop in China during the next ten or fifteen years. He believed the best hope was to attempt to divide China and Russia, and if this was not possible at least to modify the Chinese viewpoint through outside contacts and thus convince China that it need not depend entirely on Russia. FRUS 1951, vol. VI, p. 2188.

39. Dalai Lama, *Autobiography*, pp. 88–92.

40. While in Beijing the Dalai Lama became friends with his interpreter, a Tibetan named Phuntso Wangyal, one of the founders of the Tibetan Communist Party. The Dalai Lama requested Phuntso as one of the officials of the Chinese administration in Lhasa, and Mao agreed. But Phuntso was caught up in one of China's many political purges, imprisoned for several years, and never made it to Tibet on his own. He was imprisoned in Amdo. Dalai Lama, *Autobiography*, pp. 86–88, 111–112.

41. The British embassy reported that the Dalai Lama was "quite a popular hero in these parts, with his autograph in much demand," but the British still seemed nervous about reminding anyone of their former ties to Tibet. The envoy reported that "I shake hands with [the Dalai Lama], but never say more than a few words, as I think it would be unwise for me to appear to be taking more than a superficial interest in him." British embassy, Peking, to Foreign Office, letter, November 4, 1954, FO 371/110648.

Chapter 7

1. Quoted by Tsipon W. D. Shakabpa in his book, *Tibet: A Political History*, p. 311.

2. Erich Teichman's *Travels of a Consular Officer in Eastern Tibet* provides a classic account of an only partially successful attempt by the British in 1918 to mediate the historic border disputes between the local Tibetan chieftains and the struggling new Chinese Republic. The boundaries and political control over these remote areas along the headwaters of the Yangtze had come under

increasing challenge during the last century of the Ching dynasty. Its Chinese Nationalist successors were never able to establish sustained and effective political control over the region. By the time the Chinese Communists began their move into eastern Tibet in 1950, these local Tibetan domains had grown used to alternately challenging or accommodating the usually nominal authority claimed by representatives of a distant government in Beijing.

3. Gyalo Thondup said that as early as 1953 emissaries from both the Khampas and the Amdowas came to him to ask him to obtain weapons from abroad so that they might resist what they described as intolerable programs and controls being imposed on them by the Chinese. Thondup, interviews, November 1995.

4. Charles Bell, *Portrait of a Dalai Lama* (London: Wisdom Publications, 1987), p. 214.

5. Department of State, Office of Intelligence Research (OIR), *Unrest in Tibet,* November 1, 1956, NARA RG 59, box 312A.

6. OIR, *Unrest in Tibet.*

7. Dalai Lama, *Autobiography,* pp. 110–111.

8. Ngabo still resides in Beijing, where he went after the Dalai Lama fled to India in 1959. He has continued to play an equivocal role as an accommodator and sometime advocate for a moderate Chinese policy toward Tibet. Prior to the retreat in 1989 from Hu Yaobang's liberal approach toward Tibet, Ngabo and the Panchen Lama tried to promote a plan preserving the educational and cultural identity of the Tibetans. Thereafter he was quiescent.

9. "Peiping Concedes Rising near Tibet," *New York Times,* August 8, 1956, p. 6, col. 5.

10. The army commander was the man to whom the U.S. addressed its final appeal to the Dalai Lama, urging him to remain in exile in India in 1951. A descendant of the ancient Tibetan kings, he belonged to a family that had served the Dalai Lamas and the Tibetan government for generations. Following family tradition, he had escorted his young ruler back to Lhasa. There he established a reputation as one of the few officials who stood up for the interests of the Dalai Lama and his country against the Chinese. After his 1956 visit he remained in India throughout the subsequent visit of the Dalai Lama.

Ragashar's nephew, the crown prince of Sikkim, later told the British foreign office (minute, April 16, 1957, FO 371/218455) that he participated in a joint approach made by senior Tibetan officials including, surprisingly, Ngabo Ngawang Jigme, to Zhou Enlai during the Chinese prime minister's visit to New Delhi to demand the withdrawal of Chinese troops from Tibet, the independence of the country, and the reunion of the Tibetan-inhabited areas in the upper Yangtze. According to the crown prince, Zhou was reasonable during the talks, admitting that the Chinese had made mistakes, which they would rectify. He urged them to bring their grievances to the attention of the Chinese occupation officials in Lhasa.

In the words of the crown prince, "The next thing that happened was Ragashar's death." The commander died in Shigatse the following spring while escorting his leader back to Lhasa. While the general's nephew in Sikkim suspected foul play, Gyalo Thondup discounted reports that he had been poisoned by the Chinese Communists. Thondup said that Ragashar was overweight and had a history of heart disease. He noted that in any event, it was the Chinese Nationalists who poisoned their enemies; the Chinese Communists preferred more direct means. (Thondup, interviews, November 1995.)

11. "Red China Avows Caution in Tibet," *New York Times,* September 21, 1956, p. 1, col. 4.

12. U.S. consulate, Calcutta, telegram 351, June 29, 1956, NARA RG 59, 793B.11/6-2856.

13. U.S. consulate, Calcutta, dispatch 828, June 27, 1956, NARA RG 59, box 3949.

14. Department of State, telegram 23, July 24, 1956, NARA RG 59, box 3951.

15. In a British foreign office minute the following spring, R. W. Ford noted that after talking with the Sikkimese ruler in London he had arranged with Brian Crozier to include an item on the unrest and dissatisfaction in Tibet in the *Economist Foreign Report,* with the prospect of a lengthy article following the visit of his equally activist sister Kukula. Minute dated April 16, 1957, FO 371/21845.

16. There is no record that the U.S. had ever withdrawn the commitments it made to the Dalai Lama when it was encouraging him to seek asylum in 1951. Moreover, Gyalo Thondup, in an interview with the author in Kalimpong on November 1, 1996, said that he had forwarded to Phala, the Dalai Lama's chief of staff, the reaffirmation of these pledges of financial and political support that were part of a package Gyalo negotiated with the CIA during the summer and autumn of 1956. Part of this agreement consisted of training and arms support, but Gyalo said he was careful not to inform his brother of that.

17. Dalai Lama, *Autobiography,* p. 113.

18. Dalai Lama, *Autobiography,* pp. 117–120.

19. "There is a place in India called Kalimpong [where they] specialize in sabotaging Tibet. Nehru himself told the Premier [Zhou] that this place is a center of espionage, primarily American and British." Mao also referred to a group in Tibet with a "shaky organization that wants to set up an independent kingdom" and further noted that the Chinese have "advised the Dalai Lama that he'd be better off coming back: If you stay in India, then go to America, it might not be advantageous [for you or Tibet.]"

Mao also mistakenly stated that the Dalai Lama had already returned to

Tibet. When Mao made his speech the Dalai Lama was still in Kalimpong trying to decide whether to remain in India or return to Lhasa, which he did six weeks later. This was either an instance of misinformation or a bit of a premature forecast of the Dalai Lama's intentions. Roderick MacFarquhar, Timothy Cheek, and Eugene Wu, *The Secret Speeches of Chairman Mao* (Council on East Asian Studies, Harvard University, 1989), p. 184.

20. Thondup, interviews, November 1995.
21. Gyalo Thondup, interview with author, November 1–7, 1996.
22. Thondup, interviews, November 1995. The fact that this was a self-generated revolt and that the insurgents were asking only for arms to carry on their own battles weighed heavily in the Tibetans' favor, although their appeal and the U.S. response predated by a few months the Hungarian revolt, which haunted Washington's conscience for years. Three years later, when considering the National Security Directive on U.S. policy in the Far East, Eisenhower said: "A major uprising had once occurred in Hungary and everyone had been afraid to take action. In the event of an uprising in Communist China, we would have to decide what would be gained by action and what the people of China wanted. The Chinese people were not a pawn in a struggle between Mao and Chiang. If they wanted freedom and called for help that might be one thing; but a decision by the U.S. to intervene in the absence of an appeal for help would be quite another thing." Memorandum of discussion at the 419th Meeting of the National Security Council, September 17, 1959, FRUS 1958–1960, vol. XVI, p. 125.

CHAPTER 8

1. Michael Warner, *The CIA under Harry Truman* (Washington, D.C.: CIA, 1994), p. xxvii.
2. Robert Shapiro and Benjamin Page, "Foreign Policy and the Rational Public," *Journal of Conflict Resolution* 32(2) (June 1988), p. 221. Cited by Steven M. Teles in a presentation at the Fairbank Center, Harvard University, May 31, 1996.
3. U.S. consulate, Calcutta, reports of conversations with the Maharaj Kumar of Sikkim, February 4, 1955, August 1, 1955, and June 29, 1956, NARA RG 59, box 3949; the reports of resistance that originated with Thondup's organization are cited in U.S. Department of State Intelligence Report 7341, November 1, 1956, NARA RG 59, box 312A.
4. Gyalo Thondup (November 1995) and Takster Rimpoche (May 16, 1995) interviews with the author. Roger McCarthy, *Tears of the Lotus* (Jefferson, N.C.: McFarland and Co., 1997), pp. 5–6.
5. OIR, *Unrest in Tibet,* concluded that there was sufficient evidence that revolts

in various areas of Tibet were taking place, but that it could not be determined whether the resistance was cohesive and organized.

6. Evan Thomas, *The Very Best Men* (New York: Simon and Schuster, 1995), chapters 11 and 19.
7. Sam Halpern, telephone interview with the author, January 24, 1995.
8. Thomas Parrott, telephone interview with the author, January 24, 1995.
9. The moral dilemma felt within CIA over this issue is described by Thomas, *The Very Best Men,* pp. 146–147.
10. McCarthy, *Tears of the Lotus,* p. 139.
11. Ibid.
12. Ngabo's equivocal position seems typical. After the Dalai Lama fled to India in 1959, Ngabo went to Beijing, where he resides today. The Dalai Lama and his government continue to believe that Ngabo tried in his own way to work for the interests of the Tibetan people. They feel there is no comparison, however, between his contribution and that of the late Panchen Lama, who was outspoken and was punished for his courageous stands on behalf of the Tibetans. Lodi Gyari, interview, June 8, 1998.
13. Dalai Lama, *Autobiography,* pp. 120–121. Gyalo Thondup, in his interview with the author in New Delhi on November 7, 1996, described in detail what he told his brother about his negotiations with the U.S. and the commitments that were made.
14. Greg MacGregor, "Restudy of India by Peiping Seen," *New York Times,* January 20, 1957, p. 3, col. 2.
15. MacFarquhar, Cheek, and Wu, *The Secret Speeches of Chairman Mao,* pp. 184–185. The State Department's analyses of Mao's speeches are in a memorandum dated June 20, 1956, FRUS 1956, vol. III, p. 551; and an OIR report dated July 1, 1956, NARA RG 59, box 316.
16. Department of State, Office of Intelligence and Research Brief 2142, June 27, 1957, provided to NATO. Filed FO 371/127639.
17. John Avedon, *In Exile from the Land of Snows* (New York: Knopf, 1984), p. 119.
18. Account provided by one of Gompo's close associates, a former monk named Gyesang Chamatsang Ngadruk, in an interview with the author in Darjeeling, India, on November 6, 1996. Ngadruk had initially taken part in raising funds for the Golden Throne project without knowing of its covert purpose. He later participated in the follow-up meetings at which the Chushi Gangdruk was established, subsequently fought alongside Gompo, and accompanied him into exile in India in April 1959. He counted twenty-eight groups that eventually rallied to the flag of the Volunteer Freedom Fighters.
19. Gompo Tashi also describes these events in his book, *Four Rivers, Six Ranges.*
20. Thondup, interviews, November 1995.

21. McCarthy, *Tears of the Lotus,* pp. 4–5, 139, 240–241.

22. Gar T., interview with the author, May 10–11, 1995. He also commented on the great contribution that Richard Bissell made when he became the CIA's director of plans in 1958 and made available aerial photographs taken from U-2 planes of this previously ill-charted area. These photographs were used to prepare navigational charts for use by the flight crews and maps for team members. Bissell's work on the U-2 is described in Evan Thomas's *The Very Best Men,* pp. 164–178.

23. Popularly known as the "Flying Fortress," these four-engine bombers were introduced early in World War II by the U.S. Eighth Army Air Force from its bases in Britain in 1942 and became the workhorse of American strategic bombing campaigns against the occupied European continent.

24. William M. Leary, "Secret Mission to Tibet," *Air and Space* (December 1997), p. 62–71.

25. Goodman, Michael H., *The Last Dalai Lama* (Boston: Shambala, 1986), p. 268.

26. Debriefing Katsang Gyatotsang, Boston, September 1997.

27. Wangdu's experience was described by Lhamo Tsering, interview with author, February 18, 1997.

28. Gompo Tashi, *Four Rivers, Six Ranges,* chapter 6.

29. Gyesang Chamatsang Ngadruk (known as Ngadruk) to author, letter by fax, June 16, 1998.

30. Ngadruk said that when he arrived at Trigu a few weeks after Gompo he found approximately 1,500 combatants there. The larger figure may include groups that had signed on to the Chushi Gangdruk organization but were located in other areas east and north of the Lhoka region.

31. Pencho Rabgey (a former monk from Litang), interview with author, November 9, 1998.

32. Lhamo Tsering, interview with author, October 26, 1996.

33. Gompo Tashi, *Four Rivers, Six Ranges,* p. 73.

34. Ngadruk and Tenzing Tsultrim, interviews with the author's son, February 21–27, 1997.

35. Gompo Tashi, *Four Rivers, Six Ranges,* p. 74, lists his haul as two 80 mm mortars; 18 cases of shells, each containing six shells; two 60 mm mortars with 16 cases of shells, each containing 18 shells; ten Bren guns, with five packets of shells each containing 2,660 shells; 18 Sten guns; 385 .303 rifles; 378 bayonets; and 60 boxes of ammunition each containing 1,000 shells.

36. Gompo Tashi, *Four Rivers, Six Ranges,* chapter 8.

37. Tsering, interview.

38. L. Fletcher Prouty, "Colorado to Kokonor," *Denver Post,* February 6, 1972, pp. 10–17.

39. Gen. Edward G. Lansdale to Gen. Maxwell Taylor, memorandum, July 1961,

printed as Document 100 in *The Pentagon Papers: The Senator Gravel Edition* (Boston: Beacon Press, 1971), vol. II, p. 643.

40. Leary, "Secret Mission to Tibet," p. 70.

41. Gar T., interview. Prouty, in "Colorado to Kokonor," further describes the Pentagon's role and the objectives it saw served by these operations. Prouty, a former Air Force colonel, was serving in the office of the secretary of defense at the time. Leary, "Secret Mission to Tibet," describes the aircraft used and their actual operations.

42. McCarthy, *Tears of the Lotus,* p. 243. Further confirmed by Lhamo Tsering in letters to the author, July 15 and April 11, 1996.

43. Prouty, "Colorado to Kokonor," pp. 14–15.

44. Thomas, *The Very Best Men,* chapter 19, pp. 155–160, 273–284. His daughter, Frances FitzGerald, is the author of *Fire in the Lake,* one of the most distinguished early books questioning the anti-Communist activism of America in Vietnam.

45. William Colby, interview with author, March 22, 1994.

46. Dulles was the key member of a group called the 5412 Special Group. Its members were Gordon Gray, the president's national security affairs adviser, and the deputy secretaries of state and defense. The group had been created at Gray's request to make decisions on covert actions carried out under National Security Council Directive 5412 without having to hold a formal meeting of the Council itself. Thomas Parrott, a special assistant to Allen Dulles, told the author in an interview on July 3, 1996, that, as the group's only staff member and secretary, he had invented the obscure name for the powerful group, which was usually able to decide and coordinate the government's covert programs on the spot without its members having to check with their principals. In the case of Tibet, Parrott said the Group approved of the policy and continued to follow and approve the operations under the program.

47. Roger E. McCarthy, interview with the author, May 9, 1995.

48. Department of State, Bureau of Intelligence and Research, intelligence report 7985, March 31, 1959, NARA RG 59, box 3950.

49. U.S. consulate, Hong Kong, dispatch 591, January 30, 1959, NARA RG 59, box 3949.

50. U.K. High Commission, New Delhi, dispatch 293/2, May 3, 1958, FO 371/133710.

51. The approach was unofficial. Ivan Surita of the Indian home office showed it to the consul at a social event. U.S. consulate, Calcutta, dispatch G-4, July 25, 1958, 793B.00/7-2558, NARA RG 59, box 3949.

52. Walter S. Robertson, memorandum of conversation, November 24, 1958, 793B.00/11-2458, NARA RG 59, box 3949.

CHAPTER 9

1. Gompo Tashi, *Four Rivers, Six Ranges,* pp. 90–94; McCarthy, *Tears of the Lotus,* pp. 227–230.
2. John K. Greaney, CIA headquarters officer, interview with the author, January 14, 1997.
3. U.K. High Commission to the Commonwealth Relations Office, telegram, March 7, 1959, FO 371/21845.
4. "Taiwan Reports Revolts in China," *New York Times,* January 4, 1959, p. 5, col. 1.
5. In a meeting with the U.S. consul general in Calcutta, Dorji said that the Bhutanese border guards numbered fewer than thirty and that they were poorly armed. He also admitted that he had given his personal permission for the Khampa leaders to use the Bhutan route in and out of Tibet, but he had refused to allow the route to ship arms and ammunition. He had been told by Tibetans who had recently crossed from Tibet that the U.S. had been airdropping arms and supplies to the Khampas guided by U.S.-trained radio teams. U.S. consul general, Calcutta, telegram 345, March 25, 1959, NARA RG 59, folder 3949.
6. John Hart, interview with the author, November 26, 1994.
7. Called the "rice heap" because of the congeries of buildings that then housed 10,000 monks, Drepung was founded in 1416 and was one of Lhasa's three great monasteries of Gelugpa (Yellow Hat) Buddhism, the Dalai Lama's sect. Today only about five hundred monks are in residence. Sera, founded three years later, then had a population of around 5,000, which has dwindled to a few hundred today. The neighboring Ganden monastery, established by the founder of the Gelugpa order, was destroyed during the Cultural Revolution. In 1959 these three were the principal seats of monastic learning in Tibet.
8. The first "summer palace" in the Norbulingka park area was built in 1755 by the seventh Dalai Lama to use as both a refuge from the vast and uncomfortable Potala and as a base from which to administer the country. His successors continued this practice, each building his own "summer palace" there. The fourteenth Dalai Lama completed the New Summer Palace in 1956.
9. Dalai Lama, *Autobiography,* p. 130.
10. Dalai Lama, *The Memoirs of His Holiness the Dalai Lama: My Land and My People,* (New York: McGraw-Hill, 1962), p. 167. On pages 164 to 199, the Dalai Lama gives a full description of the events beginning on March 10, which culminated in his flight to India one week later.
11. Ibid., p. 195.
12. Phuntso Tashi to the author, letter, May 12, 1997. The sixth cabinet minister, Samdup Phodrang, had been injured when the demonstrations began and had to be left behind.

13. *Memoirs,* p. 209.

14. Gompo Tashi, *Four Rivers, Six Ranges,* p. 101.

15. In analyzing the order the U.S. consul general in Hong Kong noted that the short list of places held by the Chinese, their appeal to the populace for help, and the offers of very generous treatment of prisoners as well as rebel defectors, suggested that the Chinese were concerned about their military position. U.S. consul general, Hong Kong, telegram 1451, March 29, 1959, NARA RG 59, box 3949.

16. Taikhang Gomo, interview with the author, May 20, 1996.

17. Thondup, interviews, November 1996.

18. Memorandum of discussion, National Security Council (NSC) meeting, March 26, 1959, editorial note, FRUS 1958–60, vol. XIX, p. 751.

19. Dalai Lama, *Autobiography,* p. 140. References to the radio operators' messages are contained in boxes 14 and 15 of the White House, Office of the Staff Secretary files, subject series Alpha, Intelligence Matters, Dwight D. Eisenhower Library. John Greaney described the daily map prepared for the president tracing the Dalai Lama's flight (interview, January 27, 1995).

20. Greaney, interview, January 1995.

21. Message of the Dalai Lama's arrival, April 2, 1959, White House, Office of the Staff Secretary files, Intelligence Matters, box 15, Eisenhower Library.

22. Greg MacGregor, "Dalai Lama Enters India and Asks for Sanctuary," *New York Times,* April 3, 1959, p. 1, col. 5.

23. U.S. embassy, New Delhi, telegram 2210, March 24, 1959, NARA RG 59, box 3949.

24. U.S. embassy, New Delhi, telegram 2259, March 30, 1959, NARA RG 59, box 3949.

25. "Nehru Placates Indians on Tibet," *New York Times,* April 3, 1959, p. 3, col. 3. The prime minister told Parliament that after the Communists took over Tibet, Kalimpong filled up with people in the guise of technicians, geologists, bird-watchers, journalists, and some who had come "just to admire the scenery." Its population was about 15,000, of whom 3,000 were Tibetans, 500 Chinese, and the rest mountain people of Nepalese, Sikkimese, and Bhutanese ancestry.

26. U.S. embassy, New Delhi, telegram 2362, April 6, 1959, NARA RG 59, box 3950.

27. CIA report TDCS 3/396,258, April 23, 1959, contained in Papers as President, Ann Whitman file, International series, box 44, Eisenhower Library.

28. Tillman Durdin, "Peiping Reports Tibet Sealed Off," *New York Times,* April 23, 1959, p. 1, col. 6.

29. White House Staff Secretary files, subject file Alpha, Intelligence Briefing folder, box 14, Eisenhower Library.

30. Nehru's jiu-jitsu metaphor is reminiscent of the one offered by Assistant Secretary Allison to Takster Rimpoche in 1952 ("the Japanese judo expert") in rationalizing the U.S. government's inability to intervene to help the Dalai Lama then. See chapter 6.

31. U.S. embassy, New Delhi, telegram, May 6, 1959, NARA RG 59, box 3950. Nehru made this same point to U.S. National War College students who called on him on May 16, 1959. "He said that the Tibetans were tough and the methods being used by the Chinese were not those calculated to win them over. He felt it would take the Chinese a really long time to take over Tibet because the terrain was so favorable for guerrilla warfare, because the Tibetans were tough and vigorous fighters and because most of Tibet was at such a high altitude that it was extremely difficult to colonize. In fact, said the Prime Minister, 'the biggest thing in favor of the Tibetans is their country.'" U.S. embassy, New Delhi, dispatch G-395, May 16, 1959, NARA RG 59, box 3950.

32. "Chou Insists Rebels Seized Dalai Lama: Hopes He Will Return," *New York Times,* April 19, 1959, p. 1, col. 5.

33. U.K. High Commission, memorandum of conversation, May 6, 1959, FO 371/21845. MacDonald, the son of Ramsay MacDonald, the British National Labor prime minister in the thirties, was very much a Third World sympathizer, and a staunch supporter of the Commonwealth. He took a strongly critical stand against the Chinese in Tibet, even though the Beijing government contained two of the foreign leaders he most admired, Zhou Enlai and Chen Yi. MacDonald had known them since he met them in 1955 on their way to the Bandung Conference, which endorsed the Panch Sheel—the five principles (of peaceful coexistence). Of Zhou he later wrote: "During my nearly four-score years on this Earth I have had the privilege of knowing a number of the truly great men working creatively in various fields of human activity in many different lands scattered across all the continents and seas. I think that Zhou was as fine a political statesman as any among them—which is saying a lot, for the others include, for varied reasons, immortal figures such as Mahatma Gandhi in India, Franklin D. Roosevelt in America, Jomo Kenyatta in Kenya and Winston Churchill in Britain." *Inside China* (Boston: Little Brown, 1980), p. 155. He felt similarly close to Chen Yi, who shared his birthday in 1901, for which reason he said they "regard[ed] each other as brothers." He characterized Chen Yi as a "charming, jovial man, highly talented as both a soldier and a statesman" (p. 68).

34. Department of State, daily staff summary, May 11, 1959, NARA, RG 59, box 2.

35. The embassy's report of Nehru's acknowledgment that Tibet's legal status would be controlled politically and not juridically was based on Nehru's own remarks, which were frequently couched in obscure language, as in this case: "The issue is really decided by strength of nation." U.S. embassy, New Delhi, telegram 2923, May 22, 1959, NARA RG 59, box 3950.

36. "Tibetans in Peril, Dalai Lama Says," *New York Times,* June 21, 1959, p. 1, col. 6.

CHAPTER 10

1. James Critchfield, interview with author, December 5, 1996. Roswell Gilpatrick, who was deputy secretary of Defense, noted that his boss Robert McNamara "never got the Bay of Pigs off his conscience" and that he began regularly attending the meetings of the Special Group chaired by McGeorge Bundy after that fiasco. Oral history, interview with Dennis J. O'Brien, May 3, 1970, Kennedy Library.

2. Transcript of press and radio briefing, March 23, 1959, Public Policy Papers, Papers of J. F. Dulles, Health, Press and Radio briefings, box 139, Seeley G. Mudd Manuscript Library, Princeton University.

3. Department of State, statement for the press 222, March 26, 1959.

4. Department of State, daily radio and press briefing, March 28, 1959, Dulles Papers, box 139.

5. Intelligence Information Brief 125, April 14, 1959, which was apparently shared with the British Foreign Office and filed in FO 371/21845.

6. Memorandum, *April 1 OCB Luncheon Discussion: Exploitation of Tibetan Revolt,* White House, Office of the Special Assistant, Operations Coordinating Board (OCB) series, box 6, Eisenhower Library.

7. MacDonald to the CRO, dispatch 21, May 30, 1959, FO 371/141595.

8. The most admired woman in the U.S., Eleanor Roosevelt, wrote in her widely circulated column, My Day: "Neither India nor any other country has meddled in China's internal affairs. A country—Tibet—under Communist China's influence, which was promised freedom, rebelled against controls imposed by the Chinese Reds, and the leader of the Tibetans, who is still held in the warmest regard by his people, has escaped for refuge to India. Nobody incited this rebellion. The Communist Chinese, in putting it down, broke their promise to allow the country freedom for its government.... The action in Tibet should alert the Asian-African world to the true aim of communism everywhere." Anna Eleanor Roosevelt Papers, April 23, 1959, box 3161, Roosevelt Library.

9. Memorandum of the 403rd meeting of the NSC, April 23, 1959, Papers as President, Ann Whitman file, NSC series, box 11, Eisenhower Library.

10. Edwin F. Black to Karl G. Harr, memorandum, June 3, 1959, White House, Office of the Special Assistant, OCB series, box 6, Eisenhower Library.

11. Averell Harriman and Chester Bowles before the House Foreign Affairs Committee, "Harriman Urges Caution on Tibet," *New York Times,* April 17, 1959, p. 15, col. 3; "Mansfield Proposal," *New York Times,* April 13, 1959, p. 6, col. 2.

12. Text released by the Government of the Republic of China (GRC) Information Office, forwarded as enclosure 1, U.S. embassy, Taipei, dispatch 533, NARA RG 59, box 3949.

13. GRC, press release, NARA RG 59, box 3949.

14. Department of State, telegram 654, April 2, 1959, NARA RG 59, folder 3950.

15. Yeh undoubtedly remembered the fast one that the Tibetan trade mission had pulled on him in Nanking in 1948, when they pretended to agree to use Chinese passports on their onward travel to the United States and the United Kingdom and then switched in Hong Kong to the ones issued by their own government as evidence of its independent status. Memorandum of conversation, April 23, 1959, 793B.00/4-2359, NARA RG 59, box 3950.

16. U.S. embassy, Taipei, telegram 1137, April 28, 1959, 793B.00/4-2859, NARA RG 59, box 3950. The conversation was also included in the Department's daily staff summary, April 28, 1959, NARA, RG 59, box 2.

17. Department of State, staff summary, May 3, 1959, NARA RG 59, box 2.

18. Lhamo Tsering, interview with author, April 30, 1997.

19. Throughout the Eisenhower and Kennedy administrations the Nationalists attempted to obtain U.S. support for sending special forces teams into China to organize resistance activities. The U.S. government could not forget its early experience with the Chinese "irregulars" that had been placed in northern Burma with U.S. help in 1950. Their activities in the drug trade, among other nonmilitary ventures, finally caused the U.S. to request their withdrawal, and they had become a constant irritant in relations between Washington and Taipei. Roger E. McCarthy, interview with author, January 19, 1995.

20. Gyalo Thondup, interviews with author, November 1996.

21. A copy is in White House, Staff Secretary files, subject series Alpha, Intelligence Matters folder, box 15, Eisenhower Library.

22. Lhamo Tsering, the Tibetan operations chief who was then at Camp Hale, interview, October 1996. Confirmed by John Greaney on June 11, 1996, and Roger McCarthy on January 12, 1997, in interviews with the author.

23. Director of Central Intelligence Dulles to President Eisenhower, memorandum, April 1, 1959, FRUS 1958–1960, vol. XIX, pp. 752–753.

24. Gompo Tashi, *Four Rivers, Six Ranges,* p. 102.

25. Note of telephone call, Chairman's daily log, April 20, 1959, Papers of Nathan Twining, box 7, Library of Congress.

26. Memorandum of 403rd meeting NSC; and memorandum of the 404th meeting of the NSC, April 30, 1959, Papers as President, Whitman file, NSC series, box 11, Eisenhower Library.

27. Exchange of correspondence, NARA RG 59, folder 3950.

28. Rep. Stuyvesant Wainwright and Frederic P. Bartlett, memorandum of conversation, May 20, 1959, NARA RG 59, folder 3950.

29. The Dalai Lama refers to the photographer and his CIA training in his *Autobiography,* p. 140.

30. While it was noted on the State Department memorandum forwarding this proposed message to the president that he was briefed on it, there is no copy of the final message in the present NARA files. This correspondence is contained in the Papers as President, Whitman file, International series, box 44, Eisenhower Library.

31. Foreign Office FT 1015/197, August 26, 1959, FO 371/21845.

32. Department of State, memorandum for the president, June 16, 1959, White House Office of the Staff Secretary, International file, box 13, Eisenhower Library.

33. The message was also copied to Ambassador Henry Cabot Lodge, U.S. representative at the UN, on October 8 so that he would know the limits to the U.S. commitments to the Dalai Lama, whose appeal to the UN was then being considered. Department telegram 323, October 8, 1959, White House Office of the Staff Secretary, International file, Tibet, box 73, Eisenhower Library.

34. Goodpaster, memorandum for the record, June 20, 1959, White House Office of the Staff Secretary, International file, Tibet, box 13, Eisenhower Library.

35. Minutes of the 415th Meeting of the National Security Council, July 30, 1959, White House Whitman File, NSC series, box 11, Eisenhower Library.

CHAPTER 11

1. Tillman Durdin, "Nehru Doubtful Tibet Is UN Case," *New York Times,* July 8, 1959, p. 5, col. 4.

2. U.S. embassy, New Delhi, telegram 161, July 16, 1959, NARA RG 59, folder 3951.

3. U.K. High Commission to the Commonwealth Relations Office, telegram 1523, October 3, 1959, FO 371/21845.

4. J. Graham Parsons to Secretary Herter, memorandum of conversation, August 6, 1959, NARA RG 59, folder 3951.

   Unlike 1950, when the State Department's International Organization Office (IO) was reluctant to promote the Tibetans' appeal to the United Nations, most of the decisions taken at this meeting with Murphy were based on a memorandum prepared for it by the IO office. Memorandum, "Preparations for Consideration of Tibet at the 14th General Assembly," from IO to the Acting Secretary, July 28, 1959, NARA RG 59, folder 3951.

5. U.S. embassy, London, telegram 37, September 1, 1959, NARA RG 59, folder 3951.

6. United States Mission to the United Nations (USUN), New York, telegram

288, September 1, 1959, NARA RG 59, Department of State daily staff summary, box 2.

7. Memorandum of conversation, September 5, 1959, NARA RG 59, folder 3951.

8. Department circular telegram, September 7, 1959, NARA RG 59, folder 3951.

9. U.K. High Commission, New Delhi, telegram 1340, September 4, 1959, FO 371/141597 21845.

10. U.S. embassy, New Delhi, telegram 798, September 5, 1959, FRUS 1958–1960, vol. XIX, pp. 777–780.

11. Department of State to U.S. embassy, New Delhi, telegram 869, September 9, 1959, NARA RG 59, folder 3951. Brown responded with a similar priority "NIACT" (Night Action) cable informing the Department and the USUN mission that the Dalai Lama had already sent his appeal to the UN secretary general and planned to call a press conference to read it out as soon as the secretary general released it. The chargé d'affaires also reported that he had arranged an appointment that afternoon with the Dalai Lama to pass along the points that the Department had requested that he make to him. He also noted that he had issued visas to the Dalai Lama's brother, Gyalo Thondup, and an interpreter, who were being sent to New York to begin lobbying at the UN. As instructed, he issued these on the Indian letters of identity that the Tibetans were carrying instead of the Tibetan passports they wished to use.

In an earlier exchange the Department mistakenly said that the Hong Kong consulate had issued visas on the affidavits of identity carried by the Tibetan trade mission in 1948 rather than their Tibetan passports. This misstatement reflected either a misunderstanding or an incorrect official record of the event that had so aroused the anger of the Chinese Nationalist government at that time. In any event, there was to be no repetition of this embarrassing slip-up so prized by the Tibetans. Undated memorandum for the president, September 1959, NARA RG 59, folder 3951.

12. Records documenting the bitterness between Khrushchev and Mao have only recently become available. A valuable source is the report made by Mikhail Suslov, a member of the Central Committee of the Soviet Communist Party, on the trip that Khrushchev made to Beijing in early October 1959, immediately after meeting with Eisenhower at Camp David. Excerpts from Suslov's report have been printed in Issues 8–9 of the Woodrow Wilson International Center for Scholars' *Cold War International History Project Bulletin* (winter 1996/1997), pp. 258–261.

13. Suslov said in his report that during these obviously nasty exchanges with the Chinese leaders, Foreign Affairs Minister Chen Yi had claimed that the Soviet policy toward Nehru was "allegedly opportunistic and the policy of China was more firm and correct." He noted, "Naturally, we gave a resolute rebuff to these pronouncements." Suslov continued, "We are getting the impression that, while

recognizing the principle of peaceful coexistence between the two global systems, the Chinese comrades tend to regard this principle just as a temporary maneuver."

14. Facts on File, vol. XIX, No. 985, p. 296. It is discussed in Arthur D. Low, *The Sino-Soviet Dispute* (Cranbury, N.J.: Fairleigh Dickinson University Press, 1976), pp. 99–100. Suslov in his report said that neither the letter nor the TASS commentary evoked a "proper understanding among the Chinese leaders" who reproached Moscow for the TASS announcement, which they said "displayed to the whole world the different positions of China and the Soviet Union toward the incident on the Sino-Indian border, which causes a virtual glee and jubilation among the Indian bourgeoisie, and American and British imperialists, who use this to drive a wedge into the relations between China and the Soviet Union."

15. Memorandum, "Discussion at the 418th Meeting of the National Security Council," September 10, 1959, Papers as President, Whitman File, NSC series, box 11, Eisenhower Library. Dulles's statement about the Chinese unwillingness to admit the failure of the Great Leap Forward program is curious, because two weeks earlier the Beijing *People's Daily* had published the communiqué of the Eighth Plenum of the Chinese People's Congress scaling back by considerable amounts the claims for grain and steel production that had been made for 1958.

16. Parsons to the secretary, memorandum, September 16, 1959, NARA RG 59, folder 3951.

17. White House, memorandum of conversation, September 27, 1959, White House Staff notes for September 1959, box 44, Eisenhower Library.

18. E. W. Kenworthy, "Soviet Is Blamed for Acts of Bloc," *New York Times,* October 7, 1959, p. 1, col. 2, and October 8, 1959, p. 1, col. 1.

19. Facts on File, vol. XIX, No. 991, p. 342.

20. Facts on File, vol. XIX, No. 992, p. 349. Washington continued to wrestle with how to handle the growing evidence of the Sino-Soviet conflict. On October 16, 1959, the State Department's Bureau of Intelligence and Research prepared a memorandum generally taking a restrained position concerning exploitation of the possibility that "during the coming years—and this may be in some ten or twenty rather than one or two—the frequency and intensity of these frictions will increase substantially." FRUS 1958–1960, vol. XIX, pp. 611–613. A subsequent debate followed on whether the secretary should continue to exploit actively the "Doctrine of Partial Responsibility" in the context of the Sino-Soviet differences that had provoked the responses from Khrushchev and the Chinese noted above. Undersecretary Parsons contended in a memorandum to Herter on November 4 (FRUS 1958–1960, vol. XIX, pp. 622–624) that this campaign should be continued, while the Policy Planning staff argued that U. S. noninvolvement in the Sino-Soviet controversy might give Moscow a freer hand in

putting "a break on the Chinese Communists" (FRUS 1958–1960, vol. XIX, pp. 629–631). The Policy Planning staff's argument for restraint apparently won out for the time being.

21. Memorandum of conversation, September 17, 1959, FO 371/21845.

22. *New York Times,* September 18, 1959, p. 14, col. 1.

23. Lloyd, Herter, and Couve de Murville, record of conversation, September 18, 1959, FO 371/21845.

24. USUN telegram 21, September 18, 1959, FRUS 1958–1960, vol. XIX, pp. 785–787.

25. Foreign Office to U.K. mission New York, telegram, September 22, 1959, FO 371/21845.

26. Parsons, memorandum, September 16, 1959, previously cited.

27. Department telegram 659, September 19, 1959, NARA RG 59, folder 3951.

28. Department of State, telegram 1029, September 19, 1959, NARA RG 59, Department of State summary, September 21, 1959, box 2.

29. Gregerson/Murphy exchange, October 9, 1959, NARA RG 59, folder 3951.

30. Herter, telephone log, October 6, 1959, Papers of Christian A. Herter, telephone calls, box 12, Eisenhower Library.

31. Thondup, interviews, November 1996.

32. Herter, telephone log, October 8, 1959, Papers of Christian A. Herter, telephone calls, box 12, Eisenhower Library.

33. Bunker had been directed to prepare and deliver a letter by hand to the Dalai Lama on October 6, 1959. It conveyed the president's assurance that the U.S. government welcomed the initiative of Ireland and Malaya in requesting inscription of the item and would support "full consideration of the shocking record of the Chinese Communist authorities in Tibet." State Department, telegram 1247, October 6, 1959, White House, Office of the Staff Secretary, Records 1952–1961, International file, box 13, Eisenhower Library.

   The embassy reported on October 8 that the letter was being taken to the Dalai Lama at Mussoorie by his brother Lobsang Samten that evening (U.S. embassy, New Delhi, telegram 1273, October 8, 1959, which is in the same Eisenhower Library file).

34. USUN, telegram 137, October 8, 1959, FRUS 1958–1960, vol. XIX, pp. 790–792.

35. Gross to Murphy, memorandum, October 9, 1959, NARA RG 59, folder 3951.

36. Gross, interview.

37. The two members of this seemingly odd couple had, each for its own reasons, taken on the role of championing this resolution, which other more likely sponsors were avoiding. Ernest Gross recalled in an interview with the author on May 4, 1997, that at the time he and former State Department colleagues had speculated that the Irish might have felt called upon to do this out of

sympathy for another underdog that had become a victim of religious persecution. The Malayans were probably still mindful of their bitter battle with Communist insurgents earlier in the decade. In any event Lodge approved of this team.

38. Michael James, "UN Will Debate Tibetan Question," *New York Times,* 13 October 1959, p. 8, col. 3.

39. USUN, telegram 82, September 28, 1959, FRUS 1958–1960, vol. XIX, pp. 788–789.

40. U.S. embassy, London, telegram 2138, October 21, 1959, 793B.00/10–2159, NARA RG 59, box 3951.

41. Memorandum, October 14, 1959, FRUS 1958–1960, vol. XIX, pp. 792–795.

42. Secretary's Staff record, October 20, 1959, Department of State Summary, NARA RG 59, box 2.

43. Memorandum of conversation, October 29, 1959, NARA RG 59, folder 3951.

44. Gross, interview with author, September 18, 1996.

45. Parsons and Thondup, memorandum of conversation, October 31, 1959, NARA RG 59, folder 3951.

46. Thondup to Murphy, letter, November 2, 1959, NARA RG 59, folder 3951.

47. Murphy to Thondup, letter, November 4, 1959, NARA RG 59, folder 3951. Murphy's official version read: "While it has been the historical position of the United States to consider Tibet as an autonomous country under the suzerainty of China, the American people have also traditionally stood for the principle of self-determination. It is the belief of the United States Government (USG) that this principle should apply to the people of Tibet and that they should have the determining voice in their own political destiny. The USG is prepared, when a suitable opportunity presents itself, to make a public declaration of its support for the Tibetan people."

48. Department of State, Secretary's Staff record, October 20, 1959, NARA RG 59, Daily staff summary, October 1959, box 2.

Fifteen months later President Kennedy restored a variant of this assurance in a letter to the Dalai Lama dated February 4, 1961, in which he expressed the hope of "all Americans" that "Tibet will one day be governed in accordance with the manifest wishes of the Tibetan people" and "assured" him that the "United States Government will seek effective and practicable means to help speed the day." President's Office files, India 11/60–5/61, box 118a, John F. Kennedy Library.

49. The promised statement was made in the form of a letter dated February 20, 1960, from Herter to the Dalai Lama, which was released to the press on February 29, 1960. It said: "As you know, while it has been the historical position of the United States to consider Tibet as an autonomous country under the suzerainty of China, the American people have also traditionally stood for the

principle of self-determination. It is the belief of the United States Government that this principle should apply to the people of Tibet and that they should have the determining voice in their own political destiny." Editorial note 401, FRUS 1958–1960, vol. XIX, p. 809.

50. Department of State, telegram 1947, November 25, 1959, NARA RG 59, box 395.

51. Memorandum of conversation, November 3, 1959, NARA RG 59, folder 3951.

52. Department of State, telegram 1652, November 25, 1959, NARA RG 59, folder 3951.

53. Department of State, Staff summary supplement, November 23, 1959, NARA RG 59, box 1.

54. U.S. embassy, London, November 9, 1959, NARA RG 59, folder 3951.

55. The exchange is in the form of two aide-mémoire from and to the Chinese embassy in Washington, February 28 and March 2, 1960, NARA RG 59, folder 2161.

56. U.S. embassy, New Delhi, telegram 398, November 23, 1959, FRUS 1958–1960, vol. XIX, pp. 804–805.

57. "William J. Jordan, "Herter Avoids Firm U.S. Stand on Indian Border," *New York Times,* November 13, 1959, p. 1, col. 8.

58. Eisenhower to Nehru, letter, September 2, 1959, FRUS 1958–60, vol. XV, pp. 513–514.

59. Jackson's role in the Eisenhower Administration is described in H. W. Brands, *Cold Warriors,* Columbia University Press, New York, 1988, pp. 117–137.

60. Gross, interview, November 28.

61. White House, Office of the Staff Secretary, International file, box 13, Tibet (2), Eisenhower Library.

62. Secretary Herter to President Eisenhower, memorandum, April 7, 1960, White House Office files, Office of the Staff Secretary, International file, box 13, Tibet (2), Eisenhower Library.

63. Gross, interview, November 28.

CHAPTER 12

1. Special Staff Record, December 3, 1959, NARA RG 59, Department of State Daily staff summary, box 3. The Nationalist plan called for training 3,000 special forces to help "restore freedom to the mainland by political means." The only restriction imposed on U.S. support was that they could not be deployed unilaterally, i.e., the U.S. had a veto.

2. Evan Thomas, *The Very Best Men,* p. 276.

3. Victor Marchetti, *The CIA and the Cult of Intelligence* (New York: Knopf, 1974), p. 115.

4. Thinlay Paljor to the author, letter by fax, May 12, 1997. His observations are similar to those in McNallen's article, "Leadville to Lhasa."
5. Steve McNallen, "Leadville to Lhasa," *Soldier of Fortune* (April 1991), pp. 74–79.
6. The cooking problem was solved when the U.S. Army eventually assigned two noncommissioned officer cooks, "Mr. Bill" and "Mr. Joe," to join the team. They soon earned the high regard of both the trainees and the *ghegen*.
7. Some were published in the international edition of *Life* (October 12, 1959), pp. 18–19.
8. In an article in the July/August 1981 edition of *Rocky Mountain News*, entitled "Going After Wangdu," Jeff Long describes a front-page story in the *Denver Post* of July 16, 1959, headlined "Atom Unit Making Test Near Leadville," in which Rear Admiral Parker of the Defense Atomic Support Agency denied that a nuclear bomb had been placed at Camp Hale. His denial only enhanced the local legend.

    John Greaney (interview with author, May 1, 1995) recalled that one instructor set off a charge larger than usual that shattered windows in a nearby mining processing facility. The management was speedily compensated, and more modest charges were used in subsequent blasts.

    For years, a Basque shepherd conducted his flock in periodic migrations to and from seasonal pasture there. He showed no interest in the activities of the camp and moved unchallenged with his sheep.
9. McNallen, in "Leadville to Lhasa," noted "the warmth for their American friends which shone through" in every interview he conducted with the Dumra alumni thirty years later. He said the instructors "were seen as competent, dedicated sincere men."
10. Tenzing Tsultrim, interviews, February 1997. Tenzing Tsultrim said he had taken part in twenty-eight battles en route to India.
11. Previously referred to in chapter 10, and confirmed by Lhamo Tsering (interview, February 1997).
12. Gyesang Chamatsang, also known as "Ngadruk," a participant, interview with the author's son in Darjeeling on February 20, 1997.

    Tawang was traditionally Tibetan territory, and the fifth Dalai Lama was born three centuries earlier in the monastery that administered the area. In 1914 the Tibetans yielded their claim at the Simla Conference, bowing to the British desire to eliminate the "Tawang wedge." Some colonial officers saw the wedge of about sixty miles' depth as a potential staging point for the Chinese to expand their control between Bhutan and the North East Frontier Agency. The Tibetan negotiators ceded the territory as part of a package deal guaranteeing their boundaries, but the package fell apart when the Chinese refused to sign. The Tibetan negotiators were severely criticized by their government, although the British and the Tibetans did sign a secret agreement accepting the agreement as binding. In practice this meant very little in Tawang, since the British never took political control there. The Tibetan government consequently continued to administer it until 1951 when the Indian government moved in and claimed control. It was through this area that the Dalai Lama fled into exile in India in 1959.

13. Details from Lhamo Tsering, interviews, October 1996 and February 1997.

14. Lhamo Tsering, from the inventories prepared by the teams. Letter, July 15, 1996.

15. Greaney, interview, January 1995.

16. The Amdo plateau is an area of ethnic Tibet in the Chinese province of Qinghai. Lhamo Tsering provided the details on the team's activities and the arms dropped to them (interview, April 1997).

17. Nyemo Bhusang, interview with author, October 25, 1996, with additional details in response to questions by mail in August, 1997.

18. President Kennedy and Chiang K'ai-shek's son, Chiang Ching-kuo, discussed the guerrilla teams sent into mainland China by the Nationalists between October 1962 and September 1963. The younger Chiang was in charge of these operations and reported a similarly high casualty rate. Chiang argued that an 85 percent casualty rate of these teams, which contained from six to twenty-eight men, did not mean that they had been a failure because they had achieved their purpose of "causing trouble on the mainland, raising morale of the Chinese people, and upsetting the organization of the army." Chiang was accordingly asking for U.S. support to expand these operations to teams of fifty to three hundred men that could establish a foothold on the mainland. An unconvinced Kennedy responded that before considering the request, the U.S. would require more hard intelligence indicating a realistic prospect that they could ignite a revolt. Memorandum of conversation, September 11, 1963, NARA RG 59, box 3860.

19. Lhamo Tsering, interview, February 1997.

20. Stuart R. Schram, *Mao's Road to Power,* vol. III, *From Jinggangshan to the Establishment of the Jiangxi Soviets, July 1927–December 1930* (Armonk, N.Y.: East Gate Books, 1995) pp. 78–108.

CHAPTER 13

1. Lhamo Tsering, interview, April 1997.

2. Memorandum for the record prepared by the President's Special Assistant for National Security Affairs, Gordon Gray, February 4, 1960, FRUS 1958–1960, vol. XIX, pp. 808–809.

3. Kenneth Lieberthal cites a recollection by Peng that Tibet was very much on

his mind in July of 1959, when the conference at Lushan resulted in his political banishment. MacFarquhar, *The Politics of China,* p. 104.

4. Lhamo Tsering, interviews with author, November 18 and 19, 1995, October 26, 1996.

5. Michel Peisel, *Mustang, the Forbidden Kingdom* (New York: Dutton, 1967). The French anthropologist and explorer describes his 1964 trip and his findings about the origin of the Mustang kings.

6. Lhamo Tsering, interviews with author, November 18 and 19, 1995.

7. Lhamo Tsering, who was to be the operational executor for the Tibetans, described the plan in his interviews, previously cited. The CIA officers responsible for the U.S. participation agree with his description.

8. Michael R. Beschloss, *Mayday* (New York: Harper and Row, 1986).

9. Chinese troops killed one Nepalese soldier and captured ten others near the Mustang border area on June 28, 1960. The Chinese, although admitting the incident took place within the demilitarized zone of twenty kilometers established on each side of the Nepal-Tibet border in an agreement signed by Premiers Zhou Enlai and B. P. Koirala two months earlier, claimed that it occurred on Chinese territory ("Chinese Troops Kill a Nepalese," *New York Times,* June 30, 1960, p. 8, col. 4.). The Chinese later agreed to pay the 50,000 rupees compensation demanded by the Nepalese government and reported in early August that they were withdrawing their troops from the demilitarized zone. They said their troops had been stationed there to intercept Khampa resistance fighters fleeing into Mustang (*New York Times,* Aug. 1, 1960, p. 4, col. 5). The Nepalese government several months later expressed concern that the Chinese might send troops into Mustang to expel the Khampas. The Nepalese spokesman was quoted as having said that unidentified aircraft had been dropping arms to about 4,000 Khampas in Mustang. Again the Chinese seemed disinclined to turn this into a major incident (Paul Grimes, "India Fears Threat to Nepal by Red China Over Tibetans," *New York Times,* Feb. 3, 1962, p. 4, col. 2).

10. Roger McCarthy and John Greaney, interviews with author, April 9, 1997.

11. James Thomson, "On the Making of U.S. China Policy, 1961–1969," *China Quarterly* 50 (April/June 1972), p. 221.

12. Dean Rusk, recorded interview with Dennis J. O'Brien, March 30, 1970, Oral History project, Kennedy Library.

13. Dean Rusk, interview with author, May 24, 1994.

14. McGeorge Bundy, interview with author, February 11, 1993.

15. Brands, *Cold Warriors,* p. 211.

16. John Kenneth Galbraith, *A Life in Our Times* (Boston: Houghton Mifflin, 1981), p. 395. He was particularly pleased with the epithet, "deeply unhygienic tribesmen," which he repeated mischievously almost thirty years later in an interview with the author in Cambridge, Massachusetts, March 14, 1994. As

for the overflights, he admitted in retrospect that he might have overreacted to the risk of their exposure.

17. Galbraith, *A Life in Our Times,* pp. 396–397.
18. Lhamo Tsering, interviews, October 1996 and February 1997.
19. Ngadruk, interview, November 1996.
20. Lhamo Tsering, interview, October 1996.
21. Lhamo Tsering, interview, April 1997.
22. U.S. embassy, New Delhi, telegram 1099, November 26, 1960, FRUS 1958–1960, vol. XIX, p. 814.
23. Confirmed by the parachute dispatch officer on these flights in an interview with the author on April 17, 1997.
24. These documents were released to the Library of Congress for use by the press and scholars on August 4, 1963; summarized in "Ordeals in China Show in U.S. Data," *New York Times,* August 5, 1963, p. 1, col. 7; and later published in full in James Cheng, *The Politics of the Chinese Red Army* (Stanford, Calif.: Stanford University Press, 1966).
25. Ambassador to India (Galbraith) to the Undersecretary of State for Economic Affairs (Ball), memorandum, November 30, 1961, FRUS 1961–1963, vol. XXII, pp. 170–171.
26. Lhamo Tsering, interview, April 1997.
27. Editorial note 155, FRUS 1961–1963, vol. XXII, p. 321.
28. Ernest A. Gross, "Tibetans Plan for Tomorrow," *Foreign Affairs* (October 1961), pp. 136–142.
29. Foreign Office, minute, October 20, 1961, FO 371/158596.
30. Herter and Thondup, memorandum of conversation, October 27, 1960, NARA RG 59, box 2162.
31. Merchant and Thondup, memorandum of conversation, October 27, 1960, NARA RG 59, box 2162.
32. Bowles and Stevenson, letters, March 17 and 27, 1961, NARA RG 59, box 2161. Stevenson was later to tell the president that it was his "opinion that the legal grounds for objection to China's action in taking over the administration of Tibet were relatively weak" (memorandum of conversation, August 5, 1961, FRUS 1961–1963, vol. XXII, p. 113).
33. Rusk to Dalai Lama, May 30, 1961, NARA RG 59, box 2161.
34. The author was instructed by Forrestal to deliver these assurances to Thondup, who had called on the president's brother Senator Edward Kennedy earlier that day.
35. Foreign Office, minute "Tibetan Item at the United Nations," December 14, 1961, FO 371/158601.

CHAPTER 14

1. Mullik, *The Chinese Betrayal*, pp. 178–181.

2. Nehru rejected the request from free India's first Armed Forces commander-in-chief for a formal policy direction, saying: "Rubbish! Total rubbish! We don't need a defense policy. Our policy is non-violence. We foresee no military threats. As far as I am concerned you can scrap the army—the police are good enough to meet our security needs." D. K. Palit, *War in High Himalaya* (London: Hurst and Company, 1991), p. 20.

3. It was not until late 1959 that responsibility for the defense of the northeastern frontier was transferred to the minister of Defense, and the Fourth Infantry Division, trained for tasks in the Punjab plains, took on this role along the 1,000 kilometer border. Palit, *War in High Himalaya*, pp. 46–47.

4. Mullik, *The Chinese Betrayal*, pp. 135–136.

5. Nehru and Herter, memorandum of conversation, October 7, 1960, FRUS 1958–1960, vol. XV, p. 567.

6. Palit, one of the recipients of the paper, describes its contents and his reaction to it in his book, *War in High Himalaya*, pp. 97–99.

7. Ibid., pp. 105–110.

8. Galbraith noted in his diary on July 12, 1962, that "part of the trouble [on the Chinese frontier], indeed, stems from Indian troops taking more advanced positions." When the first shooting occurred on the frontier two weeks later, this time he noted only that "our policy (mine) is to keep silent and seem to take no satisfaction out of this manifestation of the Cold War." *Ambassador's Journal* (Boston: Houghton Mifflin, 1969), p. 343.

   The crisis came to a head three months later. In neither the cables coming from the embassy in New Delhi nor from the State Department in Washington, is there is any mention of the possibility that the conflicts might have originated in the provocative military policies sanctioned by Nehru, which were accompanied by his deft evasion of Zhou's offers to settle the boundaries on terms he could not accept for fear of domestic political repercussions.

   By November, Galbraith had assumed the role he professed publicly to dislike, but admitted privately he enjoyed, of a "professor master minding the war." He was accordingly contemptuous of his State Department colleagues who had met in London in mid-November and concluded that the Chinese were "going to nibble at the border and then stop," thereby assuming "the mildest of Chinese ambitions" as "they couldn't handle anything else." He, "with more experience in government, and also a better knowledge of history," kept his assumptions "on the dismal side." Galbraith, *A Life in Our Times*, p. 419.

   Whatever the source of the conflict, by the time it had escalated into a confrontation and disaster for the Indians, it had become another case of Chinese aggression in the eyes of Washington and the West. Certainly the complex reasons that had caused Mao to come "roaring back" that summer from his self-imposed semiretirement to take charge of the opportunity offered by the Indian actions to expose Nehru as an old-time "imperialist" and to convince the international community of India's aggression were unknown then to Washington and even its learned ambassador in New Delhi. (Roderick McFarquhar provides the background to Mao's role in the Sino-Indian conflict in chapter 13 of his book, *The Origins of the Cultural Revolution, the Coming of the Cataclysm* [Oxford: Oxford University Press, 1997].)

After the Indians had suffered their calamitous defeat, a CIA Geographic Intelligence memorandum issued in November 1962, (CIA/RR GM 62-10, National Security files, India, box 108, Kennedy Library), made no mention of India's "forward policy" in this background article on the origin of the conflict. There was great sensitivity in Washington about admitting that the Indians might have provoked the border fight. Some months later General Maxwell Taylor, chairman of the Joint Chiefs of Staff told a Congressional Committee that the Indians had been "edging forward in the disputed area." The Department of Defense later issued a statement noting that "General Taylor's full testimony did not imply in any way that the Indians started, or might have been responsible for starting the hostilities . . . There is no question that the Chinese Communists were clearly the aggressors." Department of State, telegram 3747, April 18, 1963, NARA RG 59, box 3861.

9. Neville Maxwell, *India's China War* (New York: Pantheon Books, 1971), pp. 297–358.

10. Maxwell, *India's China War*, p. 328.

11. Roderick MacFarquhar, *The Origins of the Cultural Revolution, The Coming of the Cataclysm* (Oxford: Oxford University Press, 1997), p. 307.

12. Palit, *War in High Himalaya*, p. 223.

13. Lt. Gen. B. M. Kaul, *The Untold Story* (Bombay: Allied Publishers, 1967), p. 383.

14. Maxwell, *India's China War*, p. 340.

15. Ibid., p. 344.

16. MacFarquhar, *Origins of the Cultural Revolution*, p. 307.

17. Palit, *War in High Himalaya*, p. 296.

18. On January 21, 1963, the minister of Defense provided figures on Indian casualties in Ladakh and the North East Frontier from the attack of October 20 to date. In the North East Frontier 285 officers and men had been killed, 617 wounded, and 5,030 listed as missing. In Ladakh there were 37 dead, 59 wounded, and 460 missing. Of the total of 5,490 missing on both fronts, 405 had been repatriated, and the Chinese identified 789 men they were holding

as prisoners, plus another 2,156 prisoners yet to be identified. This still left 2,140 men unaccounted for. U.S. embassy, New Delhi, airgram 851, February 1, 1963, NARA RG 59, box 3861.

19. Galbraith, *A Life in Our Times,* p. 378.

20. U.S. embassy, New Delhi, cable 1889, Eyes Only for the President and Secretaries of State and Defense (delivered by Indian ambassador to the president), departmental telegram 2167, November 19, 1962, National Security files, India, Nehru Correspondence, box 111, Kennedy Library.

21. Department of State, telegram 2196, November 20, 1962, National Security files, India, Nehru Correspondence, box 111, Kennedy Library.

22. Roger Hilsman, *To Move a Nation* (Garden City, N.Y.: Doubleday and Co., 1967), p. 327.

23. James Critchfield, interview with author, December 5, 1996.

24. Hilsman, memorandum for the record, Roger Hilsman Papers, Sino-Indian Border Clash 1962, box 1, folder 18, Kennedy Library.

25. The following summer an air defense agreement was worked out to provide joint training exercises for Indian Air Force personnel in the use of complex radar and ground equipment for flying supersonic fighter planes. The Indian External Affairs ministry said this was part of the defense measures the government was taking to guard against a possible "large scale air attack by Communist China." The government also announced the acceptance of the U.S. offer to provide radar installations and a communications network to cover almost the entire northern border. Britain also was to provide electronic and communications equipment. The foreign ministry said that there was no commitment by the U.S. or Britain to go to India's defense in the event of an attack, although they had "agreed to consult with the Government of India in such a contingency." "India Agrees to Western Plans for Guarding Against Air Raid," *New York Times,* July 23, 1963, p. 3, col. 5.

26. Although highly critical of Mullik's role in urging Nehru to adopt the "forward line" policy, Palit wrote that "from the day I first called on Mullik I fell under his spell." *War in High Himalaya,* p. 161.

27. Galbraith, *A Life in Our Times,* p. 436.

28. Galbraith, interview, March 1994.

29. In an interview with the author, July 12, 1998, Critchfield described this calculated diversion.

30. Memorandum for Secretary Rusk, November 17, 1962, Hilsman Papers, Sino-Indian Border Clash 1962, box 1, folder 18, Kennedy Library.

31. James Critchfield, interview, July 12, 1998.

32. Maxwell, *India's China War,* pp. 417–443.

33. The issue lingered for many years. In 1993, Indian Prime Minister Narasimha Rao signed an agreement in Beijing under which both China and India rec-

ognized the line that had separated their troops since 1962. Where there were differences, they agreed to let experts check the boundary. They also agreed to reduce their forces along the border in conformity with "the principle of mutual and equal security," and to give prior notification of military exercises and to avoid air intrusions. But they insisted that references to the actual line of control did not prejudice their positions on the boundary question. Xuecheng Liu, *The Sino-Indian Border Dispute and Sino-Indian Relations* (Lanham, Md.: University Press of America, 1994), p. 3.

34. Many of these countries showed a remarkable lack of gratitude toward their former Indian patron. A Department of State summary of November 27, 1962, noted that, although all of the European and most of the African countries were either "strongly" or "moderately" for India, five others—Afghanistan, Burma, Ceylon, Indonesia, and Laos—were "generally neutral." Cambodia was "moderately" for China, and Pakistan, India's sworn enemy, "strongly" for China as a counterweight. Bureau of Intelligence and Research (INR) Intelligence Note, November 27, 1962, Hilsman Papers, Sino-Indian Border Clash 1962, folder 18, box 1, Kennedy library.

35. U.S. consulate, Hong Kong, general 1673, April 3, 1963, NARA RG 59, box 3861.

36. CIA Information report, November 29, 1962, National Security File, India, box 108, Kennedy Library.

37. Hilsman, *To Move a Nation,* p. 339.

38. Ibid.

39. Memorandum, September 11, 1963, NARA RG 59, box 3860.

40. Kennedy mentioned Baotou, which is located in Suiyuan province. It was the site of a 100,000,000–200,000,000 kilowatt reactor then capable of producing about 10 kilograms of plutonium 239 annually. Leo Yueh-yun Liu, *China as a Nuclear Power in World Politics* (London: Macmillan, 1972).

41. The Kennedy administration had used diplomatic channels a year earlier to signal that Washington had no intention of upsetting the status quo in China. On June 26, 1962, the U.S. ambassador in Warsaw was instructed to inform his Chinese counterpart in the dialogue that had been going on since 1955 that the U.S. would not support any Chinese Nationalist attempt to invade the mainland. This had been accompanied by a public warning that the U.S. continued to oppose the use of force by either side in the Taiwan Strait. It is not known what effect this reassurance may have had on Mao's decision to make a show of force on the Sino-Indian border that autumn. Hilsman, *To Move a Nation,* p. 319.

CHAPTER 15

1. Henry Kissinger, *Diplomacy* (New York: Simon and Schuster, 1994), p. 644.
2. Hilsman, *To Move a Nation,* p. 138.
3. Avedon, *In Exile from the Land of Snows,* pp. 129–130. Ken Conboy, *Elite Forces of India and Pakistan* (London: Osprey Press, 1992), pp. 23–24.
4. Thondup, interviews, November 1995.
5. Mullik, *The Chinese Betrayal,* p. 571.
6. Conboy, *Elite Forces of India and Pakistan,* p. 23.
7. Ibid., p. 27.
8. Avedon, *In Exile from the Land of Snows,* p. 129.
9. Described by Ngadruk, one of the company commanders whom Gyen Yeshe brought with him, in the November 1996 interview with the author previously cited.
10. Editorial note, document 189, FRUS 1961–1963, vol. XXII, p. 397.
11. Memorandum for the Special Group, January 9, 1964, document 337, FRUS 1964–1968, vol. XXX, China.
12. Lhamo Tsering, the Tibetan representative at the center from 1963 to 1974, described its establishment and functioning in the interview previously cited with the author in October 1996. Thinlay Paljor and Wangchuk Tsering, who also served at the Center during this time, provided further details in interviews in Kathmandu on October 19 and 20, 1996.
13. George Patterson, in his book *A Fool at Forty* (Waco, Texas: Word Books, 1970), describes the whole venture.
14. Lhamo Tsering, interview, February 1997.
15. Lhamo Tsering to the author, letter, August 12, 1997.
16. Lhamo Tsering, interview, October 1996.
17. Kundeling Thubten Gyantsen and Tenzing Tsultrim described the operations in which they participated; interviews with author, November 4 and November 5, 1996.
18. Lhamo Tsering, interview, October 1996.
19. U.S. embassy, New Delhi, dispatch A-1113, May 7, 1964, NARA RG 59, box 2741.
20. State Department, telegram 1985, March 31, 1964, NARA RG 59, box 2741. The annual budget is listed in the January 9, 1964, Special Group memo previously cited.
21. Ford, *Wind Between the Worlds,* p. 75.
22. Thinlay Paljor, Lobsang Tsultrim, Wangchuk Tsering, and Tashi Chutter, who were members of either the first or second groups, described their training and the subsequent assignments of their teammates in interviews with the author in Kathmandu and New Delhi during October 1996. In an interview

in London in November 1996, Mrs. Takla spoke highly of the training she received at Cornell.

23. U.S. embassy, New Delhi, telegram 1143, October 29, 1965, NARA RG 59, box 2741. This official show of public support for the Tibetans indicates that Prime Minister Lal Bahadur Shastri may have moved from his earlier show of caution.

24. Shastri's offer to Thondup was reported in State Department telegram 435, August 10, 1964. Gundevia's advice to Thondup was reported in U.S. embassy, New Delhi, telegram 752, September 2, 1964, NARA RG 59, box 2741.

25. Foreign Office, minute, November 25, 1964, FO 371/176127.

26. Mountbatten–Home correspondence, May 1963, FO 371/170879.

27. Department of State, telegram 435, August 10, 1964, NARA RG 59, box 2741.

28. USUN telegram, October 30, 1964, NARA RG 59, box 2741.

29. Jonathan D. Pollack, "China's Agonizing Reappraisal," in Herbert J. Ellison, ed., *The Sino-Soviet Conflict* (Seattle, Wash.: University of Washington Press, 1982).

30. Gyalo Thondup described the negotiations in interviews with the author in Kalimpong in November 1995. An authority within the Oriental Institute of the Academy of Sciences in Moscow, who does not wish to be identified, confirmed in 1997 that it was general knowledge in those circles that the KGB conducted these negotiations with Thondup.

Chapter 16

1. This description is based on the author's previously cited interview on October 26, 1996, with Lhamo Tsering, the Tibetan representative at the Combined Operations. It has been supplemented by the notes made by Lhamo Tsering's son, Tenzing Sonam, on his father's days at Mustang, made available to the author in interviews on November 10 to 15, 1997. The information on resettlement projects was provided in interviews during October 1996 with Wangchuk Tsering, Lobsang Tsultrim, and Thinlay Paljor, three of the men who carried out the projects.

2. Lhamo Tsering, interview, February 1997.

3. Memorandum for the 303 Committee, January 26, 1968, FRUS 1968, China, vol. XXX, document 342.

4. David Anderson, U.S. aide and translator at Warsaw, interview with author, November 5, 1997.

5. In briefing the 303 Committee on March 1968, Critchfield said that "the Tibetans by nature did not appear to be congenitally inclined toward conspiratorial proficiency." This opinion was not shared by his Far East Division colleagues.

6. Marshall Green, interview with author, July 7, 1996.

7. Gyalo Thondup reemerged to play an active part in Tibetan political affairs in 1978 when he was invited to Beijing by Deng Xiaoping to open communications between China's then paramount leader and the Dalai Lama. Thereafter he made fifteen trips to China, usually accompanied by his son Khedroob, and engaged in negotiations to find a formula that would permit the Dalai Lama to return to Lhasa in a position of substance and play a meaningful role in the life of the Tibetan people. As of this writing, Thondup remains active in this pursuit.

8. Jamyang Norbu, interview with author, December 19, 1995.

9. Tenzing Sonam, interviews, November 1997.

10. Lhamo Tsering's notes report the final payment to the Mustang force was made late in 1973.

11. Telephone interview with the author, November 7, 1997.

12. Dalai Lama, *Autobiography*, p. 192.

13. Lhamo Tsering estimates that at this time there were about 1,800 active guerillas and retired veterans in Mustang.

14. Lhamo Tsering to author, communication by E-mail, December 26, 1997, and July 27, 1998. The Nepalese had been alerted to Wangdu's presence by a disaffected member of his group; Wangdu had also taken two border guards hostage but released them before setting out. None of these had known that Wangdu originally was heading for Tibet, and it was only the unforeseen presence of the Chinese troops that forced him back into the ambush laid by the Nepalese on the mistaken assumption that he had always planned to cross into India over the Tinker Pass.

15. Avedon, *In Exile from the Land of Snows*, pp. 128–129.

16. The faithful Ragra died in Nepal shortly after he and Lhamo Tsering were released from prison in 1981. Lhamo Tsering, interview, February 1997.

17. Avedon, *In Exile from the Land of Snows*, p. 130; Conboy, *Elite Forces of India and Pakistan*, p. 27.

18. William M. Leary describes the use of these fields in "Secret Mission to Tibet."

19. Sonam Palden, interview with author, September 6, 1997.

20. Jamyang Norbu, interview with author, September 14, 1997.

21. Conboy, *Elite Forces of India and Pakistan*, p. 27.

22. State Department, memorandum of conversation, December 17, 1965, NARA RG 59, box 2741.

23. Department of State, telegram 1766, March 13, 1966, NARA RG 59, box 2741.

24. U.S. embassy, New Delhi, telegram 2614, March 29, 1966, NARA RG 59, box 2741.

25. Correspondence in the Chester Bowles Papers, box 331, folder 0090, Yale University Library.

26. Henry Kissinger, *The White House Years* (Boston: Little Brown, 1979), p. 169.

27. Kissinger, *The White House Years,* p. 179.
28. Ibid., p. 180.
29. Lord to the author, message by fax, February 14, 1997.
30. Holdridge, telephone interview with author, November 6, 1997.
31. Kissinger says he recalls no discussions or communications with the Chinese concerning the support the U.S. government had or was giving to the Tibetans during the time that he served as President Nixon's Adviser or secretary of state. Former ambassador L. Paul Bremer provided Kissenger's comments in a telephone call to the author February 10, 1998.

    Deng Xiaoping did "complain about the Dalai Lama" to Kissinger when he accompanied President Ford to Beijing in October 1975. He and Deng also made a passing, laughing reference to the Dalai Lama's government-in-exile during their talks. William Burr, ed., *The Kissinger Transcripts* (New York: The New Press, 1999), pp. 403, 405.
32. Rusk, interview, May 27, 1994.
33. Kissinger to President Nixon, memorandum, *My Trip to China,* March 2, 1973, Nixon Documents file, NARA.
34. Kissinger to President Nixon, memorandum, *My Asian Trip,* February 27, 1973, Nixon Documents file, NARA.
35. Phuntso Thonden, chief of the New York office at that time, recalled the heated luncheon at which the termination notice was served and rejected. Interview with author, April 30, 1997.
36. None of the CIA directors who served before, during, and after 1973, i.e. Richard Helms, James Schlesinger, or William Colby, could recall any meetings of the Special Group that made the decision to end the subsidy to the Dalai Lama. It was suggested that the action may have taken place at the verbal request of Dr. Kissinger. Helms and Schlesinger, interviews with author, March 1998; Colby, interview.

CHAPTER 17

1. The Dalai Lama may have had an exaggerated idea of the arms dropped by the CIA up to the time he fled to India. The two drops made in late 1958 and early 1959 contained 403 Lee Enfield rifles, 20 machine guns, 60 hand grenades, and 26,000 rounds of ammunition. Only part of these weapons had been distributed before he left Lhasa in March 1959.
2. The Chinese made the Panchen Lama pay for his defiance. In 1964 he was prosecuted and then imprisoned for fourteen years. After his release and until his death in 1989, he continued to protest Beijing's encouragement of Han immigration and other policies resulting in cultural and environmental degradation in Tibet.

3. Goodman, *The Last Dalai Lama,* p. 327.

4. Response to question raised following the Dalai Lama's address at Harvard's John F. Kennedy School of Government, September 10, 1995.

5. The Dalai Lama's secretary, Tenzin Geyche Tethong, reaffirmed these views in a follow-up letter to the author dated December 22, 1995.

6. The Dalai Lama, interviewed by Claudia Dreifus, *New York Times Magazine* (November 28, 1993), pp. 52–54.

7. Thondup, interview, November 7, 1996.

8. Lhamo Tsering to the author, letter, February 4, 1998.

9. Ngadruk, interview with author's son, January 1997.

10. Tenzing Sonam, interview with Athar, June 1998; copy provided to the author.

11. Nyemo Bhusang, interview with author, October 1997.

12. Tsering Paljor Phupatsang (Tim's son), letter to the author, October 20, 1998.

13. Tenzing Sonam, letter to the author, February 4, 1998.

14. Rusk, interview, May 27, 1994.

15. Department of State, telegram 03019, November 6, 1959, NARA RG 59, folder 3951.

16. "Relations of the United States with Tibet," in *Country Reports on Human Rights Practices for 1994,* (Washington, D.C.: Department of State, October 1994). Repeated requests to both the Department's Office of Chinese Affairs and the Office of Legal Affairs for the identity of the person who made these acknowledgments have gone unanswered.

17. Morton Halperin, interview with author, March 22, 1994.

The archival documentation for this book has been obtained from the following collections of papers at these libraries and records centers:

National Archives (NARA), College Park, Md.: Department of State records; Office of Strategic Services records; Richard Nixon documents.

Library of Congress, Washington, D.C.: Papers of Averell Harriman; Papers of General Nathan Twining.

New York Historical Society: Papers of Robert A. Lovett.

Yale University, Beinecke Library: Papers of Dean Acheson; Papers of Chester Bowles.

Princeton University, Seeley G. Mudd Library: Papers of Allen W. Dulles; Papers of John Foster Dulles; Papers of Adlai E. Stevenson.

Columbia University: Ellsworth Bunker correspondence.

Stanford University, Hoover Institution: Papers of o. Edmund Clubb; Papers of Stanley K. Hornbeck; American Emergency Committee for Tibetan Refugees.

Franklin D. Roosevelt Library, Hyde Park, N.Y.: Papers of President Roosevelt; Papers of Eleanor Roosevelt; Papers of Harry Hopkins.

Harry S. Truman Library, Independence, Mo.: Papers of President Truman; Papers of Dean Acheson; Oral history of John S Service; Oral history of o. Edmund Clubb.

Dwight D. Eisenhower Library, Abilene, Kan.: Papers of President Eisenhower; Papers of John Foster Dulles; Papers of Christian A. Herter.

John F. Kennedy Library, Boston, Mass.: Papers of President Kennedy; Papers of McGeorge Bundy; Papers of Roger Hilsman; Papers of James C. Thomson.

Lyndon B. Johnson Library, Austin, Tex.: Papers of President Johnson.

Gerald R. Ford Library, Ann Arbor, Mich.: Papers of President Ford.

All documents relating to the British relationship with Tibet were obtained from the Public Record Office (PRO) in Kew, Richmond, Surrey.

Acheson, Dean. *Present at the Creation*. New York: W. W. Norton and Company, 1969.

Andrugtsang, Gompo Tashi. *Four Rivers, Six Ranges.* Dharamsala, India: Information and Publicity Office of the Dalai Lama, 1973.

Avedon, John F. *In Exile in the Land of Snows.* New York: Knopf, 1984.

Bagby, Wesley M. *The Eagle-Dragon Alliance.* Newark, Del.: University of Delaware Press, 1992.

Bailey, F. M. *No Passport to Tibet.* London: Rupert Hart-Davis, 1957.

Bell, Charles. *The People of Tibet.* Oxford: Clarendon Press, 1928.

———. *Portrait of a Dalai Lama.* London: Collins, 1946.

———. *Tibet Past and Present.* Oxford: Clarendon, 1924.

Beschloss, Michael R. *Mayday.* New York: Harper and Row, 1986.

Bhargava, G. S. *The Battle of NEFA.* Bombay, India: Allied Publishers, 1964.

Brands, H. W. *Cold Warriors.* New York: Columbia University Press, 1988.

———. *Inside the Cold War, Loy Henderson and the Rise of the American Empire 1918–1961.* New York: Oxford University Press, 1991.

Brendon, Piers. *Ike.* New York: Harper and Row, 1986.

Burr, William, ed. *The Kissinger Transcripts.* New York: The New Press, 1999.

Cammann, Schuyler. *The Land of the Camel.* New York: Ronald Press, 1951.

———. *Trade through the Himalayas.* Westport, Conn.: Greenwood Press, 1951.

Carrasco, Pedro. *Land and Polity in Tibet.* Seattle, Wash.: University of Washington, 1959.

Carter, Carolle J. *Mission to Yenan.* Lexington, Ky.: University of Kentucky Press, 1997.

Chapman, Spencer. *Lhasa the Holy City.* London: Readers Union Ltd., 1940.

Cheng, James. *The Politics of the Chinese Red Army.* Palo Alto, Calif.: Stanford University Press, 1966.

Church, Frank. *Final Report of the Select Committee to Study Governmental Operations with Respect to Intelligence Activities.* United States Senate, Washington, D.C.: U.S. Government Printing Office, 1976.

Chutter, Tashi. *Confidential Study on Deployment of Chinese Occupational Force in Tibet.* New Delhi, India: Private printing, 1998.

Conboy, Ken. *Elite Forces of India and Pakistan.* London: Osprey Press, 1992.

Cook, Blanche Wiesen. *The Declassified Eisenhower.* New York: Doubleday and Company, 1981.

Craig, Mary. *Kundun.* Washington, D.C.: Counterpoint, 1997.

Crankshaw, Edward. *Khrushchev.* New York: Viking Press, 1966.

———. *Khrushchev Remembers.* Boston: Little, Brown and Company, 1970.

Cutting, Suydam. *The Fire Ox and Other Years.* New York: Charles Scribner's Sons, 1940.

Dalai Lama. *Freedom in Exile.* New York: HarperCollins, 1990.

———. *From Liberation to Liberalisation.* Dharamsala, India: Information and Publicity Office of the Dalai Lama, 1982.

————. *My Land and My People.* New York: McGraw Hill, 1962.

————. *Tibet under Chinese Communist Rule.* Dharamsala, India: Information and Publicity Office of the Dalai Lama, 1976.

Darling, Arthur B. *The Central Intelligence Agency.* University Park, Penn.: Pennsylvania State University Press, 1990.

Davies, John P. *Dragon by the Tail.* New York: W. W. Norton, 1972.

De Riencourt, Amaury. *Roof of the World.* New York: Rinehart, 1950.

Douglas, William O. *Beyond the High Himalayas.* Garden City, N.Y.: Doubleday, 1952.

Enders, Gordon B. *Nowhere Else in the World.* London: Hurst and Blackett, 1936.

Ekvall, Robert B. *Tibetan Sky Lines.* New York: Farrar, Straus and Young, 1952.

Ellison, Herbert J., ed. *The Sino-Soviet Conflict.* Seattle, Wash.: University of Washington Press, 1982.

Fisher, Margaret W., Leo E. Rose, and Robert A. Huttebback. *Himalayan Battleground.* London: Pall Mall Press, 1963.

Fleming, Peter. *Bayonets to Lhasa.* New York: Harper Brothers, 1961.

Ford, Robert. *Wind Between the Worlds.* New York: David McKay Company, 1957.

Galbraith, John Kenneth. *A Life in Our Times.* Boston: Houghton Mifflin, 1981.

————. *Ambassador's Journal.* Boston: Houghton Mifflin, 1969.

Gelder, Stuart, and Roma Gelder. *The Timely Rain.* London: Hutchinson, 1964.

Goldstein, Melvyn C. *A History of Modern Tibet, 1913–1951.* Berkeley, Calif.: University of California Press, 1989.

————. *The Snow Lion and the Dragon.* Berkeley, Calif.: University of California Press, 1997.

Goodman, Michael. *The Last Dalai Lama.* Boston: Shambala, 1986.

Goodwin, Doris Kearns. *No Ordinary Time.* New York: Simon and Schuster, 1994.

Gould, B. J. *The Jewel in the Lotus.* London: Chatto and Windus, 1957.

Gross, Ernest A. *The United Nations: Structure for Peace.* Published for the Council on Foreign Relations. New York: Harper and Brothers, 1962.

Grunfeld, A. Tom. *The Making of Modern Tibet.* Armonk, N.Y.: M. E. Sharpe, 1996.

Halperin, Morton H. *Self-Determination in the New World Order.* Washington, D.C.: Carnegie Endowment for International Peace, 1992.

Han Suyin. *Lhasa, the Open City.* London: Jonathan Cape, 1977.

Hedin, Sven. *A Conquest of Tibet.* New York: E. P. Dutton, 1934.

————. *Trans-Himalaya, Discoveries and Adventures in Tibet.* 3 vols. London: Macmillan, 1910.

Hicks, Roger. *Great Ocean.* London: Penguin Books, 1990.

Hoffmann, Helmut. *The Religions of Tibet.* London: Allen and Unwin, 1961.

Holdrich, Sir Thomas. *Tibet the Mysterious.* London: Alton Rivers, 1906.

Holdridge, John H. *Crossing the Divide.* Lanham, Md.: Rowman and Littlefield, 1997.

Hopkirk, Peter. *The Great Game.* New York: Kodansha International, 1992.

————. *Trespassers on the Roof of the World.* London: John Murray, 1982.

International Commission of Jurists. *The Question of Tibet and the Rule of Law.* Geneva: H. Studer S.A., 1959.

Jebb, Gladwyn (Lord Gladwyn). *The Memoirs of Lord Gladwyn.* London: Weidenfeld and Nicolson, 1972.

Karnik, V. B. *China Invades India.* Bombay, India: Allied Publishers, 1963.

Kimura, Hisao. *Japanese Agent in Tibet.* London: Serindia Publications, 1990.

Landon, Perceval. *The Opening of Tibet.* New York: Doubleday, 1905.

Lazar, Edward, ed. *Tibet: The Issue is Independence.* Berkeley, Calif.: Parallax Press, 1994.

Leary, William M. "Secret Mission to Tibet." *Air and Space Magazine* (December 1997/January 1998), pp. 62-71.

Lhalungha, Lobsang P. *Tibet, the Sacred Realm.* Millerton, New York: Aperture Inc., 1983.

Li, Tieh-tseng. *The Historical Status of Tibet.* New York: King's Crown Press, Columbia University, 1956.

Liu, Leo Yueh-yun. *China as a Nuclear Power in World Politics.* London: Macmillan, 1972.

Liu, Xuecheng. *The Sino-Indian Border Dispute and Sino-Indian Relations.* Lanham, Md.: University Press of America, 1994.

Long, Jeff. "Going After Wangdu." *Rocky Mountain Magazine* (July/August 1981), pp. 36–42.

Low, Alfred D. *The Sino-Soviet Dispute.* Cranbury, N.J.: Fairleigh Dickinson University Press, 1976.

MacDonald, Malcolm. *Inside China.* Boston: Little, Brown and Company, 1980.

MacFarquhar, Roderick. *The Origins of the Cultural Revolution, the Coming of the Cataclysm.* Oxford: Oxford University Press, 1997.

MacFarquhar, Roderick, ed. *The Politics of China, 1949–1989.* Cambridge: Cambridge University Press, 1993.

MacFarquhar, Roderick, ed., with the assistance of Timothy Chhek, Eugene Wu, *The Secret Speeches of Chairman Mao: From the Hundred Flowers to the Great Leap Forward.* Cambridge, Mass.: Council on East Asian Studies, Harvard University, 1989.

Mankekar, D. R. *The Guilty Men of 1962.* Bombay, India: Tulsi Shah Enterprises, 1968.

Maraini, Fosco. *Secret Tibet.* New York: Viking Press, 1952.

Marchetti, Victor, and John D. Marks. *The CIA and the Cult of Intelligence.* New York: Alfred A. Knopf, 1974.

Maxwell, Neville. *India's China War.* New York: Pantheon Books, 1971.

May, Ernest R. *The Kennedy Tapes: Inside the White House during the Cuban Missile Crisis.* Cambridge, Mass.: Harvard University Press, 1997.

————. *The Truman Administration in China.* Philadelphia, Pa.: Lippincott, 1975.

McCarthy, Roger E. *Tears of the Lotus.* Jefferson, N.C.: McFarland and Company, 1997.

McGovern, William M. *To Lhasa in Disguise.* New York: Century, 1924.

McNallen, Steve. "Leadville to Lhasa." *Soldier of Fortune* (April 1991), pp. 74–79.

Menon, V. K. Krishna. *India and the Chinese Invasion.* Bombay, India: Contemporary Publishers, 1963.

Mullik, B. N. *The Chinese Betrayal, My Years with Nehru.* Bombay, India: Allied Publishers, 1971.

Mullin, Chris. "Tibetan Conspiracy." *Far Eastern Economic Review* 39(36)(5 September, 1975): pp. 30–34.

Nanporia, N. J. *The Sino-Indian Dispute.* Bombay, India: *The Times of India,* 1963.

National Security Archives, Laurence Chang, and Peter Kornbluh. *The Cuban Missile Crisis.* New York: New Press, 1992.

New York Times. The Pentagon Papers. New York: Bantam Books, 1971.

Norbu, Dawa. *Red Star over Tibet.* London: Collins, 1974.

Norbu, Jamyang. *Warriors of Tibet.* London: Wisdom Publications, 1986.

Norbu, Thubten J. *Tibet is My Country.* New York: Dutton, 1961.

Palit, D. K. *War in High Himalaya.* London: Hurst and Company, 1991.

Pallis, Marco. *The Way and the Mountain.* London: Peter Owen Ltd., 1961.

————. *Peaks and Lamas.* New York: Alfred A. Knopf, 1949.

Panchen Lama. Petition, 1962, printed in *A Poisoned Arrow,* London: Tibet Information Network, 1997.

Panikkar, K. M. *Geographical Factors in Indian History.* Bombay, India: Bharatiya Vidya Bhavan, 1955.

————. *In Two Chinas.* London: Allen and Unwin, 1955.

Patterson, George N. *A Fool at Forty.* Waco, Tex.: Word Books, 1970.

————. "China and Tibet, Background to the Revolt." *China Quarterly* (1) (January–March 1960): pp. 87–102.

————. *God's Fool.* London: Faber and Faber, 1956.

————. *Requiem for Tibet.* London: Aurum Press, 1990.

————. *Tibet in Revolt.* London: Faber and Faber, 1960.

Peissel, Michel. *Mustang, The Secret Kingdom.* New York: E. P. Dutton, 1967.

————. *The Last Barbarian.* New York: Henry Holt and Company, 1997.

————. *The Secret War in Tibet.* Boston: Little, Brown and Company, 1972.

Pereira, Sir Cecil. *Peking to Lhasa.* Boston: Houghton Mifflin, 1926.

Prouty, L. Fletcher. "Colorado to Kokonor." *The Denver Post* (February 6, 1972), pp. 10-17.

Ranelagh, John. *The Agency, The Rise and Decline of the CIA.* New York: Simon and Schuster, 1986.

Robbins, Christopher. *Air America.* London: Corgi/Transworld Publishers Ltd.,

1988. (Originally published in the U.K. as *The Invisible Air Force: The True Story of the CIA's Secret Airlines.* London: Macmillan, 1979.)

Rockhill, William Woodville. *The Land of the Lamas.* London: Longmans, Green and Company, 1891.

Rositzke, Harry. *The CIA's Secret Operations.* New York: Reader's Digest Press, 1977.

Schlesinger, Arthur M., Jr. *A Thousand Days.* Boston: Houghton Mifflin, 1965.

Schram, Stuart R. *Mao's Road to Power.* Vols 1–3. Armonk, N.Y.: Eastgate Books, M. E. Sharpe, 1995.

Sen, Chanakya. *Tibet Disappears.* Bombay, India: Asia Publishing House, 1960.

Seth, Vikram. *From Heaven Lake.* New York: Vintage Books, 1987.

Shakabpa, Tsepon W. D. *Tibet, A Political History.* New York: Potala Publications, 1984.

Shelton, Albert L. *Pioneering in Tibet.* London: Fleming H. Revell, 1921.

Shen, Tsung-lien. *Tibet and the Tibetans.* Stanford, Calif.: Stanford University Press, 1953.

Sis, Peter. *Tibet: Through the Red Box.* New York: Farrar, Straus and Giroux, 1998.

Smith, Warren W. *Tibetan Nation: A History of Tibetan Nationalism and Sino-Tibetan Relations.* Boulder, Col.: Westview Press, 1996.

Snow, Edgar. *Red Star over China.* New York: Random House, 1938.

Stevens, Herbert. *Through Deep Defiles to Tibetan Uplands.* London: Witherby, 1934.

Strong, Anna Louise. *When Serfs Stood Up in Tibet.* Beijing, China: New World Press, 1960.

Sun, Yat-sen. *The Three Principles of the People.* Taipei, Taiwan: China Cultural Service, 1981.

Suyin-han. *My House has Two Doors.* New York: G. P. Putnam's Sons, 1980.

Taring, Rinchen Dolma. *Daughter of Tibet.* London: Wisdom Publications, 1986.

Teichman, Eric. *Travels of a Consular Officer in Tibet.* Cambridge: Cambridge University Press, 1922.

Thomas, Evan. *The Very Best Men.* New York: Simon and Schuster, 1995.

Thomas, Lowell, Jr. *Out of this World.* New York: The Greystone Press, 1950.

————. *The Silent War in Tibet.* New York: Doubleday and Co, 1959.

Tsering, Lhamo. *Resistance, bTsan rGol rGyal sKyob.* Vol. 1. Dharamsala, India: Amnye Machen Press, 1993.

Tucci, Giuseppi. *To Lhasa and Beyond.* Rome, Italy: Instituto Poligrafico della Stato, 1956.

Varg, Paul A. *Open Door Diplomat.* Urbana, Ill.: University of Illinois Press, 1952.

Younghusband, Sir Francis. *India and Tibet.* London: J. Murray, 1910.

ACKNOWLEDGMENTS

This book had its origin at the Kennedy School of Government at Harvard University where I planned to write it as a case study for students planning to make their careers in government service. After some months of research, it became apparent that some documents needed for it were not going to be released by the CIA. I consequently decided to write a book that would be available to anyone interested in how the U.S. government became involved in Tibetan affairs using the documents and papers available in public archives and the memories and journals of those of us Americans and the Tibetans who were part of this relationship. This turned out to be a five year project, which never would have been completed without the wise counsel and encouragement of Professor Roderick MacFarquhar, for which I shall always be grateful. Professor Ernest Vogel generously granted me the privilege of association with the Fairbank Center for Far Eastern Research at Harvard and the use of its facilities, which made the whole thing possible. I can only hope that this book will reflect the high intellectual standards and stimulating atmosphere of this Center, named for one of this country's most distinguished scholars on Chinese affairs. I am also indebted to Professors Samuel P. Huntington and Ernest R. May for their continued interest throughout the lengthy period of this work in progress.

For forty years I have enjoyed the friendship that grows out of a shared endeavor with the Dalai Lama's family, particularly Mr. Gyalo Thondup. In the past four years he has spent days with me in India discussing his role in providing political leadership and support to the Tibetan resistance and representing his country's cause abroad. Subjectively, Mr. Thondup has never made any bones about promoting his own agenda of working for the return of the Dalai Lama to his country. Objectively, as an intelligence officer, I have always known him as a man of integrity and honesty and given appropriate weight to his account of the events described in this book. The Dalai Lama's oldest brother Norbu, a man of equally strong convictions and integrity, and his youngest brother Tenzing Choegyal, who has shared his family's sense of commitment, have been equally forthcoming. Gyalo's son, Khedroob, has contributed invaluable help by sharing his unique and candid insights into the events described in this book from his vantage point as both an observer and a participant. He also generously provided photographs from his family's collection. Phuntso Tashi, who played a role in several of the critical events in this history, graciously provided his recollection of several of the events in which he participated.

For the details of the operations that the CIA conducted in support of the resistance, I have had the invaluable assistance of Mr. Lhamo Tsering, who died in January 1999 after a lifetime of service to his country. I had known and respected him for four decades. His superb memory was supplemented by the detailed journal of the CIA's relationship with his people that this able and dedicated man kept. His son Sonam Tenzing and son-in-law Jamyang Norbu have extended the same courtesy and support. Over two dozen Tibetans who were resistance leaders or fighters, members of teams sent into Tibet or those who helped us train their comrades, talked freely and at length to me in Darjeeling, Kalimpong, Dharamsala, New Delhi, Kathmandu, and in Cambridge about their participation in these events. There were differences of opinion among them, and they voiced both their criticisms and their approvals for what their leaders and the U.S. government tried to do. In a very real sense it is their book, as it couldn't have been written without them.

My colleagues were extraordinarily helpful in sharing their recollections to piece together what we did and what we tried to do in the operations that were a vital part of this history. They include: William Broe, James Critchfield, John Greaney, Sam Halpern, John Hart, Frank Holober, David Hoopes, John Horton, Joan Kiernan, Fred Latrash, Roger McCarthy, Thomas Parrott, Tony Poe, Bill Smith, John Turner, Bruce Walker, Jack Wall, John Waller, and William Wells; those who must be identified only by the initial of their last names: John B., William G., Kenneth M., John R., Raymond S., and Gar T.; and others who must remain unnamed. Some were enthusiastic supporters and others were more skeptical, but they all wanted to help my efforts to keep the record straight.

Those who were making the policy that determined the objectives and scope of the U.S. government's involvement in Tibetan affairs over the thirty years covered in this book also gave generously of their time and memories. Some were there when the U.S. government first became interested in Tibet, others were there when we decided to leave the Tibetans on their own. While they had differing views on whether and how our government should support the Tibetans, they were all kind enough to share them so that I might write an accurate history of U.S. policy commitments concerning Tibet. Any failings on this score are mine, as the following persons very kindly tried to help: Donald Anderson, McGeorge Bundy, William P. Bundy, L. Paul Bremer, William I. Cargo, William E. Colby, John Kenneth Galbraith, Marshall Green, Morton Halperin, Richard M. Helms, Roger Hilsman, John Holdridge, U. Alexis Johnson, James Lilley, Franklin A. Lindsay, Winston Lord, James R. Schlesinger, Phillips Talbot, and Nicholas G. Thacher.

For the unique insights on the efforts made by the U.S. on behalf of the Tibetans in their appeals to the United Nations and on the behavior of those countries to whom we looked with varying degrees of success for support, I am deeply indebted to Ernest Gross. Over the past forty years this wise statesman has graciously shared with me his perceptive understanding of these events and the times and people that shaped them. George Patterson and I have differing evaluations of some of the events and personalities described in this book. He has, however, been unfailingly generous about sharing his recollections and reflections on his life among the Khampas that he knows and cares very much about and about the negotiations for which he acted as interpreter and middleman when the U.S. government began its efforts to influence the affairs of the Dalai Lama. I am grateful to him. I am also indebted to David Schimmelpennick, who shared his knowledge and scholarly findings concerning Russia's historic interest in Tibet and kindly aided me in obtaining verification of Moscow's reentry into the Great Game, and to Colonel David Longacre, who happily recalled his days as an OSS colleague of Ilya Tolstoy and gave me a print of an OSS film of Tolstoy's visit to Lhasa. Like everyone interested in understanding the background of the events covered in this book, I am indebted to Melvyn Goldstein for his incomparable *A History of Modern Tibet, 1913–1951.*

The documents cited in this book came from the National Archives, the Truman, Eisenhower, Johnson, and Kennedy Presidential Libraries and the papers of various participants held by the Columbia, Princeton, Stanford, and Yale University libraries and the Library of Congress in this country and the British Public Records Office in Kew Gardens. Many people at these institutions helped me, but I would like to thank particularly that great friend of all research scholars at the National Archives, John Taylor, and Dennis Bilger, Suzanne Forbes, and Paul Droghi at the Eisenhower, Kennedy, and Yale libraries respectively for their interest and assistance. I am indebted to Emily MacFarquhar, Patrick Tyler, and Esmond Harmsworth for helping me find a publisher, and I am particularly indebted to Peter Osnos who had the faith to accept a manuscript on a controversial subject. I am also grateful to Lawrence Malkin for his experienced editorial eye, which helped convert my manuscript into a book that people might want to read; to Geoff Shandler, who acted as an understanding and judicious final arbiter in the inevitably painful editorial process that made the book convey what I wanted to say; and to Robert Kimzey for his meticulous and imaginative work in pulling it all together.

Lastly, but especially, I would like to thank my wife. She understood and came to share my special regard for the Tibetans, and her love and unfailing support throughout my career enabled me to write this book. She has read and provided invaluable advice on the numerous several drafts, and the final product reflects her generous contributions, making it a joint endeavor, as our life together for the past forty happy years has been. I have also had the great good fortune of having children who have participated in this endeavor: Maggie, my cheerleader, who freely gave of her enthusiasm and artistic talents to assemble and prepare the photographs, and her husband Alex, who gave his discerning interest and advice; Holley, who has always been my moral compass; and John, with whom I had a father's rare privilege of sharing a trip to revisit the origins of my long-held admiration for the Tibetans—whom he has also come to know and respect. Thank you all.

The seven-year-old. . . : U.S. National Archives Still Picture Collection.
The Potala with a carved stone pillar. . . : Khedroob Thondup Collection (It is also on page 18 of his book *Tibet in Turmoil* [Tokyo: Nihon Kogyo Shinbun, 1983.])
Reception party meeting. . . : U.S. National Archives Still Picture Collection.
Major Ilya Tolstoy. . . : U.S. National Archives Still Picture Collection.
F.D.R.'s presents. . . : U.S. National Archives Still Picture Collection.
Reting, the former Regent. . . : U.S. National Archives Still Picture Collection.
Taktra, the Regent. . . : U.S. National Archives Still Picture Collection.
Major Tolstoy and Captain Dolen. . . : U.S. National Archives Still Picture Collection.
The Tolstoy mission. . . : U.S. National Archives Still Picture Collection.
Yangpel Pandatsang. . . : U.S. National Archives Still Picture Collection.
George Patterson. . . : provided by George N. Patterson.
Robert Ford. . . : provided by George N. Patterson.
Chamdo, the site of the final battle. . . : U.S. National Archives Still Picture Collection.
Monastery at Yatung. . . : Tseten Tashi Studio, Gangtok Sikkim.
The Tibetan delegation. . . : Khedroob Thondup Collection (also p. 25, *Tibet in Turmoil*).
Gyayum Chenmo. . . : Khedroob Thondup Collection.
Palanquin carrying the Dalai Lama. . . : Tseten Tashi Studio.
Dalai Lama's camp. . . : Tseten Tashi Studio.
Dalai Lama's retinue. . . : Tseten Tashi Studio.
The new era arrives. . . : Tseten Tashi Studio.
Lhasa residents returning. . . : Tseten Tashi Studio.
The Dalai Lama and the Panchen Lama. . . : Khedroob Thondup Collection (also p. 30, *Tibet in Turmoil*).
Gyalo Thondup. . . : Khedroob Thondup Collection.
From left to right, Lhamo Tsering. . . : Khedroob Thondup Collection.
The Dalai Lama's older brother. . . : Khedroob Thondup Collection.
Thubten Jigme Norbu. . . : courtesy Mr. Heinrich Harrer.
Gompo Tashi Andrutsang. . . : in Gompo Tashi, *Four Rivers, Six Ranges,* Dharamsala, India, Information Office of H.H. the Dalai Lama.
Members of the Volunteer Freedom Fighters. . . : Khedroob Thondup Collection (also p. 104, *Tibet in Turmoil*).
A group of Volunteer. . . : Khedroob Thondup Collection (also p. 101, *Tibet in Turmoil*).
Lhuntse Dzong. . . : Khedroob Thondup Collection (also p. 109, *Tibet in Turmoil*).
Soldiers in front . . . : Khedroob Thondup Collection (also p. 21, *Tibet in Turmoil*).
Tibetan resistance. . . : Khedroob Thondup Collection (also p. 20, *Tibet in Turmoil*).
The Dalai Lama. . . : Khedroob Thondup Collection (also p. 22, *Tibet in Turmoil*).
The Dalai Lama at the Indian. . . : Khedroob Thondup Collection (also p. 113, *Tibet in Turmoil*).
The Dalai Lama's reluctant. . . : courtesy Information Office, Embassy of India, Washington, DC.
Tibetan cavalry. . . : Khedroob Thondup Collection (also p. 100, *Tibet in Turmoil*).
C–130B flying a relief. . . : U.S. National Archives Still Picture Collection.
Site of Camp Hale. . . : courtesy Mr. Bruce Walker.
The compound. . . : courtesy Mr. Bruce Walker.
Sign to discourage. . . : courtesy Mr. Bruce Walker.
A staff meeting at Dumra. . . : private Collection.
Lessons at Camp Hale. . . : courtesy Mr. Bruce Walker.
Gyen Yeshe and Lhamo Tsering. . . : the Lhamo Tsering Collection.

Yeshi Wangyal. . . : courtesy Mr. Tsering Phupatsang.
Wangdu and his lieutenants. . . : the Lhamo Tsering Collection.
Wangdu (his back to the camera). . . : the Lhamo Tsering Collection.
The first class. . . : courtesy Mr. Bruce Walker.
The Dalai Lama with Ernest Gross. . . : courtesy Mr. Ernest Gross.
The only portrait. . . : courtesy Mr. Bruce Walker.
The Dalai Lama's family. . . : courtesy Mr. Bruce Walker.
Lhasa officials. . . : courtesy Mr. Roger McCarthy.
The Dalai Lama with the author. . . : from the collection of the author.
Gyalo Thondup. . . : from the collection of the author.
The author introduces. . . : from the collection of the author.

PublicAffairs is a new nonfiction publishing house and a tribute to the standards, values, and flair of three persons who have served as mentors to countless reporters, writers, editors, and book people of all kinds, including me.

I. F. Stone, proprietor of *I. F. Stone's Weekly*, combined a commitment to the First Amendment with entrepreneurial zeal and reporting skill and became one of the great independent journalists in American history. At the age of eighty, Izzy published *The Trial of Socrates*, which was a national bestseller. He wrote the book after he taught himself ancient Greek.

Benjamin C. Bradlee was for nearly thirty years the charismatic editorial leader of *The Washington Post*. It was Ben who gave the *Post* the range and courage to pursue such historic issues as Watergate. He supported his reporters with a tenacity that made them fearless, and it is no accident that so many became authors of influential, best-selling books.

Robert L. Bernstein, the chief executive of Random House for more than a quarter century, guided one of the nation's premier publishing houses. Bob was personally responsible for many books of political dissent and argument that challenged tyranny around the globe. He is also the founder and was the longtime chair of Human Rights Watch, one of the most respected human rights organizations in the world.

. . .

For fifty years, the banner of Public Affairs Press was carried by its owner Morris B. Schnapper, who published Gandhi, Nasser, Toynbee, Truman, and about 1,500 other authors. In 1983 Schnapper was described by *The Washington Post* as "a redoubtable gadfly." His legacy will endure in the books to come.

Peter Osnos, *Publisher*

60 —

77 —   338

96 —

105 —

112 —
    116

      136

      143

    228
    234
    246 —
      ✳ 249 —
        269
        278
          297 —
          321 —

Lhamo Tsering 384 (TR Feb 99,
                   Tib. Bulletin Mar-Apr 99)

N

CHINA

XINJIANG

TIBET

Dharamsala

TSANG

Nagchu Dzong

Purang

Dhamshung
Airfield

Ü

Shanggaden
Chokhor

Lhasa

Mustang

Brahmaputra R.
(Tsangpo R.)

Shigatse

Tsetang

H

Tingri

L

Triguthang

Nyalam

Tingye

NEPAL

Kathmandu

Yatung

Thimphu

SIKKIM

Thona

Darjeeling

Kalimpong

BHUTAN

INDIA

Brahmaputra R.

Kms.
200
0
200
Miles

EAST
PAKISTAN
(BANGLADESH)